*Barnard Castle became front-page news when Dominic Cummings
drove there 'to test his eyesight' at the height of the
2020 Covid lockdown.*

*It wasn't the first time the town had hit the national headlines. Nearly
two centuries earlier it was the scene of brutal murders that
gripped the country's attention as police superintendent
Ralph Leconby Snowden battled to bring the killers to justice.*

*This novel weaves together contemporary press and court reports with
a host of unforgettable characters in a tale of tragedy, triumph,
fortitude and farce in Victorian Britain. Much of it is true,
or could have been.*

With best wishes to
Jim McTaggart
(who, thank God, bears
absolutely no resemblance
to Hamish McQueedie)

John Smith

SNOWDEN

Jon Smith

First published 2022

Published by Jon Smith
Heath House, Barningham, North Yorkshire DL11 7DU
01833 621374 / jonxxsmith@gmail.com

Designed and typeset by Jon Smith using Adobe InDesign and Adobe Photoshop.
Text set in 10/11.5pt Times New Roman

Printed by County Print, 11 Collingwood Court,
Riverside Park Industrial Estate, Middlesbrough TS2 1RP
01642 225867 / sales@countyprint.co.uk

ISBN 978-1-3999-0853-5

220412 19

ALSO BY JON SMITH

Essential Reporting: The NCTJ's guide for trainee journalists
Around the World : An A-Z of Barningham and its neighbours
But Not Forgotten: Extraordinary local lives
Barningham Baptisms
Barningham Brides
Where Lyeth Ye Bodies: Barningham Burials
Jam Letch & Jingle Potts
Short Butts and Sandy Bottom
A Child of Hope (editor)
A Farmer's Boy (editor)
A Fleeting Shadow (editor)

Dedicated to
JO CROWE 1948-2021
A dear sister, without whose encouragement
this book would never have been written.

My grateful thanks, too, to Sharon Griffiths, Andy Kluz,
Helen McGuire, Frank Mansfield, Nigel Metcalfe
and Jay Smith, all of whom read early drafts of Snowden
and offered invaluable suggestions for improvement, and to
Sheila Catton for her extraordinary patience throughout.

CONTENTS

NORTHERN ENGLAND 1845

Carlisle
Tyne
Newcastle
Cumberland
County Durham
Stanhope
Wear
Durham
Penrith
Bishop Auckland
Shildon
Tees
Barnard Castle
Stockton
Darlington
Westmorland
Richmond
North Sea
Swale
Northallerton
Yorkshire
Lancaster
Ripon
Thirsk
Nunnington
Lancashire
Harrogate
York
Irish Sea
Railways
Under construction
Leeds
Ouse

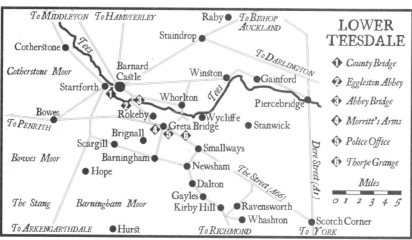

LOWER TEESDALE

To MIDDLETON To HAMSTERLEY
Raby
To BISHOP AUCKLAND
Staindrop
Cotherstone
Tees
To DARLINGTON
Cotherstone Moor
Barnard Castle
Winston
Gainford
Startforth
❶
❼
❸
Whorlton
Tees
Piercebridge
Bowes
Rokeby
Wycliffe
To PENRITH
❹
❺
❻
Stanwick
Brignall
Greta Bridge
Scargill
Smallways
Barningham
Newsham
Dere Street (A1)
Hope
The Street (A66)
Bowes Moor
Dalton
The Stang
Barningham Moor
Gayles
Kirby Hill
Ravensworth
To ARKENGARTHDALE
Hurst
Whashton
Scotch Corner
To RICHMOND
To YORK

❶ County Bridge
❷ Eggleston Abbey
❸ Abbey Bridge
❹ Morritt's Arms
❺ Police Office
❻ Thorpe Grange

Miles
0 1 2 3 4 5

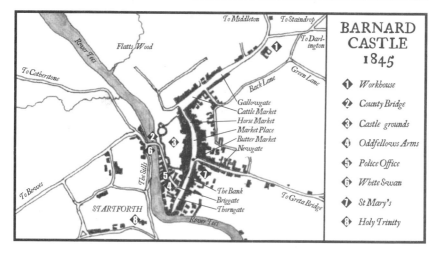

BARNARD CASTLE 1845

To Middleton To Staindrop
To Darlington
River Tees
Flatts Wood
Green Lane
To Cotherstone
Back Lane
Gallowgate
Cattle Market
Horse Market
Market Place
Butter Market
Newgate
❷
❸
❻
To Bowes
The Sills
❺
❹
❼
The Bank
Briggate
Thorngate
To Greta Bridge
STARTFORTH
❽
River Tees

❶ Workhouse
❷ County Bridge
❸ Castle grounds
❹ Oddfellows Arms
❺ Police Office
❻ White Swan
❼ St Mary's
❽ Holy Trinity

PART ONE

August 1845

Barnard Castle's carpet mills beside the Tees in mid-Victorian days, viewed from the Sills on the Startforth side of the river.

Briggate (now called Bridgegate) lies behind the industrial buildings; St Mary's church is on the skyline.

Almost all the riverside buildings have long gone.

Tuesday August 12ᵗʰ

Wycliffe, 6.26pm

ISABELLA CLARKSON, 25, unmarried kitchenmaid and a good deal plumper than she would wish, hitched her skirts above her ankles and broke into a trot. It was the first time she could remember running since she was a child, and she hadn't enjoyed it then. Within a hundred yards she was pink, breathing heavily, and cursing her stupidity. It was all her own fault, nobody to blame but herself. Oh, Bella, how could you, how *could* you?

She was due back at Wycliffe Mill by half-past six and was still the best part of a mile away, a long mile along the riverside path, muddied and puddled by days of rain. Knowing her mistress would be unforgiving if she was late back from her afternoon off, she had left her parents' cottage in Whorlton in good time, the church clock's half-dozen distant strikes fading as she bade farewell. Off she'd set, down the steep crooked track to the Tees, over the little suspension bridge, the toll-keeper fast asleep as usual, and onto the riverside path to Wycliffe.

If only she hadn't met Will Bowron coming the other way, she'd never have stopped, she'd have been back with at least ten minutes to spare. But how could she ignore him, him with that moustache and the uniform, those eyes of his, and, oh, I wonder...

And now she was late.

On she ran, one hand gripping her skirt, the other her purse, paisley shawl billowing behind as she skipped heavily over the streams that poured down through the trees and over the path into the river. It had been a wet and miserable summer after one of the coldest springs anyone could recall, and for the past two days relentless rain had turned the Tees into an angry torrent, peat-brown and laden with debris swept down from the moors. The storm had finally stopped that morning, but its aftermath would last for days.

That Will Bowron, cook said he was trouble and they all promised things like that, men, there was only one thing they were after...

She ran past the ferry cottage, swerving round the ancient rowing boat upside-down on the bank, tethered to a tree. There was no sign of old Annie Smith, who had been transporting people, goods and the occasional small animal across the river for as long as anyone could remember and she must be at least seventy now, thought Isabella, funny old woman, living here on her own under that thatched roof. Some said she was a witch but she didn't believe them. That boat must be just as old, look at the paintwork, nearly all peeled away, must be rotten, they wouldn't get her in it.

The river on her left crashed furiously over a weir, swirling and eddying, white foam clutching the banks, and she watched a tree branch swirl and spin its way downstream.

It was no good, she was going to have to stop, just for a moment. Gulping for breath, she rested a hand against a rock and fought the temptation to sit down. It wasn't that far now, she might just be able to slip in without them noticing, cook would turn a blind eye if she was lucky.

She'd have to change her mud-caked shoes before the mistress saw her. If only she'd worn her everyday pair, high-buttoned and leather-proof against the water. Instead it was seeping step by step into the Sunday-best cast-offs she'd been given by her elder sister, now doing very nicely thank you living in tally with that flash fellow from Barnard Castle. But Isabella had wanted to look her best, you never knew, just in case...

She shook her head, took a deep breath and set off again. Left, right, over the worst of the plashes, ducking under a rain-sodden sycamore branch, over another minor torrent and then catching a foot on a hidden tree-root and going giddily head over heels, arms out-stretched, face to the ground, fingernails in the earth, sliding to the water's edge.

For one terrifying moment she thought she was going to continue down the bank into the river, but she came to a halt and lay there gasping for air. She pushed herself upwards, hands and knees mired, a smear of blood on one arm but nothing broken as far as she could tell. Her purse was lying open beside her, her handful of coins scattered on the ground; her new lace bonnet, so prized, was dancing down the Tees.

Isabella began to sob as she watched it disappear round the bend and through the tears her gaze met another pair of eyes staring sightlessly from rocks in the middle of the river. She gave a muted scream of horror and scrambled to her feet. A body, a man, just a young man she thought, her mind swirling like the water between them. And dead, he had to be dead the way he was lying there, head and one arm above the surface, the rest hidden below and so firmly wedged that the Tees even in full spate was unable to move it.

She'd seen bodies before, her father laid out grey in the front room, an infant brother cold in his crib under the stair, but never one whose life had ended violently like this. Fighting back a wave of panic she decided the only thing to do was to report it to the mistress. She'd know what to do.

She picked up the purse, recovered as many coins as she could find, stared at the body again for a moment, and set off down the path towards the mill. Across the fields the double bells of Wycliffe church struck the half-hour, but Isabella, weary, wet and mud-spattered, walked the rest of the way.

Whoever it was in the river, however he'd died, whatever the reason, he'd done her a favour.

Nobody was going to blame her now for being late and having shoes caked with mud.

Barnard Castle, 6.30pm

FOUR miles upstream, Ralph Leconby Snowden, Superintendent of Police for the Greta Bridge Association for the Protection of Property and the Prosecution of Felons, walked into the Oddfellows Arms in Briggate and beckoned landlord Tom Marwood into the back bar. They sat down at a quiet corner table and Snowden pushed away a couple of empty glasses.

'Know anything about salmon, Tom?'

'Salmon, Mr Snowden?'

'Salmon, Tom. Poached.'

'As in, like, grilled or fried?'

'As in like nicked, Tom. A little bird tells me you had someone in here last night saying they could lay hands on one.'

Marwood shook his head. 'Don't know anything about that, Mr Snowden.'

'That's a pity.' Snowden pulled a battered briar out of his waistcoat pocket and began investigating the contents of its bowl. 'I heard you'd had a bit of trouble recently and wondered if I might be able to help.'

'Trouble, Mr Snowden?'

'One of my constables says your customers were fighting in here on Sunday afternoon.'

Marwood frowned. 'Just a friendly disagreement, the usual, nothing to worry about.' Like most local publicans he had to cope at weekends with lead-miners from up the dale, flush if they'd hit a good vein, eager to spend their earnings in town on their only night off and even happier if it ended in confrontation with the Irish navvies excavating for the proposed railway south of Barnard Castle. And there were also, of course, Barney's home-grown collection of rascals, rogues and booze-fuelled belligerants.

'I'm not interested in what it was all about, Tom.' Snowden dug out an ancient leather pouch from somewhere under his coat and began filling the pipe. 'Well after closing time, the constable says. His report's sitting on my desk, waiting for me to decide what to do anything about it.'

'Just friends celebrating my birthday, Mr Snowden. I'll swear to it.'

'Don't waste my time, Tom. I've better things to do than check when your birthday is and discover you're lying.' Snowden examined the contents of his pipe and packed them down carefully. 'I can get very upset when people lie to me.'

Marwood hesitated and gave a cautious glance round the bar. There were two customers in flat caps bent over a set of dominoes, a nondescript mongrel asleep at their feet, but no one within earshot. He lowered his voice all the same. 'Now I come to think of it, Mr Snowden, there was someone in here boasting he could get hold of a salmon.'

'That's better. Offering it to you cheap, was he?'

'No, nothing like that. My customers can't afford salmon, Mr Snowden, mutton pies, sheep's trotters, bit of bread and cheese is the best I can sell them. This fellow was in the front bar there, late on, arguing with some of the other lads and said he could get a fish any time.' Marwood shook his head. 'They didn't believe a word of it, wagered a sovereign he couldn't bring one in tonight.'

'Tonight? Where was he getting it from?'

'That's all I heard. I was shifting empty glasses at the time, he clammed up till I'd moved away.'

'Name, Tom?'

'Oh, come on, Mr Snowden, I've got a living to earn. If anyone knew I'd tipped you off I'd lose all my custom, and they'd probably smash the place up as well.'

'Listen,' said Snowden. 'What can you hear?'

Marwood strained his ears. 'Nothing. Just them two clicking their dominoes and the dog farting.'

'I could have sworn I heard the sound of coins on the table,' said Snowden. 'They wouldn't be playing for money, would they?'

Marwood stared at him. 'You wouldn't do me for them having a ha'penny bet on a game of doms?'

'Well, Tom, you know the law. No gaming of any kind. You could lose your licence, that and the drinking out of hours.'

'You wouldn't.'

'I might. Just a name, Tom, and I promise you no one will know where it came from. I've been round nearly every pub in town today and any one of thirty landlords could have tipped me off. '

Marwood scowled and gave in. 'Greenhow, Joe Greenhow, lives in Kirtley's Yard up The Bank. I didn't tell you that, mind, he'd kill me if he knew.'

'Joseph Greenhow.' Snowden sat back and drew an experimental breath through the unlit pipe. 'Well, well. Moving up a class if he's after salmon.'

'You know him?'

'Seen him before the Greta Bridge magistrates a couple of times. Rabbits, maybe the odd pheasant. Shouldn't be a problem picking him up.'

Marwood's face grew even more worried. 'You come in here and nab him, they'll all know it was me.'

'I won't come near you, Tom, never fear.' Snowden found a match in his pouch pocket and struck it on the stone flag beneath his chair. 'We'll find him a long way away from here.'

He took a long draw from his pipe, sent a cloud of blue smoke drifting towards the ceiling and stood up. Marwood watched him go and wondered, not for the first time, why he'd ever thought running a pub would be easy.

The dog rolled over and let out a stupendous fart.

Wycliffe, 7.05pm

'HE didn't half look awful, Mrs Siddle. All white with his arm sort of waving in the air over the water, and his eyes just staring at me.' Isabella, hanging her newly-washed stockings over the stove in the mill kitchen, shuddered at the memory. 'I thought your eyes closed when you was dead.'

'They close them for you.' Mrs Siddle, cook at the mill since long before Isabella was born, crossed mottled legs in front of the fire. 'Undertakers. One of the things they learn how to do, like straightening arms and shaving legs. Used to put pennies on their eyelids, they did, to stop them opening again. You don't want to be looking at dead eyes, do you?'

'It was horrible, like he was staring at me from beyond the grave.' Isabella gave another shiver. 'Not that he's got a grave yet, of course, him being stuck there in the rocks like that.'

'Poor devil, wonder who he was?' Mrs Siddle pondered for a moment. ' Must have come from up-river, Barney maybe or further. Probably fell in, I wouldn't wonder, drunk on his way home.'

'Could have done it on purpose. Done away with himself, broken-hearted because his girl had left him.' Isabella lapsed into a reverie, wondering if she'd ever find anyone who'd kill themselves if she spurned their advances. Just somebody who made advances for her to spurn would be a start.

'Well, too late for him now. The mistress says they're going to get him out in the morning, if he's still there. Meanwhile, there's a sink-full of dishes to be done. Back to work, young Bella, and you make sure them stockings don't catch fire.'

Greta Bridge, 7.15pm

JEREMIAH Sowerby, shoemaker and village constable, hammered a last nail into the clog and sat back. Another day over, time for a quick one in the Morritt's Arm back bar. Maybe two.

He spat out the spare nail clamped between his lips, dropped the hammer on the workshop bench and pulled on his coat. As he walked to the door he heard a horse coming fast down the road from Rokeby and stopping nearby. Some gentleman in a hurry for his dinner at the inn, Sowerby guessed. He went out and pulled the door shut behind him.

'Constable!' He spun round. Superintendent Snowden, the last person he wanted to see. 'Need you at the Abbey Bridge, fast as you can.'

'What, now?' Sowerby stared at him. 'I've not eaten yet.'

'Give you an appetite. I want you there within the half-hour.' Snowden wheeled. 'Cut across the fields, and don't forget your truncheon.' He rode off rapidly the way he'd come.

Sowerby swore silently as he walked into his house and found his wife in front of the kitchen range. 'Got to go out, police business. Bloody Snowden's just been here.'

'Don't expect anything when you get back.' She spoke without looking up. 'Get Snowden to feed you. And no calling in the Morritt's on your way home.'

Not much chance of that. He cursed again as he found his stave in a drawer, pocketed the handcuffs beside it, and hurried out of the door. God knows when he'd get back.

Egglestone Abbey, 7.30pm

GREENHOW strode along the road beside the river, stick in hand, his boots squelching in the mud as he tried to dodge the puddles. The Tees was still running high, and he hoped the stretch at Rokeby where he'd found the salmon last week had not been too disturbed. He crossed the tiny bridge over Thorsgill Beck, passed the ruins of Egglestone Abbey silhouetted against the declining sun, and cautiously approached the junction ahead where two small toll-houses guarded the way across Abbey Bridge.

He stopped to make sure there was no sign of the toll-keeper before making his way past and slithered down the steep bank to the river beyond, cursing as he came close to falling in the mud and wishing he hadn't made that wager in the Oddfellows last night. He should have kept quiet about the salmon. It was a nice little side-line taking them to his brother-in-law, a fishmonger in Barnard Castle who didn't ask any questions, and letting anyone else know about them would be stupid. He'd get just the one tonight, collect his sovereign from those disbelieving bastards at the pub, deliver the fish to his brother-in-law and keep his mouth shut in future.

He stopped for a moment to regain his breath and then set off along the path beside the river. Another mile, maybe a bit more, and he'd be there.

Snowden emerged from the shadows behind one of the toll-houses, leant over the parapet and watched him disappear. Forty or so feet below was the Tees, for much of its length the boundary between two counties, Yorkshire on the western side, Durham to the east. It must, he reflected, have been tough crossing here before the bridge was built some seventy years ago by the Morritts to enable them to get from their Rokeby Park estate to Barnard Castle without having to ford the river, difficult at the best of times, out of the question when in flood. Morritt tenants crossed free; the rest of the world paid to pass over the bridge, just wide enough for one coach or cart at a time and guarded by a zealous toll-keeper. A notice on the toll-house wall listed fees: a halfpenny to walk across, a penny for horse-riders, sixpence for a gig or cart, eightpence a score for a flock of sheep. Disputes about charges were common, and legend had it that a funeral was once cancelled after the toll-keeper came to blows with an undertaker refusing to pay extra for the body in his hearse.

Snowden walked back to the centre of the bridge, pulled out his pipe and pondered mortality.

In ten days' time he'd be forty-one. He'd paused that morning before the looking-glass in the hall and wondered if he was looking his age. No sign yet of grey in the well-trimmed side-whiskers which hid most of the old scar down his left jaw, his face was still lean and firm, but there were a few lines beginning to show here and there, he noted, and his eyes looked tired, too many late nights writing reports by candlelight. He'd stood back a few paces to see more of himself. Five foot eleven, a good height, not quite as slim as he once was but still looking fit enough to make most villains think twice before taking him on.

He'd last a few years yet, he decided as he picked up his tall black hat and police stave from the hallstand. All the same, this coming birthday was another uncomfortable milestone. Forty-one. It didn't seem any time since he was half that age, a battle-scarred and often scared fusilier with the Northumberland Fifth Foot, quelling the rebels of County Clare, bloodily avenging the death of poor Robinson, colour-serjeant beaten to a pulp by the mob. Then there were the years with the Northumbria Preventive Service, chasing footpads and highwaymen and more than once escaping only narrowly with his life, spying on Chartists fomenting rebellion in Newcastle knowing that if they penetrated his disguise he'd probably end up floating down the Tyne. And now here he was, twenty years on, collaring poachers for the well-to-do of North Yorkshire.

It was as much, he supposed, as any self-taught son of a Yorkshire blacksmith could hope to achieve. He was in charge of 32 parish constables, possessed an enviable reputation as the scourge of local villains and vagrants, and was, he had to admit, rewarded well enough for it: two pounds a week plus expenses and the occasional bonus, plenty enough to live on and put a bit away for old age if he got that far. But it would be satisfying to be remembered for more than just cutting crime rates in the Greta Bridge area, and time was passing. The new police forces they were setting up in the boroughs had an age limit of forty for superintendents, and if the government decided to introduce them in the rural areas too, as it surely would before long, he could be out of a job.

He hunched his shoulders under his greatcoat, wishing he'd brought a muffler. A thin wind was blowing across the bridge, the temperature was dropping fast and it could be a long cold night. He dipped into his waistcoat pocket for his watch. Solid gold, his initials engraved elaborately on the front, a gift from the Association's 300 members a couple of years earlier. 'Testimony of their approval of his talent, zeal, success, uncompromising integrity and faithful conduct over the past four years', the Earl of Zetland had said when he presented it. They'd given him fifty pounds in gold sovereigns as well, half a year's salary, which was even more welcome.

He flipped open the cover. Quarter to eight. He'd stick it out until dawn if need be.

Abbey Bridge, 7.58pm

FLUSHED with exertion, Sowerby hauled himself over the stile and sat down on a once-white milestone beside the road. *Bern'd Castle 1*, it read on the face below his left leg, *Greata Br 2* on the other.

He took off his hat and mopped his brow. It was all right for the superintendent, they gave him a horse. Village constables had to walk or run, and he scowled at the injustice of it all. He deeply resented being a constable, picked by the magistrates from a list of able-bodied men in his village to serve a year as the parish guardian of law and order, unpaid and unappreciated. Unpaid, and him a time-served master cordwainer even if he did spend most of his life mending clogs. How was he expected to do his job and keep his family if he was being called out by Mr bleeding Snowden every other night on some fool's errand like this? It was high time they had a proper police force, like the ones in big towns, instead of relying on people like him to keep the peace.

He sighed and shifted his buttocks on the stile. His wife wasn't happy about it, either. He ought to be at home helping her with the kids, she said in that thin voice of hers, not wandering around the countryside and dropping into pubs, she knew what he got up to. You'd think a man was entitled to a bit of compensation after a hard day's work.

And then there was his back. There was a time when he could face anybody, tall meaty fellow like him who'd even done a bit of wrestling at the fairs in his day, but his grappling days were long gone. Nobody knew what he went through now, doctor took his money and said there was nothing to be done about it, what did he expect bent over a cobbler's last all day? He'd spent a fortune on patent medicines guaranteed to cure everything from ear-ache to haemorrhoids, none of them any good. Able-bodied, they said he was, they should have a taste of what he suffered and see how they liked it.

He stood up with a grunt, and walked on. Two minutes later he realised he'd left his hat beside the milestone and retraced his steps, cursing furiously. This was turning out to be a bloody awful day.

Snowden was waiting for him at the bridge. 'Late, constable. We'll have to get you some training. Maybe a session or two with the militia in Barney barracks.'

Sowerby looked horrified. 'Came as fast as I could. I'm not as young as I was, shouldn't be doing this job at all.' He paused to get his breath back. 'What are we doing here, anyway?'

'Catching a poacher, I hope.' Snowden waved an arm down-river. 'Mr Morritt at Rokeby Park is fed up with someone who's helping themselves to salmon on his stretch of the Tees.'

'Any idea who it is?'

'Greenhow, Joseph Greenhow.'

Sowerby savoured the name. 'Don't think I know him.'

'You will. He went under the bridge about fifteen minutes ago, just after I got here.'

'Should've got him then.' Sowerby said in an aggrieved voice. 'I could be back home by now. Or in the Morritt's Arms.'

'And the most we could do him for would be trespassing, a few shillings' fine.' Snowden shook his head. 'We'll get him red-handed on the way back when he's got his catch. And it won't be just a rabbit or two either, he's after salmon and that's a different matter. Very protective of their fish are the magistrates, can't have your common felon getting his teeth into them. He'll probably get three months on the Northallerton treadmill.'

Sowerby swung his truncheon in gloomy anticipation. 'So we just wait?'

'Down by the river. You hide yourself a hundred yards downstream, somewhere off the path. Wait till Greenhow's gone past, then come out and challenge him. He'll probably make a run for it, but unless he fancies diving in the river the only place he can head for is the bridge here. I'll be waiting for him.'

Sowerby sniffed, unconvinced. 'Never fancied fishing myself, all that hanging around waiting for something to take your maggot. Boring, I reckon.'

Snowden looked at him in disbelief. 'There's a bit more to it when you're after salmon, constable. It won't take him long, half an hour at most with a gaff, then back to the pub.'

'Gaff?'

'Barbed hook, big one on the end of a pole. Stick it through a salmon and out it comes, nice and easy, bit like a harpoon. Lot easier than using a net when there's just one of you. Come on, we'd better get down there.'

Snowden led the way down to the riverside path, watched Sowerby disappear into the undergrowth and sighed. The man was useful when muscular back-up was required but a positive liability when it came to anything more subtle. But better than nothing this evening, Snowden supposed, the only constable he'd been able to find at short notice. All the rest seemed to be away, no doubt up on the moors earning the price of a few beers beating for grouse among the heather.

He perched himself on a rock in the shadow of the bridge, let his mind go back over the day and was grateful he'd had that constable's report about Tom Marwood serving out of hours. Nobody in the Briggate area of Barnard Castle helped the police unless they wanted something in return.

His thoughts were suddenly broken by the sight of a figure loping along the path in the distance, stick in one hand, a large bag in the other. Snowden drew his pistol as the man passed Sowerby's hiding-place. He'd never shot anyone yet, not since his fusilier days, but he knew from bitter experience that even the most insignificant-looking offender might be armed.

There was no sign of Sowerby.

Silently cursing his constable's incompetence, Snowden watched his quarry approach. Ten paces away, five.

'Mr Greenhow, I believe?'

The man stopped in his tracks, stared at Snowden for a moment and swung his bundle high in a long curving loop into the centre of the river where it was whipped away by the current, floating for a few moments before vanishing below the surface. Spinning round, he began to run back the way he'd come but skidded to a halt as Sowerby at last stumbled into view, fastening his trouser belt. Caught between the pair of them, he stopped, turned and gave a resigned shrug.

'Might have known it would be you. Inspector bloody Snowden.'

'Superintendent these days, Joe,' said Snowden. 'Want to tell me what was in the bag?'

'Kittens,' said Greenhow. 'Half a dozen kittens, missus told me to take 'em out and drown 'em.' He took a few steps forward. 'No crime in that, is there?'

Snowden shook his head. 'I think those kittens could swim. Do your trousers up, constable, and then search him.'

'You've no right to do that, I've done nothing.' Greenhow raised his stick as Sowerby approached, truncheon in hand, but decided that adding a cracked skull to his problems wasn't a good idea.

'There's a good lad, wouldn't want to be done for assaulting a constable in the course of his duties, would we?' Snowden smiled grimly. 'Two years on the wheel for that, Joe. Just put your hands up and let nice Mr Sowerby here see what you've got under that coat of yours.'

Sowerby rummaged among the man's clothing, gave a triumphant snort, and held out what he'd found. 'It's one of those things you told me about, a giff.'

'A gaff,' said Snowden happily. 'And if it doesn't fit neatly into that notch at the top of his stick I'll be very surprised.'

'It was lying by the path, lost property,' said Greenhow. 'I was just on my way to hand it in to one of you lot, honest. '

'Honest?' Snowden shook his head. 'You're a lot of things, Joe Greenhow, but honest isn't one of them.' He moved closer. 'Let's see your hands, Joe. Those couldn't be fish scales, could they?' He sniffed cautiously. 'I do believe they are.'

'A bit of cod for the kittens, Mr Snowden, sort of last supper for them before they was drowned.'

Snowden raised his eyes to the heavens. 'You're all heart, Joe. Come on, let's get you back to the lock-up.' He turned to Sowerby. 'Put the cuffs on him, constable, and then you can go home.'

Barnard Castle, 9.10pm

TOM Marwood stood behind his bar and counted the tankards again. Twenty-two on the shelf at the back, thirteen in use, seven waiting by the sink to be washed. Forty-two, which meant another two had gone missing since he'd last counted them on Sunday, and it looked like the thieving bastards had lifted a couple of his best ones, the round-handled pewters with the glass bottoms.

'I'm going to move all the rest of the pewter somewhere safe,' he said angrily to Eliza when she came back from the kitchen with a kettle of hot water. 'The buggers can all drink out of glass ones from now on.'

The barmaid shrugged. 'They'll only smash them. You'll end up buying new ones every week, cost more than the price of a few pewters.' She emptied the kettle into the sink at the back and started to wash the waiting tankards. 'You want to catch them that's stealing them. Have a word with the police, they've nothing better to do.'

Marwood had seen enough of the constabulary for one day. 'Just keep an eye out, Eliza, see if you can spot who's taking them.' He looked round the room. 'There's thirteen out there being drunk out of. Let me know if one suddenly disappears.'

She nodded. 'They'd nick the tables if they weren't bolted to the floor. Could you bring up another dozen Indias from the cellar? I'm almost out of them.'

Marwood left the bar and Eliza cast an eye over the customers, all men. Most were gathered round a table on the far side by the fireplace, familiar faces who came in night after night. Lord knows where they got their money from, but it wouldn't be from hard graft at one of the carpet mills nearby. Briggate abounded with petty thieves, pickpockets, fences and fraudsters living in the smoke-blackened tenements crowded down to the riverside, communal ash-closets in the yards and open drains carrying filth down to the Tees. More ale-houses and brothels per head than in towns ten times the size of Barney, they said.

She turned to serve one of the men approaching the bar. However the Oddfellows' customers got their money, enough of them spent it in there to pay her wages, and she wasn't going to complain about that.

'Another pint of the same, sweetheart.' The drinker, already flushed with alcohol and leaning unsteadily against the bar, belched as she filled his tankard from the wooden cask behind her. 'Doing anything tonight?'

'Sod off, George,' she said routinely. 'Go and find yourself one of the girls down the street, plenty there ready to take your money.' She sniffed the contents of the tankard and put it down in front of him. 'You can pay for this first, mind.'

He pulled a handful of coins from his pocket and spread them on the bar top. 'Help yourself.' She sorted out a silver threepenny piece and two halfpennies, checked automatically that they were all genuine, and dropped them into the wooden box under the counter that served as a till. George pocketed what was left and weaved his way back to the others, tankard in hand, as Marwood came back with a crate of pale ale bottles. 'Barrel's going off,' Eliza told him quietly. 'Smells like vinegar, want to put a new one on?'

'The state this lot are in, they'll drink anything. I'll leave it till tomorrow.' He began emptying the black bottles onto the shelves as the door opened and four more customers walked in. Marwood recognised them, strangers who had been in the night before. Navvies, he reckoned. One, tall with a dark-stubbled face, made his way to the bar.

'We'll have some of them.' He pointed to the bottle shelf. 'Fresher than the beer if last night was anything to go by.'

His companions were staring at the top of a small beer cask hanging on the wall, its face crudely chalked into sections. 'It's a bloody dartboard!' said one in mock amazement. He rubbed out one of the chalk-lines with his thumb and turned to the group at the table. 'Where's your mate tonight, then? Got drowned chasing his salmon?'

'He'll be in.'

'In the bloody Tees more like. Wagered he'd be here tonight with one. All mouth and no fish, that one.'

'I said he'll be in.' The speaker, a dark-bearded man in his thirties, turned his chair to face the newcomers. The rest of the table fell silent.

'Five to one we don't see him. Lying bugger, salmon my arse.'

The bearded drinker stood up, hand on the back of his chair. 'You calling my brother a liar?'

'Where is he, then? Said he'd be back, I can't see him.'

'You'll bloody see this, though.'

Eliza sighed, knowing what was coming. She edged towards the door as the chair swung through the air and smashed onto the skull of the stranger. The room erupted and she fled.

Marwood took refuge under the bar as the makeshift dartboard hurtled over his head and smashed the mirror behind him. It collapsed, bringing down his shelf full of bottles, and he crouched among the shards of broken glass, wondering why Snowden and his bloody constables were never around when he needed them.

Greta Bridge, 9.30 pm

JOE Greenhow sat on the stone slab in his tiny cell, one of three in the tiny Greta Bridge police house, and rubbed his wrists. 'You didn't have to cuff me,' he complained. 'I'd have come quietly without them things biting into me.'

'Better safe than sorry,' said Snowden from the other side of the bars. 'There's a bucket of water in there, cold but it'll get the smell of fish off you. Then you can have a peaceful night. There's nobody else around.'

A small office near the front door was manned in daylight hours by a duty constable but at night arrested felons were usually left on their own, well locked in, a cracked chamberpot in the corner and a mug of water to quench any thirst. Breakfast, a slice of bread and maybe a bit of ageing cheese, arrived when the duty constable turned up at seven next morning unless the cell's occupant had been particularly difficult about being incarcerated, in which case constables had a habit of forgetting to bring it.

Snowden made his way to the office, sat down at the desk and skimmed through a pile of papers that had accumulated during his all-day absence. Four copies of a notice about a runaway butcher's apprentice from Darlington, to be posted up in local villages. A letter from the Association secretary reminding him that his expenses were overdue, and another one from Shaw and Sons, publishers of Fetter Lane in London, saying they might be interested in his book if he ever got it finished. A note from the day's duty constable about a body being found in the Tees near Wycliffe. Two applications from publicans seeking late-night extensions which needed his approval. A list of people due to appear before Greta Bridge magistrates on Thursday morning.

Snowden paused. He'd better add Greenhow to the list, he thought, reached for a pen and dipped it in the inkwell. *Greenhow, Joseph*. What was his address? He'd got it somewhere in his notebook. Ah, yes. *Kirtleys Yard, Briggate, Barnard Castle*. Age? With a sigh he put down his pen, rose and went back to the cells.

'How old are you, Joe?'

Greenhow was lying on the slab, his coat bundled up to form a pillow. 'Thirty, maybe. Could be thirty-one, I lost count years ago. Does it matter?' He sat up. 'Ever tried sleeping on stone like this?'

'Not since I left the army. You've no idea when you were born?'

'Well, now.' Greenhow scratched his head. 'I do know my dad wanted to call me Wellington, it was the year we beat the Frenchies at Waterloo. My mam wasn't having any of it, bloody good thing too. Wellington Greenhow, can you imagine?'

'We'll say thirty, then.' Snowden turned to go.

'Hang on a moment, Mr Snowden. I've been thinking.' Greenhow paused. 'There's no chance we could do a sort of deal, is there? It's my daughter's wedding on Saturday, the missus is going to kill me if I'm in Northallerton doing six months on the wheel instead of giving her away.'

'A deal?' Snowden looked at him quizzically. 'If you're offering me money you'll be doing two years for attempting to bribe a police officer as well as everything else.'

'Nothing like that, Mr Snowden,' Greenhow assured him hastily. 'Wouldn't dream of it, not money, you being such an upright gentleman. No, I thought, well, perhaps a bit of information, like.'

'It'll have to be good, Joe. Very good. Because if I don't deliver you to Mr Morritt on Thursday morning I'm going to have some explaining to do.'

Greenhow was silent for a few moments. 'Supposing, just supposing I could tell you something that would make him even happier than sending me down for poaching his salmon?''

Snowden stopped and reached for his pipe. 'And what might that be?' His voice echoed with scepticism.

'It's good, Mr Snowden. Worth letting me out of here for.'

'Time I went, Joe. I've had a long day.' He turned back towards the stairs.

'No, wait, I'll tell you what. You put me up before the magistrates on Thursday like you say, but water it down a bit, say I didn't catch anything or it was just a trout or two. And tell them I've put you on the scent of a real criminal and I should be shown a bit of mercy.'

'Nothing doing till I've heard who this real criminal of yours might be.' Snowden put a match to his pipe, blew a cloud of blue smoke into the air and raised a questioning eyebrow. 'Well?'

Greenhow studied his face and came to a decision. 'Ever come across a Captain Bainbridge, lives up the dale in Cotherstone?' He shifted his rolled-up jacket under his backside as a cushion.

Snowden nodded. 'Went bankrupt last spring, said he'd been robbed. We were called in to investigate but didn't get anywhere.' He cast his memory back. 'I wasn't involved, I was in Leeds for a long fraud trial at the time, but I heard something about it later.'

Bainbridge, he recalled, had suddenly found himself in dire financial trouble and the bailiffs had moved in to help themselves to as many of his belongings as they could load on their carts. Furniture, clothes, books, paintings, they'd all gone off to the King's Head hotel in Barnard Castle to be sold by his creditors, and most of them vanished overnight from the locked stable at the back where they'd been stored.

The search for the thieves proved fruitless. Somehow they'd managed to sneak everything out of the stable under the nose of the hotel's night porter. He'd probably had a few drinks and fallen asleep, though he'd vehemently denied it afterwards. It turned out he'd been employed there with an unblemished record since joining as a boot-boy forty years ago and was clearly guilty of nothing worse, perhaps, than gross dereliction of duty while under the influence. The bailiff and his assistants all had alibis for the night of the theft, no witnesses came forward, and there was never even a trail to go cold. The police had long given up hope of finding the thieves or their booty, and although it hadn't been his case the failure still rankled with Snowden.

'So how can this Captain Bainbridge help you?' There was a wooden chair in the corner for anyone who came to talk to a prisoner through the bars, and Snowden pulled it over. 'You're not telling me he's your secret criminal?'

'No, not him. Look, before Bainbridge went bust your Mr Morritt was selling off stuff he didn't want after inheriting that place at Rokeby. Furniture, carpets, all sorts. It all went for auction, lots of small stuff, too, I went along to see if I could pick up a bargain or two.'

Snowden looked sceptical. 'Lost property like the gaff by the river, you mean?'

Greenhow gave him a pained look. 'You want to hear this or not?'

'Keep going,' said Snowden, tapping ash onto the floor. 'I'm still waiting to learn what it's got to do with you.'

'Be fair, Mr Snowden, it's complicated and I'm doing my best.' Greenhow paused, marshalling his story. 'This Captain Bainbridge was there and bought a picture from Morritt, bloody great big thing, gold-framed, by some foreign artist or other. Cost him a fair bit, I remember. Not my cup of tea even if I had the money.'

Snowden had visited the hall at Rokeby many a time, an impressive country pile set in wooded parkland and full of expensive furniture and paintings. He remembered meeting old Sir John Morritt there a few years back to discuss security precautions, and had admired works by Rubens, Reynolds and, prize of the collection, that extraordinary picture of Venus by Valasquez hanging over the fireplace in the hall. 'Wellington found it on a battlefield somewhere in Spain,' Sir John had told him proudly. 'I picked it up for a song, worth thousands.'

Snowden wondered which painting Bainbridge had bought. Morritt wouldn't have sold the Venus, that was certain. 'This picture,' he said, coming back to Greenhow. 'Was it among the stuff that got taken?'

'Never seen again.'

'So what's it got to do with you getting out of here?'

'I'm trying to tell you.' Greenhow leant forward. 'This Bainbridge goes bust and of course he's got no money so Mr Morritt never gets paid for the picture he sold him. And he can't get the picture back because it's been nicked.'

'So?'

'Well, Bainbridge has a lawyer called Manners, who says he should sue the bailiffs for not looking after his stuff properly, and the case goes back and forth and finally comes up at York in July just gone, you know how these things drag on. It gets put off again, of course, don't know why, and they're still waiting.'

'The painting?' asked Snowden, beginning to lose patience. He hadn't eaten since mid-day, and then only a mouldering veal pie grabbed at one of the pubs he'd visited.

'I'm coming to that, but it's a bit difficult.' Greenhow paused. 'A couple of weeks ago I was doing a bit of work up the dale at Mickleton for one of the lads who lives on a farm up there. Just don't ask what the work was, all right?'

Snowden sighed and gave a nod.

'Good. Well, this lad, call him Harry though that's not his real name, he goes off for the day at Mickleton Show and there I am on the farm on my own and I decide to have a look round. There's this big shed out the back, doors barred tight, and I wonder what's in it, as you do. I open the doors, there's nothing to see but a pile of hay on one side, old stuff, beginning to rot, and I'm just about to leave when I hear this cat up there, up in the rafters, mewling its bloody head off because it's got itself tangled up in some netting they've put there to keep the pigeons or rats out or something.'

'Got a soft spot for cats, have you, Joe?'

'Love 'em, Mr Snowden.'

'You were drowning them when we met a couple of hours ago.'

Greenhow looked hurt. 'You know that's not true, Mr Snowden... Anyway, I climb up, there's a ladder at the side, and I get the cat free and it gives me a quick claw and vanishes, ungrateful bugger. And then I sort of slide down again, not all that far and I haven't had a hay-slide since I was a kid, and part of the hay comes down with me, and you'll never guess what was hidden behind it.' He paused expectantly.

'A load of stolen property we've been looking for since the Bainbridge robbery?'

Greenhow looked deflated. 'Can tell you're a bloody detective. But it must be worth a word with the magistrates for me, isn't it?'

Snowden looked thoughtful. 'Tell me where the farm is, and I'll think about it.'

'Can't do that, Mr Snowden, you know better than that. But you let me out, I could go up there one day no-one's around and bring you the painting back, make Mr Morritt very happy, that would.'

Snowden sat back and re-lit his pipe. 'And how much of this stuff did you help yourself to when you found it in the barn?'

'I never took anything, Mr Snowden.' Greenhow shook his head. 'He's not someone you cross, Frankie, he'd have known straight away it was me.'

'Frankie?'

There was a long silence.

'Bugger,' said Greenhow.

Barnard Castle, 9.50pm

TOM MARWOOD shovelled the last of the broken glass into a bucket and surveyed what was left of his bar. One window gone, three broken tables, half a dozen chairs in bits, an empty shelf where the bottles had been, no hands left on the clock and still a pool of mixed blood and beer to mop up.

'It's been worse,' said Eliza, picking a bent spittoon out of the fireplace and putting it back beside the grate. 'They didn't take the money this time.'

'Only because that constable arrived.'

'Daft bugger, fancy walking in when that was going on.' Tom shook his head. 'I wonder how he is. Nasty head wound, that, you wouldn't think you could hit anybody that hard with a crib board.'

Footsteps sounded outside and a girl came in through the bar door, still hanging open on its broken hinges.

'Had a good night?' she asked, staring at the damage. She was dressed for the streets, frock below her cape no lower than her knees, no stockings, hair in ringlets and a smear of something red on her lips.

'Don't joke, Emma. If you're looking for trade, you'll find nothing here.'

'I'm looking for Joe Yates, have you seen him? Said he'd have my blue dress mended by today but he's not home, can't find him in any of the pubs.'

'Yates?'

'Funny little fellow down the street, does tailoring and that. You'd know him.'

'Got a high voice, bit like a woman's?'

'That's him. Nothing wrong with the rest of him, though, I've made a shilling or two out of him a few times up the backyards. I was hoping he'd give me the dress back free in return for a quick turn tonight.'

'He comes in here from time to time, but not recent. You seen him, Eliza?'

The barmaid shook her head.

Emma shrugged. 'Men, you can't trust any of them.' She turned to go. 'He'll turn up sometime. Plenty of fish in the sea.'

Thorpe, 10.20pm

SNOWDEN made his way into the kitchen at Thorpe Grange, lit an oil lamp and doused the lantern that had lit his half-mile walk from Greta Bridge. He found cold beef and a loaf in the larder and carried them through to his office, poured himself a large brandy and sat down to eat.

The Grange stood beside an isolated farmstead on the old Roman road from Scotch Corner over the Pennines to Penrith, a Georgian-style building intended to be part of a much larger and grander building to rival nearby Rokeby Park but never completed. It belonged, together with the rest of the Thorpe estate, to Colonel Sheldon Cradock, a former member of parliament and, Snowden was reliably informed, the unmarried father of at least half a dozen bastard children. In 1826, in a fit of business acumen coupled with political spite, Cradock had turned the farmhouse into a public house to steal business from the Morritts' coaching inn at Greta Bridge. It proved so successful – partly, Snowden knew, because he'd poached the Morritts' landlord to run it and connived to get the valuable post-chaise business moved there as well – that the up-and-coming young author Charles Dickens had stayed there overnight while researching grim Yorkshire schools for *Nicholas Nickleby*. Snowden wished he'd been around at the time: he could have told the writer a few things about schoolmasters who made Dickens' fictional Mr Squeers look angelic.

Cradock's inn had closed four years ago, hard-hit by the arrival of railways that made stage-coaches and long-distance postal deliveries by horse increasingly redundant, and the felon-chasing Association had turned the nearby Grange into a base for Snowden, half home and half workplace. He and Betsey, then just fourteen, had moved in after three years living above the village shop in Greta Bridge where the former police house, little more than a cottage with cells, remained in everyday use by his constables.

Magistrates met in the Grange diningroom, another defeat for the Morritts whose inn had been the local court-room for generations. The cellar became cells for prisoners brought from Greta Bridge for trial and Snowden took over the library as his office. The rest of the house, a kitchen, another large room on the ground floor and the whole of the upper floor, was Snowden's to live in. It was more than enough; three of the five bedrooms had never been slept in and a fourth stood empty every weekday night when, like tonight, his daughter was away.

Snowden finished his meal, poured another brandy and wondered how Betsey was getting on working at Barningham village school. Not much of a job, more a general dogs-body than anything else, but she'd been so keen to go when she was offered the chance last year that he'd encouraged her even though it meant she would have to live in Barningham during the week.

The grandfather clock in the corner struck the first note of eleven and he rose sadly to his feet. He knew he'd miss her, but hadn't realised how much or how empty the Grange would be without her.

Wednesday August 13th

Whorlton, 9.30am

BLACKSMITH Emmanuel Tenwick stared at the body lying on a pile of straw in the cow-house beside the Bridge Inn and nodded. 'That's him. Joe Yates, set himself up as a tailor in Barnard Castle a few years back. I've taken leather to him for stitching a few times, he did a good job on harness.'

'You're sure it's him?' Constable Matthew Johnson, who had been looking forward to a peaceful day at the magistrates court until Snowden told him to get over to Whorlton and find out about the river death instead, was not in the best of moods.

'Positive.'

'All right. Who's next?'

Tenwick took a last look at the body and walked out. A man dressed in footman's livery replaced him.

'Wappit, William Wappit, manservant to the vicar. I helped get the poor sod out of the river.' Almost the whole population of Wycliffe and Whorlton seemed to have turned out that morning to watch Wappit and fellow servant John Wilkinson haul the body from the Tees, supervised by the Rev John Headlam, imperious Wycliffe vicar and magistrate. 'Wasn't easy, he was well stuck between the rocks, but we loosed him after a while, hauled him onto a horse and brought him to the side. Then over here.'

'He was dead?'

'Course he was dead, must have died days ago.' Wappit looked at the constable with scorn. 'You don't think he could have been there all that time and still be alive, do you?'

'Just routine questions, have to give a full report. What was he wearing?'

'Same as now, jacket, shirt, trousers. One of his shoes was missing.' He glanced down at the body. 'Still is.'

'Anything in his pockets?'

'Bits and pieces. We made a list.' He pulled a sheet of paper out of his pocket. 'Knife, thimble, bodkin, little packet of needles.'

'Nothing else?'

'Nothing.'

'No money?'

'I told you, nothing.'

'Any marks on him?'

'Nothing you can't see now. Plenty of bruises, him having been knocked about in the river, and cuts where he'd hit the rocks. And his head was well battered, lot of blood on the back of his head and up his nose, too.' Wappit frowned. 'You'd think the water would have washed it off, but a lot was dried on, a right mess.'

'Anything else?'

'Nothing I can think of.' He sniffed. 'Beginning to smell a bit, his guts were all bloated up. He was dead all right, like I said, he must have been in there some time.'

'That'll do. We'll want you at the inquest, in the pub this afternoon.' Johnson consulted his notebook. 'Is Wilkinson outside?'

'He'll tell you just the same.'

'Just making sure. Send him in.'

Wappit walked out into the pale sunshine. 'You're next, mate. Watch where you go, there's cow-shit everywhere.' He began scraping the bottom of his shoes on the grass as Wilkinson disappeared into the byre. 'Waste of bloody time if you ask me.'

'Mr Wappit, is it not?' He looked up to see a short balding man in his fifties wearing a black coat several sizes too big and recognised him without enthusiasm. The man had been here only a week ago, digging around for information after poor young George Fawcett's accident.

'Hamish McQueedie from the *Yorkshire Gazette*, we met at Mr Garry's farm last week. Terrrible business, that.'

Wappit nodded. 'Saw the story in your paper on Saturday. He's a good lad, George, God knows what he'll do now with his left arm gone.'

'Never know what's in store for you, do you?' McQueedie shook his head. 'One minute you're happily taking shots at rabbits, next minute your gun's blown up in your hand and the doctor's sawing away at your elbow. Terrible thing, terrible. And now this.' His eyes lit up at the prospect of another few paragraphs in the *Gazette*. 'SHOCKING SUICIDE IN RIVER, SECOND TRAGEDY AT VILLAGE OF DEATH. I can see the headlines already.'

'Suicide? Says who?'

'Done himself in, must've done. CONSUMED WITH GUILT OVER LIFE OF SIN, that's my theory, HORROR AS SHAMED TAILOR TAKES OWN LIFE.' He took a battered notebook from his pocket. 'How well did you know this Yates fellow?'

'Never seen him before just now.'

'Looks terrrible, does he? FACE CONTORTED IN MORTAL ANGUISH?'

'Looks like you'd expect him to look. Dead.'

McQueedie's face fell and he closed his notebook. 'Think there's any chance the pub might open early?'

Barningham, 12.05pm

BETSEY Snowden stood before Miss Walton's desk and wondered how much more of this she could take. The schoolmistress's faint but fascinating moustache quivered as she spoke.

'You're a very bright young lady, Betsey, but you have to learn to respect the judgement of your betters. I took you on here last year in the hope that you might benefit from further education and perhaps in time become an assistant mistress, maybe even step into my shoes when I can no longer run this establishment.' She shook her head despairingly. 'I'm the first to admit that you've worked hard and proved to be quite valuable looking after the younger girls, but I *cannot* have you instilling them with ideas that are completely at odds with our Christian principles. Evolution of species, men from monkeys, I've never heard such a thing. I don't know where on earth you get such nonsense.'

Betsey ventured a response. 'My father says –'

'Your father! I'm sure he's an excellent policemen but he has some very strange notions. He is not responsible for the spiritual welfare of my girls and I will not have his daughter corrupting them with these heathen ideas, do you understand?'

'Yes, miss.' Betsey shuffled her feet, seething inside. How could this silly old woman think she knew better than papa, who knew everything there was to know about just about everything? Why, he'd even met that Mr Darwin down in Kent and corresponded with him.

The moustache quivered again. 'Are you listening to me, Betsey Snowden?' Her face hardened. 'I have to tell you that the school managers are meeting tonight and will be discussing applications for the assistant teacher's position. I was thinking that you might be suitable to replace Miss Wetherill when she leaves to get married, even though you are barely seventeen, but now...'

Getting married. Poor Miss Wetherill, rescued from a long spinsterhood by a stern-faced, narrow-minded old vicar from Westmorland with the scraggiest neck Betsey had ever seen. It was revolting.

'Well, we'll see what they decide,' Miss Walton was saying. 'In the meantime, no more of this ridiculous evolution talk. You can go.'

'Yes, miss.' Betsey turned and walked out, resisting the temptation to slam the door behind her. That's what papa would have done.

Whorlton, 4.05pm

NINE men rounded up from the village and sworn in as a jury at the Bridge Inn fidgeted impatiently as Dr Barrington Goodwood, 78-year-old general practitioner and Her Majesty's Coroner for the past thirty-nine years, finally finished summing up all they had heard over the past two hours.

'The deceased clearly died from drowning after falling into the Tees. Where that happened and why, we do not know, but there is no evidence that any third party was involved and the injuries on the body are consistent with it being tossed and turned among the rocks as it was transported down the river.

'This was a young man who had no reason to wish his own death, and we have heard that he appeared in normal good spirits when last seen in Barnard Castle last Saturday evening. There was, as you have heard, alcohol in his stomach, enough to impair his senses to the extent that he might well have missed his footing that night and tumbled into the water, which we know was in a tempestuous state.' He paused a moment and peered over his spectacles. 'I therefore instruct you, gentlemen of the jury, to return a verdict of misadventure. I trust you all agree?'

The jury foreman, who had been battling to stay awake for the last hour, glanced at his eight fellow jurors and nodded. Dr Goodwood reached for his walking-stick and stood up. 'Misadventure. You are dismissed.'

The jury filed out and McQueedie put his pencil away. He'd got the gist of it all but the old bugger had spoken far too fast to get it down verbatim, even using this new-fangled Pitman's shorthand. He's just have to make up what he'd missed, as usual. Pity about the verdict, accidents were ten a penny and he'd be lucky if it made more than a paragraph or two. He'd been really looking forward to a meaty suicide.

He stood up with a sigh and headed for the bar. It was a hard life, being a reporter.

Barningham, 4.50pm

BETSEY flung her books down on the bed and stared out of the Lilac Cottage window. Across the road were the gates to Barningham Park, and beyond them the drive curved up to the imposing country home of the Milbank family for the past 150 years and more. Their main residence was a very much grander house at Thorp Perrow in Wensleydale, but they used Barningham as a hunting lodge and now, the grouse-shooting season underway, it was busy with gun parties notching up kills by the brace on the moor above.

She watched as a gig carrying two tweeded gentlemen stopped at the gates and she wondered what joy they found in massacring those poor birds. She'd been told the moor would be a useless tangle of bracken if it wasn't properly managed for shooting, no good for the sheep that roamed its gorse, but she wasn't convinced.

To the left, if she leaned out of the window, she could see the front of the Royal Oak. At nights she lay in bed and heard its customers making their way home up the village. She'd only once crossed its threshold, invited in by landlady Ann Spenceley one evening last winter to take a letter to her father about a licensing problem, and had been surprised and a bit disappointed to discover it wasn't the den of iniquity she'd been led to believe. It was a cold night, and the blazing fire had been a welcome break from her chilly rented room at Lilac Cottage.

It wasn't much of a room, an iron bed, a table to put the water bowl on, a clouded mirror on the wall and a trunk for her clothes and a few bits and pieces. But it was cheap, and Mrs Eeles, the widow who rented it out, was like a substitute mother, warm and welcoming from the day Betsey arrived, and the food was far better than she'd expected. Her father was giving her seven shillings a week to pay the rent, almost a fifth of his salary, and she couldn't possibly ask for more.

She sat down on the bed and wondered what to do. She wasn't really learning anything at the school, just acting as an unpaid overseer of pre-adolescent girls who would far rather be back at home helping their mothers until they found employment on one of the farms or, better still, as a maid at the hall or the home of some other well-to-do family. Betsey wanted more than that. She'd set her heart on becoming a teacher one day, and not at a tiny school like this one in a tiny village miles from anywhere but a proper school with girls who really wanted to learn and teachers who dared to ask questions. It wasn't going to happen, she thought angrily, if she stayed under the wing of Miss Walton and her awful moustache.

Papa would know the answer. She stood up decisively. She'd go and ask him what to do.

It was only a forty-minute walk, down to Nor Beck, over the old bridge, up the fields and down to Thorpe. On a rainy day or in winter it was too far and often impassible at night, which was why she spent the week at Lilac Cottage and only went home on Friday nights, and not then if the weather was really bad. But today the evening was warm, the sky cloudless after days of sullen grey, and her frustration mellowed as she made her way through the newly-cut wheat to the stile at the top of the hill near Sander's Farm. Down through the woods, the sound of the Greta rushing to meet the Tees far below, along The Street for a few hundred paces and she was there.

She found her father at his desk, hunched over a pile of paperwork.

'It gets worse every day,' he said wearily as she sat down in one of the enormous horse-hair armchairs beside the fireplace. 'My own fault, Betsey. I started giving them facts and figures about crimes in the area and next thing I know is they want a monthly statistical analysis. How many larcenies, how many burglaries, how many of the miscreants appearing before the bench get sent to jail and how long for and how many are back at their old tricks as soon as they get out. Which is most of them.'

He came across, sat down in the other armchair and dug out his pipe. 'Trouble is, of course, that it takes up so much of my time I'm often not out there where I should be, catching them.' He gave her a wry smile. 'On the other hand, I suppose it does me no harm to show I'm still cutting crime down and earning the salary they pay me.'

'I'm sure you are, papa.'

'Well, they can't really complain.' He got up and dug out a file at random from the stack on his desk. It had a large letter V on its spine. 'Look at this lot I've had to deal with in the last month. Vagrants and vagabonds. Plus tramps, travellers, loafers, cadgers and hawkers and gipsies, itinerant beggars and all the other wanderers who think they can come into my patch and cause me problems.'

'Some of them must be honest,' Betsey ventured, opening the file. 'People who are homeless and destitute, or too ill or injured to find work. What are they to do but move around and beg?'

'Some are genuine,' Snowden admitted, 'but in my experience there are ten villains to every one whose story is true. We had three the other week hobbling through, claiming they were shipwrecked American sailors trying to make their way to Liverpool to get home. Turned out they were from Halifax, fit as three fiddles.'

'What happened to them?'

'Two months apiece hard labour at Northallerton jail. What would you have them doing?'

'I don't know.'

'The word soon gets around that Greta Bridge isn't a soft touch. I've doubled the number of vagrancy cases we've dealt with each year since I came here, and there's precious few of them come back.' He leant forward. 'You've got to be tough, Betsey, and that goes for the more serious crimes, too. There were 28 major felonies sent for trial at the assizes in 1840, the year I took over, and last year I'd got it down to nine.'

Far fewer serious offences, lots more petty ones brought to court. Betsey could see why the Association was pleased, but still felt sorry for some of the minor victims of her father's purge on crime. 'I'm sure you do what you think is right,' she said diplomatically.

'I do, and it works.' He settled back and re-lit his pipe, forgotten in his enthusiasm about cutting crime. 'The honest ones, and I admit there are some, I do my best to help. But the rest...' He shook his head and changed the subject. 'So what brings you down here? Just a nice evening for a walk to see your ageing father, or have you news of what's happening up there in Barningham?'

'Nothing much happens in Barningham,' said Betsey flatly. 'Old Mrs Macdonald's died, and Jane Lamb looks like following her, she's only 29 but been very ill since she had the twins... Her poor husband, they've got five young mouths to feed now and he'll be on his own.' She racked her brain for other news. 'The Milbanks are back and the moors are covered with men with guns and beaters killing things. Oh, and Mrs Eeles sends her regards.'

'Still filling you up with bread-and-butter pudding?' he smiled. 'You're looking good on it.'

He surveyed her, pleased she was growing up such a fine girl, almost a young woman now. She'd got her mother's hair, long and fair with a slight curl where it fell over her shoulders, the same crystal-blue eyes and slightly lopsided smile. And her brains, too, though he was immodest enough to think that he might have had something to do with that. Her stubbornness was probably down to him as well, but the occasional flashes of temper were definitely from Susannah. He smiled sadly to himself. There were times when Betsey's face lit up and his wife's long-dead face flashed into his mind and tears nagged the back of his eyes. Yes, he was proud of his daughter. She was all he'd got.

'Otherwise,' Betsey said, her supply of news exhausted, 'it's all quiet in the village.'

'And school?'

Betsey didn't answer straight away, and he frowned.

'Something wrong?'

She poured out her tale of Miss Walton, the monkeys and her doubts about the future. 'I still really want to teach, papa, it's what I've always wanted to do, you know that, but...' She stopped, fearing his disapproval, but was heartened to see a look of concerned understanding on his face.

'Go on.'

'I think I want to leave, only I don't know what I'd do instead.'

'You'd come back and live here,' he said with a tenderness she'd rarely heard. 'I'll find you something to do.'

'I don't want to spend my life washing up and making beds, not even for you.' A tear rolled down one cheek and she brushed it away angrily. 'But I can't work for Miss bloody Walton any longer.'

He'd never heard her swear before, and was faintly shocked. 'Not all washing up or bed-making, I promise. We'll share that. And I'll cook in the evenings if I'm in. It'll be just as it was before you left.' He paused as she recovered her composure. She didn't seem as pleased as he'd hoped, and he had a sudden idea. 'You've seen all these mountains of papers and files and reports I've got to deal with, and I'm beginning to wonder if I can cope with them. Suppose you help me with them? You're bright enough.'

'It wouldn't be teaching, though, would it?' she said in a small voice.

'Look, the Association's just allocated me some extra money to pay for an assistant, but I don't want another half-literate heavyweight like Sowerby. What I need at the moment is brains, not brawn. If I take you on – they'll raise their eyebrows sky-high at the thought of a woman, but I think they'll accept my advice – you'd get paid. Not a fortune, and I'm sure they'll cut the money back a bit when they discover you're not a man, but enough to save up and in a couple of years when you're old enough to go to a proper teacher training school for women – there's a good one in York – we'll be able to send you there. I'll be saving seven shillings a week on your rent, don't forget, you can have that to put in your moneybox too, and it'll all add up.'

Betsey thought about it and gave him a sudden hug. 'That would be wonderful, papa.' He disentangled himself, pleased but embarrassed.

'What else are fathers for? Go and put the kettle on, we'll have a cup of something before you go back.'

He returned to his paperwork, and the smile stayed on his face as she started to sing in the kitchen.

Thorpe, 6.45pm

GREENHOW had flatly refused to identify the whereabouts of Captain Bainbridge's stolen property but Snowden thought it shouldn't prove too difficult. He dug out a copy of the 1841 census returns for Mickleton and began to scour its contents.

The first census had been taken back in 1801, a simple population count undertaken so that the government could work out how many able-bodied men would be available to fight Napoleon. Forty years later its questions were extended to include names, ages and addresses, a change opposed by some who viewed it as an intolerable invasion of privacy. Snowden was not among them. It made finding people a lot easier.

Whoever had copied the Mickleton list had done a thorough job, but his handwriting could have been better. Snowden opened a desk drawer, found the magnifying glass he knew would come in useful one day, and examined the front page. *Teesdale Enumeration District No 5*, it read, *The east part of Mickleton, Taking both sides of the Turnpike...* That should cover it. He turned to the first entry, *Anthony Bustin, male, 95.* and stared at it doubtfully. The man probably didn't know his age; many people only had a vague idea of the year they were born though most knew the day and the month.

He flipped through the other eight pages. Each had the total number of names noted at the bottom, and he added them up. 363 altogether. It shouldn't take long to find Frankie, probably listed as Francis. He went back to the allegedly 95-year-old and started going down the list. *Anthony, Jane, Robert, Hannah, Elizabeth...*

When he reached the end he had found four males called Francis. Two were elderly, one a boy of six, and he focussed his attention on the fourth.

'That'll be him,' he said triumphantly to Constable Johnson, who had just finished his report on the Whorlton inquest and was hoping to get home early. 'Francis Ramsden. Aged 30 and lives at... what's that say? This handwriting's terrible.'

'Looks like High Gill Farm to me, sir.'

'High Gill Farm. Nobody else listed there, probably lives on his own. That makes things easier.' He thought for a moment. 'Who's on duty tomorrow morning?'

'Sowerby, sir.'

'Sowerby.' Snowden grinned. 'He's going to love this.'

Thursday August 14th

Mickleton, 8.10am

SITTING hunched inside the hansom cab Snowden had hired for the day from the Morritt Arms, Sowerby was anything but happy. Not only was he being taken yet again from his cobbler's workshop and losing a day's earnings, he was being jolted over rough stone roads on some incomprehensible wild goose chase and his back was playing up.

'Does he have to go so fast?' he grumbled as they swung round a bend at Romaldkirk, narrowly missing a cart coming the other way. 'If he did this in Greta Bridge I'd have him for furious driving.'

'Won't be long now, constable.' Snowden scanned the map in his hand and leaned out of his window to shout at the driver, a lugubrious man sitting in the open behind the cab, well-cloaked and muffled against the wind. 'Left as soon as you're in Mickleton, Jim, two miles or so up the track over the moor. High Gill Farm.'

The driver nodded.

Sowerby groaned. 'Don't know why you needed me, must be a constable up here could have helped.'

'I need a stranger, can't risk using someone who might know our man. Not all village constables are as upright as you, Sowerby.'

'I'll not be upright much longer if this goes on. I think I'm going to throw up.'

'You'll walk home if you do.'

The coach lurched onto the track and Snowden checked the pockets of his greatcoat. Notebook, pistol, truncheon, spare handcuffs in case Sowerby had forgotten his, pocket-knife, pipe, matches. And the fake arrest warrant Snowden had carefully forged late last night as part of his plan to arrest Ramsden without giving him any reason to suspect he'd been betrayed by Greenhow. It had to look like sheer bad luck.

The cab swung into the farm gate and came to a halt outside a long stone building, half house and half cow byre. Smoke drifted from the chimney.

'There's somebody in, that's a good start.' Snowden climbed out and waited for Sowerby. 'In a minute I'm going to ask you to go and search the barn. I want it done properly, every inch, see what you can find.'

'You wouldn't like to tell me what this is all about?' asked Sowerby, baffled.

'Just do as I say and don't ask any questions. And if you do find anything, don't for heaven's sake say a word to anyone but me, understand?'

He walked to the door and rapped loudly. It was opened by a tall thin man of about thirty in a bloodstained smock, a long butcher's knife in his hand.

'What d'you want?'

Snowden stepped back a pace, eyeing the knife. 'Superintendent Snowden, Greta

Bridge police. And you are?'

'Frankie Ramsden. What's this about, some of my beasts been straying again?'

'No, nothing like that. Would you mind putting that knife down?'

'Just killing the pig, right bloody mess.' Ramsden wiped the knife on his smock and put it on a ledge just inside the door.

'That's better. We're looking for a missing soldier, on the run from the militia in Barnard Castle.'

'What's he done?'

'Nasty assault on a woman. Look.' He held out the faked warrant.

'John Brown? Never heard of him.' Ramsden read laboriously through the rest of the document. 'Robbery and rape? Bastard wants stringing up.' He handed it back. 'What's he got to with me?'

'We're told he's been seen in this area, probably sleeping rough. I'm checking round all the farms.'

'You won't find anyone here.'

'Anybody else in who might have seen him? Your wife, perhaps?'

'Not married. I'm on my own here, lad from the next farm along helps me out. Lazy bugger hasn't arrived yet.'

'We'll be going there next. Mind if we have a look around here before we go?'

Ramsden's eyes shifted. 'I told you, there's no-one here.'

'Just a quick check. Perhaps you can show me the cow byre, my constable here can have a walk round the back and have a quick look in the hay barn.'

'Quick look? I don't want him clarting about with my hay, takes ages to stack up again.'

'Just a peek through the window should do.' He turned to face Sowerby as he spoke, and gave him a slight nod. 'Remember your instructions, constable.'

Sowerby trudged off, grumbling to himself, as Ramsden and Snowden headed for the byre.

'See, nobody in here. You're wasting your time.'

'Probably,' said Snowden mildly. 'We'll be off, then.'

They got back to the farmhouse door just as Sowerby arrived at as full a pace as he could muster. 'Can I have a word, Mr Snowden? In private, like. Urgent.'

'Just stay there for a moment, Mr – what was the name again?'

'Ramsden. Is he all right?'

'Bad stomach,' said Snowden. 'Had the runs all morning.'

He drew Sowerby, wide-eyed and desperate to speak, to one side.

'You'll never believe what I've found,' the constable whispered hoarsely. 'In that barn, sir, it's –'

'I know. Act as if you're ill and don't say a word.'

'Ill, sir?'

'For God's sake, Sowerby, you've managed it all morning so far. Come with me.'

They returned to Ramsden, still standing in the doorway.

'Just as I thought. Too embarrassed to ask himself. Can he use your privy?'

'Suppose so, if he must. Straight through the house, across the yard.' Ramsden stepped outside grudgingly to let Sowerby pass. 'Don't be long, mind, and leave it clean.'

'Off you go, constable.'

Sowerby, holding his stomach and looking more confused than ill, hurried into the house.

'Wait!'

Sowerby stopped and turned round. 'Now what?'

'Frances Ramsden, I'm arresting you for possession of stolen goods. Take him, Sowerby.'

Ramsden's face creased in fury. 'You bastard!' He reached for the knife on the ledge as Snowden pulled out his pistol and shook his head.

'Attempted murder isn't going to help.'

Ramsden hesitated, Sowerby smashed his truncheon down on the hand with the knife, and it was over.

Jim woke up from his doze inside the cab and looked out. 'Can't fit three inside,' he said as Snowden approached with Sowerby and a handcuffed Ramsden in tow. 'The fat one'll have to sit up here with me going back.'

Barningham, 12.05pm

'I SUPPOSE you've come to ask me what happened at the meeting last night?' Miss Walton pursed her lips. The moustache above them seemed to have grown a fraction. 'Well, you won't be surprised to learn that the school managers weren't impressed by my report on your progress.' She sniffed delicately. 'They agreed with me wholeheartedly that you have a long way to go yet before you reach the level of maturity required of a member of my staff.'

She paused for a moment and surveyed Betsey, a satisfied glint in her eyes. 'They have, however, appointed a new assistant mistress to replace Miss Wetherill, a Miss –' she consulted a half-written letter on her desk '– a Miss Charlotte Howard from York, to whom I am now writing to forward their decision. I'm sure she will be a very welcome addition to our staff.'

She sat back, awaiting a response.

'I'm sure she will.'

Miss Walton nodded approvingly. 'She commences her duties on the first of September. In the meantime I trust you will endeavour to improve your attitude and abandon those irreligious notions we spoke of yesterday. Monkeys, indeed! The foolish rantings of an ungodly pagan, Betsey Snowden, and the sooner you forget them the better.'

'I don't think so.'

'You don't think so?'

'I think you're wrong. All the evidence –'

'Evidence? Evidence? Do you not believe in the holy scripture, in the word of God?'

'Not all of it, no. How can you?'

The moustache wobbled alarmingly. 'If that's the case, my girl, I've no intention to allow you to continue corrupting my pupils with such un-Christian ideas.' She stood up. 'You're dismissed.'

'I don't think so.' Betsey stepped forward and put the handful of books she carried on the desk. 'These belong to the school. Give them to your Miss Howard, she may need them. I'm leaving of my own accord, and very happy about it.'

'Happy??'

'My only regret is leaving your girls in such narrow-minded hands. Goodbye.'

She gave an astonished Miss Walton a winning smile and walked out. Behind her the moustache began trembling in fury.

Thorpe, 2pm

THE Reverend John Headlam, his head of grey hair lightly powdered in the fashion of his youth and a spot of gravy on his otherwise immaculate white cravat, eased himself into the chairman's seat in the courtroom and hoped the proceedings wouldn't take long. He and fellow magistrate William Morritt had enjoyed a lengthy luncheon at the Morritt's Arms and the second bottle of claret had perhaps been unwise.

'Court in session,' William Watson, clerk to the magistrates, intoned. 'You may be seated.' There was the sound of a chair scraping on the stone floor as Snowden sat down. There was nobody else there.

'Much business this afternoon?' The Rev Headlam looked hopefully at Snowden as he stood up again and gave a short bow.

'Two applications for opening hours extensions, your worships, one bastardy and a trespass.'

Headlam covered a yawn. 'Let's get the extensions over with first. Who thinks they need more time to get drunk?'

Snowden sat down again as Watson cleared his throat. 'Oak Tree at Hutton Magna, harvest celebrations on the twenty-third, two convictions last year for serving after hours.'

Headlam glanced at Morritt. 'Refused.'

'Red Lion, Cotherstone. Wedding on Saturday, nothing recorded.'

'Saturday? Should have applied a week ago.'

'I gather it's a bit of a rush job, the wedding, your worship. The bride is –'

'Should have thought of that before she got herself in that condition. Refused. Next?'

'The bastardy claim.' Watson consulted his notes. 'Elizabeth Kirtley, lives in Boldron, makes a claim against a Robert Martindale, same parish, regarding her infant daughter. He's not contesting it.'

'Far too much of this going on.' Headlam shook his head and a faint shower of powder drifted onto his gown. 'Shilling a week for the first six months, eighteenpence thereafter.'

'Very good, your worship. That just leaves the poaching.'

'This my case?' Morritt looked suddenly interested.

'Yes, your worship. He's downstairs, I'll fetch him.'

Snowden made his way to the cells. 'Time to go,' he told Greenhow as he found his keys and unlocked the door. 'They're waiting for you.'

'About time. Haven't seen a soul all day and I'm bloody starving. Half a mind to put in a complaint.'

'Don't push your luck, Joe. It could have been worse.'

'Can't see how.'

'Well, for a start I could have put Frankie Ramsden in here with you.'

'You've got Frankie?' Greenhow looked horrified. 'Does he know about me and the painting? He'll bloody kill me.'

'Not yet, and won't if I can help it. I've lodged him in the Barnard Castle lock-up till you've gone.'

Greenhow gave a deep sigh of relief. 'If he finds out, I'd rather be doing a two-year stretch in Northallerton than face him, in here or out.'

'Up you go. Just remember what I told you. Plead guilty, say you didn't mean it. I'm not going to lie for you, Joe, but I might make it easier than I could.'

'Thanks, Mr Snowden.'

'And bear this in mind, too. If I ever see you in here again, even if it's just for having a piss outside a pub doorway, I'll make sure Frankie knows where you are and why he might like to meet you.'

Greenhow shuddered. 'No chance. I think I might emigrate, Canada, maybe, start again.'

'Good idea. And until you go, I want to know everything you hear on the street, every titbit that might be useful to me, understand? ' Greenhow nodded glumly, and Snowden led him up the stairs, across to the courtroom and into the tiny dock. 'Joseph Greenhow, your worships.'

Watson read from the charge sheet. 'Joseph Greenhow, you are charged that on the twelfth of this month you did unlawfully and with intent to pursue game enter the grounds of Rokeby Park, the property of William Morritt Esquire, contrary to clause 32, section 31, of the 1831 Game Act. How do you plead?'

Greenhow glanced at Snowden. 'Guilty, your lordships.'

'Mr Snowden?' The chair scraped again and Snowden took out his notebook. 'I had occasion to be on the Abbey Bridge with Constable Sowerby at approximately nine o'clock in the evening of August the twelfth, your worships, when I witnessed the accused walking towards me through the woods. Believing he had come from the Rokeby estates land, I apprehended him and he admitted trespassing.' So far, so true, Snowden told himself.

'Any game on him? Pheasants, rabbits, fish?'

'We searched him, nothing like that.' True. It had gone in the river.

'Gun, nets, pocket full of snares?'

'No.' Still true. He'd feared they might ask about a gaff and he didn't know how he'd have got round that.

'Then why did you suspect him of poaching?' Morritt was getting frustrated. 'You must have had a reason.'

Headlam interrupted. 'The man's a known criminal, seen him in here before. Bound to be poaching, why else would he be going through your property?'

Snowden sighed. Bringing up past convictions before the verdict was quite admissible, but he thought it grossly unfair to condemn a man merely because he'd offended in the past.

'Just taking a short-cut, your lordships.' Greenhow pleaded. 'Didn't know it was private.'

'But you've just pleaded guilty to going with intent.'

'Well, I might have had a go at a rabbit if I'd seen one in the woods, I can't deny I'd ever turn down the chance of one. So when Mr Snowden here charges me with intent, I suppose I might have, but not on private property. Which I didn't know I was.'

Morritt looked exasperated. 'The man's clearly lying. The Reverend Headlam says you're an habitual criminal, is that so, Mr Snowden?'

'Two convictions, your worship. Rabbits. I don't know that I'd call that habitual.'

'I would,' said Morritt. 'Guilty as charged and more, I'll be bound.'

Headlam deposited another trickle of powder on his shoulders. 'Anything the accused wants to say in mitigation, apart from claiming that he didn't know where he was?'

Greenhow looked puzzled. 'Mitigation?'

'Reasons why we shouldn't deal with you as severely as we might.'

Greenhow looked beseechingly at Snowden. 'I thought the inspector here, sorry, Mr Snowden, superintendent, might say a few words.'

'Mr Snowden? Good God, man, he's prosecuting you, not defending.'

'Yes, well...' Greenhow's voice trailed off and Snowden stepped in.

'I think it fair to advise your worships that the accused has been extremely helpful in another case which has led to the arrest of a man who will shortly be facing serious charges. I can't give the court any further details at this stage, but I'm sure you will appreciate his assistance to the police when the man appears before you in due course.'

He glanced around the courtroom. Thank heavens that *Yorkshire Gazette* reporter hadn't bothered to turn up. 'I would, of course, be grateful if this information remained between these four walls to avoid any hindrance to our investigations into that matter.' He sat down.

Headlam and Morritt held a brief whispered conference.

'It seems clear the accused is guilty of trespass,' Headlam eventually announced with obvious reluctance. 'That is a civil tort for which the landowner may claim damages through the appropriate courts, but sadly not within our jurisdiction.'

Morritt glared as he continued. 'I'm afraid, Mr Snowden, that you have failed to prove the intent to pursue game, and as that is what he is charged with we are bound in law to find him not guilty of that charge, despite his plea. You may step down, Mr Greenhow, and consider yourself very fortunate.'

'I do, your lordship, don't worry about that.' Greenhow walked out, his face a picture of relief.

Headlam watched him go. 'That appears to be the end of today's business.' He leant forward. 'We'd like a word with you, Mr Snowden, if you have a moment once the clerk has departed.'

Watson looked affronted at his dismissal, but gathered up his books and left.

'What was all that about?' demanded Morritt angrily. 'The man was clearly guilty, and you as good as got him off. He should be on his way to the treadmill, not walking free to rob me of more of my salmon.'

'Do you remember a painting by Poussin, *Mary and the Baby Jesus* I think it's called?'

'Of course I do. Sold it at auction, never got paid, never saw it again. Why?'

'I've got it in the office.'

Barnard Castle, 3.20pm

'YOU a policeman?' Constable Isaac Granton, half asleep on a stone bench beneath the Butter Market, blinked at the sunshine as he opened his eyes and focussed them on the speaker.

'Hardly be wearing this coat and hat if I wasn't, would I?' His eyes cleared and he saw a man of about forty, he guessed, shabbily dressed and smelling strongly of alcohol. He winced.

'You want to be out finding my daughter, not lying here sunning yourself. Couldn't find their way home, coppers round here.'

Granton stood up and tried to look authoritative. He'd only been a constable for four days, at 21 the youngest able-bodied man on the town list of potential candidates, astonished and proud to be picked for the job. He was standing guard over the curious octangular building at the western end of the Market Place, its tiled roof surmounted by a cupola holding the town bell and topped off with an erratic weathervane pierced by two bullet-holes, mementoes of a contest forty years ago between a soldier and a gamekeeper to prove who was the best shot. The first floor of the building doubled up as the town hall and courtrooms. In the centre of the ground floor was the lock-up, a single windowless cell known to all as the Black Hole and currently holding Frankie Ramsden. Constable Granton's role was to make sure he stayed there.

He took out his notebook. 'What can I do for you?'

'I told you, my girl, she's disappeared. Can't find her, not at home, not at Charlie Arrowsmith's, not anywhere.' He leaned forward, beer fumes assailing Granton's nose. 'I love her, best daughter a man ever had. Lovely, she is.' He reeled sideways and slumped onto the bench. 'Been in all the pubs looking, been everywhere, nobody's seen her.'

'Hang on while I find my pencil.' Granton opened his notebook and turned to the first page. It was still blank. 'Want to tell me her name?'

The man stared at him. 'What's it got to do with you? Bloody police, never leave you alone.' He closed his eyes, slid sideways and was instantly asleep.

Granton snapped his notebook shut and put it away. Stupid old fool. Three in the afternoon and drunk as a lord. Should be locked up.

His face brightened and took the notebook out again. Licking his virgin pencil, he began to write. *I was on duty in the Market Place when I occasionned...* One s or two? Make it two... *occassionned upon the accused in the Butter Market and having reason to beleive he was under the influence of alcohol I endevored...* That doesn't look right... *endevered to arouse him but*

The man rolled sideways and fell off the bench with a sickening thud. A pool of blood oozed from under his head.

Granton stared at it, paralysed. Nobody had told him about this sort of thing. A doctor, there must be a doctor nearby. He took a deep breath and ran out into the road to find one.

The coalman on the cart rounding the Butter Market was thinking fondly of the leeks he was entering in next week's Startforth show when Granton went under his wheels and became the youngest constable in the Barnard Castle force ever to die on duty.

Barningham, 4.15pm

BETSEY folded her nightdress and laid it carefully into her trunk. That was it, all done. Mrs Eeles' youngest son Thomas, who had called in on his way through the village with a load of sweet-smelling hay, could carry it downstairs.

She closed the lid and took a last look round. The sun had long passed her east-facing window but still lit up the road outside, long shadows from the sycamores reaching towards the pub. Summer was more than halfway over, she thought, another month and the first hints of brown and red and gold would be kissing the leaves, the swallows gathering on the rooftops to chatter about their departure, and the rector blessing the harvest festival fruits. She'd miss it, but had no regrets.

Mrs Eeles gave her a hug and a warm apple pie. 'Your father's paid to the end of the month, don't feel you owe me anything. That Miss what's-her-name, Hewitt?, she'll want somewhere to live in September and Miss Walton always sends them to me so I won't be out of pocket.'

'Howard,' said Betsey. 'Miss Howard. Heaven help her if she's got a mind of her own, but if she's with you, Mrs E, she'll not lack a welcoming home to come back to.'

'Trap's outside,' said Thomas, trunk in his brawny arms.

Thorpe, 5.45pm

FRANKIE Ramsden surveyed his new cell with disgust. 'Not much better than the last one,' he said, slumping down on the bench. 'Middle of bloody nowhere, silent as the grave. At least under the Butter Market you could hear what was going on outside.' He grunted. 'Like one of your lot jumping under a coal cart. Silly sod.'

Snowden, who had taken a trap to collect his prisoner from Barnard Castle two hours ago and arrived just as Constable Granton's mangled young body was being carried off to the Raby Hotel stables to await an inquest, tried to remain patient. 'Let's get this over with, Ramsden. I've had a long day.'

'Didn't have to have, you could've gone looking for your missing soldier lad somewhere he'd more likely to be than my farm. On his way over Stainmore and far away, if he's got any sense, wouldn't be hanging around in Teesdale. Just my bloody luck you turn up and start effing around in my barn.'

Snowden drew his chair closer to the bars separating them.

'Tell me about it, Ramsden. The stuff in your barn. How'd it get there?'

'No idea.'

Snowden sighed. 'Don't waste my time, lad, we both know you're lying. The question is, do I charge you simply with receiving and possession of stolen property, which will get you two or three years, maybe with hard labour? Or do I go for burglary, you breaking into the Kings Head stable and stealing the goods yourself? Twenty years ago you'd have ended up on the gallows.' He wondered whether Ramsden had ever heard of the 1827 Larceny Act, which had eased the penalty for this and a host of other hitherto capital offences that had sent men, women and even young children swinging into eternity for stealing a lace handkerchief or a shilling's-worth of turnips.

'The gallows?' Ramsden shook his head disbelievingly. 'You're just trying to scare me. They're not going to hang me for this.'

'Probably not.' Snowden agreed. 'But they can send you off to Australia for fourteen years, you'll be an old man by the time you get back here. If you survive the journey there and back, of course, and can find the money for a return ticket.'

'I didn't steal it.'

'It just turned up in your barn one day and you never knew about it?'

'Something like that.'

'So why try to knife me if I you didn't know what my constable had found? Could have been nothing, a couple of rabbits for all you knew. Come on, Ramsden, no jury's going to believe you didn't know the stuff was there.'

'All right, I knew about it. But it wasn't me that stole it and put it there.'

'So who was it?'

'I'm saying nothing more. You couldn't prove I stole it even if it was me. Which it wasn't.'

'I wouldn't stake my life on that, Ramsden.' He could be right, though, thought Snowden. There'd be no difficulty proving receiving, but burglary might be a different matter. All Ramsden would have to do was find witnesses who'd vouch he was with them in Mickleton on the night the property vanished, and there were plenty of perjurers in Briggate willing to swear their grandmother's life away for the price of a few jars of ale.

'It wasn't me, I tell you. You've got me for receiving, maybe, but you're not going to get me saying I done something I didn't and end up the other side of the world. And I'm not fingering anyone else who might face that, either.' He shook his head angrily. 'Do your worst, Mr bloody Snowden, but I'm saying no more.'

Snowden wasn't sure why, but he thought Ramsden was probably telling the truth. He wouldn't decide yet, though. The man could stay down here for a bit. A few days on bread and water might persuade him to be more co-operative.

Rokeby, 7.45pm

'EXTRAORDINARY thing, extraordinary!' William Morritt poured himself another glass of chilled madeira and another for his dinner guest at Rokeby Park. 'Took me into his office and there it was, leaning up against the wall. Bit dusty, few bits of hay and what-not, but it'll clean up well enough. Don't know how Snowden did it.'

'Worth a bit, that painting. You'll be glad to have it back.' Charles Manners sucked a last mouthful of soup from his plate. 'You do want it back, I suppose?'

'Seems the best idea. Your client, what's his name? Brainsforth? Captain fellow who bought it –'

'Bainbridge.'

'That's the man. Owes me for it, went broke. If he has it he'll sell it, and the money will get split up among all his creditors. Won't get a fraction of what I'm due.' He waved a hand at a footman to clear the soup away. 'No, I'm laying claim for it, waive my bill, forget I ever sold it. Price of these paintings is going up all the time, I'll hold onto it for a while before putting it back on the market.'

'Wisest thing,' agreed his companion.

'Glad you see it that way, Manners. You legal fellows can fight over the rest of the stuff Snowden's found, you'll make a few guineas for yourselves, I'm sure. No such thing as a starving lawyer, eh?' He laughed and turned to his butler. 'Where's that roast grouse, Jennings?'

'Running a little late, I'm afraid, sir. One of the kitchenmaids is missing, some kind of family problem, I believe. Cook has had to cope without her.' He coughed gently. 'She's not in her most amiable mood, sir. She's had to do some washing-up.'

'Good lord.' Morritt's eyebrows shot up. 'Best to keep out of her way, eh?'

'Indeed, sir.'

'May as well get the claret on the table while we wait, must be warm enough by now.'

'Very good, sir.' The butler cast a calculating eye at the decanter. A good half-pint of madeira left, he'd enjoy that later.

'Got it all back, did he, this Snowden fellow?' Manners took a pinch of snuff and sneezed delicately into a handkerchief.

'Pretty well. Few bits and pieces missing, clothes and the like, some silver but nothing else valuable.' Morritt greeted the arrival of the claret and watched Jennings pour a first glass for his approval.

'Rascals who stole it in jail, I suppose?'

'Didn't say, Snowden keeps these things close to his chest, but I'll lay good odds on him finding them. Persistent fellow, our police superintendent, doesn't give up easily.'

'Sounds like a useful man to have around. Must meet him sometime.'

'Not much for social gatherings, I gather, but knows his job. Worked wonders clearing the area of those work-shy beggars we were plagued with.' Morritt paused thoughtfully for a moment. 'Hard on poachers, too, though he missed out on one in court today, not like him.' His mind returned to his painting. 'Bainbridge still suing the bailiff, is he?'

'Him and his crew. Case comes up again at York in a week or so. Not sure what they'll do now the stuff's been found but they've been served with subpoenas ordering them all to be there. Bainbridge will get his costs, anyway.' Manners smiled at the thought. 'Not that he'll pocket much of it after he's settled my bill.'

The grouse arrived as Morritt sniffed, sipped and eventually swallowed his sample of claret. 'Damned fine year, this. Fill the glasses, Jennings, and get another couple of bottles up warm and ready.'

Barnard Castle, 9.40pm

McQUEEDIE paused outside the Golden Lion, put down his heavy travelling bag and wondered whether to go in for a swift one.

He was standing halfway along the cobbled main street where the Horse Market met the Market Place, though he could never remember which was which. When he'd arrived in the town six weeks ago he'd been further confused about the Butter Market, the odd-shaped building at the far end of the Market Place, or possibly the Horse Market, one of them, anyway, which wasn't a market except sometimes on market day. He shook his head. No wonder he needed a drink.

On the other hand, he was only a hundred yards or so from the Black Horse in Newgate, where a room was waiting for him. It would be good to get rid of his luggage and then settle down for the night in the bar. He could put the drinks on his bill instead of paying for them in the Golden Lion, and he was worryingly short of money after paying his former landlady for the damage last night.

He picked up the bag containing all his worldly goods, which were few enough but could have been a bag of bricks by the weight of them, took a deep breath and staggered on. It was a pity he'd had to leave the lodging house in Gallowgate at such short notice, but Mrs Birtwhistle had insisted, saying firmly that she could no longer accommodate guests who turned up drunk after midnight and proceeded to fall down the stairs and demolish her furniture. She'd demanded ten shillings compensation plus two pounds rent he owed and told him to be out first thing in the morning.

He reached the Butter Market, turned left into Newgate and made his way down the street to the Black Horse where he dropped his bag gratefully beside a corner table and walked to the bar.

'Mr McCormack, isn't it?'

'McQueedie. C, Q and three Es, Mrs Borrowdale.'

She looked at him sharply. 'Not come to say you don't want the room after all, have you? I told you when you came in this morning that you'd still have to pay.'

'No, no, I haven't changed my mind. I'm sure it's a splendid room, can't wait to see it.' Her expression softened a fraction. 'After I've sampled a pint of your excellent ale. Just put it on a tab, settle everything up at once, eh?'

'We don't do credit in the bar. Threepence if you don't mind.' He reached for the pint. 'Up front.'

He delved into his pockets and found a sixpence his landlady had missed. 'Your good health, Mrs Borrowdale.'

'Rent payable weekly in advance.' She looked at him expectantly.

'First thing in the morning, Mrs B, soon as the bank's open.' There must be a pawnbroker somewhere nearby. 'Any chance of a bite to eat?'

'At this time of night?' She gave him a withering look with his change and reached for a key from the hooks behind her. 'Number four, top of the stairs and turn left. No lady visitors, hot water's extra, no playing musical instruments, breakages to be paid for, no pissing in the fireplace, coal's extra, breakfast's seven sharp.'

He picked up his pint with a sigh, sat down and looked round. There were a dozen men dotted round the bar, most involved in a heated argument about Barnard Castle's chances against Raby in next Saturday's cricket cup final. Two others were throwing darts at a board over the fireplace, above which hung a notice forbidding singing, dancing and something else that had been torn off. Probably laughing, he thought.

It had been a long day, running about trying to find out about that police lad who'd gone under the cart, and his head drooped over the table. He'd have another pint, still had the money for that, and then he'd go up to his room. Buried at the bottom of his bag was a good half-bottle of Glenbuckie's Highland Malt, a nightcap when he got upstairs. He deserved it after doing a good job on the policeman story. HERO IN BLUE SACRIFICES

LIFE TO SAVE TODDLER. He yawned and closed his eyes. DRAMATIC DASH ENDS IN DEATH. With luck it'd make a page lead.

At the other side of the room Joe Greenhow, celebrating his release but avoiding the Oddfellows in case the lads there demanded the sovereign he'd wagered about the salmon, watched the balding fellow in the corner fall asleep and smiled.

Forty minutes later McQueedie awoke, decided to call it a night and looked in vain for his bag.

Over the road in St Mary's churchyard Greenhow sat behind a gravestone and took another swig of Glenbuckie's. It really had been his lucky day.

Whorlton, 11.45pm

THE DOG FOX tore another mouthful from the leg trapped among the roots of a fallen elm half-submerged in the river two hundred yards downstream of the suspension bridge. The body, bloated and grey, its eye-sockets robbed the day before by a magpie and clumps of long black hair ripped from its scalp, shifted for the first time in five days.

Breaking loose, it resumed its passage down the river, tumbling past the upturned ferry boat and the stones that had trapped Yates, spinning slowly under the single arch of Winston bridge and floating on towards Gainford.

Thursday August 21ˢᵗ

Barnard Castle, 7.0am

THE SIX BELLS in St Mary's tower hammered out the hour and McQueedie's hangover hammered back with each echoing ring. Last night's meeting of the Teesdale Poor Law Union had gone on till almost midnight as argument raged over who was to blame for impregnating two female inmates of the paupers' workhouse in Gallowgate, and he had got through at least half a bottle of brandy writing it up afterwards in his rented room above the Black Horse bar.

He found his notebook under the trousers he'd abandoned on his way to bed and tried to focus his eyes on what he'd written. WORKHOUSE MASTER ACCUSED OF GRAVE OFFENCES. That should be good enough for a top-of-the-page column. HE MADE ME DO IT, CLAIM INNOCENT YOUNG WOMEN. No, make that GIRLS, much better. He forced down a mouthful of coffee, topped up his mug with the dregs from the brandy bottle and reached for the four-day-old copy of *The Sporting Chronicle* he'd picked up on his way to last night's meeting.

He ran his eye down the front page. Advertisements for London theatres, horses at stud, Schweppe's new soda and a patent tooth brush that promised it wouldn't fall to pieces in your mouth. He turned to the main news column. Parliament had passed new restrictions on gaming houses. Twelve thousand protesters at an Orange march against Popery in Enniskillen. The mayor of Sunderland had been stoned by voters after Hudson won the by-election, and the Queen and Albert were on a visit to Germany and she hadn't been sea-sick once. McQueedie yawned and wondered what it was like working for a real newspaper.

He turned the page and a tiny headline caught his eye. AMERICAN INVENTS POWER LOOM FOR CARPETS. Hangover forgotten, he reached for his notebook and began to make notes. If he couldn't get Barnard Castle seriously worried about inventor Erastus Brigham Bigelow of Massachusetts, his name wasn't Hamish McQueedie.

Thorpe, 8.15am

BETSEY opened the file she'd picked at random from the shelves and flicked through its contents. F, it said on the spine, and inside were her father's notes on Felonies, Fraudsters, Forgers, Furious driving... it went on and on in no apparent order. Fairs (licences for) merged with Foreign Coins (utterance of), Felonies suddenly became Fraudulent Pretences. No wonder he spent so much time at his desk. It all needed sorting out.

She'd spent the past week settling back into Thorpe Grange, surprised and a little ashamed at the state it had got into since she'd moved out. Papa was so organised at work – apart from the filing which he obviously detested – but there were corners of the house that clearly hadn't seen a mop or broom for months and she'd found things in the pantry that were frankly disgusting.

Well, it was better now, and first thing this morning she had moved a table and chair into a corner of his office and begun work. Fortune-tellers. What was *that* all about? She got up and examined the books behind her father's desk, looking for one heavy leather tome she'd often seen him poring over. *Blackstone's Commentaries on the Law of England, Volume IV: Criminal Law*. She pulled it out onto the desk. It was ancient, published in 1770, so old that it was full of the lower-case letter s printed as f. She opened a page at random.

'By the ftatute 4 & 5 Ph. & M. c. 8. whofoever marrief a woman child under the age of fixteen yearf, without the confent of parentf or guardianf, fhall be fubject to fine, or five yearf imprifonment...'

She looked in vain for an index, gave up and was putting it back when her father walked in, mud-spattered boots leaving footprints across the stone floor. She grimaced.

'You're up early.' He threw his hat on an armchair. 'Looking for something?'

'Fortune-tellers. I was trying to find out about them, but that book's useless.'

'Well out of date,' Snowden agreed. 'They've done later editions, updating it a bit from time to time, but they're all as unreadable as that one. It's still about the best guide to the law we've got, though. Courts would be lost without it.' He smiled. 'They're often lost with it, too, I'm afraid.'

'Someone should write a replacement, a book even I could understand.'

He nodded. 'Well, that's what I'm trying to do when I get time.' He picked up a sheaf of papers from the desk. 'Here you are, Snowden's Guide for Police Officers and Constables and Magistrates Assistant, everything you need to know. Or it will be if it ever gets finished.' He riffled through the sheets. 'Long way to go before it gets an index, but there's fortune-tellers in here somewhere. Here you are, look.'

She took the page, covered with his sloping black handwriting and full of words crossed out and amended, scribbled notes in the margins and liberal spatters of ink.

'*Every person pretending or professing to tell fortunes, or using any subtle craft, pretence or device, by palmistry or otherwise, to deceive and impose on any of Her Majesty's subjects shall be deemed a rogue and vagabond,*' she read. 'I think I know what that means.'

'It means they're liable to do three months' inside if they're caught. Twelve hours a day breaking rocks, or keeping the treadmill busy, if it's a woman.'

She looked horrified. 'Just for telling me I'm going to meet a tall dark stranger?'

'That's the law, Betsey.' He handed her the rest of his manuscript. 'Have a look through it all, tell me what you think.'

'After I've cleaned up your mud. Where have you been to get your boots in that state?'

'Got up at five and rode over to Hurworth, village on the Tees south of Darlington. They've found another body in the river. Parts of it, anyway.'

Greta Bridge, 9.25am

CONSTABLE Sowerby stood at his workshop door, hammer in hand, and shook his head firmly. 'I don't do animals.'

'Yes, you do.' Sarah Lambert, matriarch at Ewebank Farm, mother of eight and renowned for being able to sling a sheaf of hay as well as any man, folded her arms over her ample bosom and stood her ground. 'Always getting us into trouble over straying beasts, horses running loose, dogs getting into chicken sheds. Spend more time on them than doing what you should be, catching thieves.'

'That's different, Mrs Lambert. Horses, cattle, sheep, dogs, yes.' He shook his head again and stared at the animal at the end of the piece of rope she'd looped over his door handle. 'Pigs, no.'

'Well, I'm not taking it back wherever it's come from. Lost property, that is, and it's been at my broad beans. You find out who's let it get free and tell them I want compensation.' She glared at him. 'Prize beans, they were, not fit for the compost heap now. And no salting it away for bacon, Jeremiah Sowerby, or I'll have you up before your own magistrates for stealing the bugger.'

She stormed off. Sowerby watched her go, unlooped the rope and wondered what he was going to do with the two hundredweight of Gloucester Old Spot that had just urinated copiously over his feet.

Thorpe, 10.20am

IT WAS the first time Barningham's young rector had appeared as a magistrate and the Reverend William Fitzwilliam Wharton peered nervously over his spectacles as the opening defendant was led into court.

'Francis Ramsden, your worships.' Snowden led his prisoner to the dock. 'Committal for trial, receiving goods knowing the same to have been feloniously stolen, taken, extorted, obtained, embezzled or disposed of, contrary to...'

'Committed.' John Michell of Forcett Hall, Wharton's co-magistrate, was in no mood to waste time listening to sub-clauses of the Larceny Act. 'Next assizes. In custody, of course.' He drew a firm line through Ramsden's name on his list of the day's cases.

Wharton leant over. 'Shouldn't we know a bit more about it first?' he whispered tentatively.

'Nonsense, man's guilty, wouldn't be standing there if he wasn't. You'll learn.' Wharton sat back in silence and watched Ramsden glower as he was led back to the cell. 'I'll have you, Snowden,' he shouted as he reached the door.

'Bread and water, solitary confinement for a week,' Michell ordered. 'Take him down.' He turned to Wharton. 'Contempt of court, very useful, you can pretty well make it up as you go along. Stick 'em in jail for months if you feel like it. Next!'

'Mary Dawson!'

A young woman hobbled into court clutching a bundle to her breast and stared around.

'In the dock.' She made her way across and stood there. The bundle began to cry.

'No children in court. Take it out, constable.'

The woman looked terrified. 'I've got no one to look after it, my lord.' Constable Johnson took it gently from her. 'He'll be all right with me, miss.'

'It's a girl.' The woman started sobbing.

'What's she here for?' demanded Michell impatiently as the constable vanished with the child.

Snowden consulted his charge sheet. 'Breach of contract, your worship.'

'Let's get on with it.'

Watson stood up from the clerk's desk. 'Mary Dawson, alias Alderson, residing at Gilmonby?' The woman nodded.

'Alias?' Michell demanded. 'Going under a false name, is she?'

'I understand she resides with a man named Alderson to whom she is not married, your worship.'

'Disgraceful. No wonder she ends up in court.' His moustache bristled. 'What's she done?'

The clerk turned back to woman. 'You are charged that you contracted with Mr William Dent of Bowes Hall to serve in husbandry for one year, the said contract being in writing and signed by the contracting parties, and that you did not enter into the said service and have not yet commenced the same. How do you plead?'

'I haven't worked for him, no, sir.' She was still sobbing.

'Guilty plea, your worships. Mr Snowden?'

Snowden stood up. 'I have the contract here, sir, supplied by Mr Dent. It's quite clear.'

Michell grunted. 'House of Correction, six months' hard labour.'

'If your worships will permit me to confirm this is what she signed?'

'If you must.'

Snowden took the document across. 'Is this your signature?'

She peered at it through her tears. 'That's my cross, sir, as far as I can tell.'

'You can't read?'

'No, sir.'

'Then how...' he paused for a moment. He was supposed to be prosecuting, but there was nobody else to help her. 'How did you know what it said?'

'I didn't, sir, I just wanted a few weeks' work, till the baby came, sir, and they said I had to sign the paper. And then I was so ill...'

'Is she alleging that Mr Dent trapped her into the contract?' Michell looked astounded. 'The impudence of the woman! Why, he's a member of the board of guardians, know the man well.'

'Not Mr Dent, your worship.' Snowden brought the paper back to the bench and gave it to them to study. 'Signed by someone called Garstang.'

'That's his farm manager.'

'Perhaps he was in error about the nature of the intended employment, your worship. These things happen.'

Michell turned abruptly to Wharton. 'What d'you think? Guilty, I say.'

The rector bit his lip. 'It could be the case, I suppose, we all make mistakes. Perhaps a little mercy is called for?'

'Mistakes? Mercy?' Michell looked at him with faintly disguised contempt. 'Clergymen, all the same. Oh, very well, case dismissed. But if we see you here on another occasion you'll not see your child again for a long time.'

'Yes, my lord, thank you, sir.' She walked out to regain the infant.

Wharton watched as another line was scored across the case list and decided he did have a lot to learn. He'd been given the Barningham incumbency five years ago at the age of 29 after a miserable childhood being bullied at Eton and an even more miserable three years at Cambridge wrestling with his soul, and had entered the Church in search of peace and quiet. Sitting here beside this appalling man Michell, sentencing helpless people to vicious treatment for things they didn't understand, was not what he had in mind. All he really wanted to do was look after his prize pigs and invent farm machinery. He was good at that.

'Next!'

Wharton polished his spectacles and sighed unhappily. He wasn't enjoying this, and he had enough things to worry about today already. His missing Gloucester White Spot for one.

Barnard Castle, Noon

McQUEEDIE put down his pint of Crabthorpe's Best Barney Bitter and grimaced. If this was his best, he'd hate to taste Crabthorpe's worst. Barmaid was all right, though.

He dug out his notebook and went through the morning's work. Interview with two carpet mill bosses about Erastus Bigelow inventing things to put hundreds of hand-weavers out of work. The bosses had been delighted. Far fewer hands to pay, just one painful bill for the power loom and then enough savings on labour to swell their balances at the Backhouse Bank.

He'd had a job finding any workers to talk to, with them all slaving away inside the Briggate mills. Carpets and other woollens were being turned out at five-storey smoke-blackened factories lining the street all the way from Thorngate to the County Bridge, and there was Ullathorne's just across the river and a flax mill downstream. Squeezed in between them were dye vats, forges, builders' yards and all the other premises serving the carpet-makers and, of course, the host of grubby tenements housing the workers, many living in single rooms, some holding two or even more families. Water came from open wells, streets shared communal toilets emptying into the street, and the threat of typhoid and cholera hung over it all. McQueedie thought he'd seen slums back home in Glasgow, but nothing as bad as this stinking, slimy, shit-littered corner of Barnard Castle. No wonder the beer went off.

He finished his pint, decided he couldn't face another, and walked over to the bar.

'Same again?' Eliza took his empty glass.

'No, thanks. What have you got in the way of whisky?'

'Just O'Donnell's.'

Irish, he might have guessed. 'It'll do. Make it a double.' He looked round. There were bits of wood stacked in a corner. 'What happened to your chairs?'

'The usual. Fight last week, Tom's going to chop that lot up for firewood when he gets a moment.' She handed him his drink. 'Bloody hooligans, the lot of them. Fighting over a fish or something. Stupid thing is, the fight was all about some bugger who wasn't even there.'

'Wasn't there?'

'No, never seen him since either. Seem to be a lot of people disappearing these days, him and that lad Yates and now poor Kate.'

'Kate?'

'Kate Raine, lives across the street when she's at home. Her dad's been all over looking for him. When he's sober, that is.' She smiled. 'Silly sod cracked his head the other day, drunk in the Butter Market, day that young copper went under the coal cart.' The smile faded. 'Anyway, haven't seen Kate since the night Yates went in the river, funny that.'

McQueedie's ears perked up.

'Give us another and have one yourself.' He went back to the table to collect his notebook. 'You can tell me all about it.'

Thorpe, 1.15pm

BETSEY closed the file she'd been working on, now neatly organised on an alphabetical basis, and began writing a list on its cover of what was inside. Damage, Deedforging, Deer-stealing, Defacing coinage, Disorderly houses, Dog-fighting... She'd had no idea there were so many criminal offences, and that was just the Ds.

'Papa.' He looked up from his desk across the room. 'You've got all these files with lists of people who've committed crimes. What do you do with them?'

'Well,' he scratched his head. 'Which file have you got there?'

'D.'

'Right, so I'm looking for, say, drug dealers. I just look up Drugs in the file and there they are.'

'But suppose you have somebody's name and you want to know what they've done?'

'I'd go through the files looking for them.'

'All the files?'

'Of course. They might have done all sorts of things.'

'That must take ages. Look at them.' She waved a hand at the stack of files beside her. 'And those are just the A to Gs.'

'It does.'

'Suppose we had another file, one with all the people listed in alphabetical order and saying what they'd done. Wouldn't that speed things up?'

He thought about it for a moment. 'I suppose it would.'

'And if each person's file had a marker on it, with a number or a code or something saying what they'd done, you could just go through them and pick out the ones who'd done, say, murder or whatever, and wouldn't that be useful too?'

'Yes. Yes, it would.' He glanced at the ornate grandfather clock in the corner. 'The stages will be in soon. I'll have to be off.'

Halfway to the door he stopped. 'Almost forgot, we have a guest for dinner tonight. Can you manage something a bit out of the ordinary? It's your turn to cook.'

She nodded, surprised. 'There's a leg of lamb.'

'That'll do very well.'

'Who's coming? You don't often have people for supper.' She frowned. 'I'll have to get the best china out.'

'The Reverend Wharton, met him in court today. I've come across him before, of course, but it was his first time on the bench and I thought he might like some advice. Interesting fellow, not sure he's cut out to be a magistrate, though.'

'He goes into school to keep an eye on religious instruction.' Betsey smiled. 'It made a nice change from Miss Walton. He seems a gentle sort of man, but I've never met him socially.'

'Now's your chance.'

Barnard Castle, 1.40pm

McQUEEDIE was breathing heavily by the time he reached the top of The Bank and looked desperately around for a cab. They rarely ventured down to Briggate, too likely to be robbed and nobody who lived down there could afford one anyway.

He spotted one parked outside the Kings Head and ran towards it. 'Greta Bridge, fast as you can,' he panted.

'In a hurry?' The driver put down his *Gazette* and studied him. McQueedie's coat was crumpled, his hat was awry, and he smelled of whisky. 'Cost you a shilling. Up front.' He knew what drunken Scotsman were like.

McQueedie swallowed, but he had to get to the south-bound stage before it left. Hang the expense, his scoop couldn't wait and it would earn him far more than a shilling. He dug into his pocket, found two sixpences and thrust them into the cabbie's hand. 'Fast as you can,' he repeated, clambering inside.

The cabbie bit the coins carefully and nodded. 'Do my best. Gertie's not much of a one for hurrying, mind.'

'Persuade her, man. Another sixpence if you get me to Greta Bridge by quarter past. A shilling, even.'

The cabbie brightened and reached for his whip.

Inside the cab McQueedie dug out the story he'd scribbled hurriedly in the bar and read it through. It was good, he always wrote better after a drink or two. LOVERS' DOUBLE SUICIDE. THEY LEAPT TOGETHER TO THEIR WATERY DOOM. TOWN MOURNS TRAGIC COUPLE. Oh, they were going to love this at the *Gazette* if he got it to them in time.

The cab swung over the Abbey Bridge and stopped.

'Twopence for the toll,' said the cabbie.

McQueedie swore silently as he handed over two pennies. Fifteen minutes left. They might just make it.

Greta Bridge, 2.10pm

THE north-bound stage was running late and the coachman anxious to have it ready by the time the south-bound arrived from Carlisle, due any minute. He stood by impatiently as the Morritt's ostler backed the new horses into position. Eight passengers had vanished into the inn for their allotted ten minutes to stretch cramped legs, take refreshment or queue for the privy. Some had been travelling since six that morning, and needed all three.

The ninth person to clamber out of the cab was a uniformed constable from the Leeds borough police, now standing beside it talking to Snowden.

'Usual stuff, sir.' He handed over a bulky leather bag, its handles secured by a spring lock. 'Letters and documents from Leeds, superintendents' reports I picked up when we stopped at York, Northallerton and Catterick, copy of that book you wanted, came by the London stage yesterday. I think that's it.'

'Any news along the way?'

'Murder in Ripon, pub landlord threw a customer down the cellar steps. Gentleman robbed on the Thirsk road out of Northallerton. Woman found drowned south of Darlington.'

'Yes, I know about that, saw the body this morning. Been dead a few days, probably came from round here somewhere and been washed down after the storms last week. We're asking round about anyone missing. Anything else?'

'No, sir.'

'Thank you, constable. Get yourself something from the inn to eat on the way back. The south-bound will be here any minute and you can be on your way home.'

'Thank you, sir. I'll see you here on Saturday.'

Snowden wandered past the lodge at the tree-lined entrance to Rokeby Park and onto the hump-backed bridge over the Greta. Not much of a river compared to the Tees it met the far side of the Park, scarcely a stream in a dry summer, but its romantic and in places dramatic reaches upstream had won the admiration of artists and writers. Turner had painted it, Walter Scott had wandered it while composing his epic poem *Rokeby*. Snowden, no painter or poet, had been bewitched by its beauty last summer, when he'd walked with Betsey from the back of the Morritt's Arms across the grass-covered remains of a Roman fort to the river and followed its banks upstream, discovering to their surprise and delight a tiny derelict church in a deserted village.

He turned back at the sound of the coach arriving from Carlisle. Greta Bridge was the halfway point on the stage route, and the two drivers would exchange coaches, each heading back home the way they'd come. Passengers on the new arrival poured out, fresh horses were led forward, and Snowden went to see if there was anything for him from Brough, the last staging post it had called at. There was nothing for him. The north-bound coach set off and the one he stood beside was ready to go. As the coachman climbed onto his seat a cab arrived at almost a gallop, slid to a stop alongside, and a dishevelled figure leapt out.

'Don't go yet!' it shouted. 'Exclusive hot news, stop press, must get it to York tonight.' He thrust his story, folded in four with the *Gazette*'s address scrawled on the back, into the coachman's gloved hand.

'Shilling for a letter.'

McQueedie groaned and reached into his pocket. This scoop was costing him a fortune. He watched the coach rattle over the bridge on its way south, turned and was greeted by Snowden.

'Hot news? What's that all about?'

'Buy me a drink and I'll tell you, Mr Snowden. Just promise you won't tell anyone else in the press until Saturday. It's got a what's-it, an embargo on it till then, top secret.'

Snowden emerged from the Morritt's Arms fifteen minutes and four whiskies later. Three of them were swilling inside the *Gazette*'s proud Teesdale correspondent and about to be joined by another. The cabbie was waiting patiently outside.

'Does he want taking home?' he asked hopefully.

'I don't think he's going anywhere for a while.' Snowden smiled. 'You'd best be getting back to Barney.'

'On you go, Gertie. Take it easy, girl, you've earned your keep for one day.'

Snowden pondered what he'd heard from McQueedie. The man had milked it for all it was worth and his SORROWING SWEETHEARTS IN DREADFUL DEATH was almost certainly nonsense, but there might be something in it. Kate Raine. Her description fitted the body he'd seen that morning, and it might well have gone into the river at Barnard Castle. He'd get Sowerby to investigate.

He collected his horse, tethered on the verge, and led it round to Sowerby's workshop.

His constable was inside, with one of the fattest pigs Snowden had ever seen.

'Afternoon, Sowerby. Who's your friend?'

Thorpe, 7.10pm

BETSEY stood up from the range and brushed her hair back over her shoulders. The lamb would be ready in five minutes, she'd let it stand while they opened the wine and had the soup. There were leeks and potatoes from the garden and a warm crusted loaf to go with it.

She went into the diningroom and surveyed the table. All set. She'd found the silver cruet, glasses shone, napkins were freshly pressed, and a bowl of wild flowers picked that afternoon stood in the centre. All it needed now were the diners.

She found her father sitting in one of his office armchairs, newspaper before him.

'He's late. If he's much longer the vegetables will be cold.'

Snowden lowered his paper. 'I'm sure we agreed seven o'clock. He'll be here soon, I'm sure.'

'I hope so. It's taken ages.' She went back to the kitchen and her father resumed his reading. It was yesterday's *Morning Post*, printed in London last evening and delivered to Darlington by the overnight express within six hours. Copies reached Barnard Castle by horse in mid-morning and his was ready for collection at the Morritt's Arms by noon. The coming of the railways was a marvel, he thought, a wonder of the age. Only a few years ago he'd have waited up to a week for the day's news.

There were new lines springing up everywhere. The *Post*'s front page was full of notices about new routes being approved by Parliament and even more notices urging subscribers to buy shares in ones still at the planning stage. Everybody seemed to be rushing to make money from new routes.

The railway hadn't reached Barnard Castle yet, but surveyors were already mapping a line from Northallerton that would skirt the church at Barningham and make its way to a massive marshalling yard at Scargill, with links from there to Barney and over the Pennines to Tebay. There would be viaducts over the becks, noise and steam and smoke over the moors and valleys, who knew what else. Factories, workshops, new streets for railway workers, hotels for tourists? The area would be transformed beyond belief and not, he thought, all to the good.

He shook his head. This proposed and grandly-named York, Carlisle & Durham Westmorland & Lancashire Junction Railway had already raised thousands of pounds and he'd been tempted to invest. But it couldn't go on, this railway boom. One day the bubble would burst and he didn't want to be among those wringing their penniless hands when it did.

He turned the page. An Irishman was being sued for £5,000 in a breach of promise case at Cork Assizes. That was better, and he was folding the paper for details when a knock came at the front door, the Reverend Wharton at last. Snowden cast a look at the clock as he got up. Twenty minutes late, Betsey wasn't going to be pleased.

Greta Bridge, 9.15pm

HANNAH Sowerby heard her husband open the front door and hid the gin bottle behind the family bible on the shelf. By the time he walked into the room she'd picked up her knitting and was busy on a half-finished sock.

'Waste of bloody time.' He sat down in the other chair and began pulling off one of his boots. 'Three hours traipsing round Briggate and not a word, no bugger will say anything. Oh, she lives there all right, this Kate Raine, but that's all they'll say. You should see the state of the room she shares with her father, bloody disgusting.' He started on the other boot. 'He was no use, either, half-pissed and no idea where she was. When I told him she was probably lying on a slab in Hurworth he was all over the place, sobbing and wailing.' He got the other foot free and stood up. 'Told him to get over there tomorrow and see if it was her. Anything to eat?'

His wife didn't look up. 'This time of night? You should've got yourself something in one of those Briggate pubs you've been drinking in.' He opened his mouth to protest. 'Don't lie to me, Jeremiah Sowerby. I can smell the drink from here. Good job one of us never touches a drop or we'd both be on the streets.'

She waved a needle at him. 'And what about that pig you've got in the workshop? It's not staying there, filthy thing, we'll all get God knows what kind of diseases.'

'Snowden says it has to until I find its owner.' His face lifted and he started putting his boots back on. 'I'll just go and see if it's all right, give it a feed if I can find anything.'

'It can have your supper, it's in the waste bucket under the sink. And no nipping round the back bar afterwards.'

His face fell. As the door closed behind him she put down her knitting and stretched out an arm to reach behind the bible.

Thorpe, 9.45pm

BETSEY and Wharton were in animated conversation when Snowden came back with another bottle of claret. The rector had apologised profusely for being late when he arrived, but then said little at first. He'd sipped carefully at the wine and it wasn't until the lamb had been demolished and the bottle half-emptied that he began to relax. By the end of the meal he was positively lively.

Snowden sat down, opened the new bottle and poured him another glassful.

'So kind, perhaps just another drop.' Wharton resumed his discourse with Betsey, and Snowden surveyed him with curiosity. Tall, lank, with slightly-curled dark hair falling over one eye and spectacles which he was waving in the air at that moment to demonstrate a point, he reminded the policeman of a portrait he'd once seen of the poet Byron, apart from the spectacles, of course, and the scandalous reputation. Betsey clearly found him interesting, attractive as well, probably, and for the first time he considered the possibility that his daughter might one day wish to marry. One day, a long time ahead, he hoped, and pushed the thought from his mind.

'You're absolutely right,' Wharton was saying. 'It is imperative that the Church comes to terms with all these scientific discoveries. This is the nineteenth century, for heaven's sake, we can't go on wallowing in the begats and begottens of the Old Testament and insisting the world began only four thousand years ago. We have to move with the times.'

'That's *exactly* how I feel.' Betsey nodded vehemently. 'I wish you'd have a word with Miss Walton.'

He took another gulp of claret and gave a slight giggle. 'You mustn't repeat a word of this to anyone, my dear Miss Snowden. If the bishop gets to hear of it I shall be defrocked.' He blushed faintly at the word and Snowden tried to hide his amusement. Wharton's unexpected enthusiasm was as welcome as the humanity he'd shown in court earlier in the day, and the superintendent had warmed to him increasingly as the evening drew on.

It was well past ten o'clock when the rector got up to go, a little unsteady but insistent that he could ride home in the gathering dusk. He shook Snowden's hand and gave Betsey a faint bow.

'It's been delightful, quite delightful. You must come to the rectory some evening and dine there, though I fear my domestic arrangements are a little primitive. I do have a cook, however, who does a passable shepherd's pie, and there's a cellar half-full of wine my predecessor overlooked when he left. I don't usually drink a great deal. Or dine with anyone else, for that matter.'

He went to shake Snowden's hand again, realised he'd already done it and instead gave Betsey another embarrassed bow. 'I must apologise again for my tardy arrival this evening, I was looking...' He gave another boyish giggle. 'I was looking for Ermintrude. She's been missing all day.'

'Ermintrude?'

'She's a Gloucester, you know, white with spots.'

'Spots?'

'Blue ones, lots and lots of them all over.'

Betsey looked shocked. 'How awful for her.'

'Oh, I don't think she minds.' Wharton's face fell. 'Anyway, she's my prize sow and I've lost her. It's very sad.'

'I think he's talking about a pig, Betsey.' Snowden grinned as he guided Wharton to the door. 'Ermintrude, eh? Do you know, I think I might be able to help.'

The rector on his horse and safely across The Street, Snowden returned to the Grange. 'A good man,' he said as he rejoined Betsey, finishing off the washing-up. 'He'll need a bit more practice before he can hold his wine, though.'

'I liked him.' She put the final plate away. 'That's the lot, I'm off to bed.'

Snowden poured himself a last half-glass of wine and wandered into his office. On the desk was a parcel, carefully wrapped in brown paper and tied with a red ribbon. There was a card tucked under the bow.

Happy Birthday, Papa

He'd quite forgotten, and looked at the clock. Another hour and he'd be forty-one. He took a sip of wine and opened the parcel. A book, three slim volumes bound in leather, *Sybil or The Two Nations*. It was Disraeli's latest novel, published a few months ago and hailed by the *Morning Post* as another searing political satire exposing the conditions under which the working classes laboured. Not as good as young Dickens, Snowden felt, but Disraeli was definitely destined for great things.

He took the first volume over to the fireplace, sat down and turned to the opening page. It was the eve of the Derby in 1837 and the odds were on a horse called Caravan. Snowden took another sip of wine and settled down.

Monday August 25th

Barnard Castle, 9.10am

ELIZA shook her head in disbelief. 'I never said that, he's made it all up.' She threw the *Gazette* down on the bar top. 'Sweetheart Suicides? Jumping into the bloody river together? I just said Yates and Kate might have known each other, nothing like that.'

'Typical. Can't trust 'em, reporters, say anything for a story.' Tom Marwood put the pub clock down on a table and examined its vacant face. 'Why would anybody nick the hands off this?'

'I don't know, they'll take anything that moves.' She picked the newspaper up again. 'Can't find anything in here about an inquest, we don't even know she's the one who drowned.'

'Held it on Friday, too late for the *Gazette*. It was her in the river, your reporter friend got that right at least.' He opened the back of the clock and peered inside. 'They've took the bloody key as well.'

'How d'you know?'

'Not here, is it? Should be on this little hook back of the door.'

Eliza banged the *Gazette* down on the bar. 'How d'you know it was her that drowned?'

'Kate Raine? Her father was in last night, in a right state, he was. Had to go all the way to Hurworth to see the body and everything.'

'So what happened?'

'He told everybody about it, had five pints and went home. Well pissed, he was, by then.'

'At the inquest, I mean?'

'Fell in and drowned, the coroner said. Accident.'

'Nothing about Yates and her being together?'

'Never mentioned, don't suppose they knew about him.' Tom shook his head and picked up the clock. 'Might as well chuck this out, no use with no hands and no key. Bastards.'

Thorpe, 10am

THERE were thirteen names on the list of magistrates appointed to serve on the Greta Bridge divisional bench. Four had turned up for their monthly meeting at the police house.

It was as many as Snowden had expected. Five of those missing lived far away, two of them in London, and were never seen. Of the rest, one was suffering from advanced dementia, one refused to attend anything but the annual free dinner, one was a rich industrialist too busy for daytime deliberations, and the last had stalked out after a meeting last year rejected his demand that all errant children should be whipped, and had never been seen since.

'Good morning, your worships.' Snowden took his place beside Morritt, the bench chairman, and laid his report on the table, nodding to the three sitting on the other side. The Reverend Headlam returned the nod, dislodging the day's first haze of hair powder. Michell, moustache drooping a bit this morning, Snowden thought, ignored the greeting. Young Wharton gave an uncertain smile and dropped his pencil. At the far end of the table Watson, the magistrates' clerk, was busy opening his inkpot.

'Don't suppose we'll see anyone else.' Morritt looked at the clock. 'Let's get on with it. Same apologies as last time, I presume? First item, superintendent's report. Mr Snowden?'

Barnard Castle, 11.15am

JOHN Robinson stood up from his loom, stretched and made his way outside. He'd been in the carpet mill since six o'clock, his eyes ached and he was ready for his first fifteen-minute break of the day.

Blinking in the sunshine as he stepped out into Briggate, he reached for his clay pipe. It was one of half a dozen he'd bought on Saturday night, its bowl shaped to show the head of the young queen, her hair bunched behind the crown just like on the stamps and at twopence-halfpenny for six a bargain. He lit it carefully and looked round to see who else was out.

'Morning, Sam.'

'Now, John. What's new?'

'Not a lot. See that girl up your lonning got drowned. Went into the river with young Yates, they say, on purpose. In the papers according to my missus, so it must be true.'

'That'd be when we had them big storms, week back.' John rolled back through his memory. 'Reckon I saw them both that Saturday night, up by the bridge, he had his arm round her. Could've been on their way to kill theirselves then, I suppose.'

'Look miserable, did they?'

'Happy enough the pair of them, bit tipsy, I'd say. It'd be about one on the Sunday morning, he just came down the lonning, had a word with her and off they walked together. Well, you know what she was, Sam.'

'They get younger and younger, them girls on the game. What was she, seventeen?'

'Something like that. In the family way already, my missus says, but I don't know anything about that.'

'Too old for it, eh?'

'Never too old, Sam, but I'll be damned if I pay for it.' He chuckled. 'Not on the County Bridge at one o'clock on a wet Sunday morning, anyway.'

'At it, were they?'

'Not that I saw. Dark night, I lost sight of them.'

Sam looked thoughtful. 'There was some constable going round the other day asking if anyone had seen them. You want to tell them.'

John shook his head. 'Never talk to the police, me. Been locked up by the bastards too often. They can find out themselves.'

He lifted his right boot and tapped the pipe out gently on its heel. 'Back to work.'

Startforth, 11.45am

McQUEEDIE gripped the brass rail at the back of the fire engine, his eyes closed in terror as it hurtled over the County Bridge and veered left round the White Swan on the corner. He would never, ever, do anything as stupid as this again as long as he lived, if he lived, which seemed horribly unlikely with every bone-shaking jolt of the wooden wheels spinning inches from his knees.

It had seemed such a good idea three minutes ago when the engine had thundered round the corner from Gallowgate and been forced to stop momentarily while pedestrians and horses got out of its path. A fire was always good for a few paragraphs, more if it was a fatal, and there was no quicker way of getting to the scene than grabbing a lift on the small empty platform at the back of the machine. He had no idea that it could go so hideously, terrifyingly, ball-wrenchingly fast.

He'd almost come off as the two horses and crew of six brawny volunteers tore along Briggate, blithely unaware they had a stowaway on board, the bell clanging to the cheers of passers-by. He'd long ago wet himself and worse, much worse, was going to happen if this went on much longer. He was already spattered thickly with something thrown up by the wheels which he hoped was mud but had a dreadful suspicion was steaming from the animals in front.

The engine slowed down a little as it met the challenge of the steep bank past the church and then accelerated on towards Cross Lanes. McQueedie renewed his grip on the bar and whimpered a prayer. Let him survive this, he promised, and he'd do anything. He'd even give up the drink.

The horses were reined in sharply at they reached The Street and he dared open his eyes. He never thought he'd be so glad to see a flock of sheep. There was a God after all.

The engine slowed to walking pace to negotiate the animals and he let go of the bar, his shaking legs tumbling him backwards onto the road as the firemen careered off towards Bowes. He didn't care what was on fire, it could be whole bloody village, he never wanted to see even a chimney blaze for the rest of his life.

He needed a drink.

Thorpe, 12.10pm

IT HAD been a tedious couple of hours, thought Snowden wearily as Morritt drew proceedings towards a close, even by magistrates' meeting standards. Michell had left on the stroke of noon, pleading urgent business that Snowden was fairly sure involved the Morritt's Arms wine cellar, and the remaining three were on to any other business.

'That box of new truncheons outside,' said Morritt. 'Must be half a dozen of them. Expensive thing, truncheons. Do we need them?'

'Replacements, sir.'

'How do they lose a truncheon? Big heavy thing like that, you'd notice if it dropped out of your hand. Got a wrist-strap on, anyway, can't drop anywhere.'

'Well,' Snowden began with an inward sigh. 'We've had to replace five in the past few months. Two got broken – one went under a cart and another hit a tree instead of the man it was aimed at. A third fell down a well in Boldron, another was used as a wedge to hold a barn door shut with felons inside and then forgotten about, and the fifth...' He didn't want to mention the last one and paused before continuing. 'The fifth was stolen.'

'Stolen?'

'Constable took his coat off to go down a drain, looking for a lost child. Truncheon was in his pocket and someone helped themselves to it.'

'Disgraceful.' Morritt shook his head. 'Man's been punished, I hope?'

'Haven't caught him yet, I'm afraid.'

'The constable, Snowden, the constable. Appalling disregard for police property.'

'He did save the child, sir.'

'Hmm... Any other business? Very well, meeting closed.' Morritt paused for a moment and his voice became less formal. 'Now that's over, Snowden, perhaps you can enlighten us about this Leaping Lovers nonsense in the papers? Anything in it?'

'To be truthful, I don't know. We've had the two drownings, or at least that's what the coroner decided. Both victims came from Barnard Castle, indeed from the same lonning, and –'

'Lonning?' Headlam interrupted, looking baffled.

'Local dialect, sir, for a lane, though in this instance it's no more than a narrow alley between tenements.'

'Ah. Do go on.'

'Well, although some ten days elapsed between the discovery of the bodies it seems they may well have entered the river at much the same time, probably on the night of August the ninth or early the next morning.'

'A Sunday, that would be?' Headlam asked. 'The thirteenth after Pentecost?'

'Indeed, sir. There had been stormy weather for a couple of days beforehand, if you remember, and the river was running high. Whether they fell in deliberately or by accident is unknown, as is whether they did so together.'

'One could have fallen in and the other gone to their rescue but also drowned?'

'It's possible.'

Wharton, who had been silent throughout most of the morning's proceedings, ventured a question. 'Or one pushed the other in and then fell in himself?'

'Yes, himself or herself. One was a young man, the other a girl, as you know.'

'Or...' Wharton hesitated. 'Or a third party was involved and pushed both of them in?'

'It's another possibility. As I say, we just don't know. If anybody saw anything, they're not telling us about it. You're all well aware of how popular the constabulary are in that part of the town.'

Morritt and Headlam nodded.

'I've never been as far as Briggate,' Wharton confessed. 'St Mary's is as far as I've gone in that direction. Further down it looks... is unsavoury the right word?'

'Very.' Snowden gave him an encouraging smile. 'I'll take you down there sometime, it'll certainly make you appreciate the rural peace of Barningham.'

Morritt returned to the drownings. 'What do you think happened then, Snowden?'

'My own view, at the moment, is that these were two separate accidents, young people who had probably had too much to drink on a Saturday night, wandered along the river for some reason, possibly together but we've no evidence for that, and fell in.' Snowden shook his head. 'It's not the first time that's happened and it won't be the last. It's a dangerous place to be, especially on a dark night.'

'So the *Gazette* could be right, it could have been a, what did it call it? a suicide pack?'

'Pact, sir. *Geminus mors pactum,* I believe the Romans called it, an agreement of twin deaths.'

Morritt looked astonished. 'You have the Latin?'

'A bit, sir. Have to, the law's full of it.'

'Indeed. Very handy in Briggate, I'm sure.' Morritt frowned. 'I think you should go a bit deeper into these deaths, Snowden. Too many questions about the affair, what do you think, John?'

Headlam nodded. 'Coroner was that old fool Goodwood, I suppose?'

'At both of them, yes.'

'Hmm. Yes, well, I think Morritt here's right, it's worth looking further into. Dig around, see what you can find. You agree, Wharton?''

Barningham's rector looked gratified that anyone was interested in his opinion, 'Oh, yes, absolutely. It does all seem a bit odd.'

Morritt stood up. 'Time for luncheon. More grouse at the Morritt's, I suppose. Time they changed the menu.'

Barnard Castle, 2.15pm

THE RAT looked up from gnawing what was left of the dog's carcass and watched five-year-old Patrick Malloy paddle through the open sewer running from Briggate into the Tees.

The boy picked his way carefully over the rocks, the ragged smock many sizes too big for him trailing in the filth beneath his bare feet, and stood at the water's edge. In his left hand he held a tangle of string that did for hair on a one-legged wooden doll, and he swung it idly from side to side as he looked across the river. On the far side he could see two people wading knee-deep in the water, dragging a net between them, and he knew they were trying to catch fish.

It looked interesting and he wondered how they did it, but they were too far away to see clearly. He dropped the doll, put a foot on a half-submerged rock and stepped forward. That was better, and there was another rock just a bit further out. He stretched out his other foot, slipped sideways and was suddenly being carried downstream.

Nobody saw him go.

The rat gave its whiskers a quick clean and went back to its meal.

Thorpe, 2.20pm

THERE wasn't much in the Qs. Two folders, Qualifications (falsification of) and Quays (damage to), both containing no more than their titles on otherwise blank sheets of paper, and Betsey turned to the next file

Rabbits (unlawful killing). Races (licences for). Railways and Rape and Riots. She stopped, remembering the events of last April, and began to read the *York Herald* cutting folded inside.

It was dated May 6th, a report of the Greta Bridge court case. *Before the Venerable Archdeacon Headlam in the chair and a full bench of magistrates.* That was unusual, papa said most of the time hardly any of them turned up. But it had been a very unusual occasion. There weren't many riots in Teesdale.

The headline was *Brutal Conduct of an Innkeeper and a Mob*, and was followed by a column of tightly-printed text. *On Thursday week, Barnard Castle races were held, and Mr Snowden, the superintendent of police was present, along with Sergeants Askew, Clarke and police constable Sowerby, to preserve the peace, etc. Several battles took place during the day...*

Betsey had been there, allowed to miss school to accompany her father to the races on the Demesnes, the large expanse of open land beside the river at the western end of the town where the fairs and hirings were held. They had met a former schoolfriend with her family, and she'd spent the day with them as papa went off to keep the peace. It was late afternoon when the trouble began.

The race course attracted crowds of visitors, and mingling inevitably among them were thieves, fraudsters and pickpockets having a profitable time. *Towards night, Mr Snowden received information that a person had lost £105...* An enormous amount, more than papa earned in a year! *...and from this and the number of bad characters on the ground, the superintendent directed Constable Sowerby to inform the several land-lords of the tents to cease from filling more drink...*

Poor Mr Sowerby. Most of the beersellers had complied with the order but John Westwick, 34-year-old shoemaker who ran the Four Feathers in Briggate with his wife Mary, was having none of it. 'I'll fill the bloody glasses till morning if I see fit,' he'd told the constable.

Mr Snowden and Sgt Clarke proceeded to the tent to remonstrate with Westwick, but they had scarcely entered the tent before Westwick seized Mr Snowden by the throat and said he was master there and wanted no police officer in his tent. A general rush was made by upwards of a hundred of the very lowest blackguards, and blows were struck at the officers in all directions.

Betsey and her friend were safely at the far side of the Demesnes, but Papa told her afterwards that he had feared for his life as fists, sticks and bottles rained down on him. Beaten into a corner, he had somehow managed to draw his pistol and threatened to fire at his assailants.

By this means he regained his horse, but not before he had received very serious injuries, from which he is still suffering. The officers had now got all together, and repulsed the mob for a considerable time, and also got the names of the ringleaders...

Betsey had been reunited with her father after he had been treated for three broken ribs, a broken shoulder-blade, two knife wounds, luckily not as serious as they might well have been, and a body covered in cuts and bruises. She had flung herself upon him, sobbing and causing him even more pain, but he had just held her tightly and said he'd feared she might have got caught up in the riot as well.

She read to the end of the cutting. Westwick had been convicted of gross assault on papa and fined £4 with costs or two months in jail if he couldn't pay. Ten others, including one woman, were fined or sent to hard labour for assault, larceny, or both. One was acquitted.

One name seemed familiar, and Betsey consulted her new filing system. There he was, listed under Inquests. Emmanuel Tenwick, blacksmith, the man who'd identified young Yates's body six days ago. She gave a satisfied smile. She could prove to papa, brave papa who she could have lost forever in that riot, that she wasn't wasting her time.

She folded the cutting back into its folder and picked up the next piece of paper inside. Another cutting, this one from the following week's *Gazette*, a letter from West-wick himself, no less. He must have been able to pay the fine, she thought, because he certainly wouldn't be given the chance to write from a prison cell. She read it with growing disbelief. Not only did the man outrageously claim he was innocent, but he blamed the riot on papa, saying he had been 'over-officious' and not injured at all.

They shouldn't be allowed to print such lies in the newspapers, and she knew whose version she believed. She thrust the cutting angrily back in the folder and picked up the next file.

River Banks (damage thereof). She picked up her pen and dipped it in the ink.

Over-officious. Papa? How *dare* they?

Barnard Castle, 2.30pm

McQUEEDIE limped into the Oddfellows bar and collapsed at the first table in sight. He'd had to walk the first two miles before a cart came along, and spent the rest riding in the back of it on a pile of dead sheep destined for the knacker's yard. The driver refused to let him any nearer because he stank of horse-shit.

Eliza was out of sight, busy in the other bar.

'With you in a minute.'

He hadn't dared enter any other pub on his way back, the state he was in, and had taken to the Briggate back alleys after being jeered by a crowd of snotty kids as he crossed the County Bridge. Coming along the riverside he'd passed a dozen people scouring the banks for something and was grateful they seemed too busy to see him slinking his way to the Oddfellows, desperate for a drink before he faced the long crawl up The Bank to the Black Horse. Eliza, he knew, would welcome him after their chat the last time he was in.

He looked round the room. There was a disgusting hairy dog sprawled by the door but only one other customer, an aged crone dozing over an empty glass of gin. It could have been worse. Summoning up what little strength he had left, he walked to the bar and checked the whiskey bottle was still there at the back. Plenty left, Irish of course, but he'd take anything just now.

He reached into his pocket and discovered that all his money must have fallen out during his ordeal on the fire engine. It wouldn't matter, he told himself, Eliza would understand, he'd just have to sweet-talk her a bit when she came in and she'd let him pay the next time he called by.

She walked in and stared at him.

'Hello, darling,' he said, putting on his best smile.

What happened next haunted his dreams for weeks.

'You lying bastard!' She grabbed the *Gazette*, folded on the bar-top, and waved it in his face. 'Elderly barmaid Miss Eliza Benson said this, the buxom Miss Benson said that!' He staggered back, speechless, as she rounded the counter. 'I'll have you know I'm a respectable married woman, Mr bloody Teesdale Correspondent, and I am NOT ELDERLY.'

Her eyes blazed and her teeth flashed with fury.

'You're barred! Get OUT! OUT of this bar before I throw you out, and believe me, I could.'

He believed her, he believed her. He turned and made for the door, tripped over the dog, ricocheted off the wall and out into the passage. Eliza followed him at the top of her voice.

'And if I have anything to do with it you'll be barred from every other house in Barney!'

The dog took a savage bite at his ankle before he fell out of the pub door into Briggate and collapsed on a pile of ripe privy dung that had dropped off the midden man's cart moments before.

Barnard Castle, 2.40pm

'I'VE told you a thousand bloody times not to let him go near the river, you stupid, stupid girl!' Mary Malloy was on the verge of hysteria, shaking with fury and fear. 'If they don't find him soon and alive you'll wish you'd gone in the bloody water too.'

She collapsed sobbing on the muddy bank. Her daughter, another Mary, eight years old and her face blotched red and smarting from the savage belt her mother had just given her, stood silent, stricken with horror at what she'd done. How could she have known the little sod could get out of the yard and move so far so fast? She'd only been gone a few seconds for a piss behind the wall and he'd vanished.

Although screams were common enough in Briggate, her mother's anguished howl when she found the one-legged doll at the water's edge had brought a dozen neighbours to the riverside, joined within minutes by a score and more weavers from the nearby mill. They were still searching downstream but had found nothing so far, and the mill owner was standing impatiently at its door, calculating the cost of lost production. He'd be wanting his men back soon. One of the fishermen from the other side who had seen the crowd and come over the bridge to find out what was going on had launched a rowing-boat, now checking parts of the river downstream where the boy might be caught among rocks breaking the surface.

Constable Ephraim Kipling had been in the centre of town, contentedly investigating allegations that the landlord of the Black Horse was watering his beer, and was eventually persuaded to finish his free pint and venture into Briggate. He stood there now, nervously wondering what to do and proving no use at all except as a target for abuse and the occasional rotten vegetable thrown at him from the upper windows.

A small boy with a shock of ginger hair came haring round the corner and stopped abruptly at the sight of him. 'You a fly, mister?'

'I'm a member of the constabulary, son, not a bloody insect. You mind your lip and get on home. This is a serious incident scene.'

'No bloody use here, then, are you? You want to be down the mill, they just found him there.' He stuck out his tongue and vanished.

Constable Kipling took out his notebook, put on his most authoritative look, and wondered where to go. There were half a dozen carpet mills in sight, more round the bend, two flax mills by the Demesnes and any number of corn mills down the river. He wished he'd stayed in the Black Horse.

Thorpe, 2.50pm

BETSEY picked another handful of broad bean pods and examined them doubtfully. Past their best and dotted with dark brown scabs, but they'd have to do.

She dropped them on top of the runners in the basket and wandered on past the brassica plot. Black and yellow caterpillars everywhere, on the cabbages and cauliflowers and even a few strays making a start on the sprouts despite the netting the gardener had thrown over them. She moved on, uprooted a carrot and discovered it was a parsnip.

'Thought I might find you here.' Her father smiled. 'Parsnips tonight? I didn't know we had any.'

'Nor did I. Not much of one, is it?' She brushed earth off the root, split into three strands tangled around each other. 'I thought they were supposed to grow straight.'

'Depends on the soil, too many stones and they do that. Make good wine, though, I'm told.'

She looked surprised. 'Which ones are the carrots, then?'

He bent down and picked her a couple from the next row along.

'Thank you, papa. How was the meeting?' She hadn't seen him since he'd disappeared to meet the magistrates.

'Dragged on, as usual.' He sighed. 'They'd seen the *Gazette*, want me to find out more about the drownings. I rode into town for a word with the sergeant there and asked him to pass the word round among his constables.'

'I thought you said Mr Sowerby had been investigating?' She decided she might try making parsnip wine and picked another half-dozen as they spoke.

'Sowerby? There are times when I think he couldn't find his own mother, let alone a witness to anything. I'm going to have to go to Briggate myself and see if I can do better. Two people disappear into the Tees, somebody must have seen something.'

'You want to take care down there, on your own.' She remembered the files that morning. 'You don't want to end up facing another mob like at the races.'

'I'll be safe enough in daylight. Maybe I'll take Sowerby along, show him how it's done. He's big enough to keep me out of trouble.'

'Good idea.' They began walking back to the house. 'I was reading the file, about the riot. There's a letter from one of the men who attacked you, the one who ran the beer tent.'

Snowden thought back. 'Westwick?

'That's him. He wrote to the paper saying it was all your fault. It wasn't, was it?' Her father smiled. 'I don't think so.'

'They shouldn't be allowed to publish lies like that. You should have written back.'

He frowned. 'I'm not arguing with a convicted criminal in the correspondence columns of the *Yorkshire Gazette*, Betsey.'

'But you might have been killed, people should know the truth.'

They reached the kitchen door and went in. Snowden shrugged. 'It wouldn't be the first time someone's tried to kill me. I'm still here.'

Betsey put the basket on the table. 'I know about that poacher who tried to shoot you a few years ago, it was awful.' They'd never caught the man, who had fired a gun at her father late one evening on a lane at Hartforth, missing him by only inches: the bullet had smashed into the tree he was leaning against. Although the government offered the enormous sum of a hundred pounds as a reward for information that led to the assailant's arrest, no one came forward to claim it.

'Any other narrow escapes, papa?'

'One or two. I'll tell you about them sometime.' He turned towards his office. 'Tonight, perhaps, after dinner, if you really want to know. What are we having, apart from carrots and beans?'

'There's some mutton that needs doing before it goes off.' She lifted the parsnips out of the basket. 'Mrs Eeles will know about parsnip wine. I'll ask her next time I'm in Barningham. You wait and see, I might surprise you.'

Barnard Castle, 2.55pm

HE was cold, his face almost blue and his teeth chattering, but he was alive. Mary Malloy grabbed him from the burly weaver who had found him among the reeds a hundred yards downstream, lying face-up and conscious in the shallows just short of Etherington's corn mill race. He'd wrapped the boy in his jacket and carried him back to Briggate, followed by a crowd of fellow searchers.

'The disobedient little bastard, I'll bray the daylights out of him when I get him home. And you, too.' She gave her daughter another blow across the face. 'That's just for starters, it's the whip for you.' She disappeared up the alley in which they lived, the girl trailing dismally behind.

Constable Kipling arrived, notebook at the ready, as the crowd dispersed. 'Move along now, nothing more to see.' He'd always wanted to say that.

Half a rotting cabbage missed him by an inch, and he decided to write up his report in the safety of the Black Horse. He still hadn't decided if its beer was being watered, and a couple more free pints would go down very nicely.

Barnard Castle, 4.15pm

McQUEEDIE sat with his knees under his chin in the tiny battered tub in the outhouse behind the Black Horse and tried to reach the middle of his back with the tiny remaining sliver of carbolic soap.

The bath would cost him a shilling, the soap threepence, there was an extra twopence for hot water and he knew they'd want at least a florin to launder his clothes. His rent included a shaving-mug of warm water each morning, a jug of cold to wash in, and one bath a fortnight. That wasn't due for another week, and he'd had to beg for an extra one today and only got it when he'd threatened to go into the bar smelling of horse droppings, dead sheep and privy dung. The outhouse was the only place vacant and the maid had refused to go in because of the stench. He'd had to fill the tub himself, kettle by kettle, and it was tepid at best when he finally got undressed and climbed in. By now it was positively cold.

He reached for a towel and his heart sank. He knew there was something else he should have asked for, even though it probably meant another twopence from his pocket. Which was, he suddenly remembered, empty.

He wasn't going to put his shit-ridden clothes back on. Equally, he wasn't going to walk stark-bollock naked through the kitchen. There was nothing in the outhouse to dry himself on and the only thing he could see that might be wrapped round his clean but shivering body was an empty sack. He peered inside, disturbing a writhing mass of white maggots feeding on what he guessed was once a pig's head discarded by the cook.

Perhaps there was something he could use in the stables over the yard. He peered round the door to make sure no-one was around, and scurried out, hands over his privates, a trail of cold water spattering behind him.

Halfway across a voice brought him to a heart-stopping halt.

'Well, well, well, the Newgate Flasher at last. We've been looking for you, sunshine.' Constable Kipling reached for his handcuffs. This was turning out a much better day than he'd thought.

Thorpe, 8.10pm

MUTTON gone, dishes washed and the black cat with the white spats that had appeared from nowhere three days ago and been promptly adopted and disgracefully spoiled by Betsey lay curled up on her lap before the fire. It purred gently as its new mistress put down her book and tried to divert her father from the *Morning Post*.

'Papa? He looked up. 'You said you'd tell me about being shot at and everything.'

He put the newspaper down and wondered where to start. He wouldn't tell her about Ireland, he wasn't proud of what he'd been part of there. 'No other shootings, but I thought I was going to have my throat cut back in...' He paused, working out when it must have been. Two years, perhaps, after he'd lost Susannah and baby Sarah. '1833, it must have been. When I was just a young constable with the preventative service in Corbridge.'

'I didn't know you worked there, on the Tyne.' She leant forward, intrigued, and the cat gave a gentle protesting wave of a paw. 'What happened?'

'I was riding home one night on the Hexham road, four men sprang out of a hedge and dragged me off the horse. It all happened in a moment.' He paused, his mind delving back twelve years. 'They cracked me over the head and robbed me of all I'd got, watch, money, everything. One of them had a knife and used it to slit my coat open to see if I had anything hidden inside, and I remember thinking he'd slice my throat next.' He gave a wry smile. 'It was very embarrassing.'

'Did you catch them?'

'Never saw their faces, they all had masks. They were robbing people all over the place, a blacksmith in Hexham, a farmer in Dilston. One eventually got arrested after a victim was wise enough to be carrying a pistol – they didn't issue them to us in those days – and shot him through the leg. They hanged him, but the rest got away, we never found them.'

Betsey's eyes were wide open, the hand that had been stroking the cat at her mouth.

'You must have been terrified.'

'Well, it was part of the job, you knew it might happen.'

'And where was I? I'd have been, what, five? I don't remember any of it.'

'You wouldn't. You were living with your grandmother in Nunnington.'

'After my mother died?'

'Yes.' He fell silent. Betsey had fond memories of the farm in Yorkshire, a haytime ride on a high-stacked cart, steaming cattle waiting to be milked, tadpoles in the pond and nights in the attic bedroom with mice running through the rafters. She must have been eleven when grandmama died and papa had reclaimed her, bringing her to his new home over the grocer's shop in Greta Bridge.

Her father came out of his reverie. 'Long time ago,' he said, a note of sadness in his voice. She wondered what her mother had been like. She must have been wonderful if he'd loved her so much.

She changed the subject to bring him back from the past. 'Did you find that report from Constable Kipling? I left it on your desk.'

'About the child in the Tees?'

'Yes, he said they'd found him.'

'Lucky lad. The current took him down into some shallows, he never really went underwater as far as I understand. Got stuck among reeds by the mill race.' His brow furrowed. 'I wonder...'

She waited, stroking the cat again. It needed a name. Blackie? Spats? Tibby? Matilda? Tom? It rolled over and began to purr. Thomas it was.

'I wonder if anybody else falling into the river there would end up in those shallows?' her father said at last. 'The two who drowned, they went miles downstream.'

'Maybe they went in from the other side?' Betsey tickled newly-christened Tommy under the chin.

Her father nodded. 'It's possible, I suppose. I'll ask a few questions across the bridge. You never know.' He picked up his *Morning Post* and turned to the back page. 'I see Surrey have formed a county team, not before time. I don't suppose you're interested in cricket?'

Betsey shook her head. 'Don't be silly, papa.' The cat yawned, wondered if there were still some mutton scraps left in the kitchen, and decided it would rather fall asleep.

Tuesday August 26th

Barnard Castle, 9.10am

SNOWDEN tethered his horse outside the new workhouse at the top of Gallowgate, gave a loitering urchin a penny to look after it and the promise of another if all was well when he returned, and began to walk down towards the town. He'd rejected the idea of bringing Sowerby along. He had enough on his plate without giving lessons to half-witted constables.

Gallowgate was Barnard Castle's broadest street, with a neat public park on his left and then prosperous-looking residences lining each side, a far cry from Briggate. The houses gave way to pubs and shops as the street approached the town centre, where cobbles marked the site of the weekly cattle market and narrow alleys led to yards and poorer dwellings, some not much better than the tenements down by the river. He turned into King Street, and walked towards Ullathorne's new heckling workshop, built for employees combing out flax from its mill beside the Tees. There was a line of new houses for them to live in as well, two-storey thatched dwellings each housing at least two families and already looking run-down. The third one along in Hecklers Row had been the home of the unfortunate Joseph Yates.

One of its windows was broken, and he could hear a baby crying inside as he knocked on the door. It was opened by a woman of about twenty-five, dank-haired and thin-faced, an apron tied round her waist and the baby in her arms.

'Yates?' he asked.

'Dad's not in. What d'you want?' She joggled the child, still crying.

'Police. I want to talk to someone about the drowning.'

'He's talked to you lot already, told the inquest all he knew. Not that he knew much. He was snoring his bloody head off in here the night our Joe disappeared.'

'Where is he now?'

'Outside some pub or another, waiting for opening time. All he ever does these days.' She took a grubby crust of bread from her apron pocket and stuck it in the baby's mouth. 'Chew on that, you little bugger, and shut up.'

'You're Joseph's sister, then?'

'Was. He's dead, remember? Scrafton, Jane Scrafton.'

'And where were you that night?'

'Here, of course, looking after this one.' The baby spat the crust out and started wailing again. Snowden picked up the remnant of bread and she pushed it back in the open mouth.

'Anybody else live here?'

'Husband, three kids, my sister, that's all.'

'Your husband, was he out that night?'

She scowled. 'Out every bloody night, bad as my father. He was snoring away, too, pair of pigs.'

'And your sister?'

'Up an alley with some punter, I expect, it was a Saturday night. She never said she'd seen anything, came back in before midnight.'

'Is she around now?'

'Works as a kitchenmaid at Rokeby Park, spends all week there. Comes back Saturday nights and makes the most of them.' She thought for a moment. 'She did came back the day they buried Joe, mind.'

None of the inhabitants seemed to have been near Yates when he disappeared. Snowden changed tack. 'Joseph – sorry, Joe – he was here early that night, wasn't he? Your father said so at the inquest.'

'Till about eight. Got himself spruced up, found himself some money somewhere, he was off out round the town with Tom.'

'Tom?'

'My husband.'

'Where will I find him?'

'God knows. Same as my father, I expect. Got himself sacked, didn't he?'

'Did he? What was he doing?'

'Bugger-all, that's why they got rid of him.'

'I meant, where did he work?'

'Anywhere that would have him. Labouring and that.'

'I'd like to have a word with him.' Snowden thought back. 'You said Joe had money the night you last saw him?'

'Showed me a sov, must've done something for someone. He had a workshop, more of a shed really, in the yard out the back, doing tailoring, clothes and that. Good at it, he was.' For the first time a note of emotion tinged her voice. 'I was fond of our Joe. You going to find out what happened to him?'

'I hope so.'

'Never bloody killed himself, that's for sure. Happy, he was, no reason to do himself in.' She put the baby down on the footstep and it began to crawl back in the house. 'Load of rubbish in that paper. Lovers' Leap!' She gave a harsh laugh. 'Quick screw up against the wall, maybe, but Joe wasn't the romantic sort, never had a girlfriend I know of, not since Eleanor died.'

'Eleanor?'

'His wife, died having their second kid. They were in Gainford back then, must be, oh, four years ago. He came to live with us here after that.'

'You said second child. What happened to the first?'

'Her sister's got it, over in Middlesbrough somewhere. Never seen it since. Nor did Joe, he wasn't bothered, wasn't sure it was his anyway.'

'So he wasn't in a relationship of any kind with Catherine Raine?'

'The one who got herself drowned as well? Never heard of her till now, Joe never mentioned her. Where did she live?'

'Briggate, down one of the lonnings.'

'Well, he was often down there, plenty of pubs, plenty of girls. He might have come across her, depends what she was offering. But lovers, never. More likely she pushed him in.'

She might be right, thought Snowden, maybe an argument about payment for services rendered up against the wall by the river. Yates was only a little fellow by all accounts, and the inquest report on what was left of Catherine suggested that she was a big girl quite capable of chucking him into the Tees if she felt like it. But in that case, how did *she* get into the river?

'Thank you, Mrs Scrafton, you've been very helpful. I'll be back if I can't find your husband.'

'Try the Three Horseshoes, they aren't fussy about opening times if there's money to be made. He won't know anything you don't know already, mind.' She turned back into the house. 'You'd best find him soon or he'll be too pissed to tell you anything even if he did.' She shut the door abruptly. As he turned away he heard her shouting.

'Get out of that swill bucket, you little bastard!'

He shook his head and aimed for the Three Horseshoes, back into Gallowgate and down almost to the corner. Half a dozen men lounged against the wall of the alley alongside, clay pipes in their hands.

'Any of you know where I'll find Tom Scrafton?'

'Who wants him?' A tall man with a broken nose and blackened teeth spat against the wall and eyed him with suspicion.

'Police, but he's not in any trouble as far as I know. It's about his brother-in-law.'

'Him that died?'

'Joseph Yates, yes. Know where he is?'

One of the others grinned. 'In the bloody graveyard, unless he's gone swimming again.'

Snowden held his temper. 'Scrafton?'

'He was here.' The broken-nosed man decided there was no chance of the Three Horseshoes opening early if this policeman was hanging around, and pointed down the street. 'Went off to the pie shop over the road about five minutes ago, said he was hungry.'

'If I don't find him there, tell him Superintendent Snowden wants a word.'

'Superintendent, eh?' The man gave a mocking smile. 'Must be important if they've got the big boys out looking for him.'

'I do hope you're not inside here when I come back.' Snowden smiled back sweetly and glanced at the name above the pub door. 'I'd hate to have to have to nick you all, and your accommodating landlord George Mason wouldn't be best pleased either.'

He walked down to the Horse Market, crossed the road and entered the pie shop. He knew the proprietor, a cheerful fat man in his fifties who gave visiting constables free mugs of tepid tea and the occasional tip-off in the hope that they wouldn't ask too many questions about what went into his mutton pies.

'Morning, Isaac.' There were half a dozen wooden chairs round a table at the far end, five of them occupied. 'Got a Tom Scrafton in here?'

Isaac nodded, his chins wobbling. 'In the black jacket on the left. What's he done?'

'Nothing I know of yet.' He declined a free tea and made his way to the back.

'Tom Scrafton?'

'Could be.' The man was halfway through a pie, and there was gravy dripping from his mouth. He wiped it off with a sleeve. 'Seen you before, in court when I got done for fighting in the Cricketers last year. Snowman or something.'

'Snowden. It's about Joseph Yates.'

'Joe? I told your lad all I know. Daft sod got drunk, fell in the river.'

'Maybe.' Snowden sat down in the spare chair. 'Maybe not.'

Scrafton shook his head and took another mouthful of pie. 'Must've done, obvious. Didn't go in on purpose, he was piss-happy that night, singing and dancing when I left him.'

Snowden nodded. 'Your wife said you were with him that night.'

'You been talking to her?' He scowled. 'Bitch won't even make me breakfast in a morning, have to come in here.'

'Tell me about it.'

'She and those bloody kids –'

'About the night Joe died.'

'Oh, right. Well, we had a few jars here and there, ended up in Briggate, Lofthouse's ale-house down one of the lonnings.'

'I know it. And?'

'That's all there is. I decided to go home about midnight, they were closing and I'd no money left for another drink anyway. Joe says him and Cooper were going over to Startforth, they thought Hunton's up the road would be still open.' He gave Snowden a sharp look. 'Not going to do his pub if I tell you this, are you?'

'Don't worry, that's not what I'm after.'

'So we all walk out, the three of us, and they head off towards the bridge and I went home. Least, that's what I meant to do, but I'd had a fair few and she wouldn't let me in, bitch had the door barred.' He shook his head at the memory. 'Had to spend the night in Joe's shed. Bloody uncomfortable it was.'

'Anything else?'

'Don't think so.'

'Where will I find this man Cooper?'

'Frank? He's a weaver, works in one of the mills in Briggate, just up from the Lofthouse lonning.' He licked the last smear of gravy off his lip. 'Want to buy me another pie?'

'No.' Snowden stood up. 'But you can tell your mates outside the Three Horseshoes that it's safe to go in. I won't be coming back this way till well after opening time. Whenever it is.'

Scrafton's face brightened, and he followed Snowden out into the street.

Barningham, 9.45am

ERMINTRUDE gave a contented grunt as Wharton tickled her ear and emptied a bucket of kitchen slops into her trough.

She was in fine shape, he thought proudly, not bad for a pig who had strayed at least half a mile before being caught by that terrifying woman at Ewebank Farm, carted down to the constable's shed in Greta Bridge and locked up inside for the night. He scratched her other ear. He'd given Sowerby sixpence for looking after her and another shilling to pay for the bag of leather uppers she'd eaten, and just hoped she hadn't swallowed any cobbler's nails.

He wondered briefly whether he should visit Mrs Lambert and thank her, but decided her couldn't face it. Most women frightened him, most of all his mother who despised him for not growing up to rival her brother Lord Sallow, a rugged six-footer, Knight of the Garter, Lord Lieutenant of his county, Grandmaster of the Royal and Ancient Order of Master Mercers, and owner of a string of race-horses that vied each year for the Derby and St Leger. He spent most of his life hunting, shooting and fishing anything that moved on his vast estates in the Hebrides. Wharton's mother adored him.

Wharton, on the other hand, had a double first in theology and divine studies from Cambridge, which she thought was quite ridiculous as no member of her family had ever been remotely religious unless it was critical for survival in times of civil war.

Ermintrude emptied the trough and started grubbing about at Wharton's feet. He had high hopes of her doing well at the Teesdale and District Agricultural Show next week. He'd inherited Ermintrude when he arrived in Barningham, a piglet abandoned in the Glebe Farm sty and probably destined to end up on the rectory table with an apple in its mouth had the rectorship not changed hands. He had been feeding her prodigiously ever since. Peaceful creatures, pigs, unlike so many of the people he met.

He bade Ermintrude a fond farewell and ambled back to the rectory, his mind on finding a text for next Sunday's sermon. What was it the Bible said? '*Like a gold ring in a pig's snout is a beautiful woman who shows no discretion.*' That was it, Proverbs 11, verse 22, he must be able to make something of that.

His mind wandered off. A beautiful woman. There were some, he was sure, they just didn't seem to come his way. Apart from young Betsey Snowden, of course.

Ermintrude chomped happily on, unaware that she was in grave danger of being supplanted in her master's affections.

Barnard Castle, 10.15am

COOPER added little to solve the riddle of Yates's death. Snowden found him at work in the second mill he tried, and the weaver confirmed that he'd gone with the dead man over the bridge and up to Hunton's alehouse in Startforth, a little after midnight he thought, and stayed there for perhaps an hour before walking back.

'It was dark and the wind was blowing hard when we got to the bridge. I didn't fancy staying out any more and went home.'

'Where did Yates go?'

'Left him on the bridge, looking down at the water. It was running very rapid, it was high and likely to be higher.'

'Where do you think he went next?'

'No idea, he didn't say. Another alehouse, perhaps, there were still plenty open and he had plenty of money on him.'

'Enough for a woman if he found one?'

'More than enough. He'd bought the last jar we had in Hunton's and said he'd still got a half-sov in his pocket. You could buy half a dozen women in this street for that and still have change. Not sure he was sober enough to manage it, mind.' He creased his brow. 'My bet is he wandered off along the Sills. The road dips down where the cattle drink at the end, easy to go into the water if you miss the road and it was bloody dark.'

Snowden walked out of the mill to discover it had started raining, a thin drizzle that was slowly turning the Briggate dust into mud. It looked like being the worst August he could remember. That morning's paper had been full of riots in Ireland over the potato harvest, which had failed for the second year running. The government blamed the tenant farmers, refusing to offer food or money to relieve the starving thousands; many had already died. Snowden had no idea what the solution was, but doing nothing appalled him. He turned up his coat collar and hoped his new regulation half-stovepipe hat didn't leak as much as the last one.

Catherine Raine had lived somewhere among the tenements nearby. None had names or numbers and he had no idea where to begin looking for her father. He'd be well-known, though, in the taverns and alehouses scattered along the street, and he picked the nearest with an open door.

He was surprised to find it empty. 'Not open for drink yet,' said a woman's voice. 'Unless you want water, there's a well round the back. Still cost you, mind.' She stood up from where she had been kneeling behind the bar. 'Bloody hell, it's you.'

'Morning, Mrs Brass.'

'Just laying a rat trap, place is crawling with the things.' She was in her sixties, short and stout, a cotton bonnet hiding faded grey hair. 'Just like you lot, always around and never welcome. What is it this time?'

'Looking for someone called William Raine, wondered if you'd know where I could find him.'

'Raine? There's Raines everywhere round here, must be at least half a dozen called William.'

'This one's just lost his daughter. Called her Catherine.'

'The one they found in the river? That'll be Bill you want, Bill that lives down Greenacre Lonnen. Three doors along on the left.'

'I'll find it.'

'She didn't live there, mind. Well, not often. Shacked up with one of the Arrowsmith lads last time I heard.'

'And where's he?'

'Further on down the street, next the dye shops. Charlie, they call him, works in the slaughterhouse over the road. Or did. Haven't seen him around for a while.'

'Thanks. And good luck with the rats.'

He made his way down the alley, stopped at the door she'd suggested and pushed it open. Inside was an earth-floored hallway with two rooms on each side, a narrow staircase leading upwards, and the stench of urine and rotten vegetables. An old man dozing on a bench in the corner looked up.

'Still raining?'

'A bit. Where do I find Bill Raine?'

The man stuck a thumb towards the ceiling. 'Upstairs, green door.'

It had been green once, perhaps, but most of the paint had long gone and there was a large smear across it of what could have been blood but was probably something worse. Snowden knocked loudly.

'Sod off.'

'Police, want a word with you.'

'Shit.' He heard footsteps and the door was opened by a man in his fifties with one of the finest purple noses Snowden had ever seen. The face surrounding it was a web of red veins from which yellowed eyes peered at him. 'What d'you want?'

'William Raine?'

'Might be.'

'It's about Catherine.'

'More bloody questions.' Raine looked around the landing. 'You'd best come in, don't want anyone seeing me talking to the police.' Snowden followed him in. The room was dark, sacks hanging over what was left of the window, two low beds with crumpled blankets, a table with half a loaf and some green cheese beside a half-empty bottle of beer, and three wooden chairs. Raine sat down in one. Snowden decided to remain standing.

'Found out what happened to her yet, have you?'

Snowden shook his head. 'Not yet. I'm told Catherine wasn't living here?'

'Kate, we called her Kate. Hadn't been here for years, seven or eight, maybe, not since her mother went.'

'Went where?'

'Died.' He shrugged. 'I was no use to her, Kate, I mean. She was better off with the mother-in-law over at Bowes. Then she died too, her nan, and she came back to Barney and moved in with Charlie Arrowsmith.'

'When was that?'

'Two, three years ago.'

Snowden's eyebrows rose. 'She'd only have been fourteen.'

'They grow up fast round here. Too bloody fast.' He gave Snowden a sad smile. 'Specially the girls. On the street before their tits show.'

Snowden frowned. 'She was on the game?'

'Time to time, when she needed the money. Said it was better than slaving away in the mills.'

'Since she was fourteen?'

'Bit after, maybe.' His voice took on an apologetic note. 'Tried to stop her but she wouldn't listen. Charlie didn't stand in her way, he got most of what she earned. No better than a pimp, that bastard. Started beating her up, she said.'

'Did you see her often, then?'

Raine shook his head. 'Not as often as I'd've liked. She was a lovely girl when she was little, my little darling she was, but then...' His voice tailed off.

'When was the last time?'

'Thursday before she disappeared. Came over here, said Charlie had thrown her out. Slept over there.' He nodded towards one of the beds. 'In a right state, bruises on her face, and elsewhere I wouldn't be surprised. And her in that condition.'

Snowden raised his eyebrows again. 'Condition?'

'So she said. Few months gone, didn't show, a wonder it didn't happen before.' He reached for the bottle, took a mouthful and grimaced. 'She didn't know what she was going to do, stuck with a kid. Wretched, she was. Didn't even know who the bloody father was.'

'Not Arrowsmith's?'

'He didn't think so. She said they'd had a real fight before she left. She was in a proper state, said she might as well kill herself.'

'You think that's why she ended up in the river?'

'Could be, I suppose. I told her she was always welcome here, I never turned her out of doors in my life, never shut my door against her.' He was silent for a moment. 'She'd cheered up a bit next day, maybe it helped.'

'What happened that night, the Saturday?'

'No idea. She went over to see her brother the day before, came back here next evening and said she was going out, didn't say where. I told her to watch out for Charlie, I didn't want him knocking her about again or worse, but she said he'd left town.'

Snowden's face hardened. 'I think I'll be having a word with Charlie.'

'You'll be lucky. Disappeared, and good riddance.'

Barnard Castle, 10.50am

WRAPPED in a ragged blanket smelling of something he really didn't want to think about, McQueedie lay flat on the floor of the Butter Market cell and peered one-eyed through the tiny knot-hole in the door four inches above the floor.

He could just see the bench opposite where Constable Kipling had been sitting, but in place of the policeman's boots beneath it there swung a pair of small, bare and extremely grubby feet.

'Pssst!' McQueedie tapped gently on the wooden door. 'Is there anybody there?'

The feet stopped swinging. 'Who's that?'

If he squeezed his head right down against the floor McQueedie could just see the child, a boy about eight years old. The constable must have wandered off and there was no sign of anyone else. 'Come over here.'

The boy stood up and stared around, alarmed at the invisible demand. 'Where are you? What d'you want?'

McQueedie took a deep breath and put on his deepest and slowest voice. 'I am the spirit of the Butter Market, trapped beneath the walls by an evil sprite.' He stopped to see if it was working.

'A what?'

'The dreaded Peg Powler, the Terror of the Tees.'

'How did she get you under there?'

McQueedie muttered a prayer of thanks. Every child in town was warned from infancy to keep away from the river, where Peg Powler, long green tresses hanging from her shoulders, spent her life luring unwary children to the water and dragging them down to drown.

'I'll tell you when I get out.' He'd think of something. 'But I need you to help me.'

'There's a policeman over there, I'll get him.'

'No!' The boy recoiled at McQueedie's squawk as he battled desperately for a reason why Constable Kipling shouldn't be disturbed. 'He's one of Peg's goblins, sent to keep watch over me.'

'Not much of a goblin.' The boy looked unimpressed. 'Hasn't even got a beard.'

'He's in disguise, I watched him shave it off.'

There was a long silence while the boy pondered this. He suspected the stuff about Peg was a load of rubbish, but whatever it was inside the Butter Market cell was obviously desperate to get out and in his experience desperate people paid good money to get what they wanted. This one might even go as far as sixpence. 'All right, what d'you want?'

McQueedie was tempted to command him to find a hammer and chisel so he could break his way out, but that seemed like asking too much. They wouldn't fit under the door, anyway.

'Do you think you could find a sheet of paper and a pencil?'

'What for?' The little brat was far too full of questions.

'So I can write a magic spell that will set me free!'

'What are you going to give me if I do?'

McQueedie sighed. The mercenary little bugger. 'Whatever you want.' He threw his mind back forty years. 'I can conjure up a mountain of marzipan for you if you like. Or liquorice, pear drops, jelly babies or...' He came to a halt. What else did kids stuff themselves with?

'Can you do coconut ice?'

'Cart-loads, enough to make you sick twice over.'

'I won't be long.' The child shot off across the road, narrowly missing the wheels of the same cart that had made young Constable Granton an ex-constable the week before. Its driver hauled his horse to a halt, strode ashen-faced across to St Mary's, and asked if he could have an urgent word with a priest.

Startforth, 11.15am

SNOWDEN stopped halfway across the bridge at the spot where he imagined Yates had been staring at the Tees. The river was much lower than it had been the night the man died. If he *had* died that night, and he didn't even know that for sure. Yates could have gone off, done something else, fallen asleep maybe, and lived well into the Sunday until falling into the river sometime, somewhere.

Snowden wasn't going to find any answers just standing there, and he walked on to the White Swan on the corner and turned left. Tom Rutter's smithy stood on the other side and he walked across.

'Mr Snowden.' Rutter was pumping the giant bellows beside his fire, its centre white-hot and sending flames and black smoke up the chimney. The blacksmith was bare-chested, sweat pouring down his face and upper body, and happy to stop for a chat. 'How's that Bucephalus of yours?'

'Time I had him re-shoed, Tom. I've left him up at the top of the town, but I'll bring him in sometime.'

'Could do him now if he was here. I'll send young Thompson to fetch him if you're here for a while. He's doing bugger-all else this morning.'

'Thanks, Tom.'

'Thompson!' Tom roared at the doors at the back of the smithy and his apprentice appeared. 'Up the town, fetch Mr Snowden's horse for me. Sharp, now.'

'By the workhouse, you know what he looks like.' Snowden reached into his pocket. 'Here's the penny I promised the lad who's looking after him. One for yourself, too.'

The boy took the coins and shot off over the bridge, delighted at the prospect of a penny's-worth of lemonade or maybe something stronger if he found a landlord willing to serve a fifteen-year-old, and that shouldn't be hard.

'Good lad, that Thompson Kipling.' The smith smiled. 'They call him Tom at home, but it got too confusing with two of us, so he's Thompson at work. Come on outside, far too hot in here. Fancy a quick one over the road?'

They walked across to the White Swan and climbed the steps to the front door. Snowden ordered half a pint of half-and-half, Tom a full glass of porter which he sank before the landlady had found Snowden's change. He left it on the bar. 'Better give Tom another one. I'll put it down on expenses.'

Tom didn't argue. 'So what brings you down here?'

Snowden explained. 'Don't suppose you saw or heard anything?'

Tom took a long draught at his second pint and shook his head. 'You think this lad may have gone in the river this side, somewhere along the Sills?'

'Easy enough. The wall between the road and the river is only about four feet above the road at its highest on this side, a lot lower further along, down to a foot or so. And it's a big drop the other side, straight down to the water.'

'Depends on how high the river is, can be well up after a storm. I've seen it come over the top. Easy to fall over and away you'd go, onto the rocks and away with the current. There was a lad went in only last year.' He turned to the landlady, busy stacking glasses that had dried overnight. 'What was the name of that boy fell over the Sills last summer?'

'Barton, Bartlett, something like that. Happened the week after we took over here.' She looked at Snowden. 'Copper, is he?'

'How can you tell?' Tom was amused, Snowden a little dismayed. He rarely went out in uniform, leaving the long black coat with the badge on at home in case he wanted to hide his calling.

'Been running ale-houses long enough to know one when I see one.' She grinned at him and introduced herself. 'Mary Raper, me and George moved here from Kirby Stephen six months ago.'

'Superintendent Snowden, based over in Greta Bridge.'

'Can't still be interested in that Bartlett or whatever his name was, surely? Not as if he died or anything.' She grinned. 'Got one hell of a shock, though. He'd sunk at least a gallon in here before he fell in, sober as a judge when they pulled him out.'

'Not that one.' Tom shook his head. 'The fellow who drowned a couple of weeks ago, Yates.'

'Thought he fell in the other side, that was the talk in here.'

'He wasn't in here that night, then?'

'Wouldn't know, didn't know him. Could have been, I suppose. There's always plenty come over the bridge of a Saturday night, they reckon the law's not so active on the Yorkshire side, less likely to get caught if they're up to something. Too much going on in Briggate for the town constables to bother about Startforth.'

Tom nodded. 'Licensing laws are different over here from Durham, too, they get an extra half-hour to get drunk.'

Snowden frowned. It was a source of regular irritation, the failure of local authorities to agree on common opening times and many other minor issues. Various petty offences in Yorkshire were permitted the other side of the bridge and vice versa, and at times it exasperated him.

Tom put down his empty glass and looked hopefully at his companion. 'Another one?'

'Go on, just a half. Bit early for me.'

Tom put a shilling on the counter. 'I heard that back in the old days even the age you could get wed was different. Lad got a young girl of, say, thirteen in trouble on the Durham side of the Tees, he could marry her in their church, no problem. But if they set foot this side he'd be done for under-age. Bloody silly, if you ask me.' He began work on the fresh pint of porter. 'Ever hear of Cuthbert Hilton?'

Snowden shook his head.

'Set himself up as a priest with gown and cravat and bible and did weddings in the middle of the County Bridge, where the county boundaries met. He used to marry couples whose parents wouldn't give permission or who couldn't get approval from the Church. And when he got to the bit about pronouncing them man and wife, he had this broomstick and made them jump over it just as he said the words.' He paused for effect.

'Go on,' said Mrs Raper, lapping it up. 'Why?'

'Because when they were up in the air, they weren't touching Yorkshire or Durham and neither bishop could do anything about it. The wedding wasn't legal, of course, him not really being a priest, but they didn't know that and everyone seemed happy enough. Except the parents and the bishops, of course. And Hilton in the end, I suppose, seeing they hanged him for something eventually.'

'I don't believe a word of it.' Mrs Raper picked up a glass she'd missed earlier. 'You do make up some stories, Tom Rutter.'

'It's true. You've heard of couples living over the brush?'

'Not married, you mean?'

'There you are.'

'Well, they don't come over the bridge to get wed these days. Just to get drunk and keep us awake all night afterwards.' She put the final glass away and folded her arms. 'You can hear them every night, shouting and carrying on down the Sills.'

Snowden emptied his glass. 'Hear anything that Saturday night? When this lad Yates is supposed to have died?'

Her brow furrowed. 'I remember George going on about the noise outside, must have been about two o'clock. Screaming and shrieking they were, enough to keep the devil awake.'

'Screaming?' Snowden leaned forward. ' What about?'

'God knows, goes on all the time.'

'Women?'

'And men.' She thought hard. 'There was this woman, least it sounded like a woman, shouting she'd tell something, I don't know. And something about a letter B.'

'B?'

'That's what it sounded like. I didn't take much notice.'

'And this was down the Sills?'

'Just out there.'

'I'll go and take a look when we've finished here.' Snowden nodded at Tom, who swallowed the last of his pint, looked regretfully at the empty glass, and stood up. 'Then I'll knock on a few doors. They all look out over the Sills, those cottages along from your place. You'd think somebody would have seen something.'

Barnard Castle, 12.10pm

SO much for the power of Peg Powler, thought McQueedie bitterly, still peering through his knothole in the door. The kid had obviously abandoned him.

Something ran up his bare leg and he rose in a hurry. As he hunted for it beneath the blanket there was the sound of footsteps outside, too heavy for a child, and he put his eye back to the hole. Two large boots. Constable Kipling was back.

McQueedie couldn't quite view the man's face, but he could see his knees. There was a notebook balanced on them and a hand holding a pencil was writing, with occasional sudden movements as if it was crossing out words.

'Alice, chalice?' Constable Kipling's voice came from above. 'Malice?' Nobody answered. The man was obviously deranged and talking to himself.

Something else ran up McQueedie's leg, bigger than the first invader and this one had teeth. He lost all interest in the policemen as he flung the blanket aside with an agonised yelp.

Barningham, 12.25pm

MRS Eeles handed Betsey a small jar half-full of what looked like tiny yellow grains and joined her at the kitchen table.

'There you are, my dear. That's what you need.'

Betsey examined the yeast with interest. 'You just put this in with the parsnips and it makes wine? There must be more to it than that.'

'Well, you need sugar, of course, and water. I like to add a bit of lemon juice and when Henry was alive he liked a drop of brandy in it too, said it gave it a bit more of a bite.' She shook her head and gave a reminiscent smile.

'I'll try it,' nodded Betsey.

'Don't over-boil the roots, whichever you use, if they get mushy the wine will turn out cloudy. Make sure everything's clean, give it a good stir every day, and your papa will be drinking it by Christmas.' She raised a knowing eyebrow. 'And you, young lady, no doubt. Don't take too much, it's more powerful than you'd think.'

'Thank you.' Betsey looked at the grandmother clock in the corner by the dresser. 'Time I was getting back.'

There was a knock at the door.

'Come in, it's not locked.'

The door opened and Betsey suddenly decided that she might stay a little longer after all.

Startforth, 1.45pm

BUCEPHALUS, newly-shod, was waiting for Snowden when he returned. He gave the horse a couple of affectionate pats on the neck and it lifted its upper lip a little over the top teeth, a sign that Snowden had learnt was its version of a smile.

'All ready for you.' Tom Rutter was glistening with sweat again. 'Still doing you proud, is he?'

Snowden nodded. They'd been together for more than two years now, ever since the Association had made the first of its grateful presentations to him, and he'd spent forty-five guineas on the horse. It stood a little over sixteen hands, all black but for a white scar-shaped flash of white on its face, and had proved more than once that it was capable of covering a half-mile in well under a minute with Snowden in the saddle. It was also one of the gentlest creatures he'd ever come across, and he'd never regretted a penny of his forty-five guineas.

He put a foot in the stirrup and hoisted himself into the saddle. 'Tried him on some new oats from down Bedale way, knocked another five seconds off him over the mile.'

'Any luck down the road?'

'Nothing. Knocked on just about every door, nobody saw or heard a thing that night. At least, they said they hadn't, you never know round here.'

'It's not Briggate,' Tom protested loyally. 'They're Startforth folk, Yorkshire. Bit rough, I grant you, but most of 'em honest enough.'

Snowden looked sceptical. 'You know them better than me, Tom, I'll take your word for it. Don't forget to send me the bill.' He grasped the reins and urged Bucephalus forward. 'And add that round you bought in the pub.'

The rain had stopped and he decided he'd go back the other way, up to Startforth church and down the lane to Abbey Bridge and then home. He wheeled the horse round and set off, passing the cottages whose doors he'd earlier knocked on in vain, and up the bank where across the field on his right he could see the squat towerless Norman church. A lone figure was in the graveyard, hard at work digging.

He didn't think for a moment that he'd come across a grave-robber, but the *Morning Post* had published a graphic tale of skeleton-stealing in Sheffield only that morning and he thought he should take a look. He turned right and rode up the rough church track.

'Mr Snowden.' The figure straightened up and stuck its spade into the ground. 'Haven't seen you in church for a while.'

'Wycliffe's nearer. Or Barningham from time to time.' Or nowhere. He was not a great devotee of formalised services attended out of duty rather than piety, but he approved of the man who stood beside a half-dug grave. Robert Crampton, Startforth sexton and parish clerk, had been outspoken at local meetings of Chartists, the working-class movement demanding universal male suffrage, secret voting, fairer working conditions and a host of other reforms which Snowden privately applauded. He nodded at the grave.

'Anyone I know?'

'Old Mr Fothergill.' Crampton nodded at the hole. 'Eighty-one, not a bad innings. In the navy when he was a lad, you know, served with Nelson one time.'

'Trafalgar?'

'Too old for that. It would've been in the late nineties, I reckon, Portugal war maybe.' He kicked a clod of earth to one side. 'Glad I've seen you, saves me having to write you a letter.'

'A letter?'

'Had a complaint about someone slaughtering animals on the Sills. The vestry meeting thought I should ask you to look into it.'

'Thought they were only interested in church business, the vestry.' Snowden smiled. 'Apart from deciding which parishioners they like least and naming them constables for me to put up with for a year.'

'They do a lot more than that.' Crampton sounded defensive. 'Anyway, it came up at a meeting last night. Martin Galland said his wife had seen blood near the walls, thought it must have been Rutter. Nobody else near there does any butchering.'

'Tom Rutter?' Snowden frowned. 'I suppose he might have to bleed the odd animal every so often, but he's got that yard at the back, why do it on the Sills?'

'You'd best ask him.' Crampton picked up his spade.

'I will. Where do I find the Gallands?'

'Next but one to Rutter's place, funny old couple. Martin's right enough but be careful of the old woman if you go down there, some think she's a witch.'

'Thanks for the warning. Still got her wits about her, has she?'

'Well, she was right about the blood. I went down there the morning she told me, about nine o'clock, and it was there like she said, laid about a yard from the wall and some more on the other side of the road. I went past later, after church, but it had gone.'

'Gone?'

'Puddled into the mud. It was just after the storms, fortnight ago.'

'A Sunday morning?'

'After church, yes.'

'The day Yates disappeared?'

'Who? Oh, the lad who went into the river. Yes, that would be it.'

'Thanks, Bob.' Snowden turned Bucephalus's head. 'Sorry, old son, you're going to have to wait a bit longer for more of those oats.'

Barnard Castle, 2pm

CONSTABLE Kipling was in love. The object of his affections and some disturbingly erotic fantasies was an assistant at Brown's Drapers & Mercery Emporium in the Horse Market and without doubt one of the loveliest girls he'd ever crossed eyes with. They'd been walking out for two months, he'd got as far as putting his arm round her waist going over a stile, it was her birthday next week, and he was writing her a poem to prove his intentions were, well, if not totally honourable given half a chance, certainly sincere.

If only she hadn't been called Alice.

He stared hopelessly at the open page of the notebook on his knee.

Roses are red, my love, violets are blue

Not original, he'd be the first to admit, but it was a start.

My heart is forever devoted to you

So far, so good. It rhymed, and that was half the battle.

Say you'll forever be mine, dearest Alice,

And that was the problem. Nothing remotely useful rhymed with Alice. He'd walked up and down the Market Place twice in search of ideas and gone right through the alphabet, eventually toying in desperation with

I'll make you my queen in our very own palace

but rejecting it in case it landed him with a breach-of-promise case. He turned the page over and started again. A sonnet, that might work. Shakespeare, Keats, Shelley, that randy bugger Byron, they were all at it, churning them out by the dozen before breakfast. It couldn't be that difficult.

What if I said you were like a day in spring?

He paused. Shakespeare didn't write like that. He started again.

What if I said thou ~~was~~ ~~wert~~ ~~is~~ art like a day in spring?

There were some rotten days in spring. How about

like a day in summer?

Much better. He sucked his pencil and nodded.

~~You're~~ Thou ~~are~~ art more

He was getting the hang of this.

~~beutiffle~~ ~~beutifull~~ beautifull and more

More what?

buxom ?

True, but he couldn't possibly say that. Not in a poem.

~~good-tempered~~? ~~temperamental~~? ~~tempestuous~~? tempting ?

He put the notebook and pencil down with a sigh. This wasn't going to be as easy at he'd thought.

He stood up, absent-mindedly clipped the ear of a small boy who was lurking nearby, and set off for another tour of the Market Place in search of inspiration.

Startforth, 2.10pm

THE windows were spotless, the brass door-knob shone, the doorstep had obviously been thoroughly scrubbed that morning. House-proud, thought Snowden as he dismounted and waited for someone to answer his knock. He'd tried earlier in the day during his tour of the cottages but got no answer, and was pleased when the door opened this time.

A tiny wizened creature, dressed bonnet to boots in black and clutching a walking-stick, confronted him.

'Yes?'

'Police. Mrs Galland, is it?'

She looked him up and down. 'You're standing on my doorstep.' She glared. 'It was clean till you put your muddy feet on it.'

Snowden stepped back onto the road. 'I'm sorry, I didn't think –'

'You lot never do. What d'you want?'

Snowden swallowed. The woman must be as aged as poor old Fothergill awaiting his place in the graveyard, but she looked tough enough to take on the Portuguese single-handed. 'I understand you've made a complaint about bloodstains on the Sills?'

'Bloodstains? It was more than stains, young man, a great pool of it there was, right over there.' She pointed a bony finger across the road. 'Just in front of the wall. And there was more on the stones, smeared with blood they were.'

'And when was this, Mrs Galland?'

'That Sunday morning, of course, Sunday before last. I came out of the house on my way to church and there it was. Disgraceful. There was other people about, they saw it too. What are you going to do about him?'

'Him?'

'That Rutter, of course. Who else could it be?' She gave what Snowden could only interpret as a snarl. 'Got rid of it after he saw me there, didn't he?'

'Got rid of it?'

'Gone when I came back from church, about twelve. He'd trampled all the blood into the mud, there was mud and dirt smeared over the wall as well. He'd even scratched out some of the marks on the stone, I could tell. He can't fool me.'

'Did you actually see him do any of this, Mrs Galland?'

'Has to have been him. Nasty piece of work.'

'Did you actually see him?'

'See him?'

'Yes. See him.'

The glare returned. 'Are you calling me a liar, constable?' She waved her walking-stick dangerously close to his head and for a moment he wondered how he would cope if he had to arrest her for assault.

'Not at all, Mrs Galland.' He stepped further back out of stick-reach. 'I'll see what I can do. You didn't hear anything unusual on the night before this blood appeared, I suppose?'

'Only thing I ever hear at night is my fool of a husband snoring. Any more questions?'

'I don't think so.'

'Then I'll thank you to be on your way so I can clean up your mess.' She glowered at the two muddy bootprints he'd left on her doorstep and vanished inside, leaving the door open.

As Snowden climbed back into the saddle Bucephalus deposited a steaming heap of proof that the new oats were indeed, as their Bedale supplier had claimed, an excellent remedy for equine constipation. It landed inches away from the bootprints.

By the time Mrs Galland had found her mop and returned to her doorstep, Snowden and his horse were in the smithy yard, safely out of sight but not earshot. He heard her howl of rage ring out over the river, and shivered.

Barnard Castle, 2.20pm

THE boy rubbed his ear, still smarting from the cuff he'd received as Constable Kipling passed by, and watched the policeman disappear round the corner.

All clear. He knelt down by the door. 'You still inside?'

McQueedie's heart leapt. 'Yes!' He cut his squeak of delight short as he remembered he was supposed to be the Butter Market spirit and lowered his voice several octaves. 'I mean, yes. Where have you been?'

'Waiting for the goblin to go away.'

'Goblin?' McQueedie tried to remember what he'd said four hours earlier. 'Oh, that goblin, yes. Have you got it?'

'Got what?'

'The paper and pencil, of course.' His voice rose to a most unspirit-like note.

'Yes, they're here.'

'Then pass them under the door quick before he comes back.'

'What about the coconut ice?'

The mercenary little – 'As soon as I've written the spell.'

'Promise?'

'Yes, mountains of it. Where d'you live?'

'Cooper's Yard.' Other end of the street, up Gallowgate, far enough.

'It'll be outside your house at midnight.'

'Midnight?'

'Best I can do, the sweet fairies are really busy just now.' McQueedie was getting frantic. 'Just push the things under the door and I'll see if I can't speed them up a bit.'

'All right.' The child didn't sound very convinced, but pushed two sheets of crumpled paper and a pencil stub under the door. McQueedie leapt on them.

'Right, off you go, back home, the fairies say they'll be on their way with a cartload of coconut ice any minute.'

'If you're lying I'll set my dad on you. He's enormous.'

McQueedie wasn't listening. He straightened out the paper, clearly torn from a notebook, and began to write.

His original idea had been to appeal to his editor in York, but he'd been having second thoughts. He wasn't on exactly what he'd call good terms with him, which was why he'd been sent out to the wilds of Teesdale in the first place, and he had a sneaking suspicion that the man might be quite content to leave him where he was. Instead he would aim for the man at the top: Lord Beavermere, proprietor of the *Yorkshire Gazette* and a score of other newspapers scattered across the North of England, who McQueedie knew spent most of his days during the grouse season on the Teesdale moors and his nights wining and dining in the Kings Arms Hotel only yards away up the Market Place.

Standing on tiptoe in one corner, where a dim ray of daylight from a ventilation hole high above illuminated a tiny part of one wall, he rested the first sheet of paper against the stone and began to write.

My Lord,
You probably don't know me, but we met briefly late one evening last June
at the stage door of the Lyceum Music Hall and Variety Theatre in Leeds, where

I was hoping to interview Miss Lucy Lustworthy, the exotic dancer of the seven veils with whose fame on the boards I am sure you must be acquainted.

　I say this with some confidence, my Lord, as I happened to be there when she emerged and accompanied you to your carriage awaiting round the corner. You may recall me as the man with the notebook you shoved into the gutter in your eagerness to greet her. You were, as I remember, dressed in a long black cloak with a muffler covering much of your face. You were nonetheless

He came to the end of the page and turned over. There was a short list on the other side.

　Mend stocking
　Alice birthday, must get gift
　Poem ? Chalice? Malice? Palace???
　Butter Market 8am-6
　Cobblers

McQueedie stared at it for a moment, crossed it all out and spent the next ten minutes chewing the broken end of the pencil to get a fresh point with which to write. Finally, spitting out bits of wood, graphite and what he feared was part of his left incisor, he was able to continue.

　　　　　known to me the moment you greeted Miss Lustworthy with the words 'Lucy, my dear' and kissed her cheek, as your voice is one I know well from having reported many social events over which your Lordship has presided..

He paused, wondering how to phrase the next vital paragraph. Something with more legs than he imagined possible scuttled across the page and he decided to get this over with as fast as he could. Another night in here and he'd be confessing to being the Newgate Flasher, the Gallowgate Groper, the Romaldkirk Ripper and anybody else they wanted him to be so long as he got out.

　As a loyal member of your staff I have not yet mentioned this encounter to 'Our Man in the Know' who writes on Society Affairs in our rival publication The Leeds Inquirer. He would, I am sure, be eager to publicise your Lordship's acquaintance with Miss Lustworthy were he to become aware of it. I imagine Lady Beavermere might also

He moved onto the second sheet of paper.

　　　　　appreciate the common people being informed of your Lordship's laudable interest in the arts and in particular the delights of plebeian theatricals. However, should your Lordship's modesty demand that this remains hidden from public view, I believe my memory of our encounter in June might fade rapidly were you to extract me from my current unfortunate situation. If you wish this to be the case, my Lord, I would be gratified no longer to remain
　　　　　　　　Your Humble and Obedient Servant,
　　　　　　　　　　Hamish McQueedie
　　　　　　　　　　c/o The Cell, Butter Market

He read it through as best he could, folded the two sheets together, sealed it with a dollop of something disgustingly adhesive that one of his nether assailants had left sticking to his right buttock, and addressed it to Lord Beavermere at the Kings Head.

With a brief prayer informing God that it was high time he had at least one bit of luck before August was over, he slid the letter under the door.

Barnard Castle, 2.55pm

STILL seeking synonyms for his beloved, Constable Kipling came to a halt at the end of the Market Place and wondered if he could arrest the builder whose timber scaffolding blocked the footpath.

It covered the facade of the new Witham Testimonial Hall, being built in honour of recently-deceased local landowner and philanthropist Henry Witham who had fled the country in the 1820s after running up £100,000 of gambling debts but returned to become a local hero and an acclaimed mineralogist who knew more about fossilised plants than anyone else in Britain.

Kipling, who had never heard of fossilised plants and didn't know what all the fuss was about, eyed the pair of burly hod-carriers working nearby and decided not to interfere. He manoeuvred his way instead into the front of the hall, already completed and in use. On his right a door led him to what was grandly called the Mechanics' Institute, a small dark room full of shelves housing books nobody wanted. Among them was a mouldering leather-bound copy of Samuel Johnson's *Dictionary of the English Language* in which he discovered Fallis, a hamlet somewhere in the snowy wastes of Alberta, and Tallis, a fifteenth-century choral composer. Neither seemed much use as a rhyme for Alice.

He made his way disconsolately back to the Butter Market, sat down and picked up his notebook. He couldn't see his pencil anywhere, but lying on the floor was what looked like a letter. *Urgent. For Lord Beavermere, Kings Head. Private and Confidential. Half-a-crown awaits deliverer.*

Half a crown? His imagination soared as he considered the possible contents of the letter, which must be important if it was worth that much. A tip for York races, perhaps, a forty-to-one certainty? Inside information about a new railway shares offer? A ransom demand? He was tempted to open it but it was firmly sealed with a large lump of something he couldn't identify. Whatever was inside, half a crown was half a crown and who knows, he'd be the one who had found the letter that might make Lord whoever-he-was a fortune or save him from bankruptcy or master-mind the rescue of his son from the clutch of murderous kidnappers. He wasn't so keen on the last possibility, which sounded a bit on the dangerous side, but he'd take his chance. He might even get promoted.

Sergeant Kipling.

He rolled the words round in his mind, nodded happily, and set off resolutely towards the Kings Head. McQueedie, notebook and even Alice were all forgotten.

Thorpe, 4.30pm

BETSEY looked doubtfully at the huge pan boiling away on the range and poked her fork into another parsnip. Not too mushy, Mrs Eeles had said, but there was no chance of that. She couldn't get the fork half an inch into any of them.

There were footsteps in the hall and her father came into the kitchen.

'Is that for tonight?' He peered into the pan and sniffed. 'Ah. The great parsnip wine experiment. Having any success?'

'It's taking a long time.'

'It'll be worth it. What else have you been up to today?'

'I walked up to see Mrs Eeles for her advice. She sends her regards.' There was a pause. 'And so does the Reverend Wharton.'

'Wharton? What was he doing there?'

'She was doing some sewing for him. Poor man, the holes in his stocking. You can tell he's not married.'

'Hmm.' Snowden glanced at her. 'He doesn't look the sort to have many practical skills.'

'But he's ever so clever, and funny, too, when you get talking to him.' Another pause. 'I said I might see him at evensong tonight.'

'Evensong? On a Tuesday?'

'He asked me if I was going and I just sort of said I was. He promised he'd make sure I got back all right.'

'Did he?' Her father didn't sound overjoyed. 'I hope he drives that dog-cart better than when he's has a drink or two. Keep him off the communion wine.'

She giggled. 'They don't have it at evensong.'

'That's a blessing. Make sure you're back before dark.' Snowden sat down at the table, cleared a pile of parsnip tops to one side and took out his notebook to check the list of people he'd seen during the day. 'Tom Rutter asked how you were. I left Bucephalus with him to be re-shod and then had to take refuge in his yard on the way back.'

'Refuge?'

'I was hiding from a ferocious ninety-year-old whose doorstep I sullied. Twice, in fact, with the aid of Bucephalus.'

'Who was he? The ninety-year-old?'

'It was a she, a Mrs...' He consulted his list. 'Mrs Galland, we didn't get to first-name terms and she thinks I'm a constable.' He gave a wry smile. 'She lives a couple of houses down from Tom and is accusing him of slaughtering horses on the road and leaving pools of blood everywhere.'

'He wouldn't do that.' She gave the parsnips another hopeful prong.

'I know he wouldn't, but she complained to the vestry about it and I got involved.' He closed his notebook. 'Glad I did, though. It might be important.'

'What did Tom say?'

'They've been at war with each for years, apparently. She objects to just about everything he does – the noise, the smoke, the horses, his customers, the lot. And she thinks it's obscene the way he goes about with his chest all bared for innocent young women to see.'

She laughed. 'It wouldn't bother me. The fields are full of half-naked men at harvest-time. Women too, I wouldn't be surprised.' Her face became serious again. 'I didn't think women were allowed at vestry meetings.'

'She got her husband to raise it.' He frowned. 'I don't know what the rules are about woman attending. I've never heard of one taking part.'

'We've got more sense than to waste time arguing about churchwardens and who gets the best pews or whatever they do.'

Her father shook his head. 'There's a lot more to them than just handling church matters, Betsey. They appoint people like the poor rate overseers and constables, for example, and are responsible for most local government, in fact.'

'And it's just the men who do all this?'

'The only women I've ever seen at a vestry meeting were a couple of aged paupers appealing against paying the poor rate, and they looked terrified.'

'More of us should get involved.' Betsey's face took on a determined expression that reminded him momentarily of her mother. 'And if we're not allowed to, we should do something to change the law.'

Her father smiled. 'You'll be wanting the vote next.' He looked up. 'I think your parsnips are boiling over.'

Rokeby, 7.40pm

JENNINGS waited while the footman cleared soup dishes from the table and then approached his master. 'The '39, I think you said, sir?'

Morritt took the bottle and inspected its label without enthusiasm. 'None of the '27 left, you're sure about that?'

'Quite sure, sir.'

'Can't think how we got through it all so soon. Well, this'll have to do. Get it decanted and warmed up a bit.'

'Yes, sir.' Jennings retired to a corner, took a corkscrew out of his pocket and pretended not to listen as Morritt and his friend resumed their conversation.

'So you got your man Bainbridge his money back, Manners? Damned fine show.'

'Extraordinary case, Morritt. Went down yesterday morning expecting to be in York most of the week, you know how these county courts drag things out, but it was all over by mid-day today. Caught the two o'clock stage back and was in Greta Bridge by six.'

'Gave in, did they, the bailiffs?'

'Didn't have a chance. They were all there, that Emmerson who's in charge of them and four of his men, all dressed up in their finest and ready to argue their case. Then bless me if Captain Bainbridge don't arrive and see his coat.'

'His coat?' Morritt looked confused. 'Taken it off, I suppose, too hot in court.'

'Not the coat he had on, a coat that was among all that stuff they stole. Local clip, it was, ranter style, Bainbridge tells me he was rather fond of it. Know it anywhere.'

'One of the exhibits, eh? Did the judge see the rest of the stolen property as well?'

'None of it, and that's the remarkable thing.' He paused for effect. 'It wasn't an exhibit. He was wearing it.'

'The judge? Good lord!'

'Not the judge, Morritt, one of the bailiff's lads, would you believe. Bold as brass, there in court, flaunting himself in Bainbridge's stolen ranter.'

'The audacious devil! What did you do?'

'Well, Bainbridge whispers in my ear what he's seen, and I have a word with the judge – old Moulper, you know, nice old buffer though there are some rumours about him. I'm told –'

'The coat, Manners old man, one thing at a time.'

'Yes, of course. Well, Moulper asks to see Emmerson and me in private and he asks Emmerson who the rascal with the coat is and he says he's one of his assistants, which we already knew. Called Anderson or Henderson, something like that.'

'You're not going to tell me he was the one who stole everything from the Kings Head?' Morritt looked astonished.

'Well, that's what we all thought, obviously. We were all set to have him arrested when Emmerson says it couldn't have been him, because he'd only taken him on a fortnight ago.'

'Not one of his men when the stuff was stolen?'

'No.'

'So how did he come to have Bainbridge's coat?'

'Well, we hauled him into Moulper's room as well, just a lad he was, and asked him exactly that, and it turns out he'd bought it for seven shillings at Barney market last week. That's what he said, anyway, no idea it was stolen.'

'Hmm.' Morritt frowned. 'You believed him?'

'Seemed an honest sort of lad, Emmerson said he'd known his family for years, no criminal record or anything.'

'So what happened?'

'The lad handed the coat over to Bainbridge and asked if he could have his seven shillings back.'

'The devil he did!'

'Didn't get it, of course. And that was that. We all went back into court and the case was wrapped up in ten minutes. Emmerson tried arguing that it was all the Kings Head's fault for not keeping an eye on Bainbridge's property and the hotel should be sued, not him, for letting criminals in to help themselves, but Moulper wasn't interested in the robbery, just whether the bailiffs were negligent leaving the stuff where it could be taken. And as far as he could see, they were responsible for it wherever it was.' Manners smiled triumphantly. 'Judgement for the plaintiff.'

'Quite right. Officious lot, bailiffs, think they're above the law, could do with being taken down a peg or two.'

'Moulper said Emmerson was grossly incompetent, should never have left the property unguarded, and told him to pay Bainbridge compensation for everything missing plus all costs. Including mine, of course.' Manners sat back, smiling. 'Emmerson was furious.'

'Compensation, eh? Was there much missing, then?'

'Well, Snowden had found all the big items, furniture, my picture of course, carpets and so on. But a lot of smaller items were gone, kind of thing the thief could easily take away and sell off – jewellery, watches, clothing, some nice silverware, candlesticks and the like. Worth a fair bit, according to Bainbridge.' He smiled. 'I've no doubt he'll be claiming enough to pay off his debts.'

'No valuation of it before the bailiffs took it away, I suppose?'

Manners shook his head and smiled. 'Not even a proper inventory. His word against theirs.'

'Bainbridge must have been well pleased.'

'He was. Said it was all thanks to him seeing his coat, you'd think he'd won the case single-handed. It certainly didn't do us any harm, mind. Moulper wasn't going to believe anything the other side said after that.'

'All's well, then.' Morritt had a thought. 'It was definitely Bainbridge's coat, then? He couldn't have made a mistake?'

'Recognised it immediately, even though his name-tag inside had been removed. And do you know what? He told me afterwards that the last time he'd seen that coat there was a rip in the lining where he'd caught it on a nail, but whoever took it had had it mended, proper neat patch, better than before it was stolen!'

'Extraordinary!' Morritt turned to the butler. 'That wine should be ready by now, Jennings. Bring it over and we'll drink to Moulper, bless his wig. And then, Manners, you can tell me about these rumours. Old bugger's been at it again, has he?'

Thursday August 28ᵗʰ

Thorpe, 8.20am

SNOWDEN paused halfway through his breakfast egg, coddled perfectly with ham, cheese and chives just the way he liked it, and devoted himself to the story at the foot of page four of his day-old *Morning Post.*

SUB-MARINE TELEGRAPH

CABLE LAID AT PORTSMOUTH

CONTINENT NO LONGER CUT OFF

An announcement yesterday by the Admiralty Office of a sub-marine telegraphic cable newly laid from Portsmouth to the Isle of Wight and thence to the French harbour of Caen heralds a new milestone in the history of communication between the United Kingdom and its valiant allies across the English Channel.

The installation, the first of its kind ever to be seen anywhere in the Globe, is to be hailed as a marvel of modern science and engineering. No more must our Government be compelled to wait potentless for hours, nay days, while Neptune's furies make maritime conveyance of correspondence beyond the realm of human endeavour, for the power of Electricity now ensures instant transmission of the most vital despatches across the Oceans, ensuring that Britannia's noble rule expands

Snowden was interrupted by the arrival of Betsey with a bowl of fresh coffee.

'Your egg's getting cold,' she chided gently.

'Sorry, I was just reading about this new telegraphic link to France. It's going to revolutionise our lives.'

'Communicating with France?'

'With anywhere in the world. It's already spreading all over this country – they've linked London to Edinburgh this year, with connections at the railway stations in York and Darlington. It can't be long before it gets to Barnard Castle, and just imagine what a difference that will make.'

'No more waiting for the post-chaise, or long journeys on horseback? It sounds too good to be true.'

'But it's happening, and it's making our job, the police, easier already. A month or so ago they caught that murderer Tawell, the arsenic poisoner I told you about, on a train out of Paddington using a telegraphic message to the next station along the line. Wonderful, Betsey!'

She smiled at his enthusiasm. 'In the meantime, you've got to talk to the magistrates before court this morning, and unless you finish your coffee soon you're going to be late.'

Her father regarded her thoughtfully. 'Have you ever been in a court, Betsey?'

'No, why should I?'

'I think you should come along later and see what goes on. You may find it illuminating.'

Barnard Castle, 9.05am

JOHN Longstaff allowed his weavers ten minutes away from their looms every three hours, not out of any particular regard for their happiness or to relieve their tedium, but because he'd learned that without the occasional break their productivity declined and their accident rate went up. Both made a dent in his profits, and although he told them curtly that their breaks cost him dear and granting them was an act of great charity, he knew it was worth sacrificing ten minutes of their labour in return for increased output and fewer maimed and unproductive employees.

Mary Garthwaite stood outside the factory in Briggate, took off her bonnet and scratched her head. The lice were back. She thought she'd got rid of them with the evil-smelling lotion that pikey hawker had sold her last week, but it had proved a waste of money. Two pence, the price of a good loaf. She should have known better.

'How's your bairn?' It was Ann Humphreys, the girl three looms away from her.

Mary flicked fragments of a louse into the gutter and shrugged. 'Same as usual, been sickly for weeks. My mam says he's got the croup, always coughing he is, but I don't know.'

'You should see a doctor about him.'

'Pay threepence to be told he needs stuff I can't afford? Not on Longstaff's wages.'

'Not back on the game, then?'

'Not since he was born. Too bloody painful.'

'Pity, there's plenty of punters around.'

'All right for some. Your kiddy fit enough, then?'

'Bit of a rash, shitty all the time but he'll live. Just like his bloody father.'

'They found out what happened to his sister yet?'

'Fell in the river, far as I know.' Ann turned away abruptly. 'An accident. Time we went back in.'

'Must be a couple of minutes yet.'

Ann halted and turned back, her face troubled. 'You religious, Mary?'

'What, me?'

'Like believing in God, all that they tell you about in church?'

'Suppose so. They know what they're talking about, they're priests, aren't they?'

'All that about everlasting fire and devils if you do wrong?'

Mary stared at her. 'You in trouble? You're not in the bloody club again, are you?'

'Not this month.' A whistle shrilled from inside the factory. 'Time's up. See you at mid-day.'

Mary replaced her bonnet and went back to work.

Thorpe, 9.50am

'MORNING, Snowden.' John Michell brushed a mote of dust off the top hat he kept in the magistrates' room behind the court. Weather permitting, he always rode the five miles from Forcett Hall, a fine run at full gallop across his land as far as The Street and another up the old Roman road to Thorpe. 'Much on this morning?'

'Application from the workshop guardians, a few minor prosecutions, committal for trial. Should be over well before luncheon.' Snowden handed him a copy of the court list.

'Excellent.' Michell hung his red riding jacket up with care. 'Who's with me on the bench this morning? Headlam?'

'He's away at some ecclesiastical conference in Durham. You've got the Reverend Wharton.'

Michell gave a snort of contempt. 'The do-gooder? Too wet behind the ears for my liking, Snowden. Every villain who ended up in court would be acquitted if he had his way.' He pulled on his black magisterial coat and picked up the hat. 'Any news on those drownings?'

'There may be a link between them. I've been asking around down Briggate and across in Startforth, and it seems Yates and the girl were seen together in the early hours of the tenth.'

'The Sunday?'

'Yes. I came across someone yesterday, carpet-weaver name of Robinson, who says he saw Yates in Briggate about one in the morning. The girl came down one of the alleys, talked to him, and they walked off towards the bridge. Reckoned they'd both had a bit to drink.'

'And then?'

'Nothing, Robinson lost sight of them. It was dark, there's none of the new gas lights down that part of town. They wouldn't last five minutes.'

'Anyone else see them?'

'Not that I can find. It's not easy getting anyone to talk to us, you know what they're like.' Snowden frowned. 'I don't even know if they got as far as the bridge. There were people over the other side that night, but that's not unusual, the White Swan's popular.' He glanced at the clock. 'Almost ten, I'll see how many of our defendants have turned up.'

'Any sign of Wharton yet?'

'Oh, he's been in there for the past half-hour, looking worried as usual. Don't be too hard on him, his heart's in the right place.'

'Pity his brains aren't.' Michell straightened his cravat as Snowden went out. 'Up his arse, like the rest of the clergy.'

He picked up the top hat, part of the costume designed to impress and if necessary frighten those appearing before him, and entered the courtroom.

Wharton was sitting there, twisting a pencil between his fingers. He'd been wrestling with his conscience all morning. It was, he supposed, inevitable that he might recognise some of those who appeared in the dock, but was it fair if he knew they had a criminal record? With the best will in the world, the knowledge that a man had been convicted ten times before for beating his wife made it difficult not to suspect he might be guilty when accused of doing it yet again. Even worse, suppose the prosecution failed to prove its case and he had to acquit a man he knew for certain blacked her eyes every Saturday night because he'd seen her face in church next morning? This magistracy business was a minefield of moral dilemmas and he had no idea how he was going to cope.

He fretted about it as the opening proceedings took place and stopped only when the door opened at the back of the room and Betsey tiptoed in, gave him an encouraging smile and sat down in one of the three chairs earmarked as the public gallery.

'Application for guidance from the workhouse guardians, your worships.' Watson scanned the lengthy document in his hand. 'Female pauper, able-bodied, twenty-four years old, three children, husband transported for life for horse-stealing. Guardians want to know if she can discharge herself from the workhouse, leaving her children there?'

'What does the law say?' Michell looked disapproving.

'Refer your worships to the recent General Consolidation Order and the 7th Victoria, clause 101, section 25, Relief of Paupers.'

'Never mind all that, Watson. Can she discharge herself?'

'It says she should be treated as she would be were she a widow, your worships.'

Michell wrestled with the answer. 'Yes or no, man?'

'Not unless she takes the children with her.'

Wharton looked at Betsey, summoned up his courage and ventured a question. 'Why does she want to discharge herself? Is it to find employment and then be able eventually to care for the children herself?'

Watson's eyebrows rose in surprise at the intervention. 'Probably, your worship.'

'That seems a good idea.' Wharton looked nervously at Michell, who was clearly irritated that this was taking up valuable time. 'It would save the parish money in the end.'

'Possibly, your worship, but that's not what the law says. She stays inside or she takes them with her.'

'But how can she find work or undertake it if she has three small children to look after?'

Michell broke in. 'Should have asked herself that before she married a horse thief and had three brats. Seems clear enough to me. Permission to discharge herself refused. Agreed, Wharton? Good. Next?'

Wharton opened his mouth for a moment and then closed it without saying anything. Betsey felt a sudden wave of sympathy for him, being bullied by that awful man in the ridiculously tall hat.

'Indecent exposure, your worships, plus breach of the peace, assault on an officer of the law and theft of property belonging to the Gilling West divisional constabulary.'

'This the Newgate Flasher case?' Michell's interest rose sharply.

'I believe it has been given that description, your worship.'

'Bring the man in, Mr Snowden. I've been looking forward to it.'

Betsey followed her father out of the courtroom. 'Is it always like this?'

'Like what?'

'Making that poor woman stay in the workhouse. It's wrong.'

'Somebody has to make these decisions, silly or not. That's part of what magistrates do.'

'And who picks the magistrates?'

'The Lord Chancellor, on behalf of the Queen. Any more questions?' They'd reached the top of the cell steps.

'How does he decide?'

'I suppose he chooses men he thinks are of good character, mature, with sound judgement, wide knowledge of the area... that sort of thing. It's voluntary, you know, they don't get paid. He probably just picks the best available.'

'Like that man in there, Mr Michell? But he's supposed to be fair and just and... well, anyway, he shouldn't be there.'

'I couldn't possibly comment.' Snowden gave her a smile. 'Now, let's get this indecent exposure over.' He hesitated. 'Do you think you should hear this one? Mrs Eeles would say it was most unsuitable for the ears of a young girl.'

'Nonsense. She'll want to hear everything about it when I next see her. I'll go back in, don't worry.'

Back in the court she sat down and waited. Michell was drumming his fingers on the desk, his companion on the bench staring at the ceiling as if seeking divine inspiration. The door opened.

'Next defendant, your worships, the indecent exposure.' A small ferret-faced man with a tuft of black moustache under his pointed nose stumbled into the room, followed by Snowden who directed him to the dock.

'Name?'

'Fergus Fossitt, your lordships.'

Watson rustled his papers and looked puzzled. 'Not the name I have here, your worships.'

'An alias!' Michell glared. 'Trying to keep your disgusting behaviour a secret, you blackguard?'

The man gave a terrified squeak. 'It's my real name, so help me.' His hands clutching the bar of the dock began to shake. 'Ask anyone in Newgate, they all know me, Fergie Fossitt.'

'They will now, you perverted little deviant,' Michell roared. Wharton recoiled in alarm and almost fell off his seat. Betsey looked on, entranced.

'If I can enlighten your worships?' Snowden swallowed. This was going to be a little embarrassing.

'Please do, Mr Snowden.'

'The defendant, as you will shortly hear, was apprehended only last night. Until then it was thought that the perpetrator of his crimes was another individual, for whom appropriate paperwork had been prepared for this court hearing. I fear that the name on the papers in Mr Watson's hands needs amending accordingly.'

Watson frowned, bent over his desk and picked up a pen.

'Not very efficient, Mr Snowden.' Michell was enjoying this.

'My apologies, your worships. I knew nothing of the case until a few minutes ago.'

'Let's get on with it, then.'

'As I said, this man was arrested last night in suspicious circumstances which led to him appearing before you today.'

'Suspicious circumstances? What was he up to?'

'I'm told he ran up the aisle in St Mary's Church in the middle of a Town Mothers' Guild meeting, your worship, announcing that he was the new Messiah and come to enlighten any virgins in the congregation. He then removed his hat.'

'Quite right, sacred premises. What about the rest of his clothing?'

'There wasn't any, your worship.'

Michell's eyes goggled. 'You mean the man was *naked*?'

'Stark, your worship.'

'Good God. Then what?'

'I understand the vicar fainted and several ladies attempted to take hold of him.'

'The vicar?'

'The intruder, your worship. Fossitt here.'

'And did they take hold of him? How?'

Snowden was sure he heard Betsey behind him dissolving in barely-suppressed giggles, but pressed on. 'He managed to evade capture, your worship, but was apprehended at the door by Constable Kipling, who had heard the ladies screaming on his way home and come to investigate.'

'Did he come quietly?'

'Stealthily, I imagine, your worship. Our men are well-trained.'

Michell looked at him narrowly. 'Fossitt, not the constable.'

Snowden ignored the sound of Betsey, a fist in her mouth, trying to stop laughing out loud. 'After something of a struggle, I understand. Hence the charges relating to assaulting a police officer.'

'And the theft of constabulary property?'

'He apparently managed to appropriate the constable's headgear at one stage and dance round the graveyard in it before being finally arrested.'

'Disgraceful.' Michell sat back and shook his head. 'What's the most we can do to him, Mr Watson?'

'Not a great deal, I fear, your worship. You appear to have found him guilty –'

'Too damned right I have!'

'– without asking him how he pleads or giving him a chance to offer any defence.' He scratched his head. 'I'm not sure we can sentence him to anything. Frankly, your worships, the whole proceedings have been most irregular and any conviction would certainly be overturned at appeal.'

'You mean the little bastard goes free?' Betsey thought Michell was about to explode. He stood up, his face mottled with fury. 'Court adjourned. Resumes at two.'

Barnard Castle, 12.15pm

TOM Marwood pinned the notice up beside the makeshift dartboard and stood back to admire his handiwork. 'There you are, lads. Summer Darts Trophy draw. Saturday night, seven sharp.'

There were half a dozen of them in the bar. 'Who've I got in the first round then,

Tom?'

'Geordie Barker?' He ran his finger down the list. 'You're up against Daniel Johnson.'

'That'll do me.'

'Anyone else?'

'What about me?'

'John Breckon, isn't it?' The finger went up and down again. 'You've got Jonathan Arrowsmith.'

'Shit, he's good.'

'Not as good as his brother. Good job he's not around, he'd walk all over you.'

'Charlie? Nah, I'd beat him with both eyes closed. Where is he, anyway?'

Tom shrugged. 'God knows. Just buggered off, they say. Wasn't he the one shacked up with that girl got herself drowned?'

One of the others nodded. 'Probably did herself in, couldn't stand life without him.' The rest laughed. 'Right bastard he is, Charlie, treated her like shit, even if she was a tart.'

A tall dark man who had been sitting alone in the corner stood up. 'You saying my sister was on the game?'

There was a long silence, broken by Tom. 'Take it easy, Raine. We don't want any trouble.'

'Keep out of this, Tom. This is between me and Jim Fitzgerald here. You want to apologise or do I make you?'

Fitzgerald looked round and weighed up the numbers. 'Stuff your sister. Everyone else has.'

Tom Marwood groaned and ducked down behind the bar.

Thorpe, 2.05pm

'ALL rise.' The two magistrates resumed their places, Michell replete after another grouse special at the Morritt's Arms which Wharton had declined, inventing a dying parishioner in need of last-minute rites. Snowden had shared the remains of last night's shepherd's pie with Betsey in the kitchen.

'Next?'

Watson consulted his list. 'Committal for trial on a charge of blackmail, your worships. The defendant's outside, been brought over in custody from Barnard Castle.'

'Bring him in.'

Watson put his head round the door, said something Snowden couldn't hear, and returned, followed by Constable Kipling and his prisoner. 'Hamish McQueedie, your worships. Claims to be a reporter. No fixed abode.'

Michell stared at him. 'Why is he wearing a frock, constable?'

'He appears to have no clothing of his own, your worship. When I collected him from the Butter Market cell he was wearing only a small fragment of sacking which I didn't think you would approve of in court, so I asked Mr Snowden's assistant here to find something more suitable.' He nodded towards Betsey. 'She told me this is all she could find at such short notice.'

'Is this permissible, Watson?'

'It's highly irregular, your worship, but I can't find anything in the rules about defendants' attire. Unless you deem it to be contempt of court, I suppose.'

'Never mind, let's get on, wasted far too much time already. Committal for trial, you said?'

'Yes, your worship.'

'Well, let's get this case done properly.'

'I'll do my best, your worship.' Watson turned to McQueedie, who had long since abandoned hope of anything in his life making sense ever again. 'Hamish McQueedie, you are charged that on the 26th of this month you did wilfully and knowingly utter a letter or writing with menaces including threats of action detrimental to or unpleasant to the person addressed, namely Lord Beavermere of Rotherbrook. How do you plead?'

'It's all a dreadful mistake, I'm innocent.' McQueedie stared wildly about the court in search of assistance. 'Mr Snowden there knows me, he's seen me in court. So have the magistrates.' He looked desperately at Michell and Wharton. 'Not these two, I've never come across them, but there's a fattish one who'd vouch for me.'

'Been done for this kind of thing before, have we?' Michell couldn't resist intervening.

'No, never, I'm a reporter for the *Gazette*. I work for Lord Beavermere.'

'I don't believe a word of it. What's this all about, constable?'

Kipling stepped forward, his hopes of promotion rising by the minute. 'I have here the letter in question, your worships. Exhibit A.' He held out the folded note he'd found outside the Butter Market cell door. 'It came into my possession on Tuesday and I delivered it immediately to the Kings Head for his lordship's attention.'

'Let's see that.' Michell read the letter through, his eyebrows rising line by line, and then passed it to Wharton. 'Outrageous. What did Lord Beavermere think of it?'

'He said it was a blackmail demand from a man he'd never met, sir, the accused who I'd already arrested for being the Newgate Flasher.'

'Nonsense, man, we've already dealt with him this morning.'

'There was a bit of a mix-up, sir, yes.' Kipling shuffled his feet in embarrassment.

Michell glowered at him before turning to Snowden. 'You have investigated this further, I presume?'

Snowden nodded. 'I managed to have a word with his lordship this morning.'

'And he denied these foul allegations in the letter, of course?'

'Well, not exactly, your worship.'

'You mean he admitted being in a clandestine relationship with this –' Michell grabbed the letter back from Wharton, who was still trying to find his spectacles. 'This Lucy Lustworthy woman?'

'Not clandestine, your worship. She's his sister.'

'His *what*?'

'His lordship apparently comes from very humble origins, as do other of our peers ennobled for their services to industry. Before his elevation I understand he was known as Osbert Plunkett. His sister is also a Plunkett, but prefers to employ Lustworthy as her stage name.'

'Extraordinary.' Michell shook his head and handed the letter back to Wharton. 'I assume publication of a story inferring that he was having illicit congress with a music-hall girl, as this letter threatens, would be highly embarrassing to his lordship?'

'In the contrary, he says publication in a rival newspaper such as the *Leeds Examiner* would make him a fortune in libel damages and probably bankrupt it, which would give him enormous pleasure.' Snowden smiled. 'However, he fears his sister's reputation and theatrical career would be placed in jeopardy if the public knew she had a brother was a lord who owned the *Gazette*.'

'Why on earth –?'

'It is renowned for its opposition to improving the lot of the working classes, your worship. He believes his sister's music-hall audiences would not approve of her being related to its owner. As a result, he does not wish to press charges and says he'll deal with McQueedie himself.'

'Preposterous!' Michell was outraged. 'This reporter fellow – if that's what he is – has committed blackmail! Where's that letter?' He grabbed it back from Wharton, who had finally discovered his spectacles and was beginning to read the first page. 'Look at it, superintendent. Clear evidence of the man's guilt!' He thrust it at Snowden. 'Well?'

Snowden examined it carefully. 'I wonder if I could see the constable's report. You have an accurate note of your interview with Lord Beavermere, I presume?'

'Full note, sir, made immediately afterwards as per the training manual. Exhibit B, sir.' Kipling handed over his notebook.

Snowden opened it, flicked through the pages, and frowned. 'Can you explain, constable, why these lines crossed out at the top of the second page of Exhibit A are in the same handwriting as the report in Exhibit B?'

Kipling looked blank.

'They appear to be a list. *Mend stocking. Alice birthday, must get gift* and so on.'

Kipling turned pink.

'Or why the torn sides of these two sheets of paper on which Exhibit A was written match exactly the torn fragments of two missing pages in Exhibit B?'

Kipling's vision of sergeanthood vanished in a wave of humiliation. 'He must have stolen them,' he gurgled.

'While he was locked in the cell you were guarding?'

'Yes. No. I don't know, it's impossible.'

Michell looked aghast. 'You're not suggesting, Mr Snowden, that the constable conspired with the accused to commit blackmail?' His eyes widened at another possible solution. 'Or forged the letter in an attempt to incriminate the accused?'

'I wouldn't go that far, your worship, but it is most curious. I certainly can't see how Mr McQueedie could have written the letter himself unaided, if indeed he wrote it at all. I'm not sure we can proceed any further.'

'Neither am I.' Michell almost choked with fury. 'Case dismissed.'

York, 3.30pm

THE judge at York Assizes pondered his black cap and wondered whether to put it back on. He'd sent seven to the gallows that afternoon already, five men, a woman and a boy of thirteen, and Hangman Hawkins wouldn't complain about an extra shilling dangling from his rope.

What had this one done again? He glanced down at his notes. Receiving and concealing property knowing it to be stolen. Might have taken it, too, before he'd hidden it away in his barn, though the court hadn't been offered any evidence of that. On the other hand, he'd refused to say who had taken it if wasn't him, unusual for a man facing the likelihood of a noose round his neck. Most were only too eager to blame accomplices and name them in the hope of judicial mercy.

He looked up at the prisoner, chained to the dock and flanked by two bored warders, and then at the clock. He fingered the black cap, tossed a mental coin, and decided.

'Prisoner in the dock, you have been convicted, and quite rightly in my view, of a heinous transgression against the law of this land, for which I have been minded to impose the ultimate penalty.' He paused, waiting for the gentlemen of the press to catch up and record his next words. They would go down well with the titled and extremely wealthy widow of whom he had high hopes, despite her foolish ideas about abolishing capital punishment. 'I have, however, decided to be merciful. You will serve five years in her majesty's custody, with hard labour. Take him down.'

Frankie Ramsden let out a long deep breath. Five years. It would be hell but it would pass, and when he came out he knew who would owe him a life-long favour for keeping his mouth shut.

Thorpe, 6.20pm

'YOU'RE late. I thought you'd be back hours ago.' Betsey looked up from the file she was working on. V, not many left to do. She'd done Vagrancy, Vegetables (larceny of) and Venison (suspects found in possession of) and was about to start on Vexatious Indictments, whatever they were.

'Lot of paperwork to be done.' Snowden threw himself into an armchair. 'It took an hour to persuade that McQueedie fellow not to sue us all for wrongful arrest and illegal imprisonment. And we had to find him something to wear, of course.'

She walked over to join him in the other armchair. 'I still don't understand. Did he write the letter or didn't he?'

'Of course he did.'

'But why help him, if you thought he was guilty? You were supposed to be prosecuting, not defending.'

He frowned. 'I felt sorry for him, I suppose. He'd been through a lot after being mixed up with that Fossitt man and I'm not sure he really meant any harm.' There was a pause and his voice hardened. 'And I detest Lord Beavermere and all he stands for. Not fond of Michell, either. It was a pleasure to see him explode like that.'

She looked at him, uncertain whether she approved.

'And it probably guarantees me a good press for a long time. I may need McQueedie's help one day. How about a cup of tea?'

'I'll make one.' She walked off to the kitchen. Papa never failed to surprise her.

PART TWO

July-August 1846

*Barnard Castle Market Place long before the motoring age arrived.
At the far end is the octagonal Butter Market building in which McQueedie
was incarcerated.*

Wednesday July 9th

Thorpe, 10am

CONSTABLE William Elliott stood firmly to attention as the magistrates took their seats and sorted out their paperwork. Behind him were his superintendent and Constable Richard Pearson; on the far side sat Watson, the clerk, his pen at the ready. Apart from Watson's assistant, acting as usher, there was nobody else in the room.

Headlam cleared his throat. 'Before we commence, I and my fellow justice here –' he nodded towards Morritt '– wish it to be understood that we regard these proceedings as highly irregular. I trust they will prove to be of sufficient importance to justify bringing us here this morning.' He looked at Snowden. 'I take it you are responsible?'

Snowden rose. 'Yes, your worships. I'm well aware this is unusual, unique, in fact, in my experience, but I'm sure you will agree it is necessary when you have heard the reasons for your summons.'

Headlam grunted, unconvinced. 'Well, let's get on with it. Mr Watson?'

The clerk got to his feet. 'Disciplinary hearing, sir, under section 113, 29, of the 1842 Police Constables Act. Allegation of gross misconduct while on duty and assault, sir.'

'This the officer accused?' Headlam pointed to Elliott.

'Yes, sir. Constable William Elliott, Barnard Castle Preventative Force.'

'What's he done?'

'If I may, sir...?' Snowden consulted his notes. 'This case arises from a conversation between Constable Pearson here –' he indicated the officer beside him '– and a Mrs Elizabeth Sutcliffe of Briggate, Barnard Castle. She in turn was relaying a complaint made to her by her neighbour Miss Ann Humphreys. With your worships' permission, I'd like to call both of them as witnesses.'

'Must you?'

'I'm afraid so, your worship. Both are waiting outside.'

'Very well.'

Mrs Sutcliffe was ushered into the court, a well-built woman in her late forties dressed in a frayed cloak and once-white cap, her face lined beyond its years.

'I suppose she should take the oath?'

'It might be wise, your worship.'

Snowden studied the accused man as the swearing-in ritual took place. A member of the town force he'd not come across until now, Elliott was notionally under the jurisdiction of the Barnard Castle police sergeant who had been only too happy to hand the problem over to Snowden on the grounds of impartiality. The man was forty-something, paunchy, his face showing the first mottling of over-indulgence. His uniform was smart enough, but, Snowden noted with disapproval, his boots could do with a good polish.

He turned back to the witness, now on oath. 'Mrs Sutcliffe, you live alone?'

'Yes, sir. Husband's in America and the bairns have long gone.'

'I see. Perhaps you could tell the hearing briefly what occurred on the night of July the sixth?'

'The night Ann came round?'

'Miss Humphreys, yes.'

'Well, she'd been coming round a lot ever since her bairn died two weeks back. Poor little thing. I'd been looking after her daytimes while her mother worked, she's at Longstaff's, on the looms, you know, not easy when –'

'Just what happened on the sixth, Mrs Sutcliffe.'

'Yes, well, she came round about ten o'clock and I could see she was upset, more upset than usual, and been crying. What's the matter? I ask, and she says she's sore troubled but wouldn't tell me why.'

'Had she been drinking?'

'Well...' Mrs Sutcliffe paused, not sure what to reply. 'She was in the habit of taking liquor, sir, I can't deny it, and I dare say she'd had some drink that night.'

Morritt interrupted. 'How old is this Humphreys woman?'

'Seventeen, my lord.'

'I'm not your lord. Your worship will do.'

'Yes, my lord, your worship.'

'She's seventeen and in the habit of getting drunk, you say?'

'Not a habit, just when she could afford it.'

'How does she afford it, a Longstaff's mill-girl?'

'I'm sure I don't know, sir.'

'I think I do.'

Snowden came to the rescue. 'If I may continue? You asked Miss Humphreys what was troubling her?'

'Like I said. Then she tells me about this Elliott here and what he did.'

'Hearsay, Mr Snowden.' Headlam gave him a warning look. 'We'll wait for the girl herself to tell us what happened.'

'As you please, your worship. Is there anything else you can tell us?'

She hesitated. 'Nothing Ann can't tell you if she wants to.'

'We'll come to her. And after you'd spoken to her you persuaded her to go with you to tell Constable Pearson here all about it?'

'That's right, sir.' She glanced at Pearson and then back to Snowden. 'He's one of the good ones, known him for years. And Ann, she's a good girl, sir, even if she does get into trouble sometimes. I've known her since she was a child, and always took her to be very kind. I believe what she told me.'

'Thank you.' Snowden addressed the bench. 'I know this isn't a court as we're used to, but we might wish to follow similar procedures. Should the accused be invited to question her?'

Headlam frowned. 'I suppose so. Any questions, Elliott?'

The man shook his head. 'Except she's wrong about Humphreys. Proper little tart, she is. Anybody's for sixpence on a Saturday night.'

Snowden sighed. He had no idea whether the Humphreys girl would be telling the truth or lying through her teeth when she faced the hearing, but her chances of being believed were diminishing fast. 'You can go, Mrs Sutcliffe. Wait outside.'

She gave an awkward curtsey to the magistrates, straightened her bonnet, and left.

'Let's have the other one in.' Headlam was getting bored. 'Not going to take much longer, is it?'

Ann Humphreys was led in and Snowden studied her as she took the oath. Small, more timid than he'd expected, a meagre little fair-haired girl not much more than a child with a pinched face and a mop cap that had seen many better days. Her cape was ragged at the edges and he could see stains that had defied scrubbing. He wondered when, if ever, she'd felt hot or even warm water on her skin.

'Ann Humphreys?'

'Yes, sir.'

'We've been told that you complained to Mrs Sutcliffe about Constable Elliott. What happened?'

She took several moments to answer. 'It was midnight gone on the Sunday, the one before last, the day the bairn passed over.' Her voice faltered. 'She was breathing that bad, I was lying in bed with her at Liz's place –'

'Liz?'

'Mrs Sutcliffe, she was out somewhere. And I didn't know what to do, and the candle burnt out. So I went down to get a new one from Ellery's –'

'Ellery's?' Headlam looked confused.

'Beerhouse in Briggate, your worship. Across the road, I believe, from where Miss Humphreys resides.'

'Beerhouse, eh? Just across the road?' Snowden could tell what he was thinking as clearly as if he'd announced it out loud. 'Are you telling me it was still open after midnight on the Sabbath?'

Snowden intervened. 'It is not unknown, your worship. There is a widespread distaste for the licensing restrictions in the Briggate area.'

'I don't know why we have a police force if this is what goes on.' Headlam shook his head and turned his attention back to the witness. 'So you went to this beerhouse. Have a drink, did you?'

'I believe she said she went for a candle, your worship. Is that so, Miss Humphreys?'

'Yes, sir. It was a penny but the bairn was that bad...'

'And then?'

'I'm on my way back when Elliott and him –' she pointed at Pearson '– come along the street.'

'Together?'

'Yes, but Richard – Constable Pearson, I mean, he goes off towards Ellery's, says he's looking for somebody.' She looked at Pearson for confirmation, and he nodded.

'And Elliott?'

'He comes says he's coming back with me and he's got a bottle of gin we can share.'

'And you agreed?'

'I didn't want to. I told him about the bairn but he says if I don't do what he wants he'll have me for soliciting, say he found me up the alley with a man.' Her eyes fell and her voice turned bitter. 'I'd face two months' hard labour if that happened. What would you do?'

'You said yes?'

The girl nodded. 'We go back in, and he starts drinking the gin. I go to see how the bairn is, and I'm lying with her when he appears at the door. Next thing I know he's trying to pull me out of bed and says he wants to... to use me badly.'

'And did he?'

'He was too drunk.' Her face crumpled. 'And then the baby died.' She burst into tears. The room was silent for what seemed a very long time.

'All bloody lies.' Elliott spat the words out. 'The bitch was all for it, left the bairn on its own to die while she earned her six-pennorth.'

'You admit attempting to have carnal knowledge of her?'

'Having what?'

'Sexual relations?'

'Oh, yes, well, I would've done but she's right about that bit. Too much bloody gin.' He pointed an angry finger at the girl. 'I'll admit drinking and trying to have it away when I shouldn't, being on duty, but there was no assault on her, I'll not be done for that.'

'You're lying!' She collapsed in sobs.

'Take her out.' Headlam shook his head as she was led from the room. 'Anything else you want to say, Elliott?'

'I've told you, she's lying. Soon as Pearson left, that cow comes up to me and asks if I fancy a bit of you-know-what. In we go, a couple of gins apiece and it's on the floor, she said we wasn't to wake the bairn. But I'd had a few myself before we met up, Pearson knows that, and I wasn't up for it. She goes off to see the bairn and I buggered off back on my rounds.'

'That true, Pearson?'

'The bit about him drinking gin is, sir, he was well into it when I came on duty at midnight. Can't vouch for the rest of it, of course.'

'And you saw him next?'

'About two it would be, two-thirty, maybe. Found me by the bridge.'

'I see.' He turned back to Elliott. 'That would be in your notebook, I presume. Got it with you?'

Elliott looked flustered. 'It's here somewhere.' He searched his pockets and handed it over. Snowden flicked through the pages.

'Sunday the sixth. On duty eight till eight.' He read the entry out loud. '*8pm patrolling Briggate with Con McEwen. 10pm Market Place. Midnight Pearson. Briggate. 6am Castle. 8am handed over to Con Johnson.* Busy night, was it? Too busy to make any entries between midnight and six in the morning? Or were you asleep somewhere sleeping off the gin?'

Elliott didn't answer and Pearson looked uncomfortable. 'Very well. Anything else you want to say?' Elliott shook his head.

Headlam took over. 'Then I suggest we adjourn to talk it over. You can wait outside,

Elliott, and keep well away from those women.'

Watson's usher followed the man out of the door and closed it behind him.

'Well, gentlemen. What's our decision?'

Barnard Castle, 10.50am

'SO where is she?' James Knapton, overseer at Longstaff's flax mill, stood by the empty loom and shouted above the noise.

Mary Garthwaite shrugged. 'Something to do with the police, I don't know. Said she'd be back as soon as she could, had to go over to Thorpe.'

'Thorpe? She's no use to me there. Hasn't been much bloody use here either, these past weeks.'

'She lost her bairn, had a lot of trouble.'

'That's her problem. Tell her she's finished, I've plenty who'd welcome a nice easy place in here.' He scowled. 'There's a snag in that last line, get it cleared.'

Thorpe, 11am

'PACK of lies.' Morritt turned from the window where he'd been watching the rain form puddles in the yard. 'Girl's a whore, say anything to escape a stretch in Northallerton. Got a record, has she, Snowden?'

'I've not seen her in the Greta Bridge court, but many cases from the Durham side of the river are dealt with at Staindrop. I can get information from them if you wish.'

'Doesn't matter. Can't believe a word she says.'

Headlam nodded. 'Just lost a child, does things to a woman, don't know what's going on. Wouldn't put it past Elliott to do what she alleges, mind. Nasty piece of work.' He turned to Snowden. 'Not one of yours, eh?'

'Thank heavens. But you have to take what you can get. Not many want to spend their nights patrolling Briggate never knowing when someone's going to start waving a knife in their face.'

Headlam shook his head. 'So Elliott's clear, is that what we're saying?'

Morritt nodded. 'No assault. There's still the drinking on duty, though.'

Snowden smiled. 'If we started condemning them for that we'd have no one left.' He turned to Pearson. 'Do you want to tell us what happened later that night? I appreciate you won't want to tell tales about a fellow constable, but...'

Pearson's loyalty wrestled with his conscience and lost. 'He was well away when he found me on the bridge, sir. No fit state to do patrols. I left him there, found him asleep on the far side just before six. Sent him home.'

Snowden raised a questioning eyebrow.

'Not the first time, sir.'

'Thank you, Pearson. You seem to know the Sutcliffe woman and the girl quite well, am I right?'

'Many years, sir. There's a lot worse than them in Briggate.'

'On the game, was she, Humphreys?'

'Time to time, sir, I believe. Worked at Longstaff's, wouldn't get much more than five or six shillings a week, not a lot if you're paying someone to look after your bairn. She'd likely earn a bob or two on a Saturday night, usual kind of thing. There's a lot of them at it.'

'Think she was telling the truth?'

Pearson considered. 'Yes, sir, on balance. I can believe Elliott trying it on and I can't see her welcoming his attentions, the state she must have been in, what with the bairn dying and everything, let alone go out looking for business.' He paused. 'She was in a right state for months after Kate Raine drowned, could have done without the child falling sick.'

'Drowned?'

'Last summer. Her brother's the father.'

'Of Humphreys' child?'

'So they say, sir.'

'Get on with Kate, did she?'

'Good friends, I believe. Often saw them together.'

'Well, well.'

Morritt stirred restlessly. 'Much more of this, Snowden? Can't be long before luncheon.'

'Just a couple more things, sir, if you can bear with me. This may be important.' He returned to Pearson. 'You say she was in a right state. What do you mean by that?'

'Well, sir, I think it turned her mind a bit, she's been acting odd ever since. Thinking she'd seen Kate after she'd died, a ghost, like, walking with the lad who went in the river the same time.'

'Yates?'

'That's him, sir. Said she met them walking along the Sills large as life, even took me over there to see the spot she reckoned they went over into the water.'

'Remember where it was?'

'Think so, sir.'

'You can show me this afternoon.'

Morritt rumbled. 'Told you she was deranged. All lies.' He looked pointedly at his watch. 'Luncheon, Snowden.'

'Yes, sir... Do you think I could meet you both again briefly in about an hour? You'll be in the Morritt's, I imagine? I may need your advice and assistance.'

'If you must, I suppose. Now, about this Elliott fellow. What are we doing? Drunk on duty, neglecting his patrol, failing to maintain his notebook... the man's a disgrace.'

'Can I suggest a severe reprimand for dereliction of duty, and a final warning?' Snowden smiled. 'And I'll have a quiet word with his sergeant, see if we can't find Elliott somewhere more appropriate to his talents and far removed from temptation. Permanent guardian of the new cemetery, perhaps.'

'Good idea.' Headlam stood up. 'Let's get this over with.'

'Tell the two women to stay behind, Mr Watson, if you would.' Snowden was deep in thought. 'I'd like a word with them before they go.'

Renfrewshire, 12.05pm

McQUEEDIE stared at the advertisement in the five-day-old *Yorkshire Gazette* and prayed that it wasn't a dream.

The past year had been horrific. Sacked by Lord Beavermere the day after his court appearance in a brief and terrifying audience which culminated in his lordship promising to horsewhip him if they ever met again, he'd spent the rest of 1845 discovering that he was incapable of being a butcher's assistant, an undertaker's attendant, a stand-in postman, a brothel-owner's debt collector or a bar-tender. He had been dismissed from the last post being found insensible at ten in the morning in the cellar of the Three Horseshoes clutching an empty jeraboam of '29 Bolinger that the landlord had been hoping would largely pay for his retirement. After that he had reluctantly come to the conclusion that he was really only cut out for one career, journalism, which was a pity as Lord Beavermere had spread the word about his ex-employee and as a result nobody in the north of England seemed anxious to take him on as a reporter. There was only one solution, and he'd gone back to Scotland, where it was generally accepted that the only qualifications needed to succeed in journalism were an infinite capacity for alcohol and the courage or stupidity to enter the Gorbals unaccompanied.

For the past six months he'd been deputy sanitary affairs correspondent on the *Greenock Advertiser & Clyde Commercial Journal*, investigating Scottish sewerage leaks and blocked drains. Then the news broke that Lord Beavermere had succumbed to a heart attack while doing something very surprising and extremely illegal with a curly-haired Italian waiter up a back alley behind the Grand Hotel in Leeds. Lady Beavermere, unable to face being both ridiculed and shunned by society, had fled to the south of France, stopping only to sell off her late and unlamented husband's newspaper empire to a Huddersfield wool-mill owner who thought owning the local press might enhance his chances of entering parliament and eventually getting a peerage.

McQueedie had written immediately to an old drinking partner at the *Yorkshire Gazette* office in York, begging for news, and learnt to his delight that the newspaper had changed overnight from a rabid exponent of the Tory cause to a hearty supporter of Liberalism. The editor had been replaced by the new owner's favourite nephew, a ginger-haired twenty-two-year-old who knew nothing at all about newspapers. It was music to McQueedie's ears.

And now this. His erstwhile companion on many a drunken quest for Glenbuckie's in the North Riding had not only sent him the good news, but also the latest copy of the *Gazette*, and there it was:

REPORTER WANTED, THIRSK
Diligense, Sobriety and Strict Adherance to Liberal Principals essential, Litteracy an Advantage. Apply in writing to M. Hardcastle Esq., Editer, Yorskhire Gazette, York.

He tore it out, reached for his pen, resisted the temptation to correct the spellings and began to compose his application. It was almost too good to be true.

Thorpe, 12.15pm

ANN Humphreys seated herself nervously in one of the armchairs in Snowden's office as he guided Mrs Sutcliffe to the other, pulled up a stool and sat down before them.

'Are you feeling better?' He spoke gently and she nodded. 'I just want to ask you a few questions. Not about Elliott, you needn't worry.'

'You think I was lying.'

'Not me, the magistrates. But I promise you he won't be coming anywhere near you in future.'

She looked sceptical. 'What's it about, then?'

'Constable Pearson tells me you've seen Joseph Yates and Kate Raine, is that true?'

Her eyes widened. 'Jo and Kate?' She shot a worried glance at Mrs Sutcliffe. 'I'd been drinking, it was all a mistake. Ask Liz, I told her.'

'Mrs Sutcliffe?'

The other woman looked uncertain. 'Well, it was late at night we were talking and we'd both had a gin or two. She said she'd met them on the Sills and something about Kate smelling strong of brimstone. It was all nonsense and I thought she was losing her senses, she's been that troubled. But she went on and on about it till I thought maybe she really had seen them.' She paused. 'We'd had a fair few by then, I admit, and I said we should tell the constable, perhaps it wasn't Kate who was drowned after all.'

Snowden nodded encouragingly. 'Go on.'

'So we went out and Mr Pearson was on patrol and we told him. He said we should go with him next day and show him where they were, and we did.'

'We were very drunk.' Humphreys was looking frightened. 'I told Liz and the constable next morning it was all lies, I'd been having a dream, but he made me go.'

'So you didn't really see them?'

'No. He didn't believe me, anyway, and he told me I was wasting his time.'

'You knew Kate well, I'm told?'

Her eyes brimmed with tears. 'She was my best friend. I miss her.'

'Did you see her the night she disappeared?'

'No, not at all. Really.'

Snowden studied her face. She knew something, he was sure, more than she was saying.

'You're sure?'

'I never saw her. Or any of them.'

'Them?'

'I don't know, anybody, I wasn't there.'

'Where?'

'Anywhere, Briggate, I never went out that night.' Her face set tight. 'I don't know anything about it.'

'All right, that's all for now.' Snowden knew she wasn't going to tell him anything further and she was becoming more and more distressed. 'You can take her home, Mrs Sutcliffe.'

He watched them go, reclaimed one of the armchairs, and sat deep in thought. The girl knew not only Kate but Yates, well enough to recognise him, which he hadn't known before. The ghosts and brimstone were obviously an invention or a delusion. But why would she make it up? Perhaps it was a dream as she claimed, and she was haunted by a memory of something she'd seen a year ago and cast from her mind for it only to reappear when asleep. If she had been around that night – and she'd been so quick to deny it that he was certain she'd been lying – someone must have seen her.

He sighed. He was going to have to go looking for more witnesses, and he knew how reluctant anyone in Briggate was to collaborate with the law. There was probably only one thing that would persuade them to talk.

He got to his feet and walked resolutely to the door. Ten minutes to one, Headlam and Morritt would be about halfway through their luncheon. He found them in the dining-room, a second bottle of wine newly-opened on the table.

'Superintendent.' Morritt didn't sound glad to see him. 'What's all this about?'

'I've had some fresh information about the drownings last summer, the couple who ended up in the Tees. Could be murder.'

Headlam stopped halfway through pouring the first glassful of wine. 'Murder?'

Morritt gave a satisfied snort. 'I knew we were right to insist you looked further into it. Taken you long enough.'

Snowden managed a grim smile. 'These things do take some time, sir. The thing is, I need to get people to co-operate, and there's only one way I can do that.'

Headlam frowned. 'You mean money.' He shook his head. 'You know our policy on offering inducements out of police funds. No bribes, rewards, or whatever you like to call payment to villains who'll say anything for money. Can't be done even if we could afford it, and there's precious little in the kitty.' He filled his glass and passed the bottle to Morritt. 'Damn fine claret, this. Must cost a fortune, glad I don't have to pay for it myself. You'll not join us, Snowden, on duty I suppose?'

'Indeed, sir.' He paused while a waiter served the fish course, salmon in a delicately-flavoured sauce that set Snowden's taste buds tingling. 'But if it's just a question of money –'

'Got some good news for you, though.' Headlam savoured a mouthful of salmon and nodded appreciatively. 'Association met last night and agreed to your request for a fulltime assistant here at Greta Bridge. Starts next month, fellow you recommended, what was his name, Coleman?'

'Coulthard, sir. Anthony Coulthard.'

'That's him, constable from Durham. Worked with him before, I understand?'

'Known him for years, sir. Good man.' Snowden nodded, pleased. He'd met Coulthard in 1839, the year the Durham county police force was formed, and they had become firm friends after sharing a long investigation involving a Darlington bank and an embezzling cashier from Gainford.

'Better use of our funds than squandering it on rewards.' Headlam resumed his attack on the fish.

'He'll be worth every penny, I'm sure.' Snowden tried again. 'And you may not have to dip into Association funds for money to help my inquiries. There's a new government fund to aid the investigation of capital crimes and I'd like to apply for some.'

'As a reward for information?'

'To be used as we see fit, sir. It need not necessarily be in the form of a reward.'

'Government money?' Headlam looked relieved. 'Different kettle of fish. How much do you want?'

'A hundred, perhaps two.'

'Pounds? Good God, man, that's a fortune.'

'It'll take a fortune to open their mouths in Briggate. But if it works, it won't do our reputations any harm. Your reputations, I mean, of course, sir. Tenacious magistrates bringing heartless killers to justice, you know how the papers love that kind of thing.'

'Tenacious, eh?' Morritt gave a nod. 'Well, no harm in trying. You'll need our names on the application, I trust?'

'Of course. And they're also willing to grant a free pardon to anyone who comes forward.'

'Free pardon? Don't like the sound of that.'

'Very persuasive, sir. A guaranteed escape from the gallows loosens a lot of mouths.' He reached into his pocket. 'I want to keep it secret for the moment, we don't want anyone alerted to the fact that we're on their scent if it does turn out to be murder. We may not need to use it, of course, or the money.'

'But we'd have the money anyway... just in case?'

'Of course.'

Morritt and Headlam exchanged glances. 'Very well. Bring us the paperwork and we'll see what we can do.'

'I've got it here, sir, ready for you to sign.'

Barningham, 4.40pm

WHARTON snipped the cutting carefully from the *Yorkshire Gazette*, pasted it into his scrapbook and read it again.

Awards by the Royal Society of Agriculture's show in Norwich, 1846: five horse hoes, a light horse hoe, a very light horse hoe, a horse rake, and a set of undulating harrow drills for corn, invented by the Rev. W. Wharton, rector of Barningham, and manufactured by the exhibitor (to this implement was awarded the Silver Medal)...

The Silver Medal. He looked across at it, in pride of place on his study mantelpiece. Pride was a sin, of course, but he was sure he would be forgiven this once. It was, after all, for the greater benefit of mankind, and God must be in favour of that even if his ways were often so very mysterious.

He closed the scrapbook and then re-opened it, remembering the letter that had come in the afternoon post. From the Reverend Barnabus Hill of Shrewsbury, so kind of him. *'Respecting the plough I purchased from you... a first-rate implement... confident that it economises both time and horse power...'* It ran to three sheets of notepaper and took up another page in the scrapbook, which was almost full. He'd have to get another one before long.

He turned to the front. January the first, 1841, the year after he'd arrived in Barningham. It seemed a very long time ago, but he remembered pasting in the first item, a tiny paragraph in the *Gazette* recording the bishop's visit for confirmations and to make sure he was surviving in his new rectorship, though of course the paper didn't mention that.

He turned a dozen pages over and stopped. The first note from Betsey, a year ago now nearly, thanking him for coming to dine at Thorpe. *'Dear Reverend Wharton, My father and I were so pleased you could come...'* He smiled. A lot had happened since then.

Saturday July 25th

Whashton, 10.15am

LYING flat on his stomach Snowden could just reach what remained of the body. Whoever put it there must have pushed it the last few yards to the very end of the tunnel and then squirmed their way backwards until there was room enough to turn round, which is what he was going to have to do.

He'd seen all he could by the light of the lantern at the end of his out-stretched arm. Adult, almost certainly male judging by the calf-length boot on the nearest leg; the body, what he could see of it, decomposing but still with some flesh on it. It was cold, almost icy down here, fifty yards into the hillside, and he would be surprised if any insects had got this far to feast on the body. There was a faint odour of putrefaction, but not much, and the main thing he could smell was the damp. No sign of any blood, but that would have long gone.

He moved the lantern a few inches to one side to see the other boot. It lay on its side, separated from the other remains, presumably with a foot still inside. The tibia that had connected it to the rest of the body was missing, of course. The upper bone of the leg stuck out grotesquely from beneath what was left of a heavy black cloak that covered all the rest of the body. The skull must be beyond it, out of sight, pushed as far into the narrow end of the tunnel as possible.

He took his weight on his forearms and began to wriggle backwards, leaving the lantern for whoever came down next. It was harder going up the slope, and he was breathing heavily by the time he'd covered the twenty feet or so to the point where the tunnel was wide enough for him to twist round. He did most of the rest of the ascent on his hands and knees before rising to a crouching walk for the final few yards into the sunshine that had been just a distant dot from the far end of the tunnel. He stood up and stretched.

Sergeant Reuben Clarke eyed him up and down. 'Bit clarty down there, was it, sir?'

'A bit.' Snowden had stripped down to his vest and undershorts for the crawl down the tunnel. 'Long time since my knees got this muddy.'

'So what's down there?'

'Man I think, no idea how old, probably been in there for the best part of a year. No sign of anyone going in there since he did.'

'Accident, suicide?

'More serious than that, I suspect, sergeant. The body's been shoved right to the far end, it doesn't look as if it crawled there.'

'Any idea how he died?'

'Couldn't tell. We'll have to wait until we get him out.' He looked round. There were three constables standing nearby, awaiting instructions. 'Pick the smallest of them and send him down with some sheeting and some rope. Tell him to get the body onto the sheets, careful as he can and leaving nothing behind, and haul it gently up here. Then we can have a proper look at it.'

'Right you are, sir.'

Snowden remained, pondering the tunnel the sergeant had led him to from Whashton, a tiny village tucked away beyond the road to Richmond. They had crossed a rough field full of gorse bushes and windswept trees, treading carefully through swampy ground beside a tiny beck before climbing halfway up the wooded hillside on the far side. It was part of Whashton Hagg, commonly known as the Waste, and much of it had once been limestone quarries. The tunnel must have been built when they were in operation, but Snowden had no idea what it was for. It was well-made, stone-lined above and to each side, but became progressively narrower and narrower until it came almost to a point at its end, where the body lay. Its entrance lay hidden among a tangle of briars and gorse, invisible to any casual passer-by though Snowden couldn't imagine many people setting foot near it from one year's end to the next. If it hadn't been for George Bulmer's dog the body could have stayed there undiscovered for decades.

Clarke returned with an unenthusiastic constable who started stripping off his clothes. 'One of the other lads is going for sheeting and a rope, there's a farm at the far end which is bound to have some we can borrow. Johnson here's going down the tunnel.'

'Any sign of life at the Whashton pub?' Snowden pulled on his shirt and trousers, fastened the belt and slung his jacket over his shoulder. 'I left my horse outside and could do with a wash.'

'Should be. What do you want me to do with this?'

The sergeant held out a long bone, still with a few fragments of flesh on it. 'It's the one the dog brought up. Young Bulmer took it off him, saw what it was and called us in first thing this morning.'

'Put it with the rest when Johnson's got them up. Where will I find Bulmer later on?'

'His father runs the Shoulder of Mutton, half a mile over at Kirby Hill. George helps him out on his smallholding next-door. You'll find him there having his mid-days around noon.'

'Right. I'll get changed.' He looked around. 'There must be an easier way back than ploughing through all that swamp and gorse.'

'Up to the top of the hill, sir, you'll find the Richmond road. Turn right, right again a bit further down and you're there.'

Snowden was reunited with Bucephalus in less than five minutes. 'Won't be long,' he promised, laying his jacket over the saddle and knocking on the pub door. The Hack and Spade was a tiny pub on a corner halfway down the only street, and he wondered how it survived. Whashton was more of a hamlet than a village, just a dozen or so low cottages straggling one side of a sloping village green, a couple of larger farmhouses, one three-storey building that he guessed must be the Yorkshire school he'd heard about, a smithy and the pub. It was a most unlikely place to get murdered in, but it had happened to somebody.

A large aproned woman in her sixties answered his knock. 'If you want the shop it's the other door. If you want the pub it's open at noon.' She vanished, pulling the door closed behind her.

Bemused, he tried the second door five yards to the left. It opened into a shop crammed with everything the village could possibly need, foodstuffs, hardware, sacks of flour, buckets, coils of rope and lanterns hanging from the ceiling, a tray of fresh bread and half a dozen newspapers on the counter, shelves behind piled with packets and potions, herbs and spices, boot blacking and children's sweets, a rack of clay pipes and jars of tobacco, egg-trays perched precariously on tins of biscuits, baskets of apples and plums, a cat asleep on a pile of proggy mats at the back. There was a door on the right through which the large woman squeezed and eased herself behind the counter. 'Yes?'

'I was wondering if you could spare a little water for me to wash in.' She stared at him. 'Police, we're working over the Waste, and I'm rather muddy.'

'Water? There's a horse-trough down the road, what's wrong with that?'

'Hot water would be very welcome. Or just warm would do.'

'We don't do water, hot, cold or in-between. You could try the pub when it's open.'

'But –' Snowden was baffled. 'Isn't this part of the pub?'

'It's the shop. Open eight till noon every day, bar Sundays of course.'

'And the pub –?'

'Open noon till two, six till ten, closed Sundays and Christmas Day.'

Snowden had to ask. 'What happens between two and six?'

'No business of yours, young man. Now, do you want to buy anything or are you just wasting my time?'

'I think I'll come back later.' He turned to the door, smiling. It was a long while since anyone had called him a young man.

'Closed at noon, mind. And shut the door behind you.'

He swilled his hands in the trough, hauled himself into the saddle and pointed Bucephalus towards Kirby Hill. Perhaps the man in the tunnel was a villager who had committed suicide, and Snowden wouldn't have blamed him if all his neighbours were like the woman in the shop. Or pub, if the man had decided to end it all after mid-day.

Barnard Castle, 11.50am

McQUEEDIE sat in the back bar of The Feathers and inspected the inside of the tepid meat pie before him. So far he'd found three lumps of something gristly that was certainly meat but he suspected had once had fur, claws and kittens. He pushed them aside and sampled the pastry.

'Another pint, Angus?'

There was something orange on the plate that might be carrot. He tried a bit and blenched. God knows what that was, perhaps it had fallen into the pie by accident.

'Angus! Do you want another or don't you?'

He started. 'Sorry, Gilbert, that would be very welcome.' He shook his head, wondering if he'd ever get used to his new name. 'And a Glenbuckie's chaser if you've got it.'

He pushed the plate aside and contemplated what was in store that afternoon. He was about to meet the man who had replaced him on the *Gazette* almost a year ago and he was determined to make a good impression.

His dream of rejoining the paper had, as he'd feared, been too good to be true. He'd been delighted when the reply to his job application was an invitation to be interviewed at the *Gazette*'s head office. He'd put his notice in straight away, slightly disappointed that it was accepted without argument as if the *Greenock Advertiser* was pleased to see him go, and pawned the silver pencil he'd found one tedious day on the Renfrew & District Board of Guardians' press bench to pay for a coach ticket to York.

If he hadn't decided to stay with his former drinking partner, if they hadn't celebrated their reunion with a tour of old haunts, if they hadn't ended up in Northallerton – he still hadn't the faintest idea how they got there – and if he hadn't caught the next train back to York only to fall asleep and discover himself on the wrong train and pulling into Darlington station, it might all have been so different. Leaping out and realising as the train vanished northwards that he'd left everything he possessed, including his ticket, in his bag under the seat in the third-class carriage didn't help, and the ticket inspector, officious little bastard, had taken his last sixpence as a bribe to avoid arrest for attempting to defraud the Grand Junction Railway Company of two shillings and fourpence. By the time he'd been released the last train south had long gone. He shuddered at the memory of the night spent in a derelict privy behind the station, knowing he hadn't a hope in the world of attending his interview first thing next morning.

Penniless, bag-less, and surrounded by a small swarm of flies, he'd set off for Barnard Castle, the only place he knew within trudging distance where he might find help. He'd left the town in such a hurry after the horse-whipping threats from Lord Beavermere that he'd had no time to call in on the landlord of the Golden Lion, who ran an illegal but very profitable sideline as a bookmaker and still owed him the proceeds from a two-shilling wager on Never Say Die in the four-thirty at Pontefract. It had romped home at forty to one to the surprise of everyone including McQueedie, who'd drunkenly thought he was betting on the favourite.

The trek from Darlington took seven hours, time enough from him to work out a plan of action. To begin with, he wanted to keep his past firmly behind him. The name and reputation of Hamish McQueedie was too well-known to revive, and by the time he reached Barnard Castle he'd invented a twin brother who, he vowed, would be a totally different person.

'Another one, Angus?'

Well, perhaps not totally different. 'Same again, Gilbert, with a Glenbuckie's. May as well make it a double.'

Kirby Hill, 12.10pm

AFTER his chilly reception in Whashton, Snowden was pleasantly surprised to walk into the Shoulder of Mutton and be warmly greeted by the man behind the bar.

'Superintendent Snowden? Christopher Bulmer. Pleased to meet you, don't often see you lads up this part of the world. Clarkie said you'd be dropping by. What'll you have?'

'Pint of the Swaledale, I think.' Snowden took a stool and searched for his pipe. 'I gather it was your lad found the body?'

'George, aye. Well, the dog did, part of it. They'll both be in any minute.' He glanced at the policeman's hands. 'Been down the tunnel, have you?'

'Tried to get cleaned up at Whashton pub, but I seemed to upset the landlady and had to make do with a horse-trough.'

'Funny old bird, that one.' Christopher handed him his pint. 'Been there for donkey's years, never been the same since her husband died and that must be, oh, thirty-odd years ago.'

Snowden took a draught of beer and nodded appreciatively. 'Not a bad pint, that. Tell me about the tunnel.'

'Not much I can tell. It's been there as long as I can remember, we used to dare each other to crawl down it when we were lads. You could see it clearly in those days, that area had only just stopped being quarried and there was none of the growth there is today.' He paused, thinking back half a century. 'Nobody knew what it as doing there. There was talk that it went all the way up to the church over the road here but that must have been nonsense, it goes down over, not up. But I reckon it led to some place. Did you get right to the end?'

Snowden nodded. 'It gets more and more narrow, then it stops. That's where the body was.'

'That might not be the end, superintendent. It's as far as we ever got, we only ever had a candle stump with us and we were bloody terrified, I can tell you. But I recall the end looking as if the roof had fallen in and there might be more passage beyond. You'd have to be dwarf to get any further, though.'

'Smaller than me, anyway. I had a devil of a job reaching the body.'

There were footsteps from the room beyond the bar, and a man in his early twenties walked in. Bulmer introduced them.

'My son George, he helps me run the farm at the back. Not much of one, just a couple of fields, but it helps us keep the pub running.'

'Your dog found the body, I understand.'

'That's right. Bugger shot off on his own while I was down there checking...' His voice tailed off and he looked at his father for guidance.

Snowden smiled. 'Don't worry, I'm not interested in your rabbit snares. I think I've got more important crime to sort out.'

George looked relieved. 'Well, I was down there and he disappeared for a bit and then came back, happy as could be, with this bloody bone. It was disgusting.' He frowned. 'Wouldn't do him any harm if he'd eaten anything, would it?'

'Shouldn't think so.' Snowden finished his pint and put the empty glass on the bar. 'Either of you any idea who it might be? Anybody round here gone missing in the past year?'

George and his father exchanged glances and shook their heads. 'Not that I know of.' Bulmer picked up the glass. 'Want another?'

'Maybe. Got any food on?'

'Wife does a good veal pie. And the kettle's on if you want to wash that mud off.'

'That'll do nicely. I'll have another pint, and have one yourselves, both of you.' He turned to George. 'What's the dog called?'

'Lucy.'

Snowden put a florin down on the bar. 'That's for the beers and the pie. What's over can buy Lucy a bone she can keep. She's earned it.'

Thorpe, 1pm

TOMMY stretched out a paw, batted idly at a bluebottle crawling up the windowpane and wondered if it was worth getting up to investigate what Betsey was doing across the room. It might be interesting. It might even involve food. On the other hand, it was very comfortable lying here on the windowsill in the sunshine. The cat drifted slowly back to sleep.

Betsey laid down the piece of deep purple cloth and viewed it critically. The floral red cross on its white background in the centre was proving quite a challenge. It had to match all the others in church and she wasn't sure the red was quite the same shade. She held her handiwork next to the old hassock on the table beside her and compared the two. The old one was worn and faded from years of use, and it was hard to tell if she'd chosen the right thread. Oh well, she was more than halfway through the cross now and she wasn't going to start again. A few months of offering support to worshippers' knees and it would no doubt look much the same as the rest. William would never notice, anyway.

She picked up her needle and let her mind wander as she resumed sewing. She'd always enjoyed it, ever since she was a child and her Aunt Jane in Nunnington had taught her how to mend a doll's dress. And that sampler she'd been so proud of, the one for papa's birthday. She could see it now, yellow and white daisies in each corner, the little cottage with the smoke coming out of the chimney and the tiny figures of her and papa standing outside. It had taken so long doing the words. *God Bless Our Home Sweet Home*, it said across the top, though home hadn't been a cottage then, in fact they hadn't had a proper home at all. Then there was her name under the cottage and the date. *Bestey Snowden, Aged Eight, Anno Domini 1836*. She'd made it secretly and presented it to papa when he next came to see her, and he'd looked so pleased. 'Your mama would have been proud of you,' he'd said, and she was astonished to discover than men could have tears in their eyes. It was only years later, when she found it among her boxes of old clothes and long-abandoned playthings and hung it up in their first real home in Greta Bridge, that she noticed she'd spelt her name wrong. It didn't matter, he'd said, Bestey or Betsey, it was the thought that counted. She was sure William would feel the same about his new hassock cover if the red turned out to be the wrong colour.

Tommy abandoned the windowsill, leapt effortlessly onto the table beside Betsey and started investigating the contents of the sewing basket.

'Not in there, Tommy.' She scooped the cat up and scratched its ear.

Aunt Jane. She hadn't written to her for ages.

Barnard Castle, 1.45pm

'THAT'S the last of it.' Gilbert Townsley poured the final drops of the Glenbuckie into the waiting glass and dropped the bottle in with the rest of the empties under the bar. 'Sorry, Angus, don't usually have this kind of demand for it. I'll have another one in tomorrow if you're going to be in regularly.'

McQueedie lifted the glass to his lips. 'I'll be back. Hardly worth paying for this drop now, is it?'

Gilbert sighed. 'You may as well have it on the house. Anything else instead?'

McQueedie wavered but remembered he was Angus. 'Not now, work to be done. See you later.' He walked out of the bar, came back ten seconds later to collect his notebook, and set off again with a purposeful if slightly unsteady gait to find Lancelot Fewster.

The *Yorkshire Gazette* office was above a shop halfway along the Market Place. The sign over the multi-paned glass windows each side of the shop door identified it as the premises of Beckwith & Co Printing and Stationery Works Est 1827 and a smaller notice beside the door itself offered *All Orders Promptly Attended To, Visiting Cards A Speciality, Your Custom Humbly Sought.* McQueedie ignored the invitation and made his way down the narrow passage beside the shop to enter another smaller door at its rear.

Nothing had changed. The plaster was still peeling, the pile of old newspapers was still where it had always been inside the door, only six months taller, and the smell of damp mouldering timber with a hint of urine was just as he remembered. He gave a nostalgic sniff and mounted the dark narrow stairs he had climbed so often during his former role as the *Gazette*'s representative in town.

There were two doors on the first floor landing. The one on the left, he knew, held back numbers of the *Gazette* dating back to its first publication in 1819, dumped in unsold heaps in no order he had ever been able to unravel. It was also home to generations of mice who had burrowed into the piles, created nests and raised broods who thrived on a diet of old newsprint. A horde of grey-brown rodents scampered to safety under its door as he reached the top of the stairs and turned right. The notice on the other door said Editorial Department, an ambitious description, McQueedie thought. The *Gazette* had never employed more than one member of staff at a time.

His knock brought a muffled invitation to enter, and he went in. The occupant emerged from behind an immense roll-top desk that took up half the room, a tall, gloomy and skeletally-thin man in his fifties with thinning grey hair and a mustard-tinged moustache drooping down to his chin.

'Hami– Angus McQueedie.'

'Hamiangus?'

'Angus,' McQueedie said firmly, 'Bit of a cough.' He cleared his throat noisily. 'Angus McQueedie. My brother Hamish used to work here.'

'Plays to mate yow.' There was a moment's silence as McQueedie wrestled with the words, spoken in a broad accent that he hadn't come across before. It had taken him some time when he'd first arrived in Teesdale to discover that yow was local dialect for a ewe, but the first two words had him stumped. Perhaps it was because the man clearly had a serious nasal condition. His nose had a large drop of something at the end and McQueedie watched fascinated as it dripped slowly down and sank into the moustache. That explained the mustard, but the greeting remained a mystery. 'I'm sorry?'

'Saul roight. Tyke a sate.'

The explanation slowly dawned on McQueedie.

'Come from the Midlands, do you?' There were no chairs apart from the one his replacement was sitting in, and he perched gingerly on a tea-chest that had once contained evidence for a story he'd pursued. Something to do with a butcher in Marshall's Yard who slaughtered stray dogs for their livers, he recalled. It still carried a faint aroma of dead canine.

'Black Country, Smethwick way,' McQueedie found interpretation easier as it went on. 'Ever been there?'

'Not that I remember.'

'Well, you wouldn't unless you had to.' The man held out a hand. 'Lancelot Fewster.'

'Pleased to meet you.' McQueedie enunciated the words carefully and gave the hand a shake. Fewster winced. 'Enjoying the job, are you?'

'Hate it.' He pulled a small brass snuffbox from his waistcoat pocket and took a long nose-full. Another drip began to form above his lip. 'All bloody farmers, sheep and cows and corn prices, not what I call reporting.' His voice dropped mournfully. 'I was covering sport for the *Evening Star* before, proper job.'

'Sport?'

'Horse-racing. Had my own free pass for Wolverhampton, knew all the trainers and the bookies, tips every day. The sport of kings, you know.'

'So what made you leave the *Star*, then? Want a new challenge, fresh fields to conquer, that sort of thing?'

'Thought I'd be happy there for life until –' Fewster stopped. The drip vanished into his moustache and the mustard stain spread a fraction further. McQueedie couldn't imagine the word happy came to the man's lips very often.

'Until –?'

'Had a bit of trouble over a horse.' McQueedie nodded understandingly, hoping for more details, but Fewster sniffed and changed the subject. 'Water under the bridge now. What brings you down here, something to do with your brother? Left under a bit of a cloud, I'm told.'

'All a dreadful mistake.'

'Twins, you said in your letter?'

'Peas in a pod. Even mother couldn't tell us apart. Always did the same things, school, play, work on the paper.'

'The paper?'

'Oh yes, we both joined the local rag and fought over who got the best stories. Happy days.'

'You were a reporter too?' Fewster's eyebrows rose in surprise.

'Are. Am. A reporter.' McQueedie looked round the office. 'Hamish said this was the hardest job he'd known. All on his own, massive patch, stories to cover all over and not enough time to handle things all on his own.' He leant forward confidentially. 'Between you and me, I think that's why he lost his mind and ended up in court. Overworked, under-paid, it just overwhelmed him.' He eyed Fewster cautiously, wondering how this was going down. He needn't have worried.

'That's exactly what it's like.' Fewster nodded his head in worried agreement. 'Lost his mind, you say?'

'Terrible.' McQueedie dropped his voice to a whisper. 'Ended up being found bollock-naked behind the Black Horse. Pressure of work, just couldn't cope. Could happen to anyone.'

'Yes.' Fewster took another anxious snoutful of snuff. 'All right now, is he?'

McQueedie wondered how far he could go and decided to chance it. 'We've kept it quiet, but I think you ought to know for your own sake. They had a doctor all lined up and signed him over to the asylum. Spends his days in there babbling about the workhouse urinals sub-committee.' He shook his head sadly. 'I've just been to see him, that's why I'm in town. He'll never come out, God bless his soul, mind completely gone.'

'Babbling?'

'Babbling.'

'About the workhouse urinals sub-committee?'

'Constantly.'

Fewster's nose quivered and dripped. 'I know just how he feels. Well, it's not going to happen to me. I'll tell the new editor so on Monday.'

'Monday?'

'He's doing a tour of all the offices. I'm going to tell him I need some help or I'll end up babbling like – what was your brother's name?'

'Hamish.'

'Hamish, yes. Like him. Babbling.'

'Gibbering, they tell me, on a bad day. Well, I wish you luck. Hard to find anyone willing to work in these conditions, mind, but you never know.' McQueedie sat back thoughtfully. 'I wonder...'

The gloom on Fewster's face lifted a little. 'You don't fancy giving me a hand, I suppose?'

McQueedie laughed. 'Oh, you don't want an old hack like me. Too old to be chasing hard news, I'm afraid. All I'd be good for is taking over the day-to-day boring stuff like the cattle marts, the parish meetings and the village fetes.'

'And the workhouse urinals sub-committee, I suppose?'

'Nothing I'd like more. But you'd have to do all the real stories.'

Fewster stood up. 'Perhaps we could talk about it. Fancy a pint?'

Kirby Hill, 2.15pm

THE veal pie was every bit as good as he'd been promised, and Snowden rose reluctantly from the table. 'Time to get back to work, I think.' He looked round for a clock, couldn't see one, and reached into his jacket pocket.

'Can't see my watch anywhere, can you?' The landlord glanced round and shook his head. 'Dammit, it must have dropped out somewhere.' Snowden thought back. He'd checked the time just before leaving the tunnel, slinging his jacket over his shoulder, and it could be anywhere between there and outside the Hack and Spade when he'd put the jacket back on. It was a damnable nuisance but he'd have to go looking for it.

He pondered the tunnel body as he rode. They'd have little chance of finding out who it was after all this time unless there was something surviving among the rags, a letter or pocketbook perhaps, something with a name on it. He'd find out tomorrow, when the doctor had had a chance to look at it in the morgue in the workhouse infirmary. If it turned out to be a murder investigation it would be his fourth over the past year and he could have done without it. He went back through the others in his mind. The Cotherstone poisoning. He'd only just completed the paperwork in the aftermath of that one, she'd probably still be in the York Castle cells awaiting the gallows. Before that there was the Irish navvy who'd gone berserk with a hammer in Brough as a gang of them made their way to the new railway being built beyond Carlisle. And back in December, that poor servant girl who'd stuck a knife in her mistress after being whipped for breaking an egg. And before that...

He frowned. The Barnard Castle drownings. He was convinced that was murder, one or two he wasn't sure, and his failure to make progress with it rankled. He'd spent many hours on both sides of the County Bridge trying to find witnesses or evidence that would point the finger at somebody, but in vain. The only suspect was the man called Arrowsmith who had been living with, or at least living off, the dead girl, but he'd vanished and nobody had seen him anywhere near Briggate on the night she died. From what little Snowden could find out, he'd taken flight before then anyway, though he could have been hiding, waiting for his chance to kill her. But why kill her if she was bringing in money for him? And what about Yates? There was nothing at all to link him with Arrowsmith. And this Humphreys girl, had she really seen anything?

It was still a mystery, and here he was with another one that he didn't hold out great hopes of solving. It was doing his reputation no good at all.

He arrived outside the Hack and Spade and dismounted. He had no great desire to encounter the woman inside, but it was possible he'd left the watch in the shop. Both doors were locked, and nobody answered his knocks. So what *did* she do between two and six? He walked round the side of the inn and into the yard behind. The rear door was open, and he saw her sitting on a stool on the slabs outside, a jumbled pile of old clothing and linen beside her. She had a large pair of scissors in one hand, and was busy cutting it all into scraps.

'I'm sorry to bother you again –'

'You're trespassing, and I don't care if you are a policemen, you can be Sir Robert Peel for all I care, you can get out of my yard.'

He looked down at her handiwork. She was cutting the fabrics into strips, sorting them as she went along. Blue ones in one pile, red in another, black, green, yellow, purple... anything white was discarded to one side.

'Proggy mats. My mother used to make them.'

'Proddy mats, we call them in these parts.' She sheared a length of orange rag, cut it to length and started a new pile. 'I thought I told you to go.'

'I remember watching her when I was, what, ten years old? Cutting the strips. poking them through holes in the sacking. snipping off the one side and sewing up the other. There was always one in front of the hearth.'

'Sewing?' She sniffed contemptuously. 'You don't sew them, you twist them underneath so they bind together. What did she do with the edges?'

'I'm not sure. Hemmed them round somehow.'

'Slip-stitched?'

'I've no idea. They were wonderful things, however she made them.'

The woman paused and nodded. 'I've been making them all my life, and my mother before me.' Her voice had softened and he detected a touch of pride. 'I've got over a hundred in the back bedroom.'

He tried to imagine it. A hundred, each about four feet by two, heaven knows what they weighed apiece. It was a wonder the ceiling hadn't collapsed.

'What will you do with them all?'

'No idea. Sell a few, maybe. Rest will get thrown out when I go, I suppose.'

'Could I buy one?'

'If you like. Cost you, mind. Five shillings.'

'I'll bring my daughter, she can choose the colours. Maybe want to order one made to her own design.'

'As you like. Six shillings if it's a special.' She stopped snipping at the rags and looked up. 'What did you want? You didn't come here to talk about proddy mats.'

'I'm looking for my watch. I wondered if I'd left in the shop this morning.'

'What's it look like?'

'Gold case, double chimer, inscription on the back.'

She grunted reluctantly. 'Found it outside the door when I closed the shop. Where your horse was standing.' She delved into her apron and produced it. 'Had to clean up after him.'

'Add it to the proddy mat bill.'

'I will. Anything else?'

'Well, I was wondering if you could help in any way with this body we've found?'

'In the tunnel, I heard about it.' Snowden was always surprised at how fast news spread in the smallest of communities. 'What makes you think I might have anything to do with it?'

He attempted a smile. 'I'm not suggesting you're a murderer, Mrs...' He realised he didn't know her name.

'Mattock, Edna Mattock.'

'Mrs Mattock. But you might have some idea who it may be. Nobody missing from the villages round here in the last twelve months or so?'

'I'd know if there was.'

He'd put money on it. 'And I don't suppose you get many people passing through, it's a bit of a dead-end.'

'Don't see a lot of strangers, keep ourselves to ourselves. And when they do come they just cause trouble. Making a mess, getting in the way, running up bills they don't pay. We're better off without them.' She started snipping at the rags again. 'If you're wanting one of these made up, it'll be money up front. I don't do credit, not after the last time.'

'Been let down?'

'Gentleman ordered one back last summer, reds and green made to his own design, fiddly job. Never came back for it, no use to me unless someone else wants it.'

It was unlikely, but possible. 'What was he like, this gentleman?'

She stopped snipping and frowned. 'Nothing special. Forty, fifty maybe, well enough dressed, rode a horse. Came into the shop one day, mid-morning, bought a couple of pies and saw the mats in there. Tallish fellow, wasn't local.'

'How could you tell?'

'I'd have known him. Anyway, he didn't speak Teesdale, came from down south, I'd say.'

'Was he wearing a dark cloak, black maybe?'

'Could've been. Why?'

'He didn't give his name?'

'Didn't ask. Said he'd be back to collect it, never saw him again.'

'Riding a horse, you said?'

'Had it stood outside.'

'Any baggage, packs, saddlebags, anything to suggest he was a pedlar?'

'Selling stuff, you mean? No, nothing like that. He did have a bag over his shoulder, though, he put the pies in it.'

'And which way did he go?'

She wrinkled her brow, trying to remember. 'Up over, heading for Kirby Hill.'

'And you've got the mat still?'

'Not a lot of call for ones with bees and jays on them.'

'Bees and jays?' Snowden looked puzzled. 'A nature lover, was he?'

'Letters B and J, all twined together. He must've been called Bernard or Joseph or something, I don't know. Took a long time doing it, I can tell you, and all for nothing.'

'And this was when?'

'July, August maybe.'

Thorpe, 4.30pm

Thorpe Grange
Saturday

Dearest Aunt Jane,

I must apologise for taking so long to reply, but you would not believe how <u>busy</u> we are this summer. Papa seems to be working every hour of the day and sometimes long into the night as well, and there are times when I fear he will do himself no good unless he takes more rest, but you know what he is like! I continue to do what I can to help and have managed to get most of his files in order, though he will insist on taking them down to peruse and then forget to put them back, and now I am trying to organise a system by which we can link them all to speed things up.

The garden has run riot with all this good weather and I have a <u>wonderful</u> collection of vegetables, apart from carrots which I can't seem to grow, try what may. You were right about the parsnip wine, it did taste <u>very</u> sweet and though papa did his best I know it was not truly to his liking. Papa is fonder of red wine than white so I propose to *attempt some elderberry too when they are ready.*

You asked in your letter for more information about the Reverend Wharton and I have to confess to you that we are now on first-name terms and, I dare to say, hold each other in the <u>greatest</u> affection. However, dear Aunt, you must not, on any account think it is anything but the sincerest of friendships as I have <u>no</u> intention <u>whatsoever</u> of entertaining the idea of any more serious relationship for many years yet, if indeed ever!

How is dear Uncle John? You must be <u>very</u> proud of his promotion to inspector and

Betsey broke off at the sound of footsteps outside the office and put the pen back in its tray. She'd finish it off later. There was a knock at the door.

'Come in.'

Sergeant Clarke appeared. 'Sorry, Miss Snowden, I thought your father would be back by now.' He took a folded sheet of paper from his pocket. 'Could you give him this when he returns?'

'Of course.'

'It's a report on the body at Whashton.' She looked at him enquiringly. 'Have you not heard about it, miss?'

'He's not been back all day, I haven't seen a soul.'

'Man dead in an old tunnel, the super thinks it might be foul play of some kind. We've shifted the body to the morgue and had a look at the clothes and so on. It's all in the report.'

'I'll make sure he gets it.'

'Thank you, miss.' He wiped a sleeve across his brow. 'Been a warm day out there.'

She smiled, knowing him well. 'Time for a cup of tea while you're here?'

'Well, since you're asking...'

She put the unfinished letter into a drawer and stood up. 'Or I could find you some iced parsnip wine?'

'Cup of tea will do nicely, miss, if it's all the same to you.'

Barnard Castle, 5.15pm

FEWSTER had become almost cheerful after his third pint of Crabthorpe's Best, which just went to show, thought McQueedie as he ordered a fourth, how appalling the beer must be in Smethwick. 'And another large Glenbuckie's for me.'

The barmaid in the Golden Lion reached for the bottle and looked at him closely. 'Aren't you that reporter that used to get in the Black Horse? I did shifts there last year, remember seeing you.'

'Twin brother. Not me.'

'You don't half look like him.'

'Different ears, look. His stuck out like jug handles.'

She peered at his head. 'Oh, yes, see what you mean. Just fancy.'

He rejoined Fewster at the table. 'You're sure about this new Hardcastle fellow?'

His companion nodded and dipped the ends of his moustache in Crabthorpe's best froth. 'Called Marmaduke. They say he's a complete muttonhead, witless when it comes to newspapers. Hasn't a clue.'

'I've known editors like that.' McQueedie grinned. 'Does what his uncle tells him, though?'

'Favourite nephew, inherit the lot when the old bugger goes. He'd crawl up his own arse to keep him happy.'

'And what'll make old man happiest of all is winning the North Riding by-election?'

Fewster nodded. 'If the *Gazette* can do anything to get him into parliament he'll do it. You've seen it since he took over?' He passed a copy over. 'This is the latest issue, out this morning.'

McQueedie looked at the front page. *The Voice of The People* was splashed across the top. The rest was the usual collection of advertisements and he turned to the editorial section inside. *Chartism – The Way Forward. Tories Must Make Way For Modern Thinking.* A whole page of *Profile Of Your Next Member of Parliament – Arnold Hardcastle, The Liberal Man's Choice.* 'I see what you mean.'

'It'll go down well on the Briggate shopfloors, I'm sure, not that many of them get a vote. But there'll be plenty of bourgeoisie who'll back him.'

'Bordge-what?'

'New word, means middle-classes. No idea where it comes from, but the Chartists are full of it.'

McQueedie returned to the editor's visit. 'So when he comes on Monday, this young Hardcastle lad, we know what we're going to do?'

'Can't fail.' Fewster drooped his moustache into the last of his beer. 'My turn, I'll get them in.'

Thorpe, 8.20pm

BETSEY was intrigued. 'I've seen them, every cottage seems to have one in front of the fire. I've never thought about how they make them.'

'They cost nothing, old rags, a bit of old hessian sacking as a base, and a lot of long hours prodding away at night. Can't be a worker's wife in the dale who hasn't made one. Or in Mrs Mattock's case, hundreds. My mother must have made a dozen or so, one every couple of years maybe as the old ones wore out or got too filthy to clean.' Snowden looked reminiscently back three decades. 'I can see her now, prod in one hand, hook in the other, working away in front of the fire on a winter's night.'

'Is it difficult?'

'Not once you know what you're doing. She had a special tool she swore by, carved out of an old ram's horn.' He sighed, pushed his plate back and rubbed his eyes. Betsey frowned. He really was looking weary some evenings and she worried about him.

'Go and sit down with the paper, I'll bring you the coffee.' She started to clear the table. 'Oh, I nearly forgot, Sergeant Clarke brought a report in. Something to do with the body you said you'd found, I left it on your desk.'

'I'd better have a look at it.' She watched him leave the room. So much for getting him to relax for the night.

Snowden picked up the report and scanned through it. The body had been brought out, as instructed, without disturbing it any more than necessary, and delivered to the morgue. Beneath the cloak the man had been wearing a jacket, waistcoat, shirt and riding breeches; there were what the sergeant thought were the remains of a muffler and a cravat, and the boots were leather with little signs of wear on the soles and heels. No hat, but that didn't mean anything, it could have fallen off before he was dragged down the tunnel. A gentleman, Mrs Mattock had said, and it looked as if she was right.

There were no obvious signs of injury apart from the missing leg and, Snowden read with a sigh, nothing in the pockets to identify the man. No money, no watch, no ring or other jewellery. He'd almost certainly been robbed. Snowden got to the last paragraph of Clarke's report.

'I also discovered the renmants of what I disserned to be a travling bag made of lether, it was empty apart from a pare of gloves and a scrap of paper. Signed Reuben Clerke Sgt.'

Not a lot to go on. The only possible clue to the dead man's identity was Mrs Mattock's mat with the initials prodded into it. Snowden put the report back on the desk and went to find Betsey.

'How are you getting on with linking all those files together?'

'It's a long job, but I'm well past halfway. Why?'

'Got past the Ms?'

'Weeks ago.'

'Good. Do you think you could go through the missing persons and do me a list of those who disappeared last year, say between July and October? I'm looking for someone who may have the initial J or B or possibly both, a man, probably from somewhere south of here.'

'I'll see what I can do tomorrow.'

Sunday July 26th

Barningham, 9am

WILLIAM Wharton. He signed his name at the foot of the page, wiped the pen with a scrap of blotting paper and replaced it carefully in the glass holder on his desk. That was the register up to date.

He ran his eye down the new entries. One baptism, Isabella Craggs, daughter of, agricultural labourer John Craggs and his wife Elizabeth on July the fifth. Wharton didn't enjoy baptisms. Babies worried him, fragile little things he knew nothing about, and he was terrified that he might drop one in the font or hold it the wrong way up. They tended to smell rather, too.

He wasn't that fond of marriages, either, and was glad there hadn't been one for a couple of months or more. There always seemed to be problems, even if both parties were in favour of their union, which wasn't by any means always the case. He'd seen several grooms glaring at their new inlaws as brides tottered down the aisle in dresses designed but failing to disguise their delicate condition, and though he'd never yet had one go into labour while taking the vows he feared it was only a matter of time.

Funerals, on the other hand, he quite enjoyed. There was something satisfying about the neat finality of it all, the centre of attraction no longer able to have any say in the proceedings, the congregation behaving itself in the comforting knowledge that it wasn't their turn yet and there was a wake to look forward to. There had only been one burial, poor Elizabeth Fawcett on the sixth of June, just forty-three, unmarried and hardly a soul to mourn her. Her interment in an unmarked grave in the corner of the churchyard on a summer's morning had been peacefully uneventful.

He closed the register, put it back on its shelf, and began to worry about his sermon. It had been a struggle once again. The temptation was to find a simple, undemanding text – Matthew 5.5, *Blessed are the meek* was always a safe choice – and spend fifteen unprovocative minutes advising his listeners to be content with their lot as it would all turn out right in the end, which kept both the poor and the rich happy. He had an uneasy feeling, though, that he ought to be doing more. Not fire and brimstone exactly, but at least pointing out that there was more to Christian charity than just dropping a penny or two in the collection tray. On the other hand, he really wasn't made for pulpit-thumping and evangelical fervour. He sighed. It was very difficult.

He wondered how many would be there this morning. Attendance always dropped during the summer, and he couldn't blame farmers and their families who had so much to do, but there should be the usual dutiful parishioners with no Sabbath tasks to deflect them, filling the tall box pews. The Milbanks would be there at the front, well installed in the hall for the past week and preparing for the grouse season. Maybe he'd see Betsey, though she often attended the church beside the river at Wycliffe or the tiny building, scarcely more than a chapel, beside the Street at Rokeby.

Betsey. There was another subject troubling his mind. He'd had another of those disturbing dreams about her the other night, the ones from which he awoke in a state of mortifying physical excitement. The first time he'd dived into a cold bath, which certainly relieved the bodily symptoms but left the memory haunting and taunting him. Now he got up and buried himself in work, alarming old Mrs Middleton when she arrived at six-thirty to light the fires. It was all a test of some kind, he was sure, God in his wisdom challenging him to endure and resist the temptations of the flesh. He was doing his best, but it wasn't easy.

And then there was Ermintrude, who seemed to be off her food and only a fortnight to go before the agricultural show. He looked at the ornate marble clock on the mantelpiece. Another hour before the first worshippers arrived, plenty of time to walk round to Glebe Farm next-door and see how she was getting on. He usually found she soothed his troubled mind.

Barnard Castle, 10.40am

A FILE of disconsolate paupers were making their way out of the workhouse on their way to St Mary's for the first of the three services they were ordered to attend each Sabbath. Snowden stood aside to let them pass, the workhouse manager chivvying them along, men and women kept strictly apart here as they were the rest of their lives, the children clutching prayerbooks and staring around at the only glimpse of the outside world they would have until next Sunday.

The last straggler scurried through the gates and Snowden made his way across the yard and into the building. The corridor to the left led to the male quarters and the punishment block, the one on the right to the rooms, little more than cells, where the women and children spent their lives. Ahead lay a third corridor with work-rooms on each side, empty today but the other six days of the week hives of dismal activity. Snowden strode past them, turned left at the end and reached the infirmary. He peered into the small, dimly-lit ward in which three of the five beds were occupied, each by a silent blanketed figure too close to death, he assumed, to be put to work or transported to church. At the far side were two doors, one an office used by any visiting physician, the other the morgue. He knocked on the first, got no answer, and pushed open the other.

Dr O'Neill straightened up from the table he was bending over and greeted him. 'Snowden, good to see you again.' A small, wiry Irishman with a thin pointed face that reminded Snowden of a weasel, he lived in Gallowgate and supplemented his earnings by calling in at the workhouse when needed. He also made a few shillings a month as the constabulary's official physician in charge, with access to the mortuary where Snowden knew he dissected bodies and sewed them up again with a delicacy that put Betsey's needlework to shame.

'Thought I'd find you here.' Snowden smiled. O'Neill was a long-lapsed Catholic who hadn't stepped foot in a church for years unless he was being paid for it. 'Busy?'

'Too busy. You'll have seen the latest death figures.'

'Cholera, yes. It seems to be even worse this year.'

'It is.' O'Neill looked grim. 'Lost three patients last week and I've got no answers.

There'll be plenty more. If they've not caught it crowded in the mills and tenements during the week they'll be catching it kneeling together today.' He gave Snowden a sombre smile. 'Thought I'd be better off in here with the paupers but I see they've been dragged out to church, heaven help them. What brings you here?'

'I skipped prayers myself to see if you'd got round to my body yet.'

O'Neill stood aside and waved a hand. 'Come and have a look.'

It lay on the table, each bone neatly laid in place including, Snowden noticed, the one the dog had found. There was still a clutch of hair, light brown and ageing grey, on the skull, its eyesockets dark and empty, and bits of what he assumed was flesh clinging to the rest of the skeleton. At its feet was a pile of ragged clothing. The unforgettable, cloying smell of death hung over it all.

'Male, but you knew that already. Aged about forty, maybe a bit older, five foot seven and a half tall, must have weighed about eleven stone, I'd estimate. No physical abnormalities except one which I'll come to in a minute. Internal organs long gone, of course, nothing I can tell you about what he'd eaten or the state of his heart. One forearm broken long ago, possibly as a child, touch of arthritis in one foot.' He picked up two small bones. 'You see the growth on the metatarsus?'

Snowden nodded, unsure what he was looking at. 'Anything else?'

'Fairish-haired as you can see, blue eyes like as not. A few teeth missing, no more than you'd expect, and the rest fairly good. I'd guess he could afford a good dentist, not some butcher with a barber's chair.'

'You mentioned an abnormality?'

'Patience, Snowden, patience. All in good time.'

'What about the clothes, then?'

O'Neill went through the pile of rags piece by piece. 'Cloak, thinnish summer one. Jacket, good quality wool. Waistcoat with three silver buttons, or there were once, there's two missing. Thick riding trousers, linen shirt, scarf, cravat, underclothes, long woollen stockings, black leather riding boots not long since new.' He paused. 'He had a small leather travelling bag with him, hardly more than a satchel.' He held it up. 'It was under the body, buckles undone.'

'Anything in it?'

'Just these.'

He held up a pair of white riding gloves. 'Kid, well-made. Interesting, aren't they?'

Snowden examined them and frowned. 'The right-hand one's missing two fingers, the little finger and the one beside it.' He looked more closely. 'Not torn off, it's been made that way. There's stitching across where the holes should be.' He thought for a moment. 'You mean he'd lost two fingers from his hand? But...' He looked at the skeleton. 'There's a full set there.'

'*Palmar fascial fibromatosis.*' Snowden looked blank and O'Neill gave a gleeful chuckle. 'Thought that'd have you stumped. Not uncommon, especially in men in later life. Tendons in the hand seize up, fingers contract, eventually they're permanently bent over so the tips press into the palm. Known as the Norwegian disease, that being the country with far the most cases. Hereditary probably, though it's found among most of the white races. Not among the Chinese, though, oddly enough. Not usually painful, but a nuisance. Well documented in *The Lancet* a few years ago by a Frenchman called Dupuytren.'

'A nuisance?'

'Especially, my dear Snowden, when it comes to wearing gloves. You can't get those fingers in, you have to pull the glove over them bent double.'

'So he has these gloves...'

'And the fingers get worse, so he gets someone to modify them. Much better than having two empty glove fingers flapping about and getting in the way.'

Snowden looked suitably impressed. 'Not sure how it helps me, all the same.'

O'Neill chuckled. 'Well, for a start you know your man would have had a serious problem playing the piano. Anyone who knew him well would know about his hand, and somebody might remember doing that stitching on an expensive glove.'

Snowden looked doubtful. 'There's a lot of fair-haired men with blue eyes about, O'Neill, and you said this isn't rare. It'll help, maybe, if we want a positive identification but you'll have to do better than that. I don't even know how he died, let alone who he is.'

'Well, I might be able to help you with the cause of death.' The doctor's eyes sparkled mischievously and he reached across the table to pick up the rib-cage. 'I've saved the best till last.' He turned the bones over. 'There, see those cuts underneath, one in each rib? Clear as a bell. Someone stuck a knife in his back, nicked two ribs and went straight through to his heart. He'd have been dead in seconds.'

'Murder.'

'No doubt about it.'

'That's better.' Snowden, pleased, studied the bones with interest. 'Any more surprises for me? The sergeant's report mentioned some paper.'

'Ah, yes, it's over here.' O'Neill went to a side-table and brought back a creased sheet of newsprint. 'Crumpled into a ball, found it inside the bag. I've flattened it out as best I can.'

Snowden examined both sides. 'Bottom half of a newspaper page. All advertisements on this side, a report of some parliamentary debate on the other. Pity there's no date or anything to identify it.' He frowned. 'Not torn out, carefully cut, which is odd.'

'Maybe he wanted to keep one of the advertisements. Then didn't need it any more, crumpled it into a ball and dropped it in the bag to get rid of later.'

'Perhaps.'

'Well, that's my theory. You're the detective, Snowden, I'm just the sawbones round here.'

'You've done a good job, thanks.' He was still staring at the newsprint. 'I'll take this unless you think you can do anything more with it.'

'Couple of small stains on it, nothing I can identify. Help yourself.'

'Thanks.' Snowden paused for a moment. 'Tell me, what normally happens when a body is brought in here, someone who's died in the workhouse, perhaps, or a tramp found dead on the moors? Would you give it the sort of thorough examination I asked you to do on this man?'

O'Neill considered. 'Too many bodies to give every one that kind of attention.

They'd get a brief once-over and then be sent off for burial.'

'No inquest?'

'Only if there was anything obviously suspicious or the police asked for one.' O'Neill gave Snowden a quizzical look. 'Why?'

'Well, word will get out about this body being found, of course, but I don't want whoever stuck a knife in him alerted to the fact that we're treating it as murder. Much better if we appear to think it's a death from natural causes and not worth investigating. I'll request an inquest when we've identified this man and with luck know who murdered him. Meanwhile, can you keep your findings quiet?'

'If that's an official instruction, yes. I'll have to do something with the body, though.'

'Where do they usually go?'

'There's a corner of the cemetery set aside for the destitute. No one who dies in here can afford a proper funeral, of course, and usually several are buried together in one unmarked grave to keep costs down. No ceremony as such, though they do get a priest to say a few words.'

'That should do nicely. Just note where he goes in case we eventually find relatives who want him back.' Snowden contemplated the body for a few moments and turned to go. 'Many thanks for your help, O'Neill. Don't forget to send me a bill.'

He rode back thoughtfully. What did he know for certain? Not a lot, he feared. Middle-aged man, fairly well-to-do with a couple of bent fingers on one hand, rides past Whashton sometime in the past year, gets stabbed in the back, almost certainly robbed, and his body dragged down the tunnel. What happened to his horse? Was he the caller at Whashton shop who didn't pay for a proddy mat? Why carefully cut a square out of a newspaper and then discard it? And above all, who was he and, of course, who killed him?

He reached the Street, crossed the Greta and came to a halt outside the police house. Perhaps at least one of those questions could be answered fairly swiftly. He dismounted and walked into the office.

There were two men at the desk, one Daniel Craven who had taken over the role of Greta Bridge constable from Sowerby in May, a great improvement in Snowden's opinion. A Scargill farmer's son in his late twenties with bushy brown side-burns threatening to meet below his chin and a broad grin at the slightest excuse, he had undertaken the job with enthusiasm. He stood up at the sight of his superior and nudged his companion sharply in the ribs. 'On your feet, lad, for the superintendent.'

Snowden eyed the second man inquiringly. He looked a little younger than Craven and shared his indulgence in the latest fashion for extended facial hair. His, however, was ginger, as was the circle of hair below a surprisingly bald skull tanned deep red by the sun.

'Simon Alderson, sir.' Craven was standing to attention. 'Replacement for Constable Taylor up at Boldron, not likely to be back for a while, I'm told.' Snowden nodded. Taylor, a thatcher, had fallen off a ladder and broken a leg a fortnight ago.

'Showing him the books?' Snowden indicated the ledger on the desk before them.

'Yes, sir.'

'Need him for anything?'

'Not if you do, sir.'

'Right, Alderson. Ride a horse, can you?'

'He's a hind for the Mountfords, sir.'

'Good. Get one from the Morritt's, tell them it's police business, and go over to Whashton for me.' He dug a shilling out of his pocket. 'There's a Mrs Mattock keeps the Hack and Spade, bring me one of her meat pies.'

'A meat pie, sir?'

'And have one yourself.' He checked his watch. 'She'll be opening any time now. Bring it to the Grange, you should find me there.'

He turned for the door

'Mind how you go, Alderson. She bites.'

Barningham, 12.10pm

THE echoes of the last *Amen* faded among the rafters. Wharton genuflected towards the altar, turned, and led the choir up the aisle. They disappeared into the sunshine outside while he waited at the door for his flock.

Milbanks first, of course. Mark and Lady Augusta, a handful of offspring, a nurse with the latest infant bringing up the rear.

'Kept it brief again, rector, well done, well done.'

A dutiful nod, the rectoral equivalent of a tugged forelock. 'Master Sussex not here this weekend, sir?'

'Struck down with the hay fever again. Poor boy's a martyr to it.'

'Of course.'

The rest of the well-to-do followed. The Todds, the Hartleys, Coates and Clarksons, Lawsons from Eastwood, old Mrs Swire, widow of the last rector but four and still going strong. No Betsey, he'd scoured the congregation from the pulpit during the hymns in vain for a glimpse of her. The farming families trooped out next, much depleted by the demands of haytiming. Browns, Metcalfes, Harrisons, Mrs Lambert in a preposterous hat... and then the rest of the faithful. Nods, greetings, inquiries about ailing parents, approving examination of wailing babies. Miss Walton from the school and two much younger companions, one the rather mousy assistant teacher Miss Howard he'd seen from time to time on his weekly visits to ensure pupils were receiving adequate religious instruction, the other a stranger.

'Not the best choice of hymns, rector, if I may say so.' Miss Walton sniffed above her faint moustache. '*There Is A Happy Land*, really! Sunday service is not a glee club.'

'The children seem to like it.'

'Church is not the place for liking things.' She looked at him sharply. 'You know Miss Howard, of course?'

'Indeed.'

'This is her cousin Harriet Brunskill from Richmond, with whose family she usually resides at the weekends. She has come over to Barningham to keep Charlotte company for a week or so.'

'Delighted to meet you,' She was tall and slim with dark curls peeking from under her bonnet and a hint of amusement in her eyes, and Wharton found it hard to believe that she was related to Miss Howard. 'You're staying with Mrs Eeles?'

'She's been most kind.' She gave him a smile and he realised he had been staring at her. Embarrassed, he turned back to Miss Walton.

'I'll see what I can do about the hymns, but we do have to move with the times.'

'You may move as you wish, rector, but the rest of us can do without these non-conformist sing-songs in future. Come along, girls.' She swept them down the churchyard path and he watched them disappear.

Harriet. He wondered what her full name was and whether she liked pigs.

Barnard Castle, 2pm

McQUEEDIE stared at himself in the small cracked mirror in his room beneath the Jolly Farmers eaves and wrinkled his nose experimentally. The clutch of hair pasted to his upper lip slipped sideways and fell to the floor.

He picked it up with a sigh. He'd have to use proper horse glue, though it smelled terrible and he wasn't sure he'd get the fake moustache off again afterwards. The spectacles, narrow oval lenses in a blue steel-rimmed frame, worked well even though they did make everything more than a foot away a hazy blur. He shifted them down his nose and peered over the top. That was better, and his image in the mirror stared back with exactly the mournful expression he'd hoped for. What else should he practise?

He toyed with the idea of packing some kind of wadding in his cheeks, which he understood was a useful trick among professional thespians, but decided he'd probably end up swallowing it.

He couldn't do much about his voice, perhaps soften it down a bit to a genteel Edinburgh. He tried out a few phrases. 'How *do* you do? One lives in Morningside, naturally. Have you not had your tea?' It got up his nose and he gave up.

Just the moustache to sort out, then. He picked up the scissors and started snipping another clutch of hair from behind his ears. This time he'd try not to cut himself.

Thorpe, 2.15pm

SHE was proud of the way the filing system was working out. The *M – Missing Persons* folder lay open before her, and she flicked through the pile of cards inside.

Each one was six inches tall by eight wide, with the top half-inch marked off in one-inch segments. The first segment carried the missing person's surname and beneath it the year they disappeared. People with unknown surnames were listed under U.

The second segment was neatly cut out if the missing person was female; the third segment was missing if he or she was a child; the fourth if the person came from beyond the Greta Bridge or Barnard Castle area. The remaining four segments were blank.

'You see, papa,' she'd explained to her father, 'if I want to find, for example, a young girl called Johnson who disappeared in Darlington, all I have to do is go to the letter J, find Johnson, and pick the cards with the second, third and fourth segments missing, and there you are. Then on the cards are the details of each one, full name, address, anything else you know. It saves ever so much time.'

He'd looked sceptical. 'What about the blank segments?'

'They're for further categories if they're needed.'

'And dates?'

'We've still got your original weekly logs if we want to search chronologically.'

'Hmm.' He sounded impressed. 'Let's try something more difficult than missing people. Have you done Thieves?'

'Of course. There's hundreds of them. Their cards will be divided into a lot more segments, twelve, I think. But the way it works is just the same.'

'Let's see...' He thought for a moment. 'Find me the ones who've been convicted of burglary at night, local men aged about 30, known to use violence.' He paused. 'And let's say they're dark-haired.'

It took her less than a minute. 'There you are.' She did a quick count. 'Nineteen. And if you want to know just the ones who are left-handed, for example, I can get it down to four.' She picked them out. 'Stephen Best, Joseph Cartwright, Matthew Simpson, George Taylor.'

Papa had looked astonished. It made all those hundreds of hours she'd spent collating the files worthwhile, and now she was using it in a real search.

Men, middle-aged papa had said, who disappeared last summer, possibly with names beginning with B or J. She flicked through to the B cards, concentrating on the ones with 1845 beneath their names and the second segment still in place. Eight of them. There were five aged between thirty and fifty, and only two were from some distance away, probably south, papa had said. She reached for a sheet of paper and listed them.

Andrew Barnett, aged about 35, Richmond, missing since July 13 1845.

Thomas Botton, aged 42, Thirsk, missing September 9th 1845.

This was going to be easy. She turned to the Js and frowned. Did papa mean surnames or first names? Or both?

She gave a sigh and turned back to the first cards.

Barningham, 3.30pm

CHARLOTTE tossed another pebble idly into the stream and watched it sink to the bottom. There was hardly any water this time of year and instead of the small gushing torrent she'd seen pouring off the moor in less clement times there was no more than a trickle making its way down to the Scargill road and on into Nor Beck. She leaned back against the coarse grass of the bank and gazed around. Across the valley to the north, a mile or so away, she could see the farm buildings at Crooks House, the field below dotted with white sheep, and beyond the land rising to hazy blue Pennine hills. There was hardly a cloud in the sky, only the slightest of breezes off the moor, the only sound the murmur of the stream and a skylark singing invisibly high above her.

'I wonder why they think it's lucky?' She turned her head at Harriet's voice and watched her cousin pin a sprig of purple heather to the lapel of her cape.

'I'm not sure the purple one is.' Charlotte yawned. 'Brides wear white, don't they? I think it's something to do with the queen, didn't she bring some back from Balmoral and make it fashionable?'

'They've called her new baby Helena, I like that. Charlotte sounds so old.'

'How many's that?'

'Five, I think.' She sat up. 'I can't imagine having that many children. I can't even imagine having one.'

Harriet giggled. 'I don't think you'll have much choice when you're married. Mother says you've hardly walked back down the aisle before you're expecting.'

'You don't have to be married, though, do you? There are plenty of girls with babies who aren't. One of the servants at the hall had one.' Charlotte frowned. 'She lost her place, of course. I don't know where they are now.'

'Poor thing.'

'I wonder what it's like?'

'Having a baby?'

'Yes, and all the rest of it. I just can't imagine... doing that with a man.'

'Mother says it's not as bad as you'd think.' She grinned. 'In fact, I think she rather enjoyed it.'

'Enjoyed it?' Charlotte sat up. 'You mean she didn't mind, even if she didn't have to do it to make a baby?'

'Especially when she wasn't likely to.' Harriet looked at her quizzically. 'You do know about all this, don't you?'

'Well, sort of. But there's a lot I don't understand.'

'I think it's all different when you're in love.'

'Perhaps.' Charlotte looked doubtful. 'I've seen dogs, you know, and it all looks rather... well, animal. And I once saw a horse. It was unbelievable.'

Harriet gave another giggle. 'Well, we'll find out one of these days. All we need is a couple of wonderful young men and we'll be mothers of five in no time. Come on, it's time we were going back. The trap's coming for me at six.'

Charlotte rose slowly to her feet and brushed the grass off her cape. 'Not much chance of that, the wonderful young men, I mean. I've been here nearly a year and still haven't seen one.'

Harriet gave her a sly glance. 'How about that rector of yours? He's a bit, well, rector-ish, but he seemed very pleasant. You could do worse, a nice easy life in the rectory.' She grinned. 'I bet it's got an enormous nursery upstairs.'

'Oh, I couldn't. Not the rector.'

'Hmm.' Harriet turned back towards the village. 'I think I could. Never mind, someone will turn up eventually. Maybe the heather will bring us luck.'

'It'll take more than a sprig of heather to find me a husband.'

'Nonsense. Come on, I want some tea before I go.' She looked around. 'There's nobody else about, race you to the moor end.'

Thorpe, 4.40pm

'REALLY, Tommy, I don't know *what* we're going to do with you.' Betsey waved a finger at the cat in mock severity. 'If you go on like this we'll be over-run with them.'

Tommy gave a yawn and a stretch, ignoring her and the three kittens practising pretend fights on the kitchen floor.

'For a start, we should change your name. How do you fancy Thomasina?' She shook her head. 'Perhaps not. But we're going to have to stop you roaming about at night. I mean, look at them. One black, one half-white and one ginger. I can't imagine what you've been up to.' Well, she could, she said to herself, but the cat wasn't to know that. 'And you're all costing us a fortune in fish.'

She heard the door open and her father walked in.

'I thought the gardener was going to do something about those kittens?'

'Oh, I couldn't, papa. They're so sweet.'

'Not always. Tell their mother to get them trained or they're going down the well.'

She thought for a moment that he was serious, and then saw the smile on his face. 'You're as soft as they are. I've seen you playing with them when you think I'm not looking.'

'Nonsense. Anything to eat? I'm famished, had to miss lunch.'

'Oh, I forgot. A constable came with a pie for you.'

'Alderson, new lad, I'd forgotten about him. Where is it?'

'Over there, on the side of the range. I kept it warm for you.'

'Let's see.' He walked across the room. 'Where's the wrapping?'

'The what?'

'Whatever it came in. He hardly carried it all the way from Whashton like that.'

'Whashton? Why do you want a pie from there?'

'I'll explain when I find the wrapping. What was it, a cloth? Brown paper?'

'It was wrapped up in newspaper, I think. I threw it in the compost bucket.'

'In there?' He bent down to find it under the sink. 'It's full of peelings.'

'I've been doing the vegetables for this evening. If you want the bit of paper it'll be underneath.'

Snowden grimaced and delved below the bits of potato, carrot and cabbage. 'This is worse than the kittens. Aha!' He pulled out a soggy ball of newsprint. 'Wet through and covered in stains. What's this?'

'Gravy, I think. The pie was leaking a bit.' She watched him bring the paper over to the table and begin smoothing it out. 'What on earth do you want that for?'

'Show you in a moment.' He vanished towards his study and came back a few moments later. 'There.'

'Another piece of crumpled newspaper. Are you starting a collection?'

Instead of answering straight away he smoothed the second piece of paper out and laid it by the first.'What do you see?'

'Two bits of newspaper, pages torn in two. One fairly clean but old, the other probably newer but it's hard to tell with all the mess on it.'

'What else?'

'I don't know... they're both about the same size and...' She looked more closely. 'They've both been cut out, not torn as I thought.'

'Correct. And I think if we put one on top of the other, without spreading the mess on that one onto the other, we'll see that they're not *about* the same size, they're almost *exactly* the same size. Not a coincidence, Betsey. This one –' he pointed to the one he'd dug out of the bucket '– came today from Mrs Mattock's shop in Whashton, and this one –' he pointed to the one from his study '– from a bag belonging to the man found dead in a tunnel there yesterday. And he'd bought something to eat at Mrs Mattock's shop.'

Betsey nodded uncertainly as he continued. 'My guess is that Mrs M gets so many papers to sell each week, and when she puts them on her shelves she removes the previous week's unsold papers, if there are any, of course. Have we got a copy of the *Gazette* handy?'

'Yesterday's is somewhere about. I'll find it.'

'And see if you can find my magnifying glass, in the top desk drawer, I think. And a pair of scissors.'

'Yes, sir.' She grinned. 'I'd hate to be one of your constables.'

'You'd make a very good one, I imagine.'

She was back in less than a minute. He unfolded the paper, lifted out the front page and put the rest to one side. 'Mrs Mattock lays it out like this, front page and back page together, of course, and then neatly cuts up the middle.' He picked up the scissors and snipped the front and back pages apart. 'Then she puts one on top of the other, folds them over like this, and does another cut along the fold. Hey presto, four pieces exactly the same size, just right for wrapping pies.'

Betsey nodded. 'Then she does the same with the other pages?'

'Yes. She puts them in a neat pile, and back they go on the shelves to wrap up her pies and anything else that needs protecting – meat, bread maybe, candles, whatever.'

Bestey looked doubtful. 'Why go all that trouble? Much easier just to tear them.'

'You haven't met this woman, or you'd understand. She's organised, neat, methodical, I've seen her making proddy mats and she wouldn't be able to live with rough-torn bits of paper all shapes and sizes. And besides...' He grinned. 'I remember seeing a pile of these on the counter when I visited her shop.'

'All right, I'm convinced. So...'

'So we know the dead man had one of her pies, and is almost certainly the person she saw about a year ago, who never came back for his proddy mat. The one who wanted Bs and Js. Not some other stranger about whom we know nothing. It's a start.'

She stared at him. 'Are you going to explain all this, or just go on talking in riddles?'

He ignored her. 'It would be useful to know which newspapers all these pieces came from. The obvious first choice is the *Yorkshire Gazette*, it's the main one round here. Let's see.' He picked up one of the newly-cut pages from the *Gazette* and put it beside the ones from the tunnel and the compost bucket.

'Magnifying glass?' Betsey handed it to him. 'Thank you.' He bent over and studied the papers closely. 'Good.' He handed her the glass. 'Have a look.'

'I'm not sure I know what I'm looking for.'

'Start with the typeface, the one they use for their smallish text.'

She peered at them one by one. 'I think two of them are the same. The type in the other one's narrower, and the bits on the tops and sides of the letters sort of slope more.'

'They're called serifs, and you're right. And the good news is that the two identical ones are yesterday's *Gazette* and the torn piece found with the body. The one the pie came wrapped in today is some other publication. If it had been the other way round we'd have had to search every newspaper in Britain but as it is, we've just got the *Gazette* to deal with.'

'So where do you go from here?'

'Upstairs. You know that great pile of old newspapers in the far bedroom?'

'The ones I'm always telling you to get rid of?'

'You're about to see why I take no notice. I don't keep every one, it would be impossible, but I do keep all the *Gazettes* because they're full of local detail, especially crime and the courts.' He gave her a smile, pleased at their progress. 'Run upstairs, constable, and bring me down all the ones you can find from last summer, say July to September. There'll be about a dozen of them. It shouldn't take long to match them with the dead man's piece of paper, and we can narrow down the date he died. About a week or so after its publication, I think, if Mrs Mattock is as efficient as I think she is.'

'No longer?'

'She'd never keep old bits of paper on her shelves. They'd be thrown out every week to make space for nice new clean ones.'

'Yes, sir.'

'And I'll have my pie while you're gone.'

'I'm not sure you will.'

He looked at her, puzzled.

'The cat's got it on the floor and sharing it with the kittens. Aren't they lovely?'

Barnard Castle, 10.15pm

THE day had turned from blue to grey around six o'clock, dark clouds had scudded over the western hills, and by now rain was coming down heavily, bouncing off the Briggate cobbles and into the sewer which began to overflow, spreading a layer of detritus down the alleys. Ann Humphreys, dressed in no more than a thin frock and barefoot, was drenched by the time she'd scurried the two hundred yards to her friend's home. She stood huddled on the tenement doorstep awaiting an answer to her knock.

'You poor thing, come in.' Mrs Sutcliffe ushered her in. 'I've got the fire going. Get your clothes off and I'll find you a blanket while they dry out.' She saw Ann look round anxiously. 'There's nobody else in, love, don't worry. And I'll find the gin.'

Settled before the fire, a meagre collection of old cinders and bits of driftwood from the river that flickered occasionally into uncertain flame, Ann still shivered. 'I'm sorry to be bothering you, Liz, but I'm that mixed up. I can't sleep, and if I do I get the nightmares again, and then I wake up thinking the bairn's still there and I can't help it and...' She broke into tears. 'What am I to do?'

'Have you eaten today?'

The girl shook her head. 'There's nothing in the house. Dad's out getting drunk somewhere, and I've no money to buy food since I lost the job.'

'I'll make you something. You sit here, read the paper or something, and I'll be right back.'

She returned with a bowl of soup and slices of bread. 'It's only beans and a bit of potato, and I've nothing to go on the bread, but it'll do you good.'

'Thank you.' Ann seemed to have recovered a little and wiped her eyes. 'Did you see that in the paper about Matty Carlock being done for thieving?'

'Never was any good, that lad.' Sutcliffe found the gin bottle in a cupboard, brought two glasses and poured each of them a large measure. 'He'll end up on the gallows, mark my words. His father was no better and as for his mother, well, you know what she was like.'

'He's being transported, it says.'

'Good riddance. Did you read about that murder up at Auckland?'

'No.'

'Next page, I think. Awful it was, man cut to ribbons right there in the street. It's all there.'

Ann turned the page and went silent. The rain was hammering on the only window and Sutcliffe wished not for the first time that she'd got rooms on the eastern side. True, there was no sun there after mid-day but it couldn't be as depressing as a full-scale storm threatening to break the glass. She put another damp piece of driftwood on the fire as the girl looked up from the paper.

'It says they don't know who did it.'

'They keep their mouths shut in Auckland, just like Briggate. It's not right, they get away with anything for want of people with the courage to speak out.'

'If you knew about a murder, would you tell?'

'Course I would, even if it was my own father did it.'

'Suppose...' Ann faltered. 'Suppose you knew and had sworn a solemn oath never to tell, do you think God would strike you down dead if you broke it?'

Sutcliffe stared at her. 'Course he wouldn't. Why would anyone swear an oath like that, anyway?'

'Suppose the murderer said they'd kill them too if they didn't swear to keep it a secret?'

'God isn't going to punish you for breaking an oath if you made it to save your own life, Ann. He'd understand.'

'You really think so?'

'I'm sure he would.' Sutcliffe went down on her knees beside her and took her hand. 'Tell me what this is all about. What do you know that you're so scared to tell? It is you, isn't it?'

Ann nodded. There was a flash of lightning and she leapt from her chair as if it had struck her, with a scream that drowned the following clap if thunder.

'It's him, it's him!'

'Who?'

'God, it's God, he's going to strike me dead if I tell you. Oh Jesus and Mary, what am I to do?' She sank to the floor sobbing with fear. 'I don't want to die, I won't tell, I won't, I promise.' The sobs subsided and she lay there silent, panting for breath. There was another flash of lightning, another peal of thunder, but she didn't move.

Sutcliffe took her hand again. 'Nobody's going to kill you, nobody's going to harm you. God isn't going to be angry if you say something that stops evil people doing evil things. You'll be doing something good, he'll be pleased with you, Ann.'

'Something good?'

'Something to be proud of. You don't need to be frightened.'

'But what about them? If God doesn't kill me, they will.'

'If you speak out they'll be punished, whatever it is they've done that's made you like this. They won't be able to hurt you.'

'I want to tell you but... will you promise to keep it secret?'

'That won't stop the evil, will it?'

'I don't know.' Ann took a long rasping breath. 'I don't know. But I'm going to have to tell someone, because I'm losing my mind.'

Monday July 27ᵗʰ

Thorpe, 6.10am

A THIN RAY of sunshine piercing the gap in the almost-closed curtains gave enough light for Betsey to see by as she rolled back the bedclothes and swung her feet onto the floor. It had been a stormy night but the rain had cleared and there was blue sky outside.

She pulled on her dressing-gown and went down the stairs, trying to miss the boards that creaked in case she woke papa. She had left him just before eleven, working at his desk, and he had probably stayed there into the early hours and would need an hour or two more in bed this morning. She went into the kitchen, wondered about lighting the stove for a cup of tea and decided to leave it until Mrs Avery came in at seven. Tommy gave her a muted greeting and she laid out food for her and the kittens, all three still asleep in an intermingled ball of furry bodies. She wandered yawning into the living-room.

The door to her father's office was open. That was odd, and she went across. He was there at the desk, pen in hand and a pile of papers before him, a haze of tobacco smoke hanging in the air.

'You haven't been here all night?'

He looked up. 'No, I got a few hours' sleep.'

'Oh, papa!' His face was drawn and she looked at him severely. 'You can't go on like this, working every hour God sends.'

He smiled apologetically. 'It's only until I get the book finished. They want it by the end of next month.' He picked up the sheet of paper he was working on. 'Page 414, lunatics. There's not far to go.'

'Lunatics?' She gave a sigh of despair. 'You'll be a lunatic yourself if you're not careful. Is it worth it?'

'I think so, Betsey. Every policeman and magistrate in the land needs a guide to the law and how the courts should operate. You've seen how it is at the moment, people making judgements using books that were written decades ago and are hopelessly out of date.' He waved a hand at the shelves behind him. 'Look at them. What hope is there of proper justice when they're relying on these?'

'I'm sure you're right, papa, but...' She shook her head. 'I'll make you a cup of tea and some breakfast.'

'It won't be for ever, just a few more weeks and it'll be off to the printers. I promise.'

She went back to the kitchen and began laying the fire beneath the range. As she put the last piece of coal on the criss-crossed sticks there was a tentative knock on the back door. Too early for Mrs Avery, and anyway she knew where the key was hidden in the porch. She stood up, put the fire tongs back in the bucket and went to investigate.

On the doorstep stood a small boy in a grubby jerkin, a pair of ragged trousers several sizes too big for him and muddied boots held together with string.

'What on earth do you want at this time of the morning?'

He looked apprehensive. 'I wouldn't of woke you, miss, but I looked through the window and saw you was up. Mr Pearson said I was to give you a message.'

'Mr Pearson?'

'The constable, miss. He said it was...' He hunted for the words. 'A matter of something, miss. Urgency, that's it.'

'Urgency? Is it for Mr Snowden?'

'That's him, miss.' He hesitated. 'He said you'd give me sixpence, miss, if I went straight away.' A look of pride crossed the grime on his face. 'I got here as fast as I could.'

'Where from?'

'Barney, miss. Briggate.'

'You'd better come in. Get those boots off first and wait on the chair over there. I'll go and find him.'

Barnard Castle, 7.15am

SNOWDEN left Bucephalus in the care of a sleepy ostler at the Kings Head and made his way down The Bank. The morning shift at the mills was already well under way, a few late stragglers hurrying towards Briggate. Snowden followed them and found Pearson waiting for him in the police house halfway along the street.

'What's this all about? It had better be important, I've missed my breakfast. The boy said it was to do with a murder.'

'I'm sorry, sir, but I thought you'd want to see her as soon as you could, before she changes her mind.'

'Her?'

'Ann Humphreys, sir, you'll remember, the girl at the Elliott hearing.'

'Not more ghosts, I trust? What's she know about Whashton?'

'Whashton, sir?'

'The body in the tunnel.'

'Nothing, sir. It's the other ones. Yates and the Raine girl.'

'What about them?'

'She says she saw them being killed.'

Snowden stared at him. 'She saw it?'

'So she says, sir, and I think she's telling the truth. She's in a bit of a state, you need to talk to her before she changes her story or clams up altogether.'

'Indeed I do. Where is she?'

'Just up the lonning over the road, sir, where her friend lives.'

Snowden searched his memory. 'Sutcliffe?'

'Yes, sir.'

'Let's go, then. You're right, the sooner the better.'

They found the two where Pearson had left them, Ann sitting at the table in the tenement room with Sutcliffe opposite her, an empty gin bottle between them. Both got to their feet as the men entered, Ann with terror on her face, Sutcliffe with a look of relief.

'Mrs Sutcliffe, Miss Humphreys.' Snowden crossed the room. 'Sit down, there's nothing to worry about.' That wasn't true, he thought, as he sat down between them. If the girl had seen a murder, two murders, she had plenty to put the fear of God in her. 'Tell me all about it, take your time, we're here to help.'

He looked expectantly at Ann. She was trembling, her hands clasping and unclasping and he could see the stains of tears on her cheeks. The first to speak was her companion.

'Just tell him what you told me, Ann.'

'You said you wouldn't tell anyone.' She looked at Sutcliffe in despair. 'You promised.'

'It'll be all right. They know, they just want to hear it from you.'

'They'll kill me.'

'We'll make sure you're safe, whoever they are.' Snowden held her frightened gaze. 'You were there that night, weren't you?'

Ann's voice sank to a tearful whisper. 'Yes.'

'On the Sills? Where you showed me, where the ghosts were?'

'Yes.'

'But this was real?'

She nodded. Snowden caught Pearson's eye, nodded slightly, and the constable moved behind her, producing his notebook once he was out of her sight. 'Tell me what happened, right from the start.'

She began to talk, and it all came out in a flood of pent-up relief. 'I was in bed, about midnight, I kept thinking about the bairn and everything and I couldn't sleep. I got up, I hadn't bothered to undress, and I went down to the door and saw them out in the street.'

'Saw who?'

'Joe and Kate, they were talking and saw me and I went over to them. Then the others came along.'

'The others?'

She hesitated. 'Breckon and Barker and Thomas Raine.'

'Kate's brother?'

'No, the one from up the dale. He put his arm round my waist, Thomas, and says would we all like to walk to the bridge, and we did.'

'All of you, to the County Bridge?'

'Yes, we went over to the Sills.' She bit her lip as she remembered. 'Joe and Kate went in front and Thomas says he knows Joe has some money and asks how are we going to get it. I said they should leave him alone, poor man, he was only a little fellow and I liked him, but Thomas said no, they'll have his money and he and Geordie go up to him and says he has to hand it over.'

'Geordie?'

'George Barker.'

'Go on.'

'Well, Joe says he's willing to spend it among us but he'll not give them it, and then Geordie starts asking Joe about going to York, I don't know what that was about.'

'York?'

'They were arguing about a coat, I don't know, I was with Thomas, we were...' She stopped.

'Never mind, what happened after that?'

'They took his money. Just knocked him down and took it from him, I saw them. Thomas went over and they counted it, eleven or twelve shillings. And then they all started hitting him again and kicking him, it was so cruel, he couldn't get up and he started to cry out for help. He was screaming, murder, will no one help me, I can still hear him.' She came to a halt and started crying. 'There was nothing I could do.'

'It's all right, you're doing very well. Just take your time.' Snowden waited as she recovered.

'Kate was screaming too, as hard as she could, and they told her they'd do the same to her if she didn't stop and she did. And then...'

'Yes?'

'Then they threw him over the wall.'

'Into the river?'

She nodded, her eyes wide at the memory. 'It was very rough and dark and it was raining. They just... threw him in.'

'And?'

'And they took us, me and Kate, back to the bridge and asked if we would tell and Kate says yes, she'd tell the first policeman she saw, but I was so frightened. They swore me, there in the middle of the bridge in the rain, and made me say so help me God that I would not tell, and Thomas said I would drop down dead straight away if I did, and I never did till now.'

'What about Kate?'

'They told her she had to swear the same and she wouldn't, and God forgive me, I just stood there and they threw her over as well.'

'Over the bridge?'

'Right in the middle, Breckon had hold of her feet over the wall and then she went, I watched her go, poor Kate, poor Kate.' She began sobbing again. 'I didn't know what to do and I was so scared, and they just walked away as if it was nothing.'

'And you didn't say anything to anyone?'

'No. Never. I didn't want to die as well.'

Barnard Castle, 9.10am

HE'd never, ever do that again. McQueedie cupped another handful of cold water from the bowl, splashed it onto his forehead and groaned. He felt dreadful.

He'd done everything he'd promised himself. Not a lot to drink, well, nowhere near as much as usual, and gone to bed early, knowing it was vital he was at his best next morning. For the next five hours he had lain there, his mind whirling at the unprecedented sobriety, his body refusing to sleep, counting the chimes as midnight passed, one, two, three o'clock... He'd given up at four and reached for the Glenbuckie's, fallen into a stupor an hour later, and would still be asleep if it hadn't been the morning the Jolly Farmers landlord noisily threw his empty bottles out for collection by the drayman.

He dragged his clothes on and looked for his notebook. He'd made a neat timetable out for the day and he stared at it through bleary eyes.

9.45am	Bycroft
10.30am	Board of Guardians mtg, Butter Market
11am	Hardcastle arrives Gazette office
12pm	B/G mtg lunch.
12.30pm	Hardcastle, Fewster arrive Bmkt
1pm	B/G back

It had to work. He checked his pockets. Spectacles, moustache, carefully-stoppered pot of glue, pen. All there, just one more thing to get.

St Mary's clock chimed the half-hour and he winced. If, heaven forbid, he ever had to find yet another pub willing to accommodate him, it would have to be as far away as possible from those bells.

He made his way down the back stairs, skirted the bar where he might just bump into the landlord and have to explain why he hadn't paid this week's rent, made way for a hefty drayman carrying yet another crate of empty bottles, and stepped out into the street. One thing St Mary's did have in its favour was a curate called Simon Bycroft.

Barnard Castle, 9.35am

FOUR hundred yards away in Briggate, Snowden stopped outside the tenement block and turned to Pearson.

'You got everything down, all she said?'

'Think so, sir. Not word for word, you'll understand, but good enough for court.'

'Good.' Snowden wondered momentarily whether it might be worthwhile encouraging bright young constables who fancied a career in the police to discover Pitman's shorthand. 'Write it up as soon as you get the chance. Meanwhile, stay with those two. You needn't worry too much about Sutcliffe, but I don't want Humphreys talking to anyone or even meeting them. I've promised her she'll be safe, and anyway I don't want word getting around that she's named anyone, or they'll be away before we know it. That goes for possible witnesses, the people she said were around that night, as well as the three men we're after. Understood?'

'Yes, sir.'

Snowden thought for a moment. 'Put her somewhere safe, in the cell in the police house if necessary but keep her comfortable. She's got no job, no way of making money, has she? Apart from on the streets, that is?'

'Not that I know of, sir.'

'She probably won't mind us looking after her for a while. I'll see if I can get her a place somewhere away from here, York jail maybe, where she'll get three square meals a day and a decent bed.'

'In York Castle?' Pearson looked incredulous.

'You'd be surprised what they can do if there's money to be found. She'll get roast beef and feather pillows if it's paid for, and I've got more than enough to pay for it if it makes sure she's around to give testimony in court.'

'Money, sir?'

'Never mind. And not a word from you, either, until we've got them. You know any of these men, George Barker, Thomas Raine and – what was the other one?'

'John Breckon, sir. Know him well enough, he's in Durham jail.'

'That's handy. What's he there for?'

'Aggravated assault on one of our lads in Staindrop, sir. Smashed a chair over his head in a pub there last New Year, got twelve months. Nasty piece of work. Known as Pot-eye.'

'Pot-eye?'

'Lost the sight in one, it's gone white. Another pub fight, probably.'

'We'll have no trouble finding him, then. Check with Durham that he's still there and alive. What about the other two?'

'I've come across them both, local lads, in trouble from time to time for causing late-night bother, but nothing serious like Breckon. Haven't seen either of them for a while.'

'I'll check the court records, but I can't recall them. Any family connection between Raine and the dead girl? They've both got the same surname.'

'No, sir, I asked. It's a common enough name round here and she did have a brother called Thomas, but they're not related.'

'Very well. You've done a good job here. What time did you come on duty last night?'

'Usual, sir, eight o'clock.'

'You must be ready for bed.'

'I'll manage, sir. Won't be the first time I've worked on.'

'Good man. I won't forget it.'

'Thank you, sir.'

'Back you go then, before they disappear.' He reached into his pocket and produced a half-crown. 'Take them a bottle of gin, that should do it. And when you've got them sorted out, you might have a glass or two yourself. You've earned it.'

Snowden walked back along the street to the police house. Like the one at Greta Bridge, it consisted of one large office which served as a base for local police and a couple of cells useful as back-up for the one in the Butter Market. Two constables looked up from the desk as he entered.

'Sergeant about?'

'Just gone out the back, sir. Shouldn't be a minute.'

Snowden surveyed the noticeboard on the wall as he waited. Fifty-pound reward for the apprehension of two highway robbers at Catterick. A pound for anyone who found and returned a runaway apprentice joiner from Appleby. A list of regulations for the proper conduct of constables, a notice about expenses, old court lists, a faded timetable for the Darlington to Penrith stage-coach.

'Superintendent Snowden, good morning, sir!' Sergeant Clarke came in, fastening his belt. 'What brings you down these parts?'

'A word in private, sergeant?'

Clarke turned to the pair at the desk. 'Off you go, lads, early start for you.' They stood up reluctantly and left. 'Ten till tens, nice easy shift, all over before the pubs get too boisterous. Come and sit down.'

'This has to be kept secret, Reuben.' Snowden knew he could trust Clarke to keep quiet, but his underlings were another matter. 'The drownings last year, Yates and Raine. We've got three suspects.' Clarke's eyebrows rose. 'One's easy, he's inside, but the other two could be anywhere. and I want you to raise every man you can muster to track them down. '

'Names, sir?'

'George Barker, Thomas Raine.'

'Which one, the Raine? More than one round here called that.'

Snowden dug out his notebook and found Ann Humphrey's description. 'Tall, five ten or eleven, well-built. Black hair, beard. Broken nose. Local accent.' He closed the notebook with a snap. 'Comes from Mickleton way, I'm told.'

'Ah, that lot. Thomas Routledge Raine he's known as by us, sir, that being his middle name. His mother was a Routledge from further up the dale.'

'Is there anyone in Teesdale you don't know, sergeant?'

Clarke grinned. 'Not many, sir, been around a few years now.' The grin faded. 'There's Barkers up that way, too, could be your George is one of them.'

'Mickleton?' Snowden racked his memory. 'Haven't come across Barkers from there.'

'Any idea what he looks like, this George?'

Snowden opened his notebook again. 'Smallish, five six maybe, thin, light brown hair, thin moustache. Smallpox scars on his face. Wears a ring on one hand, not sure which.'

'Shouldn't be too hard to track down.'

'Send a man up to Mickleton, see if they know where Raine is, Barker too if he's from that part of the world. Bring them in if you find them.'

'Yes, sir.'

'And don't tell your lads what it's about, I don't want Raine or Barker scared off. Just routine inquiries, you understand.'

'Understood, sir.'

'And when we've found out all we can about them, I want every man, woman and child in Briggate to be asked if they were out and about the night Yates and Raine disappeared, and if so whether they saw them. We've asked before, but we only covered a handful of people and got nowhere. This time I want it done thoroughly.' He paused, wondering whether to add an incentive. 'They can hint – hint, mind, not promise – that there may be money in it for witnesses who come forward.'

'Reward, sir?'

'Perhaps. And tell your lads there'll be something extra in their Christmas box this year if they come up with the goods.'

'Sure they'll do their best, sir.'

'Let me know the minute you track either of them down. I'm up to my eyes in another murder or I'd be here with you. I'll call in again later if I can.'

'Keeps you busy, sir, does murder. Makes a nice change.'

Barnard Castle, 10am

SIMON Bycroft arrived as St Mary's struck the hour and McQueedie, standing in the church doorway, winced at each chime.

'Mr McQueedie, how delightful to see you.' Bycroft was in his twenties, a tall slim figure in full curatorial regalia, black gown, immaculate surplice and a cravat starched to perfection. He offered McQueedie a limp hand and ushered him into the church. 'I was so sorry to learn about your brother when we met yesterday. Such a nice man, he gave our little group of thespians such favourable reviews in the *Gazette.*' He gave Mc-Queedie a sympathetic glance. 'A sudden death, was it?'

'Very.' McQueedie nodded sombrely. 'Instantaneous, I'm told.'

'So very much better than a long lingering wait to enter the Kingdom, I always think. And so young. It must be very hard, losing a twin like that.' He paused in the aisle. 'You must have been very close, you're so very much alike.'

'Apart from the ears.'

Bycroft inspected them. 'Yes, of course, far bigger.' He resumed walking and led them on to the vestry. 'This is where we keep all our bits and pieces, and I think we'll have just what you wanted.'

McQueedie waited as the curate delved into a cupboard, and hoped his sojourn in the church the day before had not been a waste of time. The sermon had lasted well over an hour, and he'd almost given up hope before Bycroft, sitting with the choir and demonstrating possession of a fine if slightly off-key alto delivery, had noticed his presence with a welcoming nod. He was renowned in the town for his involvement in theatrical productions – an involvement which some of the congregation regarded as a little too enthusiastic, perhaps – but McQueedie, in his previous incarnation as Hamish, the *Gazette*'s theatre reviewer, had found him amusing. On the church porch after the service he had been happy to allow McQueedie access to the Teesdale Players' collection of props and costumes. Not on a Sunday, of course, the Lord would not approve and the vicar even less, but tomorrow would be lovely.

Lovely wasn't quite the word McQueedie would have used to describe what emerged in Bycroft's hands from the depths of the cupboard.

'There you are.' He held out what looked like the fleece of a very small grey sheep with a bad attack of mange. 'You did say a wig? The man playing a judge wore this in our last production, it's the best I can do, I'm afraid. '

'Oh.' McQueedie stared at it. Something wriggled out from among the locks and dropped to the floor.

'For your brother's funeral, you said. An unusual sort of thing for such an occasion, I would have thought?'

'Old Scottish custom.' McQueedie examined the wig with increasing dismay. 'We all wear them. With the kilt and sporran, essential part of the outfit. Bagpipes, Rabbie Burns, och aye the noo and all that.'

'Oh, what *fun!* Can I come along?'

McQueedie's mind raced. 'Terribly sorry, Highland Presbyterian Congregationalist

Methodists, private ceremony, they'd never let you in.'

Bycroft's face fell. 'It's the only wig we've got, unless you fancy the ginger one I wore last Christmas in our production of The Rivals. I made a very popular Mrs Malaprop, though I say it myself.'

'Ginger?'

'With an *ador*able little pigtail.'

McQueedie sighed. 'I think this will have to do.'

Thorpe, 11.10am

BETSEY dropped what was left of the mouse in the compost bucket and decided there was no point in berating the cat. 'Sorry, Tommy, you'll have to find another toy, this one's not working any more.'

She left the cat looking puzzled and went back to her table in the study. She'd done what papa had asked, the results lay on the desk nearby awaiting his return, and she wondered whether to stay until then. But she'd promised Mrs Eeles she'd call in today and she couldn't let her down, not on her sixtieth birthday.

She sat down, took up her pen, and wrote him a note.

Papa, I've finished going through the names and they're here. I'm afraid there's an awful lot of men with J or B names but we may be able to cut them down to just a few if we know when the man in the tunnel died and you'll be glad to know I've found a match with the Gazettes. The paper with the pie was the issue published on Saturday July 19th last year. If you're right about Mrs Mattock she would have turned it into wrapping paper a week later, Saturday the 26th, and the tunnel man must have got it after that and before the next Saturday when she would have thrown it out to make way for new old ones.

She stopped. This was becoming very difficult to explain, and she was staring at the last sentence trying to work out how to put it more clearly when her father walked in.

'Papa, I'm glad you're back. I was just leaving you a note. Here, the first bit of it makes sense, I think. Did you get any breakfast?'

'No time, and I won't be here for more than a few minutes.' He scanned the note. 'Between July the twenty-sixth and, what? August the second? And you've got a list of men reported missing between those dates?'

'Yes, on the desk. There's four of them. None local, not the Barnard Castle or Richmond area you'd know about.'

He went across and found it. 'Shildon, Brough, Hawes, Bedale. Well done. How big an area does this cover?'

'We get notices about missing people from all the police and crime preventative forces between Weardale and Wensleydale, and those just over the border in Westmorland. We get some, too, from further away, but I didn't think you'd want those.'

'So let's see what we can work out.' Snowden was silent for a minute or two, thinking. 'There's a good map in the drawer over there, can you find it?'

She brought it over and started to unfold it. 'Too big for the desk, it'll have to go on the kitchen table.' He followed her through.

'There.' It was beautifully hand-drawn, clearly many years old, with the words *Ebo-racensis et Dunelmens Episo* in extravagant lettering across the top. 'Yorkshire and the Bishopric of Durham,' translated Snowden as Betsey admired the intricate coloured drawings of sailing ships in the North Sea, the miniature green trees and the brown humps of hills scattered across the two counties. Every settlement, even the tiniest village, was marked in red. 'It's wonderful,' she said.

Snowden nodded and looked at the tiny writing at the bottom. 'Made in 1759. No railways around then, of course, but I don't suppose a lot else has changed.' He switched his attention to the centre of the map. 'There's Richmond, and there's where we're looking for.'

She peered at the dot by his finger. 'Wostun.'

'I suppose they just asked the first person they came to what its name was, and that's what they heard. Look, there's Newsum and over there Berneycassel. But it's good enough for our purposes.' He pondered for a moment. 'We know this man was travelling light, one small bag Mrs Mattock told me. He's not staying overnight anywhere or he'd have a change of clothes with him.'

Betsey nodded. 'So he's set off from somewhere to go somewhere else a few hours' ride away and knows he can get back again the same day?'

'It would seem so. He wasn't in a hurry or he wouldn't have wasted time buying pies or ordering proddy mats. A man on horseback trotting along, walking from time to time with maybe the odd canter, he'd be doing, what, about seven or eight miles in an hour?'

Betsey thought about it. 'Yes, I'd think so. Probably less if he was going up and down a lot of hills.'

'That's true, and there are a lot of hills around here. So if he'd started first thing in the morning, seven o'clock perhaps, he'd have covered maybe twenty miles by the time he got to Whashton. Mrs Mattock said it was mid-morning, which I take it means around ten.'

'How far is that on the map?'

'There's a scale at the bottom, about four miles to the inch as far as I can work out.' He drew a imaginary circle on the map with his finger, stopping at places on its circumference. 'Bishop Auckland, Darlington, Northallerton, Leyburn, Askrigg, Middleton. He's set off from somewhere within there.'

'Which way did he come into Whashton?' Betsey was enjoying this.

'Mrs Mattock said he left her shop and went up the village, and I think he then turned left at the crossroads, towards Richmond, and was killed on the road some fifty yards or so further on, just above where the tunnel entrance is. The killer hauled him down through the trees and into the tunnel. Nobody would have tried to drag a grown man up that slope.'

'But which way –?'

'I'm coming to that. He's a stranger, he doesn't know there's a shop in Whashton, why go there unless he's coming from the east and comes across it by chance? The only road in the village runs east-west, there'd be no reason for anyone travelling north or south to take that route.'

'He could have been coming from Kirby Hill.'

'Then he wouldn't have gone into Whashton and turned round.'

Betsey began to think she wasn't cut out for detection. 'No, of course.'

'For want of anything better, I think he's heading for Marske and then to Swaledale or possibly Wensleydale.' He paused, considering places within the circle. 'Didn't you say there was somebody missing from Shildon? What's he called?'

Betsey consulted her list. 'Vayne. Joseph Vayne. He's the only one from the east side of your circle.'

'Vayne... So he comes down Dere Street to, say, Piercebridge, cuts across to Whashton by the back roads and plans to be at his destination comfortably by noon. He'll do whatever he has to do, and will be home again for tea.'

'Hmm.' Betsey wasn't convinced. 'I've never heard of Shildon before.'

'Village south of Bishop Auckland. Not much there, apart from the railway. It shouldn't be hard to find out if someone's missing from it.'

'Well, you might be right.'

'This is all conjecture, Betsey, I could be completely wrong.'

'Wrong, papa? You?' She laughed. 'I never thought I'd hear you say that.' She glanced up at the clock. 'Good heavens, I'm late! I promised Mrs Eeles I'd be up there by twelve, I'm going to have to gallop all the way.'

'Don't you dare. I didn't buy you that pony to get you killed on the road to Barningham.'

'Road? I'm going over the fields.'

'Just be careful. Can you come back via Whashton and put your head round the door at the Hack and Spade? Ask Mrs Mattock about the wrapping paper and the time the man called, see if we were right.'

'Go into a public house on my own? How exciting!'

'I think you'll be disappointed. I may be late back tonight, there's been a development in the other murder case, the drownings last year.'

'A development? So they *were* murdered?'

'I'll tell you later, don't mention it to anyone else. Which reminds me, there's something else you can do to help.' He pulled his notebook out, found a pencil and wrote a few words. 'These are the names of three people I want you to find out about. Another chance to prove how good your filing system is.' He tore out the page. 'I'll leave it on my desk.'

'I'll do it this evening. If you're not back before I go to bed, don't stay up all night again writing your book. You need your sleep.'

'How else am I going to pay for all that pony feed?'

She laughed, and he watched her disappear towards the stables.

Barnard Castle, 11.48am

McQUEEDIE had known in his heart that something would go awry with his plan. With plenty of time before the Board of Guardians' finance sub-committee meeting was due to start, he'd gone back to his room at the Jolly Farmers to try the wig on in front of the cracked mirror. Deciding it would just about do, he'd sneaked down the back stairs straight into the arms of the landlord, who was in no mood to listen to fresh excuses about missing rent. It was well over an hour before McQueedie had been let out of the pub cellar, and then only after giving the landlord his watch to take to the pawnbrokers up the street and return with a tenth of what it was worth, which the landlord decided was exactly the amount he was owed.

Now freed, running late and breathing heavily, McQueedie hauled himself up the stone steps to the first floor of the Butter Market and stopped outside the meeting room door. A low drone from inside reassured him that the guardians were still engrossed in the mysteries of workhouse accounts. His plan had been to enter the room before anyone else arrived and hide in the tiny cubbyhole beside the office door at the far end. He would then emerge after the guardians adjourned for lunch and the rest would be easy.

He hadn't a notion what to do now, but he might as well get inside at least. With luck they wouldn't notice him. He opened the door as quietly as possible and slipped in. The drone ceased and ten heads turned towards him.

'McQueedie? I thought you'd been fired a year ago?' Watson, clerk of this as well as almost every other worthy organisation in the town, stared at him from the far end of the table.

'Ah yes, poor Hamish. I'm Angus, his twin brother.' McQueedie stepped forward confidently and stretched out his hand. It had never failed yet. 'Pleased to meet you.'

'Nonsense, man.' Watson ignored the hand. 'Know all about you, read the reports when you were up in court. Found on a pub doorstep, brought up by nuns in an orphanage, never had a brother in your life.' His eyes narrowed. 'You've got a three-inch scar on your left leg from falling off a pub table in Glasgow, it's all in the medical records. Do you want to pull your trouser leg up and show us it isn't there?'

Ten heads awaited McQueedie's response. His hand dropped and he gave a gurgle of despair. There was, he realised, only one thing he could possibly do.

'Good God!' Ten guardians stood up as one. 'The man's collapsed.'

'Apoplexy.'

'Struck down by the Lord for his sins.'

'Drink, more likely.'

'Had an uncle did just the same in Halifax.'

'Still breathing, is he?'

'Never recovered, poor soul. Had to be buried there.'

'God moves in mysterious ways, I always say.'

'Shall we have a look up his trousers while he's down there?'

'I blame the nuns. Funny things, nuns.'

'It's drink, take my word for it.'

'Glass of water, that's what he needs.'

'Never cared much for the man myself.'

'There's a glass-full here, turn him over and we'll force it down him.'

McQueedie decided it might be an idea to recover a bit. He gave a muffled groan and rolled over.

'He's coming round.'

'Give him some air, let him breathe.'

'There's brandy in the office. Full bottle in the cupboard.'

McQueedie, who was about to sit up, had a sudden relapse which lasted until the brandy arrived and a glass of it had been forced through his lips.

He sat up and gave a shaky smile. 'I'll be all right in a moment, gentlemen. Happens all the time, doctors baffled, martyr to it all my life, not really contagious.' The guardians drew back. 'A little more of that brandy, perhaps? And then if I might find somewhere to sit for a while, a darkened room always does the trick. That cubby-hole in the corner looks ideal.'

He staggered to his feet.

'No need.' Watson shook his head. 'I think this might be an opportune moment to adjourn for luncheon, gentlemen. Mr McQueedie here, whichever one he thinks he is, can remain if he must until he recovers. Back at one o'clock?' There was a general nodding of heads and gathering of hats, and they moved towards the door. 'The curtain can be drawn if you want darkness, McQueedie. No funny business while we're away. If I come back and find you wearing a frock like the last time I saw you, you'll be back in the cell underneath here before you can say Hamish McQueedie. Or Angus, for that matter.'

McQueedie was alone. The plan was back on course, more or less, and it deserved some kind of celebration. He sat down at the table, pushed a pile of workhouse minutes to one side, and reached for the brandy.

Barningham, 12.05pm

FIVE minutes late, but of course it hadn't mattered. Mrs Eeles welcomed her with open arms, the bonnet Betsey had worked and decorated so carefully was hailed as the perfect gift, and the slice of fruit cake that accompanied the celebratory glass of sloe wine ('well, it *is* my birthday, my dear, and it's purely medicinal, of course') was a triumph of her host's culinary skills.

'Such a pity Charlotte isn't here to see you.' Mrs Eeles cut another slice of cake. 'She has a friend staying with her, her cousin, such a nice young lady. They've gone off for a long walk together.'

Betsey had met Charlotte at Lilac Cottage from time to time, exchanged guarded views about Miss Walton and discovered very politely that they didn't agree. The teaching assistant's absence was not something she greatly regretted.

'I do so wish I'd seen them.' She accepted the fresh slice of cake and another glass of sloe wine. It really was remarkably good. 'Miss Howard is *such* a dedicated mistress. Her devotion to the school principles is quite remarkable.'

Mrs Eeles chuckled.'You can't stand her, can you?'

Betsey looked affronted and then broke into a smile. 'If she can put up with Miss Walton, she deserves my whole-hearted admiration.' She finished the sloe wine and gave a slight hiccough. 'I wonder how long she'll stay at the school?'

'She'll find a husband like the rest of them.'

'You think so?' She topped up her glass. 'Not the prettiest of girls, is she?'

'They say she plays the piano ever so well.'

'Ah, Brahms before beauty.' She giggled. Medicinal, Mrs Eeles had said, and she was certainly feeling better for it.

Barnard Castle, 12.25pm

HE should have remembered to bring the mirror. McQueedie sat at the enormous desk in the office at the far end of the Butter Market meeting room and tried to imagine what he looked like.

He'd found the cloak, the gaudy cravat, the red and blue sash and the gold chain where he knew they would be, in the cupboard where the Grand Master of the Teesdale and District Chapter of the Loyal and Ancient Order of Antediluvian Buffaloes stored his regalia between meetings. There was also an interesting selection of French engravings which he had put to one side to take back to the Jolly Farmers. They had to be worth a week's rent at least, and the Buffaloes were hardly likely to tell the police about someone stealing their collection of artistic poses.

He'd had a problem with the moustache, squinting down his nose to see if it was straight and dropping glue down the Grand Master's sash, but it was stuck on now and there was, he discovered painfully, no way of removing it. The wig was in place, and above it a top hat that had been lying on the desk and which he assumed Watson had forgotten to take with him in all the excitement.

That just left the spectacles. He put them on, pushed them down his nose so he could see over the top, and waited.

The door was open, and on the stroke of half-past twelve Fewster came into view, followed by a tall stringy ginger-haired young man in an equally ginger checked suit and a bowler hat.

'Mr Mayor?' Fewster came to the office, the gingery man in tow. 'May I present Mr Marmaduke Hardcastle, editor of the *Yorkshire Gazette*?'

McQueedie stayed seated, partly because he was uncertain about civic protocol when it came to mayors meeting the masses but also because his wig wobbled alarmingly if he moved very much. 'Delighted to meet you. All is well, I trust, Mr Fewster?'

'Very well, your worship. I have acquainted Mr Hardcastle with the existence of our little arrangement for passing select items of news to the *Gazette* and he is most interested in extending your activities.'

'Excellent, excellent. Always happy to assist the press and the money comes in very useful. All goes into my charity for the promotion of local democracy, you know.' McQueedie looked at the editor expectantly. 'How can I help you?'

'Not me, Mr Mayor, my uncle. He's running for Parliament and I understand you're returning officer for this part of the world.'

'I have that honour.'

'You call out the results on election night, on the town hall steps?'

'Well, I would if we had a town hall. But the balcony on the new Witham Hall will do well enough.'

'So how much?'

'I'm sorry?'

'How much? To make sure my uncle wins?'

'Well, now, that's asking a lot, Mr Hardcastle. I'd be risking my position if I went round doing that sort of thing.'

'How much?'

McQueedie shot an enquiring look over Hardcastle's shoulder and Fewster held up five fingers.

'Fifty pounds.'

'Fifty?' Hardcastle looked astonished.

'Well, I might settle for forty. Thirty, perhaps?'

Fewster was jumping up and down behind Hardcastle's back, waving frantically. He'd overdone it, McQueedie thought, too greedy. 'Twenty-five and a job at the *Gazette* for my brother-in-law Ham, er, Angus McQueedie, worth every penny of two guineas a week.'

'Hammer Angus?'

'Brilliant thrower in his time. Ran rings round them at the Highland Games. And a brilliant journalist, of course.'

'You've got yourself a deal.' Hardcastle held out a hand and McQueedie shook it carefully. The wig teetered ominously and the last of the wriggly things dropped into his lap.

'I'm sure you can sort out the little details with Mr Fewster, used notes and brown envelopes and so on.' McQueedie threw caution to the winds and stood up. 'So sorry I can't give you more of my time, but duty calls, you know.' He looked pointedly at the door. 'Good to do business with you.'

McQueedie watched them go with a puzzled look behind the false moustache. He'd thought Fewster would look delighted but he'd given him a positively furious glare as he led the editor away. It was all very odd, and he pondered it in vain as he put the hat and the Buffaloes' bits and pieces back where they came from, stuffed the wig in his pocket, picked up the French engravings and let himself out.

Barningham 2.30pm

'YOUR housekeeper said I'd find you here.' Wharton gave a startled leap and Ermintrude grunted in annoyance as his ear-tickling came to a sudden halt.

'Good lord, Miss –' He realised he didn't know the full name of the extraordinarily good-looking girl standing at the gate behind him.

'Brunskill. But do call me Harriet.'

'Yes, of course.'

'And you are –?'

He looked even more confused. 'Well, I'm the rector. I thought we met yesterday outside church?'

'We did. But if you're going to call me Harriet...'

'Am I?'

'Of course you are. Then I can hardly call you the Reverend Witton or whatever it is.'

'Wharton, William Wharton.'

'William! How lovely.'

'Is it?' He had no idea why she'd think so. The only religious William of note he'd ever heard of was a saint who became Archbishop of York in 1143 and died after drinking from a poisoned chalice, and nobody said he was lovely.

'Do they call you Will or Willie?'

He blenched. 'Just William will do, if you must.'

'Well, William, aren't you going to introduce me? She's a fine-looking animal.'

Wharton relaxed a little. She liked pigs, or at least knew a good one when she saw it. 'Ermintrude. She wins prizes every now and again.' He began tickling the pig's ears again. 'I've high hopes for her in the show. If she starts eating again properly, that is, I'm quite worried about her.'

'She looks fit and fat enough to me.' She reached in her pocket. 'Does she like fruit cake?'

'I've no idea.'

'Mrs Eeles' finest. She gave us a chunk for our walk, far more than I could eat.' She took it carefully from the cloth Mrs Eeles had wrapped round it and offered it to the pig. It was gone in a second, and both she and Harriet squealed with delight. 'There you are, she's got a sweet tooth. Plenty of sugar and she'll win the show hands-down, or whatever pigs have.'

'Trotters.'

'Yes, those.' She looked round at the sty. 'Are you in the middle of cleaning her out or something?'

'Just going to give her some fresh straw.'

'Can I help? Where is it?'

'In the barn over the yard.'

'Come on, then.'

She set off without waiting for him, and after a moment's hesitation he followed. It was dark in the barn after the sunshine, though enough of it came through the ventilation holes in the wall and gaps in the thatched roof for them to see what they were doing. One side of the building was stacked high with hay, the other half-full of straw.

'Doesn't it smell wonderful?' She picked up a handful of hay and put it to her nose. 'I love it. The best scent of summer, much better than flowers. Imagine a pillow full of it instead of musty old duck feathers.' To Wharton's astonishment she threw herself onto the hay and lay there on her back, staring up at the cobwebs far above. 'You'd sleep for ever.'

'I'll just get the straw.' He gathered a large handful and made for the door. 'I think you should come out, the dust won't do you any good.'

'I'm coming.' With a most unladylike whoop of sheer joy at being alive she leapt to her feet and ran after him to the door.

Barningham, 2.30pm again

BETSEY put the empty glass down on the table and stood up at the second attempt. 'I'll have to be going, Mrs Eeles, papa asked me to make some inquiries for him in Whashton at the Shack and something.'

'Hack and Spade.'

'That's it.' She weaved her way across to say farewell. 'It's been lovely to see you.'

'Are you sure you're all right riding back?' Mrs Eeles eyed her uncertainly.

'Absolutely, never felt better.' The cottage walls seemed to move about a bit, which was curious. She gave Mrs Eeles a farewell kiss and walked across to the pony.

'You know what, Millie? I think we should walk round and say hello to William. He'll be so pleased to see us.'

She led the animal unsteadily up the rectory drive. The sun was warm on her back, birds were singing drowsily in the trees, bees buzzed in the flowerbeds. She smiled happily. 'You stay here now, and I'll go and find him.'

She peered through the study window. Nobody. He'd be round with that pig, or in a shed somewhere tinkering with one of his inventions. She wandered round the house to the farmyard gate and leant over. He wasn't at the sty as far as she could see, perhaps...

There was a shriek from the other side and William came out, followed by a girl she'd never seen before who was laughing as she ran into the yard, shouting 'That was wonderful!' as she reached the rector and turned to face him. The back of her cape was covered in hay.

The sun went in, the birds and the bees went silent, and the world turned suddenly very cold.

Barnard Castle, 2.50pm

IT had taken a good half-hour back in the Jolly Farmers' attic bedroom to get most of the moustache off, and there were still bits of it clinging on. He gave them another scrape with the cut-throat razor, nicked his upper lip and gave up. Fewster must have got rid of Hardcastle by now. Time to divide the spoils. He stuffed the wig in his pocket and set off.

Fewster, his partner in what he supposed was undeniably crime, was waiting for him in the back bar of the Golden Lion, sitting with his head in his hands and staring blindly at the ringmarks on the table-top.

'That went well.' McQueedie greeted him jovially. 'Not got a drink to celebrate?'

'Celebrate?' Fewster repeated the word in a voice that McQueedie thought unexpectedly menacing in the circumstances. 'What have we got to celebrate?'

'Well, twenty-five pounds to start with.'

'Do you know how much they charge for a full top-of-the-menu meal for six at the Kings Head ?'

McQueedie shook his head. He'd never been able to afford a sandwich there. 'For six?'

'Six. Hardcastle and five of his buddies who are swanning round the north with him on this newspaper inspection beano. I treated them all to an early lunch before I took him over to see you, I thought it would warm him up nicely when you got to negotiating your price. A bottle of best claret apiece, cigars all round, no expense spared, I thought we'd be rolling in it soon enough.' Fewster was positively snarling by now. 'And as for the tip, their *maitre d'hôtel*'s one of the biggest brutes I've ever seen. He wanted another two guineas before he'd let me out of the room when I went to settle the bill.'

'But we did it in the end. How much have we got left?'

Fewster reached in his pocket, produced two half-crowns and tossed one of them across the table. 'Don't spend it all at once.'

There was no doubt about it, he was bitter about something. McQueedie sat down beside him, concerned. Perhaps it had all been too much for the poor fellow. 'Well, always look on the bright side. At least I've got a job, you'll have me to help you in future.' Fewster groaned. He certainly didn't look as delighted at the prospect as Mc-Queedie had hoped. Perhaps he had other problems. 'Something else the matter, old chap?'

'Oh, nothing much. Just the loss of a fortune because some Scottish idiot doesn't know what five fingers mean when he sees them.'

'Scottish idiot? Who –?' McQueedie stopped, bewildered. 'You don't mean me?'

'You're the only one I know, thank God, and that's one too many.' Fewster gave McQueedie the sort of look he recalled being given by an editor once in his early days as a reporter, when he'd explained there was no story about a church bazaar because the spire had collapsed on top of the tea tent, killing the vicar's wife and a small dog, and he'd gone for a pint instead.

'But you waved five fingers and I counted them.' McQueedie was astonished. 'If you didn't mean fifty you should have waved four for forty or whatever it was Hardcastle had told you he was prepared to go to.' He frowned. 'Well, it can't be helped. Even half-a-crown apiece is a profit, and we've got my two guineas coming in every week.' Fewster still didn't look happy. 'Look, I'll settle for two pounds, you can have the extra two shillings, how's that?'

'Two shillings?'

'Yes.'

Fewster gave him a long, long stare. 'When I waved five fingers I didn't mean fifty. It was five for five hundred.' Fewster sunk his head back in his hands. 'And you knocked him down four hundred and seventy-five.' He began to sob.

'Ah.'

There was a long silence before McQueedie picked up his half-crown and edged cautiously away. 'Can I get you a drink?'

Whashton, 3.20pm

STONY-faced and shocked into sobriety, Betsey rode into the village and brought the pony to a halt in front of the Hack and Spade.

She'd ridden the first mile at a furious pace before stopping at the roadside to give Millie a rest and burst into tears of fury. Back in the saddle, wiping the tears from her eyes, she'd vowed never again to trust a man, not *any* man, wondered how long it took to join a nunnery, thrown the pretty little brooch he'd given her for her birthday into the hedge, spent ten desperate minutes searching for it among the brambles and rosehips so she could send it back to him with a letter telling him *exactly* what she thought of perfidious rectors who went rolling about in the hay with shameless young women she'd never seen before, burst into tears again, and finally decided the only thing to do was spend the rest of her days helping the only man she would *ever* have faith in again, dear papa, who she hoped would go straight over to the rectory and horsewhip the man who had broken her heart.

The pub was closed. She led Millie round to the back, threw the reins over a gatepost and hammered on the back door. A large woman in an immaculate apron appeared.

'Open at six, and we don't allow girls on their own.' Mrs Mattock regarded her with disdain. 'And certainly none in the state you're in. You look as if you've been dragged through a hedge.'

Betsey plucked a few stray strands of bramble off her cape and tried to sound authoritative. 'Police business. I've been sent to ask you a few questions.'

Mrs Mattock looked disbelieving. 'Employing women constables now, are they? Couldn't do a worse job than the men, I suppose. Useless, all of them.'

'I couldn't agree more, Mrs Mattock. Untrustworthy, immoral, better off without them.'

'My feelings exactly.' Her eyes narrowed. 'How d'you know my name? Never seen you before in my life.'

'I think you met my father. Superintendent Snowden.'

'Don't know the man.' Mrs Mattock looked her up and down again. 'I think you're making all this up, my girl. On your way before I have a proper constable take you in for begging. Superintendent indeed! I don't know what you take me for.'

'No, please don't shut the door.' Betsey was sure real policemen, or policewomen if there ever were such things, didn't have to plead for help like this. 'He was here on Saturday, he talked to you about proggy mats.'

'Proddy mats?'

'Sorry, yes, proddy. He said you made them and they were beautiful.'

'Did he now?' Mrs Mattock melted a fraction. 'Him that got the body out of the tunnel?'

'That's right.'

'Wanted to buy one of my mats, said he'd ask you what they should look like.' She became almost friendly as the untidy young beggar before her transformed into a potential customer. 'Two he wanted, if I remember right, six shillings apiece. Have you decided?'

'Not just yet, I wondered if I could see what you can do.'

'Anything, my dear. Fancy edging, any colours you like, initials extra of course.'

'Initials?'

'People like them, wrapped round hearts, that sort of thing. I could put yours on one.' She looked at Betsey suggestively. 'You'll have a sweetheart, pretty young girl like you?'

Betsey's world went cold again.

'No,' she managed. 'Just plain will do.'

Barnard Castle, 4.35pm

SERGEANT Clarke held up his hands in despair. '*Please*, Mrs Elliott, will you just calm down and tell me what this is all about?'

She stood at the police house counter, arms folded over her substantial bosom and her face a picture of outraged fury. Four small children stood behind her, wide-eyed. 'You know very well what he's been up to, don't you try to pretend my husband hasn't been taking advantage of every little slut on the streets behind my back and you didn't know about it. Talk of the town, it is, I don't know how you can stand there and deny it.'

'I assure you, Mrs Elliott, I know nothing about it. All I know is that the superintendent told me that your husband had requested a move to less arduous duties, and I followed his orders.'

'Orders? I don't believe a word of it, a cover-up, that's what it is. You're all the same, you lot, protecting your own.' The smallest of the infants behind her began to wail and she turned round savagely to deal with it. 'Stop your snivelling, young Albert, or you'll feel the back of my hand. Get outside, the lot of you.' They shuffled out and she resumed her tirade. 'Well, you're not going to be able to keep this quiet.'

She reached down, picked up a large bag and emptied it on the counter. Clarke stared at it. There were necklaces, bracelets, rings and brooches, cigar-cases and cravat-pins, watches and watch-chains, two enamel snuff-boxes and a silver powder-pot. 'You just ask him where this lot came from.'

'I really don't see –'

'Hidden in the closet where he kept all the rest of his police rubbish. I've thrown everything else out. And him, of course, the cheating bastard.' She shook the bag and a last brooch fell out onto the pile. 'Well, I'm not having you lot find it and accusing me of stealing it, I'm a respectable woman. You ask him where it all came from.'

'Are you telling me that Constable Elliott –'

'I want him sent down and if you don't stop gawping like a dead fish and start doing something about it, Reuben Clarke, I'll not be answerable.' She swung round, headed for the door, and came face to face with Snowden on the doorstep. 'And you're no bloody use, either.' She stormed past him and he watched her collect her offspring and give Albert a sound clip round the ear as they disappeared up the street.

'What was all *that* about?'

'Elliott's missus, sir.' Clarke grinned. 'Seems somebody told her about his disciplinary.'

'Surprised she didn't know about it earlier.' Snowden wondered who had spread the word. Probably Pearson, and he could hardly blame him. 'Any news for me?'

Clarke nodded, looking pleased. 'Sent a man up to Mickleton, I was right about George Barker. Hasn't been seen for a few weeks, though, they think he's working up Weardale way in one of the ironstone works. Lot of local lads up there, good money they say.'

'Stanhope, that area?'

'Yes, sir.'

'Right. Find me two of your best men, good horsemen, get them armed. Got enough pistols and ammunition in the safe?'

'Should be, sir.'

'And they know how to use them?'

'Practice with the militia every month, sir.'

'Excellent. I'll pick them up at seven. You, too.'

Clarke looked gratified. 'Going after him, are we?'

'That's the idea.' Snowden turned to go and stopped. 'What's all this lot?' He gestured at the pile of items on the counter. 'Caught a burglar red-handed?'

'Not sure, sir. She brought it all in, said Elliott had it hidden away.'

Snowden toyed with one of the bracelets. 'Expensive. Nice watch, too. Gold, I think, well-worn, though.' He picked it up, turned it over and peered at it, suddenly interested. 'Some sort of engraving on the back... Well, well, well. Where is he now, our Constable Elliott?'

Clarke shrugged. 'She's chucked him out and he's not on duty at the crem till eight. Probably in one of the beerhouses, nursing his wounds. She's a big woman.'

'Find him and bring him in. I want a word with him about a murder.'

Barningham, 5pm

CHARLOTTE stood up crossly as Harriet came into the Lilac Cottage kitchen. 'Where on earth have you been? You said you'd race me round the churchyard and vanished. I couldn't find you anywhere.'

'I just dropped by to say hello to your rector.' Harriet gave a conspiratorial smile. 'I met Ermintrude.'

'Ermintrude?'

'His prize pig. She likes fruit cake.'

'You went to see him on your own?' Charlotte looked disapproving. 'The Reverend Wharton?'

'William.'

'*William?* Do you think that was wise, Harriet? I mean...'

'Oh, he's quite harmless. Terrified of women.' She laughed. 'But interesting. He invents things, you know.'

'What sort of things?'

'Oh, machines for farms, I don't know, but he wins awards for them.' She looked her cousin thoughtfully. 'If I come back next weekend, would you come with me to the show in Barnard Castle? He's entered Ermintrude and I asked if I could go with him.'

'Harriet! You didn't?'

'I did. He looked positively frightened, poor man, but I wouldn't take no for an answer. The thing is, I'll need a chaperone for the day.'

'A chaperone?'

'Well, I'd go without one but I don't think father would approve.'

'I'm sure he wouldn't. And I wouldn't let him know you and the rector are on first-name terms. Mrs Eeles would have one of her turns if she knew.'

'Probably.' Harriet nodded, amused. 'Where is she?'

'Upstairs asleep. She was in a very strange mood when I got back. When I said I'd been looking for you in the graveyard she asked if I'd seen anybody and then burst into giggles.'

'Giggles? Mrs Eeles?'

'She spluttered something about plenty of bodies in there to find, burst into laughter and fell over. I had to help her up to bed.' Charlotte shook her head, mystified. 'If I didn't know better I'd say she'd been drinking.'

Thorpe, 5.45pm

THE wasp crawled angrily up the windowpane for the third time, fell down when it reached the top of the glass and started once more. Betsey eyed it malevolently, rolled up the *Gazette* and gave it a determined thwack. She'd like to do that to William, preferably with a hammer. Often.

She reached down gingerly, picked up the remains of the wasp by one lifeless wing and dropped it into the grate. She hated wasps. Nasty, untrustworthy, dangerous, pointless things and the world would be a lot better without them. Just like men.

She sat down and stared disconsolately out of the window. If she'd been born a boy she could have run away to sea or gone to London or at least Darlington and made her fortune or done *something* instead of sitting here miserably swatting wasps.

She looked at the body in the ashes and felt a twinge of remorse. It wasn't the wasp's fault it was born a wasp, it probably wished it had been born a bee and everybody would have loved it. A tear trickled down her cheek. Life was just so unfair.

There was a rattle of horseshoes, a clatter of boots on the cobbles, and her father came in, obviously in a hurry.

'Betsey, I can't stop, any water on the boil? I could do with a quick cup of tea.' He rushed into his study and started rummaging through his desk. 'No, don't bother, give Bucephalus something to eat, heaven knows when he'll next get fed. Or me, for that matter. Where the devil is my other pistol?'

By the time she returned he had changed, packed a saddlebag with his heaviest cloak and a bottle of cold water, tucked a flask of brandy into his jacket pocket and the spare pistol into his belt, and was at the door ready to leave.

'Can't you spare me a minute or two, papa? It's important.'

'Of course. Mrs Mattock, what did she say? Were we right about the paper?'

'Yes, and the man called by just after ten, she thinks. But –'

'Any luck with those names?'

'There's a John Breckon in Durham Jail –'

'Yes, know about him. Barker? Raine?'

'Nothing on Barker I can find. Caution or two for rowdiness, that's all. And there are so many Thomas Raines –'

'This one's got a middle name, Routling or something.'

'Just a minute.' She ran to get her notes and returned as he finished buckling the extra saddlebag. 'Routledge.'

'Yes.'

Her face fell. 'Nothing on him either, really. One court appearance a year ago in Staindrop for affray, fined with costs. I'm sorry.'

'Never mind.' He got into the saddle. 'I may be back very late, don't wait up.'

'I do know he's left-handed, but I don't suppose that's much use.' He was already on his way, and she wasn't sure he had heard. 'Bye, papa. Take care.'

He vanished up the road, dust rising behind him, and she walked slowly back inside.

Barnard Castle, 6.50pm

'IN you go.' Clarke pushed Elliott into the cell. 'I'd sober up fast if I were you. Snowden's on his way.'

He swung the door shut, turned the lock and peered through the hatch. 'He's not fond of thieves, especially when they're masquerading as constables. Wouldn't be surprised if he had you hanged.' He smiled grimly as he heard Elliott groan, closed the hatch and went back to the office.

Snowden had arrived and was waiting for him.

'Your men ready?'

'Meeting them at the bridge, sir.'

'Any sign of Elliott?'

'In the cells, not very happy.'

'Well done, well done.'

'In no fit state to be interviewed, I'm afraid.'

'No time now, anyway. Leave him overnight, we'll see what we can get out of him tomorrow. Tell your duty constable there's no need to over-feed him.'

'Yes, sir.'

'Time we were off, then.'

Tuesday July 28ᵗʰ

Stanhope, 3.30am

THERE were seven of them now, joined by Superintendent John Browne of the Weardale rural force and two of his constables at Bishop Auckland. It had been a long journey up the dale to Stanhope, a market town scarcely more than a village straggled along the north bank of the Wear but in its time a major leadmining centre and one of the richest settlements on the river.

The night had been clear, but with only starlight and a three-day-old moon to guide them they had ridden slowly and sometimes been reduced to walking, lanterns in hand, to avoid horses catching their hooves in hidden potholes. Now dawn was breaking and for the last mile they had made better progress.

This was largely new territory for Snowden, but Browne knew it like the back of his hand. They had met several times over the years, and each held the other in genuine respect as professional policemen with reputations for integrity, efficiency and a belief in justice. 'High time I helped you out,' Browne had said when Snowden hauled him out of bed in Bishop Auckland. 'Not forgotten what you did for us when that bastard from Eastgate fled to Teesdale. I wouldn't have faced him unarmed like you did.'

Snowden had waved this aside. 'I didn't know he had a gun, John. Wouldn't have gone near him if I had. Anyway, this is your patch, I'd feel I was trespassing if I hadn't roped you in.'

They had broken their ride for a convivial and useful hour in Wolsingham's White Swan, whose landlord had been surprised and much relieved when seven police officers arrived in his bar just after midnight and instead of querying his still being open for business had ordered food and drink for themselves and their horses and paid well over the usual price for his fare without question.

'Dozen or so places he might be,' Browne had said, 'but most of them are small affairs with local workers, no need for outsiders. My money would be on the ironstone works at Stanhope, big operation and expanding fast. It's full of itinerants, Irish and navvies and lads from other dales. They're even talking about running a railway up there to get their stuff down to the new port at Middlesbrough.'

'And where do all these workers stay at night?' Snowden had wondered. 'I don't imagine the company provides accommodation.'

'No chance of that. Some sleep on site, mostly in makeshift shelters open to all weathers. All right for the Irish and navvies, they're used to it working on the railways, but the local lads like their home comforts. The money's good, they put up in boarding houses in the town.'

'What do you suggest? We can hardly search every one of those.'

'The works are a bit further up the dale. First shift starts at five and if we position ourselves at the western end of the town we should see men making their way there.'

Arriving at Stanhope just before three, they were now leading their horses silently along the main street past the Queen's Head, the Cross Keys and the arched entrance to Stanhope Castle on their left. Browne came to a halt. 'Phoenix Arms, last pub this end of town.'

The inn stood silent, its sandstone facade turning a faint pink in the day's first tentative rays of sunshine. Snowden pulled out his watch. 'Three-forty.' A church bell struck once as he spoke. 'Vicar's clock's running late.'

'Stanhope time. It's different everywhere round here, no railway timetables to put us right. Other end of the dale, Wearhead, it'll still be three o'clock.'

'Whatever it is, we've got maybe an hour or more before the first men set off for work?'

Browne nodded. 'I suggest we make ourselves comfortable in the Phoenix and keep watch as they go past. I know the landlord, he'll not complain about being woken up early if it means the price of an extra seven breakfasts in his till.'

Barnard Castle, 3.50am

SAMUEL Eddison stopped at the next Briggate doorway, raised his eight-foot-long stick, and gave four firm taps on the first-floor window above. A few moments passed before the ragged curtain inside twitched apart and then fell back. He lowered the stick and shuffled on.

'Morning, Sam.'

'Now then.'

'Anything going on out there?' Constable Daniel Laike shifted his feet on the police house doorstep and gave a yawn.

'Not a lot. Anybody new inside?'

'Quiet night Mondays. Just the one, and he'd been in since yesterday sometime. Still snoring, must have had a skinfull.'

'Lucky sod. Long time since I had a full night's sleep.' Eddison sniffed, pulled a rag out of his pocket and blew his nose loudly.

'Hey up, Sam, you'll wake the whole of bloody Briggate.'

The knocker-up gave a toothless grin. 'Save me walking round 'em. Spare a cup of tea?'

'Come on in, bit of company will be welcome.'

They sat down together inside. Emmerson cocked an ear and nodded. 'See what you mean. Noisy bugger, isn't he? Anybody I know?'

Laike hesitated and lowered his voice. 'One of our lads. Elliott.'

Eddison's eyebrows shot up. 'There's not many round here will be sorry about that. What's he been up to, shagging the superintendent's wife?'

'Hasn't got one, widowed I think. But he would of if he did have, if he'd half a chance.'

Eddison sorted out the pronouns and nodded. 'So what's he done?'

'Not sure. Something to do with a load of stuff they found when his missus threw him out, jewellery mostly. Box full of it, look.' He pointed to Mrs Elliott's haul in the corner.

Eddison looked thoughtful. 'You want to ask my brother-in-law about that.'
'Brother-in-law?'
'Isaac Greenborne, pawnbroker up The Bank. Any more tea in that pot?'

Stanhope, 4.30am

'BROWNE sat back, his eyes never leaving the road outside. Snowden was on the other side of the window, equally concentrated on the figures passing by outside. So far there had just been the occasional one tramping by, bait bag in one hand, most with a pick or hammer in the other.

'Nobody leaves their tools on site,' Browne said. 'Never see them again.'
'How long are they there for?'
'Most do ten hours, eleven maybe. Some go right through till five this evening when the night shift starts.'
'So if we don't see him now he'll be among the others on their way back in an hour or so?'
'Let's hope so... What about him, one on the left?'
'Too tall.'

One of Browne's constables came into the room. 'Excuse me, sir. Sergeant Clarke and his two men are in position further down the road. I'm off to join Davis back over in case our suspect makes a run for it back to his lodgings.'
'Good.'
'And I've just been talking to the landlord, sir. Don't know if it'll help, but he says he's got two of the works foremen staying here.' He ventured a smile. 'Reckons they don't get on too well with their men, not sure they'd be safe among a dozen of them in a lodging house.'
'Here, now?'
'Yes, sir. Just about to set off.'
'Bring them in here, I'd like a word with them.'

The constable returned with two men dressed a little better than the workers they'd so far seen on the road. No caps for them, Snowden noticed with an inward smile, bowler hats in each hand. He wasted no time.
'Police. Either of you know a George Barker? Works for you, fairly small man, thin, brown hair, smallpox scars. Maybe a moustache.'

The first man shook his head, but his companion nodded. 'Might do. Calls himself Geordie, got a beard, but could be him.'
'Wears a ring.'
'That's him.'
'I want you outside, by the door. Both of you. Moment you see him, give me a sign. I'll be here, at the window.'

The foreman shook his head. 'We'll be late at the works.'
'You'll be a damn sight later if you end up in Durham jail for obstructing the police and assisting a murderer to escape.'
'Murderer?'
'You heard. Outside, if you please.'

Now they waited. The trickle of men grew to a steady stream moving more urgently than the early birds as their five o'clock deadline grew nearer, and Snowden's eyes swept the passers-by one by one. Beside him Browne concentrated on the foremen at the door, who were trying without much success to look as if they were engrossed in conversation.

'Looks as if he'll be among those coming back.' Snowden turned his gaze in the opposite direction as the stream turned to a trickle. 'Must be almost five by now.'

'Maybe.' Browne kept his eyes on the doorway. 'It would be very handy, you know, if we had some record of who's working in places like this.'

Snowden nodded. 'I don't suppose those in charge have any more idea than we have. Men just turn up, get taken on with no questions asked, and –' His sentence ended abruptly as Browne leapt to his feet.

'They've seen him! The one with the blue cap just passing. Come on!'

Snowden hurried after him into the road. Barker halted momentarily at the sound of their footsteps, turned to see what was happening and began to run, his hammer clattering to the ground as Snowden put his whistle to his lips and blew two sharp blasts. Sergeant Clarke and his two constables down the road stepped out and Barker came to a halt as he realised he was trapped.

'Stay where you are.' Snowden produced a pistol and walked across to face him. 'Superintendent Snowden, Greta Bridge police. I have a warrant for your arrest for the murders of Joseph Yates and Catherine Raine on or about the tenth of August 1845. Handcuff him, sergeant.'

Barker stood stony-faced as his wrists were pinioned behind his back. 'So you're Snowden. I've heard about you.'

'Anything to say?'

'I know where this has come from.' His face twisted in sudden anger. 'That little bitch, I knew we should have –' He stopped. 'No, I've nothing to tell you.'

'Know where Thomas Raine is?'

'No idea.'

'Never been here with you?'

'No.'

Browne stepped in. 'We'll find him fast enough. Where is he, hiding in Teesdale somewhere?'

'Not likely, is it? Not with you lot looking for him.'

'He doesn't know we are.' Snowden paused. 'Are you saying he's on the run for something else?'

'I'm saying nothing.'

Snowden sighed. 'You're going on trial for murder, Barker, and that means you'll almost certainly end up dancing at the end of a hangman's rope. Your only chance of escaping the gallows, and it's a very, very slim chance, is by telling us everything you know. Where's Raine?'

'Ever seen a man hanged, Barker?' Browne reached out a hand and gripped the man's neck. 'They put the noose round you, not quite as tight as this, and then they drop you. If you're lucky your neck breaks straight away. But if you're not...' He tightened his grip and Barker's eyes bulged. 'You can't breath, your head's being torn out of your shoulders, you're kicking away at nothing and spinning round shitting yourself with terror, and it goes on and on...' He let go and Barker collapsed to his knees. 'Where's Raine, you little bastard?'

The captive's bravado crumbled. 'I don't know, God's honest truth I don't.'

'But you might have some idea?'

'He was with Breckon when one of you lot was done over at Staindrop last New Year.' Barker had started trembling. 'He's wanted for that, you should know.'

'Raine?' Browne shook his head. 'I was involved in that case, nobody of that name I remember. You're lying again, Barker.' He lifted the man up by his throat. 'You could have a very nasty accident all of a sudden if you don't start telling me the truth.'

Barker squealed in fright. 'It's true, he told me he was there. Your lads came looking for him and he did a runner.'

'Where to?'

'I don't know. He could be anywhere.'

'If you're lying you'll be begging for a nice easy hanging by the time we've finished with you.' Browne dropped Barker back on his feet. 'Where do you want him, Snowden?'

'Greta Bridge cells, ready for the magistrates. Bind him securely, sergeant, and get your constables to take turns guarding him while we all find some breakfast. We've earned it.'

Shildon, 9.30am

HE'd told Betsey it was not much more than a village, but it had changed dramatically since he'd last seen Shildon, fifteen years or more ago. Then it was two small settlements, Old Shildon to the north, a much smaller New Shildon half a mile away at the western end of the Stockton and Darlington Railway, the world's first steam-driven public railway. Now the view was dominated by New Shildon, chosen as the site for William Hackworth's Soho locomotive works. Railway lines stretched out in all directions, a tunnel had made redundant the stationary engines formerly needed to haul wagons up steep inclines, and tentacles of sidings spread east and west over acres Snowden dimly recalled as being swamp and wasteland. There were at least four pits in sight, each with a tall skeletal tower for the winding gear, a sprawl of shaft-top buildings and a collection of spoil heaps. Rows of terraced cottages had sprung up, with pubs on many a corner, schools and a chapel. It was a thriving hub of activity, wrapped in clouds of smoke and steam and echoing to the constant sound of locomotives, clanking wagons and works machines.

Snowden stared down at it from the top of the hill. There must have been hundreds, no, thousands of coal tubs gathered there, some piled high with the black gold from the collieries, some waiting beneath a line of coal-drops to be filled. He'd anticipated a brief detour on his way back from bidding Browne farewell in Bishop Auckland, maybe half an hour or so to find out whether Betsey's Joseph Vayne was the missing man who ended up in a disused tunnel in Whashton, but it looked like taking longer than he'd hoped.

He rubbed his eyes. Losing a night's sleep wasn't a rare experience, but he'd ridden a lot of miles and was feeling distinctly weary. One murder inquiry was enough to deal with, let alone two – three if the drownings weren't connected, though he was sure they were – and they were threatening to get confusingly entangled. Both committed at much the same time, a year ago; one with suspects known though not all yet caught and without any clear motives, the other with a motive which must surely be robbery, but with not even the victim identified, let alone the perpetrator. It was tempting to abandon the Vayne search which, he thought with a fairly humourless smile to himself, was probably going to be in vain, but now he was here... He nudged Bucephalus forward and headed for what was definitely now much more than a mere village.

He rode down to the centre of New Shildon, where the railway crossed a road junction, and realised that he had no idea where the police house was or even if there was one. There was a pub on one corner, the Masons' Arms, a pinafored matron with a broom standing in the open doorway.

'We don't do them any more,' she said as he pulled up outside. 'You get them over there.' She nodded towards what looked like a new building across the road.

'I'm sorry?' Snowden looked puzzled.

'Tickets. For the trains. We did them for years, ever since it started, but not now. Proper ticket office at the station.'

'I'm not after a ticket. Is there a police house somewhere?'

'Up the street, next to the butcher's. But if it's the constable you want, you won't find him there.' She jerked a thumb in the direction of the pub interior. 'He's inside.'

'I'll find him.' Snowden dismounted.

'Leave your horse on the other side, I've just cleaned round here.'

Snowden obeyed, encouraged by a faint memory of his encounter with Mrs Galland in Startforth, and went into the bar. The only occupant was a small middle-aged man with a ragged moustache who was reading a newspaper by the window. He glanced up, gave Snowden a noncommittal grunt of welcome and resumed reading.

'Constable?'

'Could be, who wants to know?'

'Come across anybody called Vayne in these parts?'

'Vayne?'

'Joseph Vayne. Reported missing a year ago.'

The man looked up briefly. 'Before my time. Only started last spring.'

'There'll be some record of him at the police house, I imagine.'

'Maybe.'

'Any chance I could have a look?'

'Busy right now, call in this afternoon and I'll see.'

Snowden decided to stop playing games. 'On your feet, constable, and stand to attention when you're addressing a senior officer. Now.'

The man stared at him. 'Who the hell do you think you are?'

'Superintendent Snowden, Gilling West Police.'

'And I'm Prince bloody Albert. What are you dressed like that for, then? Where's your uniform?'

'Outside in my saddlebag, together with my truncheon, handcuffs and everything else I need to sort you out, constable, if you don't get out of that chair right now.'

'Shit.' The man got hurriedly to his feet. 'I'm sorry, sir, don't often see real policemen round here. Apart from them on the railway, that is.'

'And you are?'

'Constable Yardley, sir.'

Snowden was about to berate him for idling in the pub when he recognised the newspaper. '*Police Gazette*, is it?'

'Yes, sir, the old *Hue and Cry*. I pick it up from here, soon as it's delivered. First thing I do is go through it to see if there's anything of use.'

Mollified by Yardley's answer, Snowden picked up the paper and glanced at it. Published by the Home Office since 1772, its purpose was printed in a prominent panel on the front: '*Containing the Substance of all Informations received in Cases of Felonies, and Misdemeanors of an aggravated nature, and against Receivers of Stolen Goods, reputed Thieves and Offenders escaped from Custody, with the time, the place, and every particular circumstance marking the Offence...*'

Also in it, Snowden knew, were the names and descriptions of everyone charged with a serious offence anywhere in the country and detailed descriptions of stolen property. A copy of the paper arrived each week at Greta Bridge, and there were times when it was invaluable.

'Looking for anyone in particular?'

'Just keeping up to date, sir.'

Snowden nodded approvingly. Local constables weren't noted for such devotion to duty. 'Well, I am. Let's have a search through your records.'

'Might be worth asking Mrs Dowson first, sir.'

'Landlady I just saw outside?'

'Yes, sir. She knows just about everybody.'

They found her on the doorstep, broom abandoned, deep in conversation with a neighbour. She broke off as they approached.

'You found him, then?'

'Police business.' Yardley sounded surprisingly authoritative.' Looking for a Joseph – what was his name?'

'Vayne.'

'Joe Vayne?' She gave a grim chuckle. 'Well, that'll be easy enough. Up there in the graveyard, six feet under.'

'Dead?' Snowden took over.

'Vicar's never buried a live one yet, far as I know.' She gave another throaty laugh.

'What happened to him?'

'Staggered out of the Royal Oak late one night and vanished. They found him two months later under a pile of coal in Stockton, must have fell asleep in one of those tubs waiting to be filled next morning. Silly bugger.'

Barningham, 10.45am

AUGUSTUS Milbank stood before the leather-topped desk in his father's study at

Barningham Park and tried to look contrite. Eighteen years old, he was known to everyone by his middle name Sussex, bestowed to please his godfather the Duke of Sussex, sixth son of George the Third. The only person who ever called him Augustus was his father, and then only when he was in serious trouble. Like today.

'I'm sorry, pater. It won't happen again.'

Mark Milbank regarded him grimly. 'That's what you said the last time. At least you haven't got this one pregnant. You haven't, have you?'

'It didn't quite get that far, pater.'

'Thank God for that. And you can stop all that Harrovian pater nonsense, I'm your father, dammit.'

'Yes, father.'

'Laundry-maids, scullery girls, any servant in a skirt you can lay your hands on. I don't know what's to become of you.'

'No, father.'

'Complete waste of money sending you to Harrow. You've not got the brains to go to Oxford, or even Cambridge. You clearly aren't suited for the Church and they won't take you in the Army because of that damned – what do they call it?'

'Asthma, father.'

'Foreign nonsense. It was lung cramp when I was your age and we bled it out of you. You can't add up, the only Latin you appear to remember is *amo amas amat* which rules out the law, and your political leanings make those damned Chartist revolutionaries look like fanatic royalists, so you can forget about entering Parliament. Thank God you're not my eldest. The only thing you seem capable of doing is seducing wenches in the kitchen.'

'Yes, father.'

'Your mother's upstairs in hysterics, convinced you're going to start ravishing her lady's maids at any moment. What *do* you want to do?'

'I quite fancy farming, actually.'

'Farming?' Mark stared at him aghast. 'Ten generations of Milbanks have fought to get where we are today and you want to go back to grubbing about in the soil for a living?'

'It's not like that these days, pater, father, I mean. There are all sorts of new ideas about agricultural management, fresh ways of doing things, scientific advances. Take manure, for instance –'

'Manure?' His father sank back, appalled.

'Yes, I was reading about it in *The Times*. If you –'

'Be quiet, Augustus.' Mark fixed him with a steely eye. 'I think it might be a good idea to send you off abroad for a while, France maybe, and get some civilised ideas in your head, away from all this nonsense. And if you must go groping young servants, at least they'd be French ones and from what I've heard they're all in favour of it.'

Sussex's face brightened. 'When can I go?'

'I've paid for you to do another year at Harrow and that's what you'll do, like it or not. And until you go back there after the summer you can indulge your enthusiasm for manure by helping Will Coates clean the dung-heaps down at Hawsteads farm. He's short of a man, but I suppose you'll do instead.'

'Dung-heaps?'

'Your allowance stops till they're done. And leave my maids alone or you'll be out of your godfather's will. And mine, dammit.'

Barnard Castle, 2.15pm

THERE were 252 blocks of neatly-cut stone in the wall opposite, another 82 behind him, 62 in the wall with the two tiny windows and another 36 each side of the door plus eight across the top. Elliott had counted them all, added the 48 foot-square paving slabs on the cell floor, the number of bars on the windows just below the ceiling (four apiece) and the boards making up the wooden solid wood door (six, plus four cross-pieces and two diagonals), wrestled with the sums and given up. Apart from the stone slab he was sitting on and the pail in the corner that he was trying hard not to use, there was nothing else in the cell to count except the legs on the dead spider high up in one corner. His hands were still cuffed behind his back, which meant he couldn't haul himself up to see out of the windows which in any case were made of thick glass that distorted what little light came through them. The food hatch in the centre of the door was bolted from the outside, the ceiling was a featureless stretch of flaking plaster, the walls were newly lime-washed and there wasn't even any desperate graffiti left by previous prisoners going out of their minds with boredom.

It was easy to see why people signed confessions, true or false, just to get out of there. Or hanged themselves. He was wondering morosely how he might manage that, his belt and boots having been taken away and the only other possible noose material the single rough blanket too thick to be torn into strips, when he heard the bolts on the hatch being drawn back. It was his first contact with anyone since getting his slice of dry bread and cup of water at six that morning, and he struggled gratefully to his feet.

'Sit down.'

The hatch opened, there was a pause while he was inspected from outside, and the door was unbolted. Snowden walked in, closing it behind him.

'Mr Elliott. Sobered up, have we?'

'I've done nothing, I don't know what you want.'

'I want to tell you a little story, constable. Or ex-constable, depending on whether it's true or not. Are you sitting comfortably?'

Elliott glowered. 'No bloody chance in here with my hands like this. What story?'

Snowden leaned against the back of the door, took out his pipe and lit it slowly. 'I heard it from a Mr Greenborne about an hour ago. Nice old fellow, married to Sam Eddison's sister. Do tell me if you've heard it before.'

Elliott's eyes grew wary. 'Get on with it.'

Snowden blew out a cloud of smoke and began.'Once upon a time there was a policeman who decided it would be a clever idea to go round all the pawnbrokers in town to see if they were the recipients of stolen goods.'

'So what's wrong with that?'

'Nothing at all. Very sensible, in fact, they're an obvious place for thieves to exchange their acquisitions for cash. And when our policeman found something dubious he took it away, saying it was evidence to be used in court. Quite right, too, just what I'd expect him to do.'

'So?'

'The problem was, the court cases never took place. The policeman started pocketing the things he found for himself, and if the pawnbroker asked about it he was told to keep quiet or he'd be charged with receiving stolen goods. Are you sure you haven't heard this before?'

'Don't know what you're talking about. I never –'

'I haven't quite finished yet. After a while our guardian of the law starts helping himself to all sorts of things he finds, whether they might have been stolen or not, and he builds up a nice little collection. And where do you think he hides it?'

Elliott stared at him, swallowing hard. 'How would I know?'

'In a closet where he thought his wife would never find it.' Snowden's voice hardened. 'Your closet, Elliott.'

'The bitch.' Elliott shook his head violently. 'She's lying.'

'I don't think so.' Snowden tapped his pipe out on the slab. 'Now, either I can go round all the pawnbrokers in town showing them what we've found and ask them who took it from them, or you can save me all that time and trouble by telling me now. Starting with this.' He reached into his pocket and took out a watch. 'You'll recognise it, I think. It's the one with the initials on the back.'

Barningham, 3.10pm

JOHN Coates watched in disbelief. 'Haven't you ever used a gripe before, lad?'

Sussex stuck the fork back into the manure heap, wiped the sweat from his brow, and shook his head. 'Is that what this thing's called?'

'Gripe, muck rake, cowl fork, all the same, bloody great thing to shift muck from the midden. You're doing it all wrong.' Coates picked up the fork to demonstrate. 'One hand on the handle, fingers underneath, see? Other hand halfway down the shaft so you can give the tines a good shove sideways in.'

'Tines, Mr Coates?'

'Prongs on the end there. Mind where they go, knew a lad once stuck one through his foot, died of lockjaw.' He grinned. 'Then you scoop it up, back smooth as you can, and swing it forwards, up and over into the coup cart. All in one movement, not farting about like you were. Here, try again.'

Sussex took the fork back gingerly. 'I suppose coup means muck?'

'Cow-shit, but your mother won't thank you for using good old English words like that.'

'I don't know.' Sussex sounded doubtful. 'I don't think she's ever called it anything. In fact, I'm not sure she knows it exists. She puts horse-droppings on her roses, though, or at least she tells the gardeners to. I think she calls them horsey-doos.'

'Does she now? No good for me, too full of seeds for my liking.' Coates grinned again. 'This cowsy-doos will do me on the back fields, if you ever get it shifted.' He nodded as Sussex threw another fork-full into the cart. 'That's better. We'll make a farmer of you yet.'

'I suppose it's all worth it, spreading it over the land? I'm not doing all this just to clear space for another load?'

'Worth its weight in gold, lad, full of goodness. Brings on the grass a treat, and anything else it goes on.'

'There was something in *The Times* about it. All to do with chemicals, nitrogen and potash and stuff.'

'Wouldn't know about that, but it works. Got to know what you're doing, mind. Not too little, not too much, mix in some well-rotted chicken shit if you like. Pig shit's good, too, if it's not full of maggots.'

Sussex blenched. 'There's a lot of things wriggling around in this.'

'Worst you'll catch is a dose of ringworm. Apple cider vinegar's a good cure, but I wouldn't tell your mother why you want it.'

Barnard Castle, 4.15pm

THERE were at least five pawnbrokers in the town, but Snowden knew which he wanted. Halfway along the Horse Market he turned into a narrow alley, promised a loitering urchin a penny if he kept an eye on Bucephalus, and walked into a dimly-lit shop.

'David Cohen?'

'At your service.' An elderly figure with a long white beard emerged from the back. 'How can I help?'

'Police. I wonder if you remember this?' Snowden handed over the watch.

Cohen's face grew wary as he examined it. 'Maybe.'

'Don't worry, I'm not here to get you into trouble. I just want to know who brought it in.'

'Your constable said it was stolen, I didn't know that.'

'That's all right, nobody's accusing you of anything.'

'Let me see.'

Cohen reached below the counter and produced a well-thumbed ledger. 'It would be a year ago, perhaps?' He flicked back the pages and ran his finger down the entries. 'June... July... yes, here, first week in August, Saturday the second. Pocket watch, gold casing, engraved initials H J.'

'H J? I thought it was B J.'

Cohen took the watch, found a magnifying glass and examined it. 'Hard to tell with this ornate script, all lines and flourishes. The start of the first letter's clear enough but the rest's worn away. It could be a B, I suppose, but E and F and H start much the same way. P and R, too. And the second letter's not much better. J is possible. Or an F, maybe.'

Snowden took the glass and watch, tried himself and gave a disappointed nod. 'I thought it was too good to be true. But it could be B J... Is it valuable?'

'I gave him eight shillings for it, redeemable within three months.'

'Him? You've got his name?'

'Said he was called Smith, that's what it says here.' He looked apologetic. 'Lot of them give a false name, all sorts of reasons. Husbands don't want wives to know they're pawning stuff to pay for their drinking, other way round sometimes, people ashamed the neighbours will know. It makes no difference to me, if they've not come back for whatever they've pawned within six months I can claim it for myself.'

'Which is what happened with the watch?'

'Never saw him again. Then your constable takes it and I'm eight shillings out of pocket.' He eyed the watch again. 'Do I get it back now?'

'It's evidence, but maybe when I've finished with it.' Snowden wasn't sure who it belonged to right now, the pawnbroker, the police, or the widow of the dead man, who-ever he was. 'This man who called himself Smith, can you remember what he looked like?'

Cohen's brow wrinkled. 'Young fellow, dark hair, nothing special. Only thing I remember is that he had marks on his face, as if he'd been in a fight.' He looked at Snowden uncertainly. 'I'll be honest with you, it wasn't the sort of watch I'd expect someone like that to own and I did wonder if he'd robbed someone of it.'

Snowden nodded. 'He had.'

Barnard Castle, 5.45pm

MARY Hall refilled her glass and pushed the gin bottle across the table. 'All I can say, Hannah Elliott, is that you're well shot of him.' Mary-Ann Dalkin and Margaret Walker, the two other visitors in Hannah Elliott's kitchen, nodded vigorously. 'I told you he was a bad 'un before you married him.'

'Didn't have much choice, did I? My Sarah was well on the way by then.' Hannah reached for the bottle. 'My father would've killed him if I hadn't. Me too, probably.'

'Pity there's another one on the way. When's it due?'

'Back end of the year sometime.' Hannah filled her glass. 'Well, there won't be any more after that.'

'You never know.' Mary-Ann gave her a sly glance. 'Plenty more men out there.'

'Not for me, there aren't. I'm done with them.'

'Well, you can have mine if you change your mind.' The others laughed.

'Reckon they'll do him for stealing all that stuff?' Margaret Walker looked dubious. 'Look after their own, the police.'

'That Reuben Clarke's all right, he'll throw the book at him. You should've seen his face when I emptied it all on his desk.'

'Give him everything you found, did you?'

'Everything.' Hannah paused. 'Except the money, of course, half a dozen sover-eigns there were. How d'you think I paid for this gin?'

Mary wagged a finger at her in mock reproach. 'Receiving stolen property, Hannah? You'll get locked up too if you're not careful.'

There was a crash from the yard outside and Hannah rose to look through the open window. 'Bloody kids.' She stuck her head out and shouted. 'Behave your bloody selves or you'll get no supper. And if you don't stop Albert crying like that, our Sarah, you'll feel the back of my hand.'

She began to shut the window and paused. 'There's another of those constables over the way, knocking on the Thompsons' door. Place is crawling with them.'

'Had one round our place earlier on.' Margaret finished her gin and reached for more. 'Asking a lot of questions about them drownings last year.'

'You didn't tell them anything?' Hannah closed the window and sat down.

'Well,' Margaret looked faintly guilty and lowered her voice. 'I wouldn't of done normally, but it seems there might be a reward going.'

'Reward?' The other three leant forward, suddenly interested.

'That's what they said. Well, not in so many words, but they were hinting like. It got me thinking about what we heard that night, the shrieks and that. You'll remember we talked about it, Mary?'

'Nothing special about people carrying on over the Sills, happens all the time.'

'All the same, it may be worth mentioning it to them if there's a few bob to be had. What do you think?'

'Worth a try.'

'Don't leave me out, girls.' Mary-Ann frowned. 'I heard something going on that night too. And what's more, I saw them next morning.'

'Saw who?'

'People over the river by the Sills wall.' She gave a shiver. 'Could've been murderers returning to the scene of their crime, haunted by guilt.'

'You've been reading too many Sunday newspapers, Mary-Ann Dalkin. Nobody's said that couple was murdered.'

'But if they was...' She looked at her companions for support. 'They wouldn't be going round asking all these questions if there wasn't more to it than just drownings. I think we should go and talk to your Sergeant Clarke, can't do any harm.'

Hannah stood up. 'Well, I don't know anything about it. But if you get a reward it'll buy us all plenty of gin for another day.' She reached into the cupboard behind her and produced a fresh bottle. 'Those sovereigns won't last long at this rate.'

Thorpe, 9.15pm

'SO where do we go from here?' Betsey lifted the ginger kitten gently off her chair and sat down in its place. 'You're still convinced the dead man was coming from the east?'

'I'm not sure I'm certain about anything at the moment.' Her father sighed. 'I've got three murdered people and no sure evidence who killed any of them. Discovering that my constables are filling their pockets with stolen goods doesn't help.'

'Only one of them, papa.'

'One too many.' He yawned. 'I was talking to Browne, the superintendent up at Bishop. He was impressed by your work on my files and wondered if you'd like to do the same sort of thing for him. We could share the results.'

'Perhaps. I'd rather be working for you, though.'

'And there was something else...' He hunted through his memory. '*Hue and Cry.*'

'Hugh and who?'

'Old title of the *Police Gazette*. There's a great pile of them at the police house, full of appeals about missing people. Might be worth having a look at last summer's editions.'

'I'll go over tomorrow and see. I'm not doing anything.'

'No exciting social events?' He gave her a sideways look. 'Or was Mrs Eeles' birthday enough for one week?'

'Quite enough.' She hoped he didn't notice the quiver in her voice at the memory.

For a moment she thought of pouring out her heart to him about William's fall from grace, but he had enough to worry about tonight without her problems as well. 'Come on, what you need is a good night's rest, things will look better in the morning. Up you go before you fall asleep in that chair.'

'You're probably right.' He pulled himself to his feet and gave her a wry smile. 'You usually are.'

Wednesday July 29ᵗʰ

Barnard Castle, 9.15am

McQUEEDIE walked warily into the *Gazette* office and sat down at his desk, an ancient table he'd moved in the day before from the mouse-infested room next-door. The top was covered in stains he didn't care to investigate and one leg was shorter than the rest, giving it a wobble that he'd tried to cure by sticking a book underneath, but it was the best he could do.

Fewster, poring over papers at the roll-top desk opposite, ignored his arrival. Mc-Queedie wasn't surprised. Their first day together had been spent in frosty silence and he suspected it would be some time before the anguish of missing out on almost five hundred pounds subsided. Still, he'd make an effort.

'Much on?'

'No.'

'Quiet, then?'

'Yes.'

'No news anywhere?'

'No.'

'Anything I can do?'

'Yes.'

'Ah, good, fire away.'

'Shut up.'

There was a long pause as McQueedie wondered what else to offer.

'Silly season, I suppose. Same every year, isn't it? Everybody who's anybody off on holiday, no meetings, courts empty, criminals sunning themselves instead of keeping us busy, no news anywhere.' There was no response. 'Just have to make it up as usual, eh?' He tried a chuckle which turned it into a cough when this fell flat, and gave up. 'Where's the diary?'

Fewster pointed at the floor without looking up.

'Ah, yes.' McQueedie eased it out from under the deficient table-leg and thumbed through its pages. They listed forthcoming events, times of meetings, names of con-tacts, and, if anyone ever remembered to enter them, notes of incidents that had made the news. He flicked through to July, found nothing of interest, and went on into August. It was blank.

He stood up and wandered across to the bookcase, a ramshackle structure that held long-forgotten minutes, out-of-date handbooks, reports that should have been returned to their owners months or even years before, unopened letters from readers, a battered trophy that had been awarded but never presented to the winners of the *Gazette*'s 1829 Cricket Tournament, half a ham sandwich so old that not even the mice had touched it, ragged folders marked 'Cuttings' containing aged brown snippings from the paper in no discernible order, and, what he was looking for, a row of old diaries. He found last year's and sat down with it.

August 1845, his first month on the paper. He'd been keen enough to start with to keep a meticulous note of what was going on, and he found his first entry, the lad who blew his arm off at Wycliffe. Then there was the inquest on that young tailor they found in the river. There'd been another drowning not long after, a girl, and some rumours about a suicide pact which, he recalled painfully, had been largely of his own making and meant he was still probably not welcome in the Oddfellows.

He closed the diary and stood up purposefully. ONE YEAR LATER – POLICE STILL BAFFLED BY DOUBLE DEATH MYSTERY. DID LOVERS LEAP TOGETHER? Perfect for the silly season.

'Just going out,' he announced. There was no reply, and he set off. First stop the Oddfellows. With luck the barmaid – what was her name? Elsie? Edna? something like that – would have forgotten about it by now, and anyway that was in the days when he was Hamish and she could hardly blame the newly-arrived Angus for the sins of his brother. There was only one way to find out, and he fancied an early pint.

Barnard Castle, 9.40am

SNOWDEN couldn't recall the last time he'd slept beyond seven o'clock and felt curiously guilty as he walked into the Briggate police house. He was greeted by a cacophony of female voices aimed at the constable behind the desk.

'Never here when you want them.'

'Always the same.'

'Probably out robbing pawnbrokers.'

'Ee, Mary-Ann, d'you think so?'

'When's he coming back, then?'

'Don't trust any of them, knew this was a waste of time.'

'You tell him, Margaret.'

Snowden took a deep breath and stepped forward to rescue the hapless constable. 'Can I help you, ladies?'

Three red-faced matrons turned as one to face him, followed by a faint wave of gin. 'Who are you, then?'

'Proper policeman, look at his hat.'

'Sir Robert bloody Peel, that's who he is.'

'Show us your truncheon, big boy.'

'Ee, Mary-Ann, you are a one.'

'Where's Sergeant Clarke, then?'

Snowden recoiled slightly. 'I'm sure the sergeant will be back soon. But I'm his superintendent. What's this all about?'

All three started to talk and he held up a hand. 'One at a time, please. You first. Name?'

'Walker, Mrs Walker.'

'First name?'

'Ee, Margaret, he fancies you.'

Snowden had had enough. 'Constable, take these two and make them a cup of tea. Mrs Walker, follow me. I'll talk to the others in a minute.'

He led her into one of the cells. 'Not very comfortable, I'm afraid, but it'll have to do. Now, what do you want to tell the sergeant?'

Mrs Walker perched herself on the stone bench. 'It's about the reward.'

'What reward?'

'For the drownings. I heard them shrieking, awful it was.'

There was a knock on the cell door.

'Sorry about this, sir, had to sort something out down the street. A domestic,' Sergeant Clarke nodded at the woman on the bench. 'Morning, Margaret. You in trouble?'

She bridled. 'Certainly not. I'm a witness, and if you'd been here when you should be you'd know why.'

'Well, as you're here now, perhaps you could join us, sergeant?' Snowden invited him to sit beside the woman, who shifted as far away as possible. 'Got your notebook? Good, you can run up a statement from her to sign when I've finished. And from the other two you saw waiting,'

'Yes, sir.'

'Now, Mrs Walker, tell me what you know. You live in Briggate, I presume?'

'Just up the street, in the middle, in one of the houses facing the water.'

'On your own?'

'Since my husband died two years back. There's just the one room, all I need at my age.'

Snowden guessed she was in her mid-fifties. 'And you think you heard something the night Joseph Yates disappeared?'

'I don't think so, Mr Snowden, I know I did. Nothing wrong with my hearing.'

'I'm sure there isn't. So what did you hear?'

'Well, I was up late that night, it would be after one o'clock and I couldn't sleep. There was this awful shrieking from across the river, three shrieks there were, and I thought they came from the middle of the Sills. So I opened the window and looked out.'

'And what did you see?'

'Nothing. It was wet and windy, really dark, and the water was very rough.'

'So you just heard the shrieks?'

'Yes.'

'A man or a woman?'

'I took it to be a woman. But then all of a sudden, it must have been a quarter of an hour later, there was a man's voice, he gave this cry, oh dear, oh dear, oh dear, just like that, he sounded like he was choking.'

'And?'

'Nothing else. I listened on for a while but I heard nothing else and I went to bed. Hardly slept all night, never do.'

'It's not unusual to hear people shouting and screaming over the river, though, is it? A lot go over there, I'm told.'

'Goes on all the time, disgraceful what they get up to. I've heard shrieks many a time, but never so awful as they were that night.'

'But you didn't mention it to anyone? A constable, perhaps?'

'No.' Mrs Walker became defensive. 'Like I say, it goes on all the time, your lot don't do anything about it. But I did speak to Mary Hall next-door in the morning, and she'd heard it too. She'll tell you, she's here.'

'So what's prompted you to come forward now, a year later?'

'Well, you know...' She hesitated. 'I could do with the money. The reward. How much do I get?'

Snowden shook his head. 'Nothing just yet, Mrs Walker. But if we need you as a witness I'm sure there will be something.'

A worried frown crossed her face. 'Witness?'

'In court, if necessary. But at the moment we're just making inquiries and you've been very helpful. Put her on the list, sergeant.'

'List, sir?'

'For the rewards.'

'Ah, yes, sir, the list.'

Mrs Walker's face brightened. 'Is that all?'

'For now. Perhaps you'd like to get a cup of tea and ask Mrs Hall to come in to see me?'

She left, looking pleased.

'Very helpful, sir?' Clarke turned to a new page in his notebook.

'Just confirming what I'd already been told. Not exactly here out of public duty, was she?' Snowden gave a resigned smile. 'It's amazing what money can do.'

'Do you really want a list, sir?'

'Might as well, it'll encourage the others.'

Mrs Hall came in, a short wispy-haired women some years younger than her neighbour.

'Margaret's told you about the shrieks, then?' She sat down and stared around. 'Never been in one of these before. Not very cosy, is it?' Her eyes fixed on the bucket in the corner. 'Where do you put the women?'

'In here if we have to.'

'With the men?'

'If necessary.'

'Bloody hell.' She tapped the stone slab beside her. 'Wouldn't fancy any how's-your-father on this bed.'

'The shrieks, Mrs Hall. I'm told you heard them too.'

'That's right. Loud and shrill they were, from over the river. And the man.'

'Calling out?'

'Oh dear, he kept saying, oh dear me, and then his voice got weaker and weaker. I was working by the window, I had the candle burning and I looked out but I couldn't see anything.'

'Working?'

'I'm a milliner, sewing a bonnet as I recall. Poor Joe, do you think it was him we heard?'

'Possibly. Did you know him?'

'Seen him from time to time. He was only small, you know, gentle sort of man with a very soft voice.'

'It wasn't him shrieking, then?'

'Don't think so, that was more like a woman's voice. And really loud, I could hear it over the noise of the river. Rushing down, it was.'

'And you talked about it with Mrs Walker next day?'

'That's right.'

'And you both heard the same thing?'

'Like I told you.'

'Thank you. Who's the third person out there?'

'Mary-Ann, Mrs Dalkin.'

'Send her in. And wait with Mrs Walker until I've finished.'

'What about –'

'The reward?'

She nodded hopefully.

'You're on the list.'

She left happily and was replaced her a few moments later by a tall woman, in her sixties, Snowden judged, with a bony nose and thin lips beneath a flowered headscarf.

'On the list, am I?'

'Of course, Mrs Dalkin.'

'I should hope so.' She parked herself gingerly on the slab and sniffed. 'What's in that bucket?'

'Nothing.'

'Must be the sergeant, then.'

Snowden tried to keep a straight face. 'We won't keep you long, Mrs Dalkin. You heard the screams as well, I take it?'

'Of course I did. And what's more, I saw them.'

'The person screaming?'

'Not then, next morning. There were three of them on the Sills looked like they were searching for something. Moving about and looking over the wall into the water. They must have been there for an hour.'

'Men or women?'

'Men, I think, Young men.'

'Any idea who they were?'

'I don't know, couldn't make them out. My eyes aren't so good these days.'

'So they could have been anybody? There must be lots of people walking along there on a Sunday morning.'

'Well, yes.'

'Hmm.' Snowden regarded her doubtfully. That old woman in Startforth, the one on whose doorstep Bucephalus had disgraced himself, had said there were other people around when she'd found the pool of blood by the wall. Perhaps he should have another word with her. 'Well, thank you, Mrs Dalkin. You and the other two ladies can go now. If any of you know anyone else who might be able to help us, tell them to get in touch.'

'Go on the list, will they?'

He nodded. 'Plenty for everybody.'

'We'll pass the word around.' She turned to Clarke. 'You make sure my name's on that list, sergeant. And change your socks before you come round with the money.'

Barnard Castle, 10.20am

ELIZA gave the spittoon a final polish and put it back by the Oddfellows grate. She knew exactly where it went, in the perfect circle of clean hearth surrounded by years of stains from near-misses.

The door opened, first visitor of the day.

'Morning, Edith.'

She turned round and her mouth fell open. 'You've got a bloody nerve coming back in here.' She reached for the spittoon, decided it would be a pity to throw it at him after all that polishing, and looked for something else.

'Wait!' McQueedie held up a protective arm. 'It's not me, I'm his twin brother.'

'Brother?' She looked at him in disbelief, ash-tray in hand.

'Angus. Come to offer my apologies, better late than never, eh?' He moved cautiously forwards. 'Terrible things Hamish wrote about you, wasn't right in his head, you know, poor fellow. Better off where he is now.'

'And where's that?' She put the ash-tray back on its table and approached him suspiciously.

'Dead, alas. All too much for him, Ena.'

'You look exactly like him. And it's Elsie.'

'Ah, yes, Elsie, he told me all about you on his death-bed. Lovely woman, he said.'

'Peas in a bloody pod.'

'Except for the ears, you must remember his ears. Big flapping things. Juggles they called him, poor soul.'

'Not what I called him, the lying bugger. Made me a laughing stock. I hope he suffered.'

'Oh, he did, terribly. Racked with remorse, a happy release in the end.'

'Yes, well. Come to apologise, you said?'

McQueedie gave an inward sigh of relief. 'The least I could do. Buy you a drink?'

'Suppose so. He got sacked from the paper, didn't he?'

'Indeed, indeed. I've taken his job.'

She poured herself a large gin and looked at him expectantly.

'Glenbuckie's is it for you?'

He wondered if it was a trap and reluctantly shook his head. 'Never touch it. A beer will do.' She seemed convinced and poured him a pint of Crabthorpe's which he sipped with forced enthusiasm.

'Ninepence.'

'Of course.' He put a shilling on the counter, told her to keep the change and hoped his story was worth it. 'Must be a year now since Hamish was in, I suppose. Never sorted all that out, did they?'

'The drownings? Not that I know of.'

'Still think it was suicide, do they, people round here? ONE YEAR ON, TOWN MOURNS

LOST LOVERS, that sort of thing?'

'I wouldn't know about that.' She gave him a warning look. 'Not going to put me in the *Gazette* again, are you?'

'Wouldn't dream of it. Strictly off the record, no names.'

'Nothing to tell anyway. Nobody's mentioned it for months.'

'Perfect.' He took another mouthful. HEARTLESS TOWN FORGETS DROWNED DUO AS PITILESS POLICE ABANDON SEARCH FOR TRUTH. 'Just perfect.'

'You feeling all right? Not many people say that about our beer.'

He forced the rest of it down and decided not to push his luck too far. 'Well, must be off. Nice to see you again.'

'Again?' She looked at him closely. 'What d'you mean, again?'

He battled for an answer. 'It will be, I mean. When I come back. Nice to see you.'

She was staring thoughtfully after him as he went out of the door, stepping aside to let three young men enter. One came to the bar and ordered a pint apiece.

'What's up, then, Elsie, seen a ghost?'

'I'm not sure. Him who just went out, he was asking about the drownings last summer.'

'Well, he wasn't Joe Yates come back from the dead, that's for sure.' The others laughed. 'What was he, a copper? They're all over the place asking questions. My mam says they were at her door yesterday. '

'About the drownings?'

'Right.' He downed half his pint. 'They think it was murder.'

'Never.'

'God's truth, both of them, Yates and the girl. Mate of mine who works up Stanhope way is back in town and says they arrested someone up there the other day for it, Geordie Barker. He saw it happen.'

'Little Geordie?'

'Hauled him off at five in the morning, my mate says. Bound to be in the *Gazette* on Saturday.'

Eliza smiled. 'I wouldn't put money on it.'

Halfway up The Bank on his way back to the office, McQueedie dived into the Three Tuns to avoid coming face to face with Simon Bycroft, to whom he had yet to explain that he'd lost the borrowed wig. He ordered a large Glenbuckie's to wash away the taste of the Oddfellows' beer, dug out his notebook and settled down in the back bar to compose his scoop.

A year has passed since broken-hearted lovers Joshua Yates and Kate Paine leapt to their deaths in the foaming Tees, little knowing that they would so soon be shamefully forgotten by the callous citizens they left behind.

Yes, that would do nicely. Our Teesdale Correspondent was back in business.

Barningham, 11.45am

'NOT another Victoria Sponge?' Sarah Carter, the eldest of widowed Tommy Carter's two unmarried daughters who ran the village shop, stared at the rector, perplexed. 'I don't know what you do with them. That's four since Monday.'

'Oh, they're not for me.' Wharton gave an apologetic smile. 'It's Ermintrude. She loves them.'

'You've giving them to *pigs?*'

'Not just any pig.' Wharton sounded hurt. 'She's a prize-winner. Put on at least six pounds since I discovered she had a sweet tooth, right back on her food. It's wonderful.'

'Well, I don't know what the Queen would think about it, her favourite cakes going to waste like that.'

'Oh, it's not wasted, I assure you. And I don't suppose her majesty follows the gastronomic habits of her porcine subjects.'

'I'm sorry?' She shook her head in baffled amusement. 'You do talk funny sometimes, rector. Well, if you keep paying for them, I'll keep making them, whoever they're for. Same again tomorrow?'

'If you'd be so kind. And please don't mention it to my housekeeper. She thinks it's all down to her fruit cake, but Ermintrude seems to like a choice.'

'You've got poor Mrs Middleton baking for you as well?'

'I tell her I eat most of it and just give Ermintrude the crumbs.'

The bell over the door jangled and Sussex walked in. ,

'Afternoon, reverend. Having a tea-party?'

'With his pigs.' Sarah laughed. 'Silver service in the sty at Glebe Farm next, I wouldn't wonder. Go on, tell me you want an Osborne Pudding for one of your cows.' She looked Sussex up and down. 'Don't go near any of my food in that state.'

'Still mucking out, I'm afraid. Did you say pigs?'

'Just the one.' Wharton tried to keep sinful pride from his voice. 'She wins at shows, you know, got to keep her fattened up.'

'What d'you do with all the muck?'

'Muck?'

'Pig-muck. Coates says it's good added to cow...' he paused, slightly embarrassed in front of the girl. 'Cow-coup, he calls it.'

'Shovel it out, heaps of it behind the byres. Do you want some?'

'Maybe. I was thinking about doing some experiments, different mixtures on a spare bit of ground, see which works best.'

'Interested in agriculture, are you?' Wharton's eyes lit up with enthusiasm. 'You can have as much as you like, I'd be most interested in the results. How do you spread it around?'

'Throw it out from the cart, I suppose. We haven't got that far yet.'

'I've got an idea for a mechanical spreader you might like to see. Based on my undulating drill harrow, you know. If you've got a moment I could show you.'

'Well, I've got half an hour for lunch.' Sussex nodded. 'I'll just get a pie from Sarah and come with you.'

'Mutton or pork?' She held up a couple to choose from.

'Pork, I think.'

Wharton winced.

Barnard Castle, 12.05pm

McQUEEDIE swallowed the last drops of his fourth Glenbuckie's, made his way unevenly to the door and blinked in the sunshine.

It was a beautiful day and he wasn't going to waste it arguing with Fewster about the merits of his story. The man would probably claim all the credit himself, anyway. No, he'd take a gentle walk along the river to Greta Bridge and hand it over to the stage to deliver to York. Maybe call into the Morritt's Arms while he waited for it to arrive.

He crossed the road, turned right at the Butter Market and set off towards the Abbey Bridge.

Barningham, 12.13pm

'SO with the floor on the cart sloping backwards like this, the muck will fall down onto these sort of propellers at the back, turning round of course – the speed depending on the gearing to the wheels axle – and out it would come, left, right and behind depending on the angle of the propellers.' Wharton put down his pencil. 'You'd cover a lot more area each run up and down the field and much faster than throwing it out with a spade.'

Sussex nodded, intrigued. 'It could work.'

'Oh, it would. The same sort of principle as the drill. I could build a prototype if you were interested.'

'I'll help.' The church clock struck the quarter-hour as he spoke. 'I'm going to be late back, I'll have to go.'

'Good heavens, so must I. I'm due in court at one and I need to change.' Wharton ushered Sussex to the door. 'I don't suppose you fancy coming to the agricultural show on Saturday? It's full of quite fascinating implements and Ermintrude will be there, of course.' He hesitated. 'And I'd rather welcome a companion.'

'Going alone?'

'Well, no, actually. The truth is, I'd agreed to take Miss Snowden and now it seems another young lady is joining us. I'm not sure quite how it happened but she just said she was coming and I couldn't say no. She'll have a chaperone, but it's all a bit difficult.' He looked at Sussex appealingly. 'I'm really not very good at this sort of thing.'

'A chaperone? Old aunt or somebody, I suppose? Sorry, I don't think I'll be available.'

'No, no, it's another young lady. I thought you might be able to entertain them all while I was busy with Ermintrude.'

Sussex beamed. 'Three of them? Young ladies?'

'It would be terribly good of you.'

'I'd be delighted.'

Thorpe, 12.50pm

SNOWDEN strode into his office with only ten minutes to spare before the magistrates returned to court. He hadn't been needed for the morning session, a lengthy succession of routine applications from publicans, hackney cab owners, funeral directors and public entertainers seeking licence renewals and extensions, and this was the first time he'd had an opportunity to see what lay ahead. He picked up the paperwork and scanned the list of cases scheduled for the afternoon.

They looked fairly straightforward. Robert Marwood, landlord of a pub in Gayles and probably related in some way to Tom at the Oddfellows, had been caught selling liquor at two o'clock on Sunday morning. Two sisters called Lee were accused of keeping a 'most disreputable house' in Newsham. Thomas Wilkinson, another defendant from Gayles, was charged with assault and battery upon Sarah Hutchinson, which Snowden thought might be serious until he noticed both were in their late seventies. He scanned the accompanying notes. The assault and battery consisted of Wilkinson throwing a bucket of water over his next-door neighbour during a dispute over her cat digging up his leeks, and Snowden sighed. They'd probably both be bound over to keep the peace.

What else was there? Daniel Dixon of Cotherstone, wilful damage to a fence, five-shilling fine maybe. William and Mary Middleton of Brignall, jointly charged with breaching the peace. A domestic row, another binding-over. Mary Raper, innkeeper's wife of Startforth, accused of –

Mary Raper? Wasn't she the landlady he'd met in the White Swan? He read on. Accused of assaulting her servant Sarah Bussy. He bundled the papers together and wondered what all that was about as he made his way to the courtroom.

He reached the door just as Wharton arrived, pink-faced and looking as if he'd run the last half-mile. 'Not late, am I? Got rather involved and didn't notice the time.' He stopped to gather his breath and straighten his cravat. 'How is Miss Betsey?'

'Very well, I believe. I haven't seen her today, she was out before I woke up.'

'Ah. I just wondered if she might be away. She said last week she'd see me at evensong last night but there was no sign of her. It's very odd. Do you think you could give her a message?'

'Of course.'

'We agreed to go to the show together this weekend and I thought she'd like to know I'm bringing a couple of other girls about her age. I'm hoping Sussex Milbank joins us. It'll give her some company while I'm involved with Ermintrude – it's her big day, you know – and I'm sure they'll all get on well together.'

Greta Bridge, 1.50pm

McQUEEDIE made it in plenty of time, sneaking over the Abbey Bridge when the toll-keeper wasn't looking, across the fields to the Street and down the slope to the Morritt's Arms. Just the one drink before the coach was due, he promised himself. It would be so easy to have more than that, fall asleep and miss it, the sort of thing Hamish would have done. But Angus, he told himself, was made of stronger stuff.

'Large one, is it?' The barmaid, a healthy-looking woman he'd never seen before who looked capable of shifting barrels with one hand while carrying a crate of ale in her other, reached for the Glenbuckie's. He nodded. Just the one, he'd vowed, but it might as well be a good one.

'Here for the stage, are you?'

'That's right.' They were the only ones in the room. 'Nobody else around?'

'Quiet as the grave.' She handed him his drink. 'Never many taking the stage these days, not with all these railways opening up. Runs empty some days, can't be long before they give up.'

'Not good for trade, I imagine.'

'Put us out of business, I wouldn't be surprised. Hard to imagine, no stages arriving day and night. Another one?'

McQueedie looked at his empty glass in surprise. It was tempting, but a vow was a vow and the Angus in him stood firm. 'No, thanks.' To prove it, he'd go and wait outside away from temptation.

He walked round to the rear of the inn and leant over a stone wall. The field beyond rose to a flat grassy plateau, the site, he'd read somewhere, of a Roman fort. There was time for him to have a quick look at it. He'd once earned a week's worth of Glenbuckie's by selling stories about hidden treasure in a castle near Kirkcudbright, and all it had taken was burying a single well-worn coin where it was bound to be discovered. He might try it again round here.

He found a small gate in the wall, walked up the slope and was disappointed to find the flat grassy plateau was no more than that. No foundations, half-buried statues or Latin inscriptions, just grass and a few sheep munching away in the sunshine. He wandered across to a stunted hawthorn tree and sat down. The sun was shining, birds were warbling happily above the drone of a thousand insects, and all was well with the world. His eyes drooped.

Ten seconds later something stung him viciously and very painfully on the back of his neck.

A millisecond later a dozen more joined in.

By the time he had leapt to his feet there were hundreds of them. The distant drone of insects was an angry hum, the sky was filled with diving attackers, his hair was alive with them and every inch of his body, it seemed, was being targeted with agonising accuracy. He fled down the field, screaming in pain and terror, his arms flailing madly in a vain attempt to ward them off, shot through the gate, tripped and did a double somersault through a flowerbed, cracked his head against a gatepost and hurtled into the bar, slamming the door behind him. A dozen or so miniature assailants who had made it inside with him buzzed furiously around his ears as he dived below the settle, cracked his head again on the wall and lay there waiting to die.

'Anybody there?' The well-built barmaid came into the bar, swatted a lone wasp crawling along the counter, and went in search of more. Halfway round the room she came across McQueedie's left foot.

'You can't sleep it off there, whoever you are. Out you get.'

McQueedie tried to say something. His sting-filled lips had swollen to twice their size, his throat felt as if he'd swallowed at least a million of the things, and all he could manage was a faint whimper of utter despair.

'Come on, or I'll pull you out.' She bent down to investigate. 'Bloody hell.'

She dragged him out into the middle of the room and he lay there while she summoned help. By the time he'd regained enough consciousness to open his eyes he was surrounded by half a dozen figures offering advice.

'Get a blue bag from the laundryroom, rub it all over him.'

'Ammonia, my mother always said.'

'Onions is the only thing that'll stop the stinging.'

'Or was it baking soda?'

'Knew a man in Scunthorpe died of wasp stings.'

'Anyone smoke a pipe? Old dottle's supposed to work.'

'My old granny swore by rhubarb.'

'Leeks might do.'

'Poppy leaves, any in the garden?'

'Or was it Grimsby?'

'What about garlic?'

'Shot of brandy might help.'

'Think we should get a doctor?'

McQueedie shook his head, flinching with the pain, and did his best to speak. What he needed was the brandy, not a doctor. 'Go gogtor, grangy.'

'Delirious, poor fellow.'

The barmaid elbowed her way to the front and held out a purple bottle. 'This is the stuff. Old Mother Agnes' Universal Elixir.'

'Is it any good, Martha?'

'Works a treat on my mam's varicose veins and Uncle Jim's piles.' She peered at the label. 'Guaranteed remedy for constipation, ladies' problems, sore throats, weevil infections, lugworm, thinning of the blood, consumption, chronic diarrhoea, baldness, liver fluke and toothache. It must do wasp stings.'

'Worth a try, give him a spoonful.'

'Needs more than a spoonful, give him the bottle.'

McQueedie recoiled as the bottle approached his swollen lips. It smelt terrible.

'Come on, be a good boy.' Martha fixed him with a steely eye. 'Good for you. Then we'll try the brandy.' She forced the bottle into his mouth and poured. He swallowed, rolled his eyes and began to pray.

'There we are, soon be better. Pass the brandy, someone.'

She poured a large measure into a glass and handed it to him. 'Get that down you and you'll soon feel different.'

He drank it eagerly and she was right. He did feel very different. Something remarkable was going on inside him and his brain began to swirl as the conversation continued above him.

'Good stuff, that Elixir. Bottle's empty, look.'

'What else does it do?'

Very, very different. The room was beginning to spin in multi-coloured circles.

'Goes on and on. Heart disease, flat feet, bunions, insomnia. That's handy if you can't sleep at nights.'

Very, very, very different. Spinning very, very fast.

'Adult dose, half a teaspoonful twice a day. Not to be taken with alcohol, can cause drowsiness or unconsciousness.'

The room disappeared in a rainbow vortex and McQueedie passed out.

'What are we going to do with him?'

'Well, he can't stay here. This is a hotel, not a hospital.'

'Where's he from?'

'No idea. Just turned up and said he was waiting for a coach. Have a look in his jacket pocket, see if he's got a ticket.'

'There's an envelope here.'

'Who's it for?'

'Just says *Gazette – Urgent.*'

'Must be delivering it. Ask the coachman, it's just arrived. He might know.'

'Let's get this fellow outside into the fresh air.'

'Good idea. Look out for wasps.'

McQueedie's comatose body was carried out to the front of the inn.

'Coachman says he knows the *Gazette* office. He could drop him off nearby.'

'Better than nothing.'

'Has he got any money for the ticket?'

'Try his trouser pockets.'

'You look, Martha, you're a married woman.'

'Half a crown and two halfpennies.'

'See what the coachman says. Stage is empty, tell him two and seven's better than nothing.'

'Come on, let's load him in.'

Thorpe, 3.15pm

'MUCH more to come, Mr Snowden?' Morritt was getting impatient.

'One more case, your worships. Sarah Bussy, servant girl, alleges assault by her employer, Mrs Mary Raper, landlady of the White Swan in Startforth.'

'Both parties present?'

'The girl is waiting outside, I believe, but no sign yet of the defendant.'

Morritt grunted. 'Can't hang around waiting for her. Let's hear the girl first.'

Bussy, a sullen-looking girl of about eighteen in an ill-fitting cloak, was led into the witness box and sworn in.

'You're under oath, so you'd better tell the truth.' Morritt glared at her. 'You claim Mrs Raper assaulted you, is that right?'

'Slapped me hard, she did. Twice.'

'Where?'

'In the kitchen, by the table.'

'No, no.' Morritt shook his head irritably. 'Where on your body, girl?'

'Oh, across the face, once each side. It bloody hurt.'

'And why was that?'

'Because she slapped me, I told you. Came up in a big bruise later, I looked a right sight.'

Morritt gritted his teeth. 'I mean, why did she slap you?'

'Given in my notice, hadn't I?'

'I'm asking the questions here, Miss Bussy, not you. Then what happened?'

'Well, I wasn't stopping there to be knocked about by that old witch. I went and found a constable, put in a complaint.'

'Anything else?'

'She owes me four days' wages. That's nearly three shillings. It's robbery, that is, she wants locking up.'

'That's for us to decide. Where's the landlady got to?'

Mrs Raper walked in as he spoke, looking almost as annoyed as Morritt. 'Sorry I'm late. Had a job clearing customers out of the pub.' She was led to the dock, looked round and saw the girl. 'Costing me a fortune in lost trade, she is. Should be her standing here, not me.'

The charge was read out and she gave a firm plea of not guilty. Snowden stepped in hastily before Morritt had a chance to start questioning her.

'You employed Miss Bussy as a servant, is that right?'

'More's the pity. Took her on in May, no use from the day she started. Then last Thursday she comes in two hours late, says she's got a job at that new mill in Thorngate starting straight away, and wants her wages. Well, I told her she'd stay and work out her notice, not leave me shorthanded, and she wasn't getting paid till she did.'

'And?'

'Well, she started swearing, saying things I'll not repeat before you gentlemen, shocking it was. She went on and on about wanting her money, hysterical, I'd call it. So I slapped her face a couple of times to bring her to her senses.'

Morritt pounced. 'You admit the assault?'

'You'd have done the same, anyone would.'

'I think we've heard enough. What do you say, Wharton?' His companion on the bench opened his mouth but too late. 'Agreed, case proved. Gross provocation, mitigating circumstances, no penalty, don't do it again.'

'What about my bloody wages?' The girl stood up at the back. 'Call yourselves magistrates, you're no better than she is.'

'Judgement of one shilling in favour of Miss Bussy.' Morritt smiled at her icily. 'And she'll pay a shilling fine for contempt. Two shillings if she says another word. Court adjourned.'

Snowden followed him and Wharton into the magistrates' room. 'There was one other thing, your worships.' He laid a form on the desk and pushed the pen and ink bottle across. 'If you could just sign this, the pair of you?'

'What is it, more expenses?'

'Exhumation order. I want to dig up a body.'

Greta Bridge, 3.45pm

'THERE'S more here.' Constable Daniel Craven added an armful of newspapers to the pile on the police house desk. 'I think that's the lot.'

Betsey sighed. Searching through the back issues of the *Police Gazette* was taking much longer than she'd expected.

Craven pulled up a chair beside her. 'I'll give you a hand if you like. What are we looking for?'

She gave him a grateful smile. 'A man who disappeared last summer, first name probably beginning with J though it might be B. Or neither, if he was getting it for someone else.'

Craven looked blank. 'Getting what?'

'A proddy mat. And he must be from somewhere fairly near because he didn't have any luggage and he wouldn't order it if he had to make a long journey back to collect it.

It's very complicated.' She gestured at the notebook in front of her. 'I'd had no idea so many people went missing. Why do they do it?'

'Running away from us, a lot of them.' Craven grinned. 'Then there'll be those fleeing debt, husbands running away from wives, absconding apprentices, lads being press-ganged into the navy, jobless people looking for work... must be far more than we know about, not all of them leave anybody behind bothered enough to go looking for them or tell the police.'

Bestey looked dispirited. 'You're saying this is a waste of time?'

'We might be lucky. What did this one do, the one we're looking for?'

'He got himself murdered in Whashton.'

Craven's eyebrows rose. 'I heard about that. How far have you got?''

'I'm halfway through the missing people notices. Then I thought I'd do the Hue and Cries – you know, those who are on the run from the police.'

'I'll make a start on those. Fancy a cup of tea?'

Thorpe 3.55pm

MARY Raper was waiting for Snowden when he emerged from the courtroom and accosted him indignantly. 'Disgraceful, I call it. If you can't slap a foul-mouthed servant to bring her to her senses I don't know what the world's coming to.'

Snowden tried to look sympathetic. 'I assure you I knew nothing about it until this afternoon. I've been too tied up chasing suspicious deaths to keep an eye on some of the more petty offences.'

Her umbrage gave way to curiosity. 'Deaths? Navvies been fighting each other down Briggate again, have they?'

'Probably, but they haven't managed to kill anyone recently that I know of. No, I'm still trying to get to the bottom of those drownings last year – you'll remember we talked about it at the time.'

'Oh, that.' She looked disappointed. 'I heard your lads were going round asking questions again. There was talk of it in the pub the other night. A reward, they said, for new information.'

'Perhaps.' Snowden eyed her cautiously. 'Any of your customers think they might have some?'

'Plenty said they'd been around that night, but they'll say anything if there's money to be had. You'd think they'd all seen them.'

'Them?'

'The lad and the girl and whoever was with them, I don't know. You should ask them.'

'I might. Who are we talking about?'

She gave him a calculating look. 'Does this count as new information?'

Snowden sighed. 'I suppose it might.' He took out his notebook. 'Give me some names and we'll see.'

Greta Bridge, 4.15pm

'BEST thing you could do, sending him off in the stage.' John Ward, landlord of the Morritt's Arms, pondered the story his barmaid had just related. 'I'd have done the same if I'd been here. Scotsman, you said?'

'Sounded like it. On his way home, I suppose.'

'And drunk, I suppose?'

Martha wondered whether to mention the Universal Elixir and decided it might be unwise. 'Oh yes, sir, very. That and the wasp stings, he was out like a light.'

Ward helped himself to a large brandy and picked up the day's *Morning Post* lying on the bar. There was an envelope underneath. 'Gazette – Urgent? What's this doing here?'

She stared at it in dismay. 'Oh, lord! I took it out of that Scotsman's pocket and never put it back. D'you think it's important?'

Ward shrugged. 'Give it to the boot boy – he's going into Barney later to collect some shoes for me. He can put it through the *Gazette* door.'

Thorpe, 6.40pm

'THAT'S about it.' Snowden led Anthony Coulthard from the courtroom. 'It's not ideal – it would be better if this place was next to the police house up the road in Greta Bridge – but it works fairly well. There's usually a couple of constables on duty along there and of course there's always one or two here when the court's in session to handle prisoners transferred across to the holding cell you've just seen.'

'Still relying on the stage for post, I suppose?'

'It'll be a while before the railways get to this part of the world, but it'll happen. I read in the *Gazette* last week that they've linked it all the way from London to New-castle now.'

Snowden opened the door to his office and Coulthard surveyed the room approving-ly. 'Plenty of space to work in. It'll make a nice change from Durham, we're crammed in like sardines up there.'

'I'll get a desk sorted out for you in here. You'll probably divide your time between this place and the police house, which should keep you fit going back and forth.'

Coulthard grinned. 'Ann will approve of that. She reckons I'm getting far too lazy these days and could do with losing a few pounds.'

Snowden eyed him up and down. Nearly six foot tall with dark hair receding a bit, perhaps a mite heavier than when they'd last met but still as muscular as ever and look-ing fit in his mid-thirties. 'You'll do. Come and meet Betsey. She's grown up a bit since you last saw her.' They went across the hall to the kitchen and found her busy at the range. 'Remember Anthony Coulthard?'

'Of course.' She greeted him warmly. 'We met at your wedding in Barney, five years ago, was it? How's Ann?'

'Very well. Just the pair of us still, of course.'

Betsey nodded understandingly. His bride had been a striking-looking woman some ten years older than him and it was no great surprise that they'd had no children. 'She's happy with the cottage? It has been empty for a while.'

'Very handy, couple of doors from the police house. We'll soon get it into shape.' Coulthard glanced at the clock above the range. 'I'd better be on my way back, she'll have our meal ready.'

He bade his farewells, promised Snowden he'd be in first thing next Monday morning, and left.

'You're glad he's joining you.' Betsey sounded pleased as she produced a leg of mutton for him to carve. 'I like him.'

'Very glad. He's a good man, and I could do with more help, especially if you're off to York next year. I've been lucky to get him, Betsey. Durham were about to promote him when the post here came up and I asked if he'd like to join me.'

'He's still a constable, then?'

'For the moment. But if he does as well as I expect, I'll be pressing for him to be made up to sergeant. Assistant superintendent in time, maybe.'

Betsey added vegetables to the table and joined him to eat. 'I take it you've had a busy day today?'

'Three women who say they know something about the drownings case. I've got just about every law enforcement officer in the north looking out for Thomas Raine, wherever he might be.' He told her about meeting Mrs Raper in court. 'After that, I was showing Anthony around. Not enough time in the day, and tomorrow will be the same. I've got another list of possible witnesses lined up for interview in the morning – and a body being dug up.'

'The Whashton man?'

'No, I want to have a look at what's left of Yates. Our man from the tunnel is still lying in O'Neill's morgue as far as I know, and heaven knows what state he'll be in by the time they get round to burying him if this weather continues.' He helped himself to food. 'We don't even know who he is yet.'

'Well, I might have some news about that.' She leant forward, pausing for effect. 'We think we might have found him.'

Snowden's fork stopped halfway to his mouth. 'We?'

'Constable Craven's been giving me a hand.'

'Really?' He raised an eyebrow. 'And what have you two discovered?'

'I went all through the missing persons and he did the hue and cries. There were lots of names but none that seemed to fit the person we were after and I was just about to give up when he came across this.' She reached for her notebook lying at the far end of the table and opened it. 'In the *Police Gazette* Wednesday August the thirteenth last year. I made a copy.' She handed it across.

'*Five Pounds Reward,*' Snowden read. '*Any Person furnishing information leading to the Apprehension & Conviction for Theft & Fraudulent Dealing of one Henry Franklin of London or thereabouts, some forty years of age, clean-shaven and of fair complexion, who on 29th July hired a chestnut and grey switch-tailed roan mare, about fourteen hands high, the mane plaited and leaded, together with valuable leather saddle and accompaniments, from the Station Hotel, Darlington, and has not since been seen, shall be rewarded the sum of Five Pounds Sterling. – Application to the Proptr Jno Alderson or to any Police Officer.*'

'And that's not all. Go back a few pages to my list of missing persons.' Snowden looked dubious but did as he was asked. 'There, papa, halfway down. From the *Gazette* a fortnight later.'

He went dutifully through the list headed Wednesday August 27th. '*Atkinson, Maurice, reported missing Doncaster. Ayresom, Henry, Nottingham –*'

'Further on, papa, the ones starting with F.'

'*Farnbrough, Martin, London. Fuerberg, Ludwig, Portsmouth. Frankland, Henry, Deptford. Furber, Christopher –*'

'Frankland!' Betsey brought him to a halt. 'It's almost the same, Franklin, Frankland. Deptford's in London, isn't it? I'm sure it's him.'

Snowden looked doubtful. 'This is a month after we think he died. He'd have been reported missing long before then.'

'But he hired a horse and never came back, just like our man.'

'That's not unusual, Betsey, I've got files full of horse thieves. And others ride off and have accidents – there was one in Bowes only a few months ago, left his horse at the Unicorn and vanished. Found dead weeks later after falling down a gully on the moors.'

'But there's something else.' Betsey played her last card. 'Daniel says there are Franklands up on the moors, leadminers at Hirst. He's even arrested one once.'

'All right, I'll look into it. But don't hold out too much hope.' Snowden helped himself to another slice of mutton. 'So it's Daniel, is it?' He gave her a quizzical smile and she flushed slightly. 'What would the Reverend William think?'

'I don't care.' Betsey's face crumpled suddenly. 'I won't be seeing him again.'

'That's awkward. He thinks he's taking you and two other young ladies to the show on Saturday. What's gone wrong?'

'Nothing.' For a moment she thought she was going to burst into tears but fought them back. Papa had quite enough on his mind without worrying about her.

'If there's anything I can do –'

'No, it's all right, I'll sort it out myself. Somehow.'

Somewhere, 11.25pm

McQUEEDIE screamed silently as he battled in vain to find a way out of the Glasgow tenement. The ceiling was falling all about him, the walls were crumbling, the floor swaying in great waves beneath his feet. There had to be a way out, a door somewhere in the darkness, a window, surely there was a window? The floor lunged sideways again, throwing him against a wall, and he flung out an arm to stop his fall.

Something, somebody, gave his face a powerful slap and he juddered into consciousness.

'You do that again and I'll have you thrown off.' He opened one eye and his assailant swam hazily into view. A woman in her sixties, her outraged face glaring beneath a black bonnet. 'You should be ashamed of yourself.'

He managed to open the other eye and reality slowly returned. He was in a corner of a coach swaying side to side, it was dark outside and he felt terrible. The woman on the seat beside him was sitting as far away as possible, a stout walkingstick in her hand, and there were two more passengers opposite, a hefty-looking man in a tall hat and tartan cape, fast asleep, and a small boy staring at him open-mouthed.

McQueedie struggled to sit up, tried to speak and discovered his tongue and lips were numb. All that came out was a strangled groan that made the boy shrink back in terror.

'You leave him alone!' The woman waved the stick at him threateningly. 'Assaulting women and frightening children, you should be locked up. Just stay where you are till we stop.'

McQueedie, quite certain he would be incapable of moving anywhere for a long time, subsided into his corner and tried to work out how on earth he'd got there.

He was still wondering when the coach rattled onto cobbles and came to a halt outside the dimly-lit entrance to what he assumed was an inn. The woman gave him a final warning wave of her stick and clambered out of the far door, muttering to herself, followed by the man and his son. McQueedie waited until the postboy had hauled their luggage down from the roof and all three had gone inside before inching his way painfully to the open door and looking out. The inn was in the middle of a long street he didn't recognise.

'Woken up at last, have you?' The coachman came from the front of the coach where he had been helping to unleash the horses. 'About time. This is the end of the run, mate, out you come.' He gave McQueedie a helping hand as he half climbed, half fell to the ground. 'The office is just up the road.'

'Office?' McQueedie stared at him wildly. 'What office?'

'Gazette. Them at the Morritt said you were delivering something there.'

'That's not the Gazette office.'

'Course it is, bloody great sign outside says so. Go and see for yourself.'

McQueedie staggered up the street. He wasn't in Barnard Castle, that was certain. Or York. Or anywhere else he knew where the *Yorkshire Gazette* might have an office.

There was just enough moonlight for him to make out the name spelt out in foot-high letters across the facade of the building.

The Cumberland Gazette. McQueedie sank to his knees in despair. He was in bloody Carlisle.

Thursday July 30th

Carlisle, 6.0am

'A LL yours, Sarge.' Constable Matthias Higson handed over control of the cells in Carlisle Castle at the end of his shift and yawned. 'Been a quiet night for once.'

'Any new faces inside?' Sergeant Henry Billings hung his cape on a nail behind the guardroom door and sat down at the desk.

'Four more for the petty sessions this morning. Couple of poachers in number one, young lads found down by the river. A navvy in number two, brought in after a pub fight in Gretna. Watch out if you go near him, he's a big fellow with a temper.' Higson grinned. 'And there's a drunken Scot vagabond found wandering the streets in the early hours, I put him in with the navvy to sober up. Funny old sod, couldn't understand hardly a word he said. Kept going on about losing his scoops, whatever they are.'

'Any trouble?'

'All fast asleep when I looked by just now. I'd let them stay that way for a while and then tell 'em they've missed breakfast.'

Thorpe, 7.10am

DUTIES of Constables, Section X, Part 48.

Snowden underlined the words at the top of a fresh sheet of paper, refreshed his memory and began to write.

Incorrigible Rogues. Every person wandering abroad, not having any visible means of subsistence and not giving a good account of himself or herself, shall be deemed a rogue and vagabond within the meaning of the Vagrancy Act 1824 (clause 83, section 5) and upon conviction before one or more justices may be committed to the House of Correction for three calendar months to hard labour.

He read it through unhappily. That was the law and there had been many times when he'd had to enforce it, but for every person arrested for wandering abroad who deserved three months' hard labour – thieves, fraudsters, bogus beggars and the like – there were many more who ended up on the streets through no fault of their own. What was a woman deserted by her husband, homeless and penniless, to do as she was rejected by parish after parish and told she must abandon her children to find relief in the workhouse? He had no answer, but was convinced there had to be a better way of dealing with the problem.

He shook his head, picked up his pen again, and added another sentence.

By section 6 of the same statute, all constables are bound under the penalty of five pounds to apprehend and take before a justice of the peace all such idle and disorderly rogues and vagabonds.

Only a few pages of the book to go and then it would be just a matter of checking it all through, compiling an index – an arduous but essential task, perhaps something Betsey could do? – and he could send it off to the publishers. It had taken him the best part of two years, and he would be glad to reach its conclusion.

DUTIES of Constables, Section X, Part 49.
Regulations as to the whipping of juvenile offenders. In the case of
offenders whose age does not exceed fourteen years, the number of strokes
inflicted shall not exceed twelve –

He broke off at the sound of Betsey entering the room, tea in her hand and a concerned frown on her face.

'I know, it has to be finished by the end of the week.' She put the cup down before him. 'I suppose you've been up for hours working on it.'

He took a grateful sip and smile apologetically. 'Just since six. It's almost finished.'

'Thank heavens for that. I suppose you've got another busy day ahead?'

'Interviews all morning with people claiming to know what went on a year ago. You wouldn't believe how many memories have suddenly been restored.' He nodded. 'A busy day, Betsey, you're right. And I want another chat to that woman in Startforth, the one who says she saw blood on the Sills.'

'Nothing so far about – what's his name, Raine?'

'Not yet, but we'll find him.' He sounded more confident than he felt. 'Like Barker. They'll both be in York jail before long, awaiting trial. The third one, Breckon, is safe for now in the cells at Durham.' He frowned. 'I need to have a word with him sometime.'

'What about the Franklands? You haven't forgotten them?'

'I'll try to fit them into the day somehow, though I think it'll be a waste of time. Maybe I'll take young Constable Craven up to Hirst with me– you did say he knew people up there?'

'Yes.' She hesitated. 'I've never been up that way, might I come with you?'

He smiled. 'I don't see why not.'

Carlisle, 7.25am

McQUEEDIE awoke slowly from a nightmare of disintegrating stagecoaches, eagle-sized hornets and murderous old ladies to the thunder of his cellmate emptying his bowels copiously into the slop bucket.

He opened a cautious eye, was greeted by the sight of a hairy buttock inches from his head, and closed it again. There was a final explosion and he heard the buttock-owner stand up.

'Who the hell are you?'

McQueedie opened both eyes, took a deep breath to explain, and threw up.

'You can clear that sodding lot up for a start.' His companion loomed above him, a six-foot-something man in his twenties with a thick unkempt beard, a scar down one cheek, a villainous look on the rest of his face and what looked like dried blood spattered down the front of his shirt. He also had hands the size of shovels, one of which reached down and plucked McQueedie bodily from the slab on which he lay. 'Or your head'll go in the bucket with the rest of the shit.'

'Whatever you say.' McQueedie, his feet dangling a foot above the cell floor, wasn't going to argue. 'If you could just put me down –'

He was dropped heavily to the floor and looked round desperately for something with which to wipe up his vomit. He was surprised how much there was, given that he hadn't eaten for twenty-four hours.

'Use your bloody stockings.'

McQueedie swallowed hard, removed his boots and began mopping up as his companion glowered over him.

'That's better.' The man seemed to mellow slightly now he'd proved who was in command. 'Scotsman, are you? On your way home?'

'I hope so.'

'You won't be going anywhere for a while once the magistrates have done with you. What you in here for?'

'It's all been a mistake.' A note of indignation crept into McQueedie's voice. 'They just arrested me in the middle of the night and threw me in here.'

'Burgling, were you?'

'Certainly not.'

'Robbery? Assault? Poaching? Fraud? Beating up the missus?' He appraised McQueedie and shook his head. 'No, you wouldn't dare.'

'They said it was for resisting a police officer in the execution of his duty.'

'Well, well. Proper little Rob Roy, aren't you?' The man seemed almost amused. 'Resisting arrest, that's a month's hard labour for starters unless you can pay the fine. A pound at least, plus costs. Got any money?'

'Nothing.'

'How d'you plan to get back home, then – once you're off the treadmill?'

The treadmill. McQueedie shuddered. 'I've no idea. I've nothing worth selling.'

'Have to find work, then. Won't be easy, you having been in jail.' He gave a guffaw. 'The only work round here is for us navvies up on the railway, and I don't see you wielding a pickaxe all day.'

Barnard Castle, 9.15am

THERE were five envelopes lying on Lancelot Fewster's desk when he arrived in the *Yorkshire Gazette* office, and he eyed them without enthusiasm. The paper didn't get much mail, and what it did get tended to be unwelcome.

He opened the first, which confirmed his fears. It was a lengthy and vitriolic complaint from the town's Congregationalist minister about the *Gazette*'s report on his summer fete, which, he claimed, had misspelt his wife's name, omitted the winner of the best flower arrangement suitable for a double funeral, and mixed up the hymn numbers with the day's takings. The minister was demanding a front-page apology.

Fewster sighed, dropped it into the wastepaper basket, and opened the second envelope. The note inside was a good deal shorter, a terse demand from the news editor in York to be told why he had received nothing worth printing from Teesdale for the past week. Fewster shook his head irritably as he added it to the basket. What did they expect in late July, when everyone who was anyone in town had disappeared on holiday and the rest spent their time organising summer fetes? It was the silly season and that meant no news, everybody knew that.

He quickly discarded the next two letters — one signed *Pro Bono Publico* accusing the *Gazette* of being disgracefully biased in favour of the Whigs, the other from *Man O'The People* lambasting its rabid support of the Tories – and picked up the final envelope. It was addressed simply to 'The Gazette' in a scrawl he immediately recognised. McQueedie. Some feeble excuse for not turning up for work, Fewster was sure, which must have been thrust drunkenly through the door the previous night. He ripped it open angrily and began to read.

A year has passed since broken-hearted lovers Joshua Yates and Kate Paine leapt to their deaths into the foaming Tees...

His anger had faded long before he reached the final fullstop and sat back, a thoughtful look above his drooping moustache. McQueedie might have many faults, but you had to hand it to the man, he could certainly make a story out of nothing. The harrowing description of the orphaned Yates' brutal childhood in the workhouse was masterly – Fewster had no idea they sent naked five-year-olds down to clear the sewers – and the paragraph about finding the girl's heartbroken young sister beside her grave, a single faded rose in her hand and her pet dog howling with grief, was guaranteed to have readers sobbing over their breakfasts. There were 730 words of it, and every one a gem. The editor was going to love it.

Fewster allowed his conscience a moment's protest but no more. Taking up his pen, he drew a thick line through the words *By Our Teesdale Correspondent*, substituted *Exclusive By Lancelot Fewster*, and looked for a new envelope.

Startforth, 12.30pm

SNOWDEN parked Bucephalus in Tom Rutter's yard, walked down to Mrs Galland's front door and hoped she'd forgotten their previous encounter. His knock was answered by a shuffling noise inside and she appeared on the immaculate doorstep, as far as he could tell in the same black garb as last time but without the bonnet. She was completely bald and the top of her head looked as if she polished it as fiercely as her doorknob.

'Where's your horse?' She looked piercingly up and down the road. 'And you keep your feet back there in the road.'

'Of course.' He gave her an ingratiating smile that she met with a cold stare. 'I just wanted to ask you a few more questions about the blood you saw over there.'

'Taken your time, haven't you?'

Snowden abandoned the smile. 'We've got a witness who says she saw three men here that morning, and I wondered if you remembered them?'

'Three men?'

'Yes. Young men, searching for something.'

'I never saw three men there.'

'Ah. Well, thank you all the same.' He turned to go.

'Saw one of them, mind.' She spoke reluctantly. 'He was further on, at the end, and I passed him on my way to church. Leaning on the wall, he was, staring into the water.'

Snowden turned back with a sigh. He'd had a long morning interviewing alleged witnesses, and he was getting weary of asking the next question. 'Why didn't you mention it before?'

'Never asked, did you?'

'You could be an important witness in a murder case.'

'Important, me?' The idea obviously pleased her. 'Well, I'm telling you now. He was very pale, I remember, I'd say he was labouring under a great distress of mind.' Her eyes widened. 'And there was me bidding him good morning and all the time him a murderer. It doesn't bear thinking of.'

'We don't know that for certain, Mrs Galland. Can you tell me who he was?'

'Never seen him before. They all look alike anyway, these young 'uns in their fancy jackets and hats, carousing round here all hours. I could tell you a few things –'

'And did you see anyone else here that morning?'

She delved back into her memory. 'Not till I got up the hill, nearly to church. I remember sitting down for rest, my legs aren't what they were, till Mr Solomon came along.'

'Solomon?'

'Jacob Solomon from over in Well Yard. He was on his way to church too. Funny, you wouldn't think it with a name like that, but he never misses a Sunday.'

Carlisle, 1pm

'STAND in line, you lot, eyes front, hands down your sides and not a word unless you're spoken to.' McQueedie shuffled into place with a dozen other prisoners. A burly constable stood on guard and four gowned officials were waiting at the foot of stairs leading up to the courtrooms.

The warder consulted a list in his hand. 'Thomson and Birkett, found abroad by night for the purpose of unlawfully taking fish from the Eden, let's be having you.'

Two boys in their early teens, one barefoot, stepped hesitantly forward.

'Where's your shoes, lad?'

'Down by the river, sir. Didn't have a chance to get them when we was nicked, sir, I was in the water.'

'You'll wish you had them, where you're going. Court one, follow the usher, on your way.' The pair were led off up the stairs.

'Court two, Routledge, drunk and disorderly, causing affray, assault.' McQueedie's cellmate stepped forward. 'Good night out, was it?'

'Till your lot got involved. Bit of a dispute with the landlord, that's all. Thieving bastard over-charged me.'

'Not as much as this will. You'll need a bob or two in your pocket if you want to get out of here today, sunshine.'

'I've plenty.'

'Up the stairs.' McQueedie watched Routledge depart and hoped his turn would come soon. The only thing he'd had to eat was at noon, a slice of dry bread and a bowl of rancid gruel with gobbets of something unrecognizable, indigestible and, his stomach was already warning him, almost certainly a health hazard. He was feeling distinctly queasy and having a pocket full of vomited-soaked stockings didn't help.

The warder looked at his list. 'Court three, Davies, cruelty to domestic animal and unlawful carnal knowledge of a –' He stopped abruptly. 'Bloody hell, haven't had one of those before. Where is he?'

'Still in the infirmary.' The burly constable grinned 'Did himself a damage, I'm told.'

'I'm not bloody surprised.' The warder went back to his list. 'Who's next, then? McRoody, vagrancy, resisting arrest.'

McQueedie stepped forward. 'It's McQueedie, actually.'

'You saying I can't read?'

McQueedie's stomach lurched alarmingly. 'No, just that they've spelt it wrong. McQueedie. With a Q, not an R.'

'Bit of a trouble-maker, are we?' The warder turned to the burly constable. 'You hear that, Joe? Gentleman of the road here says we don't know how to write.'

McQueedie shook his head. 'I didn't say that –'

'And now he's calling me a liar.' The warder gave a malevolent smile. 'You can get your arse back in the queue then, Mc-whatever-you-bloody-are, and go in last. If they get round to you today, of course.'

McQueedie stepped back into the line. There was a worrying rumble somewhere deep within his bowels and he wondered dismally what the penalty was for fouling the courtroom floor.

Barnard Castle, 2.30pm

SNOWDEN crossed the Horse Market cobbles and turned through the narrow archway that led to Well Yard. It was a long passage between tall buildings that blotted out the sunshine, tenements with a smattering of small workshops and dingy-looking shops on the ground floor. Five doors down on the left-hand side, squeezed between a joinery and an empty butcher' shop, a faded sign read *Jacob Solomon, Dealer in Fine Cutlery.*

Through the grime of a small-paned window Snowden could make out a thin display of Solomon's wares: an open box of table knives and forks, a handful of teaspoons, a ladle and what looked like a well-used fish slice. Snowden decided he'd seen better cutlery in the workhouse and pushed open the shop door.

The room was empty apart from small boy who leapt from a stool in the far corner and vanished through a doorway at the back. There was the muffled sound of voices and a thin bespectacled man in his early thirties appeared.

'You are wanting to buy something?' The man spoke with a slight accent that Snowden couldn't place.

'Jacob Solomon?' The man nodded. 'Police. I want to ask you a few questions.'

'Police?' A momentary flicker of concern crossed the man's face. 'How can I help you?'

'I understand you attend Holy Trinity church over in Startforth?'

'Every Sunday, yes. It is a problem?'

'No, not at all. Can I ask why you go there? St Mary's is just down the road, much nearer.'

'I am Catholic, you understand? We have no church here yet, though they say they will build one soon.' Snowden nodded. A site had been found in Ware Street, not far away, and work was said to be starting on it within a year. 'When we came to this town, when I was no older than my son George you have just seen, my father says we must go to Holy Trinity. There we have candles, incense, communion, what you call high church, more like the church back home. St Mary's does not do these things. I have gone to Startforth ever since.'

'Back home?' Snowden was curious about the man's background.

'It was Poland when my father was born. Now it is ruled by Russians. Many of us fled to England.'

'Your father is here?'

'He died last year. He was a fine silversmith, he made wonderful things.' Solomon shrugged sadly. 'I have his shop but I do not have his skills. Only a little of his knowledge, enough to make a living.'

Snowden glanced dubiously at the window display behind him. 'This is what you sell?'

'No, no.' Solomon smiled. 'It is pitiful, of no value. It is there so no-one thinks I have anything in my shop worth stealing. You are a policeman, you will understand.'

Only too well, thought Snowden. A window full of expensive silverware wouldn't last long on the town's main streets, let alone one down a dark alley. 'So you keep your stock out of sight? Very wise.'

'Upstairs, we have two rooms. You would like to see?'

Snowden was already running late and had yet to start questioning Solomon about last year's events, but his curiosity triumphed. 'If it's no trouble.'

He followed Solomon through the rear door and up a wooden staircase. There were two rooms on the landing. 'We live in that one.' Solomon pointed at the room on the left. 'I would offer you tea but my wife is in there asleep. She works at night in the flax mill.' He led the way into the other room. On the left was a workbench littered with tools and a trestle table holding heavy boxes, some empty, others secured and labelled. On the right more trestle tables stretched the length of the wall, covered in an astonishing array of tableware,

Snowden walked slowly down the room, marvelling at the collection. There were intricately-carved presentation cases, their dark blue cushions holding knives, forks, spoons of all sizes and purpose, There were sugar tongs and sugar nips, ladles and marrow scoops, an enormous tureen, dazzling candlesticks, caddy spoons and knife rests, grape scissors and crumb trays and a host of other devices and decorations to ensplendour the tables of the rich and well-fed and give their servants plenty to polish. Some was steel, some silver, some perhaps the new and still expensive electroplate. Snowden couldn't imagine what it was all worth.

'Extraordinary.' He picked up a small oval container and examined its short curling legs, lid, handle and delicately-engraved flowers entwined round the sides. 'What's this for?'

'You fill it with hot water and warm your spoon in it until your soup arrives. It is supposed to stop it congealing, I'm told.'

'A spoon warmer?' Snowden shook his head in disbelief. 'Where do you find such things?'

'Country house sales, bankruptcy auctions, unclaimed goods from pawnbrokers. I spend much time travelling around the region. And people come to me to sell privately, of course, not wanting anyone to know they need the money.'

'And who buys them round here?'

'Not many.' Solomon smiled. 'Few people in Barnard Castle can afford such things, or even want them. But in London they will pay a great deal for fine pieces.'

'You take them down there?'

'No, I have relations in London, my father's brothers and their sons, who have a good business buying and selling such things. They call here perhaps two, three times a year, they see what they like, we haggle over prices and they take what they buy.' He waved a hand at the boxes on other table. 'I know what they will want and have it awaiting their next call.'

Snowden wondered momentarily whether Betsey would appreciate a silver lobster cracker or toothpick holder, decided she was far too sensible, and turned his attention back to the purpose of his visit. 'Holy Trinity. I think you were there on Sunday August the tenth last year?'

'I have been every Sunday for many years.'

'Alone?'

'My wife works every night during the week and does not attend as regularly as I would wish.' He shook his head sadly. 'I fear she has lost her faith. But, yes, I would have been at Holy Trinity on the day you ask.'

'It was the day after we believe two people fell into the river. A Mrs Galland tells me she saw you that morning, you know her, I believe?'

'Indeed, a very fervent woman.'

She would be, Snowden thought. 'You remember meeting her?'

'The day of the drownings, yes. It was a few days after my father died and I remember telling her about it. She was sitting on the seat outside the church.'

'What time of day was that?'

'Perhaps a little before ten.'

'And did you see anyone else, on the Sills? A man, perhaps?'

Solomon's brow furrowed. 'I do not think so.'

'You're sure?'

'Not that morning, no. But when I go to church on Sundays, I first take a walk, up the hill to above Startforth and round the back along Dark Lane. I do not go by way of the Sills.'

Snowden wondered whether he was wasting his time, but persevered. 'You say not that morning. Did you go there later?'

'Not then. But I returned next day. I wished to talk to the vicar about whether my father could be buried there.'

'At Startforth?'

Solomon's face brightened. 'Yes, it was agreed, although he was a Catholic.' He paused. 'You ask about a man on the Sills. I went along past there that morning and there was someone by the wall.'

'Go on.'

'I saw him as I got past Rutter's, the smith's shop. A young man, standing with his face towards the water. I remember bidding him good morning but he turned round and walked on to a thorn bush beyond the wall end. He stood with his back to me until I got by. It was curious.'

'You knew him?'

'Yes. Not well, but we had met and done business together.'

Snowden looked surprised. 'Business?'

Solomon hesitated. 'I do not want to get into trouble. In this line of work, I meet many people who want to sell things without too many questions.' He looked questioningly at Snowden. 'You understand?'

'I think so. Don't worry, I'm not here looking for stolen property, at least not today. Who was this man?'

'I keep a record of all my dealings, I could look for it.' Solomon went to the workbench and dug a large blue notebook from under a pile of papers. 'He came here perhaps two or three times, brought me things, pieces that he said he had found. Most of it was of no great interest and worth very little, but the last time...' He turned the pages of the notebook as he spoke, searching for the right place. 'Here it is, May last year. Two candlesticks, silver, twelve shillings I paid him.'

'And his name?'

'He did not tell me, I did not ask, but my wife was here at the time and she told me afterwards she knew him. His mother, I think, also works at the mill. My wife said he was called Thomas Raine, and I wrote it here.'

He handed the notebook to Snowden who nodded, gratified that another piece of the jigsaw had been slotted into place. With luck, Raine would be the person Mrs Galland had seen, returning, perhaps, to the scene of the crime on both mornings.

'Have you seen him since?'

'Only by the river, as I told you. He has not been here again.'

'And the candlesticks? Do you still have them?'

Solomon shook his head. 'I sold them a few weeks later. They were fine pieces, Georgian, with eagle crests on the pillars and fine quilted bases. I remember them well, they were made by William Solomon of London.'

'A relation of yours?'

Solomon shrugged 'It is possible, there are many of my name in England. But sadly I do not know of any family connection.'

Snowden frowned, trying to recall when he had heard of William Solomon candlesticks before, but failed. 'Do you know who bought them?'

'It will be on the list.'

Snowden turned to the entries for June 1845. 'These?'

'Sold for eight pounds, yes.' Solomon looked defensive. 'I have a living to make.'

'And these initials for the buyer, J.M. – who is that?'

'Ah, Mr Michell, he often buys from me. A gentleman with fine taste, from Forcett Hall, you may know him.'

'The magistrate? Yes, I know him well.' A smile crossed Snowden's face. 'I think I may be seeing him again before long.'

He ran his eyes down the entries in the notebook, wondering if there were other names there he should know about. Solomon watched him, a worried look on his face. 'Is this man Raine important?'

'I think so.' Snowden was about to hand the notebook back but stopped suddenly. 'This entry here, July the twenty-ninth last year. *H.F. – Cruets.* What does that mean?'

Solomon frowned, took the notebook and looked relieved. 'It is nothing. A man who wrote to me saying he collected silver, salt and pepper pots and the like, and would call by that day to see what I had that might interest him. My uncle Marek in London had told him of me. I waited all day, but he never came.'

'Those are his initials?'

'Yes.'

'And his name?'

Solomon shook his head. 'I am sorry, I cannot remember.'

'You have the letter?'

'I fear not, it was a year ago.' He looked apologetic. 'It was from London, I do remember that. He said came up here from time to time to visit relations.'

Snowden tried to remember the name Betsey had come up with. 'Could it have been Franklin? Or something like that?'

Solomon looked astonished. 'You know about this man too?'

'No, but I think I will. You've been very helpful, Mr Solomon. Very helpful indeed.'

Carlisle, 4.02pm

'OH dear, oh dear, what a shame.' The warder gave McQueedie an evil grin. 'Looks like we've got the pleasure of your company for another night. And with you the only one left in the queue, too.'

McQueedie watched dismally as a procession of judges, lawyers and assorted court officials traipsed down the stairs and headed for the door.

'Always finish dead on time at four.' The warder folded up his list and stuck in a pocket. 'Thank your stars it's Thursday, sunshine, if it was tomorrow you'd be waiting for them till Monday.' He gave McQueedie a sniff and grimaced. 'And God knows what you'd smell like by then. Come on, back to that lovely cell of yours.'

As they turned to go a final figure came down the stairs, a tall slightly dishevelled man in an ill-fitting brown jacket with a notebook in one hand. He glanced across at them, gave a another longer look and stopped in his tracks.

'Hamish? Hamish McQueedie? What the hell are you doing here?'

McQueedie looked up and stared at him. 'Sandy?'

'No talking to the press, McCordie.' The warder gave him a shove in the back. 'Eyes front, on you go.'

McQueedie staggered forward. 'Sandy McLeod! You old bastard!' Tears came to his eyes. 'Jings, am I glad to see you. Get me out of here and I'll buy you Glenbuckie's for life.'

Barnard Castle, 4.30pm

SEPTIMUS Lampitt stuck his spade into the heap of soil beside the grave, cursed and wiped the sweat from his brow. He had no idea why he was doing this. He'd dug many a grave in St Mary's graveyard in his time, but never before been asked to dig one up again.

It had taken him long enough to find it, far over in the west corner among the many graves hurriedly created there during the last cholera outbreak. But this one, they'd promised him, wasn't a cholera victim and there was no chance of him catching the dread disease from the bones they wanted him to exhume. He hoped they were right.

He stared at the flimsy wooden cross that had stood above the grave. At least he hadn't had to shift a bloody great slab of granite or marble to get at it. Whoever it was down there – the name carved roughly into the crosspiece was Joseph Yates, a name that rang a bell but he couldn't remember why – the man hadn't been worth forking out money to a stonemason for.

Lampitt picked up his spade again and got back to work. A shilling they were paying him, and another shilling to put it all back again after they'd done whatever they wanted to do with the body. God knows what they hoped to find.

His spade struck something solid and he reached down into the earth. A bone, covered in rotten rags, aslime with what had once been flesh and guts. The bastards hadn't even bought the man a coffin.

Thorpe, 5.30pm

BETSEY sighed. 'How can I possibly draw you properly when you keep moving, Tommy? Do sit still while I try to get your whiskers right.'

The cat yawned, stretched and turned its back on her.

'It's no good.' Betsey pushed her drawingbook to one side and stood up. 'Heaven knows how real artists do it. Perhaps they use stuffed cats, I don't know.'

'What don't you know?'

She hadn't heard her father return and gave a start. 'Papa! I thought you'd be back hours ago. You said we'd go to find the Franklands.'

'There's still time.' He crossed over and examined her half-finished drawing. 'Not bad, but the eyes are a bit small.'

'She will keep falling asleep. I wish there was a quicker way of making a picture of her.' She picked up the day's *Morning Post*. 'There are people in London who say they've got a machine to do it, look. It's called a daguerreotype. They're offering to make people's portraits in minutes. Just imagine!'

'Just now all I can imagine is the sight of tea on the table. I'm hungry.'

'Oh, papa, you're hopeless.' She shook her head. 'There's cold meats and salad, I didn't think we'd want to be wasting time if we were heading up to Hirst. We are, aren't we?'

'As soon as we've eaten.' He grinned. 'Your Constable Craven is waiting for us.'

He was sure he saw her blush as she vanished into the kitchen.

Barnard Castle, 5.45pm

'THAT'S the lot.' Lampitt jerked a muddy thumb towards the heap of rags and bones on the cart beside the grave. 'Now where's it going?'

The Reverend John Davidson, vicar of St Mary's, stared at the mortal remains of

Joseph Yates and had one of his disturbingly frequent moments of doubt about the afterlife. 'Up to the morgue at the workhouse, for Dr O'Neill, I'm told. The police want to have a look at it, though the Lord knows why.'

'Nobody said anything about carting it about. It'll be another sixpence. Each way.'

'If you insist.' Davidson nodded, comforted by the knowledge that the police were paying for the whole exercise and he'd warned them they would owe his church at least five shillings. 'Take it away.'

'I'll just clear up a bit first.' Lampitt began shoring up the sides of the soil mound as the vicar disappeared, decided it was more effort than he was being paid for, and wandered off into the bushes beyond to relieve himself.

On his way back he spotted a mouldering travelling bag among the undergrowth and went to investigate. It was disappointingly empty apart from an empty Glenbuckie's bottle which he threw back into the bushes before returning to the cart.

Three dogs leapt from it, each with a bone in its jaws, and vanished across the graveyard.

Hirst, 7.35pm

IT must have been idyllic, Betsey thought. A tiny hamlet high up on the moors beside the packhorse track to Swaledale, with a farmstead, a couple of labourers' cottages and a drovers' inn beside a meandering stream.

Then came the leadminers. First a handful, then in their hundreds, spreading from Arkengarthdale to the west and burrowing into the hills, building mineshafts and worksheds, mills and chimneys, heaping their spoil beside the dams and spring-fed hushes, their days spent underground, their nights in slate-topped hovels and sleeping shelters scattered across the moor. The mines' owner extended the farmhouse and called it a hall; the cottages housed his foremen; the inn became a riotous centre for miners' drunkenness and violence. Now it was in decline, the lead petering out and the miners moving to fresh pastures to rape in Teesdale. Most of the mills and workshops and hovels lay derelict, their roofs falling in, the spoilheaps beneath smokeless chimneys gathering wiry grass on which a handful of sheep were trying to graze.

'Not pretty.' Snowden nodded, reading Betsey's thoughts. 'Watch out for old mineshafts. They're everywhere.'

Craven led them carefully down the track to one of the few dwellings from which smoke drifted into the still evening air. 'I think this is the one.' He stopped outside, dismounted and the others followed suit. Snowden knocked on the door.

It was answered by a small man in his fifties, his face grimed with dust.

'Frankland?'

'Police?' The man eyed them suspiciously.

Snowden, who like Craven had left his uniform behind, was faintly annoyed to be so easily recognised. 'Yes.'

'Next down but two.' The man's face creased into a twisted smile. 'You're wasting your time. She was mad enough before her husband died, and she's worse now.' The door shut behind him.

They moved two doors down and Snowden tried again. The woman who opened the door was one of the oldest and ugliest Betsey had ever seen, and her mind leapt to a book of fairy tales she'd had as a child, with pictures of haggard witches who bewitched and ate children. This figure, too, was dressed in black, her sparse hair wild upon her bony shoulders, her hands gnarled and her fingers long and barbed. Betsey recoiled in fright.

'I knew you'd come for me.' The woman's voice was exactly what Betsey thought the fairy tale author had meant when he wrote of witches cackling gleefully as they enticed infant victims to their doom. 'I'm ready.'

'Ready?' Snowden stared at her. 'For what?'

'Our wedding, John. I knew you'd come back.'

'I'm sorry, but I'm not –'

'I forgive you. Come in, come in.' She vanished inside and they followed warily. There was one room, the walls little more than piles of rough stone, the roof pitted with missing slates. A heap of blankets lay on the floor in a corner, dry bracken and thin logs were piled beside the hearth, and a home-made table on one side held the remains of a meal on a platter and, to Betsey's astonishment, a pile of books. A door at the back stood open to a yard in which she could see a lean-to privy.

'Have you got the ring?' The women looked at Snowden expectantly and then turned to Craven. 'You can't marry us without the ring, can you, father?'

Craven's mouth stood open, Betsey resisted the temptation to take his arm for protection, and Snowden decided it was time to take control.

'We're here about Henry. Henry Frankland.'

'Not Henry. Harry.' She spoke sharply and waved a finger at him. 'You must get his name right, he's a witness. He'll be here in a minute.'

'Harry, yes.' Snowden nodded. 'Tell me about him.'

'But you know Harry, John.' She shook her head impatiently. 'My nephew, he comes to see us. All the way from London, every year, he should be here by now.' She moved towards the front door. 'I'll just see if he's coming.'

The others stared as she disappeared from sight.

'The man said she was mad.' Craven spoke in a whisper and gave a snort of stifled laughter. 'She thinks you're going to marry her, sir.'

'I think it's very sad.' Betsey looked at him severely. 'Poor old thing, we should humour her.'

'So long as I don't end up with a ring on my finger.' Snowden walked across to the table and examined the books. 'She, or her husband, were well-read. There's Pope, Adam Smith, Milton, Dickens, the family Bible, of course.' He picked it up and turned over the front cover. 'Here we are. The family tree, all the births and marriages and deaths.' He scanned down the page. 'John Frankland and Beatrice Akers, married November the first, 1795. Then John Frankland, died September the eleventh 1845. The last entry.'

Betsey joined him. 'No children, how sad. But there's John's brother Joseph, married Mary Browning 1798, and... yes, their children, Mary 1799, Ellen 1800, Charles 1802, poor woman, three in four years... and Henry 1804. That's him, Henry Frankland, the man in the tunnel!'

'Perhaps.'

'Proddy mats!' Betsey gave a sudden squeal of excitement. 'The names in the Bible, Beatrice and John, B and J. He was going to give them a Mrs Mattock proddy mat as a present.' She did a quick calculation. 'It would have been their fiftieth wedding anniversary last November.' She gave another squeal. 'And that watch, the one that policeman took –'

'Elliot?'

'You thought that had B J engraved on it, but it could have been H F for Henry Frankland.'

'You could be right.' Snowden gave her a congratulatory smile. 'Now all we've got to do is find out who murdered him.'

'And did you notice her hands? The fingers were all bent, like claws.'

Snowden nodded and looked worriedly at the front door. 'I'm going out the back before she returns for another wedding. Keep her talking till I've got away. I'll meet you down the road.'

He left.

'Don't worry, I'll look after you.' Craven gave Betsey a smile. 'So long as she doesn't want to marry me instead. I think I can do better than that.'

She returned the smile. 'I'm sure you can.'

Friday July 31ˢᵗ

Thorpe, 8.15am

'DON'T tell me, I know. I should still be in bed.' Snowden laid down his pen and rubbed his eyes. 'But I've got another busy day ahead and I want to get this lot sorted out before I leave.'

Betsey sighed. 'What is it?'

Her father waved a hand at the pile of papers before him. 'I told you last night about Mrs Galland and Solomon. These are notes from the other interviews I did yesterday. I've been at it since six o'clock.'

'Is there any way I can help?'

'Well, you could check what I've done so far, if you're sure you've nothing better to do.'

'Nothing.' Betsey took the handful of papers he offered. 'But first I'll make you some breakfast.' She went to the kitchen, put a kettle of water on the range Mrs Avery had lit an hour earlier, and settled down at the table to read the first report.

Thursday July 30 1846, 9.20am. Statement by William Graham, 37, mason, Barnard Castle

I was in Mrs Brass's beerhouse in Briggate on the night of Saturday August 9 1845 and saw Joseph Yates there. He had ten shillings on him which I saw him twice take it out of his right-hand pocket. I left about half-past eleven. I am not sure whether Yates was still there then. I did not see him alive again. I have been in Barnard Castle eight years and know the river very well. There are many rocks on the sides and also on the bottom. I have seen the river very rough when it dashes about. When the water is high, it is too rough for anyone to go into it with safety. Wm Graham.

Betsey wasn't sure this revealed anything that her father didn't already know, apart from the money, and that didn't seem very important. She glanced at the kettle, still waiting to boil, and moved on to the second sheet of paper.

Thursday July 30 1846, 9.43am. Statement by Frances Cooper, 24, weaver, Barnard Castle.

I recollect being in company with Yates on the night of his death, at twelve o'clock. The night was dark and very windy. The water was running very rapid, it was high and likely to be higher. The wall at the Sills is a yard high at the lowest. We call it the tram-wall, there are wooden beams laid down there to ease the passage of wagons. There is a road down to the water and if you miss the road you will go into the river.

Betsey paused. Did that mean it could have been just an accident after all? Yates had just wandered along, lost his footing, and gone into the river? She read on.

I went with Yates to Startforth to try to get into some public house. We went straight up the Bowes road to Hunton's place, in the opposite direction to the Sills. When we returned I parted with Yates on the top of the bridge at one o'clock. He had money in his pocket. I was not down by the tram-wall that night. F Cooper.

Tram-wall. Betsey had heard it called that and often wondered why. She turned to the next sheet. A woman this time.

Thursday July 30 1846, 10.04am. Statement by Ann Braithwaite, 17, unemployed, Barnard Castle

I was with my friend Hannah Todd in Briggate about one o'clock on the night I last saw Joe Yates. He came down the street from the bridge. He was rather fresh in liquor but not intoxicated. He asked us to go and have a glass with him but we refused. He pressed us to go and said we need not be afraid as he had money. He got some money out and I saw ten or twelve shillings, there were two halfcrowns, some shillings and a single sixpence. We still refused and he put the money in his pocket and left us. Ann Braithwaite.

The kettle started boiling. Betsey got up thoughtfully, moved it onto the cool plate and went to look for eggs in the pantry. She found two large brown ones, took them back into the kitchen, and carefully pricked the end of each one so they wouldn't crack open while cooking. Neither Cooper or Braithwaite had mentioned seeing anyone else that night, and she wondered if her father had asked them. It probably wasn't important.

She put a small pan on the hot plate, half-filled it with hot water from the kettle and gently added the eggs. Four and a half minutes by the clock on the wall above should do it. She sat down, cut a couple of slices of bread and picked up the fourth statement.

Thursday July 30 1846, 10.32am. Statement by John Robinson, carpet weaver, Barnard Castle.

I live with my father in Freeacre Lonning, off Briggate. I was standing on the top of the lonning between one and half-past on the Sunday morning, that would be August the tenth. I saw Kate Raine come up the lonning. At the same time I saw Joseph Yates. He came over and put his arm round her and they went towards the bridge. I did not speak to them but I heard them speak to each other. I think they were tipsy, because I saw them stagger.

Betsey glanced at the clock and jumped up to take the eggs off the boil. She hastily buttered the bread, found a couple of egg-cups, added a plate, knife and teaspoon, and took it all through to her father.

'Thank you. There's another statement here.' He handed it to her. 'What do you think so far?'

'You had a busy morning yesterday. They must have been queuing to see you.'

Snowden smiled and began attacking the eggs. 'It's astonishing how the prospect of a reward loosens their tongues.'

'I wonder how much of it is true? Bother, I've forgotten the salt.' She went to find it and brought the earlier papers back as well. 'Why do they keep mentioning Yates having money?'

'I asked them to. I'm looking for motives, Betsey, and robbery seems an obvious possibility. Ann Humphreys seems to think it was. I need to know that he was worth robbing.'

Betsey went over to her own desk and resumed Robinson's statement. There wasn't much more to it.

I could not see them far, it was a very dark night. After I lost sight of them I went home. I had known Kate long and often seen her. I can't say she seemed in distress and she didn't have at all the appearance of being with child as I was later told she was. Jno Robinson.

Betsey had forgotten about that. Perhaps Yates was the father and they had a dispute about it? No, not if Humphreys was telling the truth. She shook her head and moved onto the next statement.

Thursday July 30 1846, 11.05am. Statement by George Dobson, 42, accountant, Barnard Castle

I live in Thorngate. I knew Joseph Yates and saw him last alive on the night previous to when they say he went into the river. I was about twelve yards from my father's door, he lives in Briggate about fifty yards from my home. The girl that went missing was in company with Yates. I saw them, walking towards the bridge and spoke to them. It was late but I cannot fix the time. Afterwards I also saw George Barker.

Betsey had been about to skip the rest of the statement because it seemed to be repeating what the earlier ones had said, but now it had her full attention. Barker, the first mention of him apart from Humphreys' story.

He was not a great distance from where I saw the others, and only a short time after the other two passed me. He was going in the same direction. There were three or four young persons with him. I do not know who they were but I am sure Barker was the person I saw. I went into the house immediately after and saw no more. Geo Dobson.

'So we've got a witness saying Barker was there.' Betsey looked across at her father. 'That's a start, isn't it?'

He didn't look up. 'Keep going, it gets better.'

Thursday July 30 1846, 11.05am. Statement by Robert Windlass, 22, carpet weaver, Barnard Castle

I live about halfway down Briggate. I recollect the night of ninth of August 1845. I was in my lodgings all night till about twelve o'clock when I went to the porch, and after I had had my supper I walked towards Thorngate. I met three men I knew, two of them together, George Barker and Thomas Raine, and John Breckon a yard or so behind.

'All three of them!' Betsey almost shouted with excitement. 'It must be true!'

'Just because they were around that night doesn't prove they had anything to do with the murders – if they were murders.' Snowden gave her a warning smile. 'But I agree, it's progress. How about a cup of tea while I write up the next one?'

'In a minute, I'll just finish with Windlass.'

They were on the opposite side of the street. I went to Sarah Proctor's between twelve and half-past, before I had my supper, and I saw Breckon and Kate there. Rbt Windlass.

'It would be easier if they didn't keep hopping backwards and forwards.' Betsey went back through the statements. 'We seem to be able to trace all of them – Yates, the girl, the three you think killed them – in Briggate until about half-past one that night. But it's still just Humphreys' word that they went over the bridge.'

'That's true. We know somebody was there, more than one person – Mrs Raper heard them, we've got the witnesses who heard screams. We just haven't found anybody except Humphreys who says it was Raine, Barker and Breckon.'

'Raine was back there next morning, Mrs Galland told you. And according to Mr Solomon he was there again the day after. Looking to see if he'd left any clues behind. It's got to be him.'

'Perhaps. I've still got to check that it was Raine Mrs Galland saw. That's not going to easy until we catch him and she can identify him face to face.'

'You can describe him to her.'

'Tall, dark, aged about 18? There must be scores of young men in Briggate who fit that description. What I need is a picture of him.'

'One of those darregotypes, you mean?'

He gave a wry smile. 'Daguerreotypes. Where's that cup of tea?'

Darlington, 8.50am

CONSTABLE Craven stood on the platform entranced, his astonished eyes wide with excitement as the machine drew slowly out of the station, smoke and steam belching high above him, the noise greater than anything he had ever heard, puffing and hissing and clanking and spitting and suddenly a tremendous shriek of a whistle that made him spin round in exhilarated terror. It was wonderful, beautiful, unbelievable, and he watched enthralled as the carriages dwindled into the distance, over the Stockton and Darlington line crossing, and vanished towards Newcastle.

He had never seen a railway locomotive before. Or Darlington, for that matter, or any town further from home than Barnard Castle. As he'd ridden in that morning he had marvelled at the size of the place, so many streets, so many houses, the great mills with their chimneys soaring above the church spires, the multitude of shops offering wonders he could not imagine. And so many people crowding the thoroughfares, hundreds of them, thousands perhaps, to whom all this was home and normal and nothing to stare at the way he was staring now.

'Make way if you please, sir.' He stood aside for a porter pushing a cart laden with trunks and boxes and a small cage full of terrified chickens and made his way slowly along the platform in search of the electric telegraph office.

Forcett, 10.15am

THE butler led Snowden into Michell's library and disappeared to find his master. The shelves were packed with dark-leathered books which, if the other country house libraries Snowden had encountered were anything to go by, nobody ever read. Most of those here, he discovered as he wandered round the room, were old estate ledgers recording every purchase and payment for generations.

He pulled out a volume at random and was wondering why the Forcett estate wanted to buy a cartload of pig manure in 1771 when Michell walked in.

'Morning, Snowden. Police business, I suppose?'

'Indeed, sir, but it may involve you personally.'

'In what manner?' Michell sounded affronted. 'Nobody questioning my magistrate's expenses, I hope?'

'Nothing like that, sir. I believe you purchased a pair of silver candlesticks last year from a Mr Solomon?'

'Dealer in Barnard Castle?'

'Yes, sir.'

'Foreign-sounding fellow, bought a few things from him in my time. What of it?'

'You still have them?'

'Certainly. Pride of place on my dining table.'

'Could I see them?'

'Why on earth would you want to do that?'

'I'll explain once I've been able to examine them, sir. If you would be so kind...'

Frowning crossly, Michell rang a bell beside the door and the butler re-appeared so swiftly that Snowden was convinced he had been listening outside.

'Sir?'

'Bring me the candlesticks from the diningroom, the silver ones in the centre.'

'The candlesticks, sir?'

'Yes, the candlesticks, dammit. Both of them.'

'Yes, sir.'

Snowden and Michell waited in uncomfortable silence until the man returned, a candlestick in each hand.

'Well?' Michell watched as Snowden inspected them. 'What's this all about? Out with it, man.'

'They're stolen property, sir.'

'Stolen? Stolen?' Michell was outraged. 'Are you daring to accuse me of theft, Snowden?'

'Not you, sir, of course. I'm sure you bought them in good faith.'

'Damn right I did, paid a good price for them, too.'

'Eight pounds, I believe.'

'How the devil do you know that?'

'And probably worth a great deal more. They're on a list I have of items stolen last year from a Mr Bainbridge of Cotherstone and he estimates their value at considerably more than eight pounds.' Snowden paused, relishing his next words. 'I'm afraid I'm going to have to take them away.'

'Take them away?' Michell looked as if he would explode.

'Evidence, sir. I'll give you a receipt, of course. Perhaps your butler here could find me a cloth to wrap them in? It would be a shame if they got damaged.'

York, 10.40am

MARMADUKE Hardcastle viewed the fresh page proof and nodded happily. 'TORIES BLAMED FOR TRAGEDY TOWN COVER-UP' it shrieked across four columns.

He read it through once again. Most of it was that man Fewster's story, but he'd made one or two additions. Getting the North Riding's Tory MP to say he'd never heard of Barnard Castle, let alone young sweethearts drowning themselves there, had added icing to the cake, and the cherry on the top was a strident demand by Hardcastle's Uncle Arnold, would-be Liberal MP, for a full-bloodied parliamentary inquiry into why the affair had been swept so far under the carpet that nobody in the town dared talk about it any more.

'If that doesn't sell papers, nothing will.' He beamed at his head printer. 'Just one more alteration, I think.' He crossed out *Exclusive by Lancelot Fewster* and substituted *Yorkshire Gazette Exclusive by Marmaduke Hardcastle, Editor.* 'That should do it. Print an extra five hundred for Teesdale. They'll snap 'em up.'

Uncle Arnold would be proud of him.

Barnard Castle, 11.25am

'THERE'S a fair bit missing.' Dr O'Neill led Snowden into the morgue. 'Left femur for a start, right tibia and a rib or two. No idea what's happened to them, the fellow who brought them in said he'd never seen them. A few fingers and toes missing, too, but they're probably still lying about in the grave, easy to miss. I've had a look at the rest for you.'

Snowden peered at the heap of bones on the slab. 'Injuries?'

'Minor skull fracture, back of the head, but not surprising if he'd been knocked about on the rocks after falling in the river. That's what the coroner reckoned, anyway. I've read his report, for what it's worth. I've got a copy here.'

'Could it have been caused before he went in?'

O'Neill shrugged. 'It's possible.'

'Anything else?'

'Not that I can see.'

'That's a pity.' Snowden picked up the report. 'There's mention of blood coming from the head after he was found. Does that mean anything?'

'Not to me, but I'm no expert in that kind of thing.' O'Neill frowned. 'There's a man I know in York, he specialises in post-mortem haematology. You could ask him, I suppose.'

'It's an idea. Where would I find him?'

O'Neil scribbled the name and address on a scrap of paper and handed it over. 'Sorry not to be more help.'

Snowden shook his head. 'I was hoping you'd find evidence of Yates being dead or at least injured before he went into the water, but it looks as if I've wasted five shillings digging him up.'

'Time for a drink?'

'Thanks, but no. I've a lot of people to find.'

Darlington, 11.45am

TWENTY-EIGHT. Craven watched the last coal truck clank past and shook his head in disbelief. Twenty-eight, hauled by a single locomotive, on their way to the coal staithes at Port Darlington or perhaps the new iron mill at Middlesbrough. There must, he thought, be at least ten tons of coal in each one, and he tried to calculate how many horses it would take to do that. Fifty, perhaps? A hundred?

He tore his eyes away from the last truck, a red flag fluttering behind it, and wondered how much longer he'd have to wait for an answer to come back from London. He'd be happy spending all day at the station but felt faintly guilty doing nothing and was beginning to feel hungry as well. He looked up and down the line in case another train was coming, saw empty tracks in all directions, and went in search of something to eat.

The first building on the road into town had been a single-storey inn called the Drovers' Arms until the railway arrived, when its owner astutely converted it into a three-storey building offering food and accommodation for weary travellers and re-christened it the Station Hotel. Its new name rang a bell with Craven and he looked up at the name over the door. John Alderson, Purveyor of Fine Ales & Porter. He stepped purposefully inside, made his way to the bar and ordered a jug of ale and a mutton pie.

'Fivepence.' The woman behind the bar eyed his uniform curiously as she gave him the change from a shilling. 'You're new.'

'Just visiting. From Barney way, Greta Bridge.' He took an appreciative sip of ale. 'Is the landlord in?'

'Gone into town. Can I help? Polly Alderson, I'm his wife.'

'Maybe.' Craven dug out his notebook. 'Your husband put a notice in the *Police Gazette* about a year ago, asking about a man who stayed here, hired a horse and never came back.'

'That's right.' Her eyes lit up. 'Have you found him? Our best horse, it was, Marigold. And the saddle and the rest of the gear, never saw any of it again. Bastard.'

'We think we've tracked him down, a man called Henry Frankland. From London.'

'That's him. Should be hanged, when's he up in court?'

'Never, I'm afraid. He's dead.'

'Dead?'

'Murdered. The day he left you, that's why he didn't come back.'

'Poor sod.' She shook her head. 'What about our horse, though, and the rest of it? Are we getting it back?'

'Not much chance of that, Mrs Alderson. They'll have long gone.'

'Robbed, then, was he?' He nodded. 'Have you got who did it?'

'Not yet.'

'Nor likely to, after all this time. We should have asked him for a deposit, we normally do, but he left his trunk behind and we didn't bother. Haven't done that again, I can tell you.'

'Is the trunk still here?'

She shook her head. 'We put the notice in the paper, nothing happened, we sold it a month or two later. And what there was in it, not that there was much, just a few clothes.' She shrugged. 'Didn't make much, not enough to cover his bed for the night, let alone the horse.'

'I wondered if you could tell me anything you remember about him, this Frankland? What did he look like?'

She paused, throwing her mind back a year. 'Tall, fair hair, forty-ish maybe? A bit of a gentleman I'd say.'

'Did he mention anything about having family in the area?'

'Said he'd been north before but this was his first time by the railway. He didn't say why he was here.'

'Anything else?'

'Not that I recall. We didn't talk much, he spent most of his time at a table over there, reading his paper and chatting with the locals, even had a game or two of dominoes with them.'

She leaned over the bar and called to an elderly man sucking on a long church-warden pipe in the corner. 'Remember that fellow from London, Joe, the one who disappeared with our Marigold?'

The man looked at Craven and grunted. 'Found him at last, have they?'

'Got himself murdered.'

The man stopped in mid-suck. 'Murdered? Silly bugger.'

'Didn't you play dominoes with him?

'Me and a couple of the other lads, yes, fives and threes. Played a good hand, I remember.' He started smoking again and gave a cackle which turned into a cough. 'Least, he would have done if he hadn't got a bad 'un.'

Craven looked baffled. 'A bad hand?'

'Had to line his tiles up on the table.' He cackled again. 'Couldn't straighten his fingers to hold them, could he? Proper cack-handed, he was.'

Cotherstone, 12.25pm

JOHN Whorton, landlord of the Red Lion, brought a bucket of beer slops out of the inn for Bucephalus as Snowden tethered him to the railings outside.

'Bainbridge? Big house up on the left, fancy gate outside. What's he done now, gone bust again?'

'Not that I know of.' Snowden smiled. 'In fact he'll probably be pleased to see me.'

He made his way up the village, found the gate and walked up a flight of stone steps to the front door. Bainbridge answered it, a well-fed forty-something in a checked jacket who sported a pair of the most flamboyant muttonchop whiskers he'd ever seen.

'Mr Bainbridge?'

'Could be, who wants to know?'

'Superintendent Snowdon, Greta Bridge police. I think these may belong to you.' He held up the candlesticks.

'I'll be damned!' Bainbridge looked amazed. 'I never thought I'd see those again. Where on earth did you find them?' He reached out a hand.

'I'm afraid you can't have them back just yet, sir, but you can confirm they're the ones stolen from you?'

'Of course they are. Well, well, well. First the painting – that was down to you, wasn't it? Manners told me about you – then that coat the bailiff lad was wearing, then all the rest of stuff, and now the candlesticks. Is there any more to come?'

'Not that I know of, sir.' Snowden frowned. 'You mentioned a coat and a bailiff's lad. What was that about?'

'County court case in York. I sued the bailiffs and won hands down. Didn't you hear about it?'

'I don't have much to do with the civil courts, more than enough to do keeping pace with the criminal ones.'

Bainbridge beamed through his whiskers. 'Come in, have a drink and I'll tell you all about it.'

Barningham, 1.50pm

'OH, fiddlesticks!' Wharton picked his cravat out of the mud just in time to stop Ermintrude helping herself. 'Clean on this morning, and I'm not sure I've got any more back from Mrs Eeles.'

The pig gave an uninterested grunt and wandered off to the far side of the sty. Wharton sat on the low wall and eyed her fondly. She was in prime condition, well over 700 pounds by now, he reckoned, though he had no scales big enough to weigh her. He'd have to invent some. Whatever her weight, he was sure there wouldn't be many to challenge her at tomorrow's show.

He frowned. He still hadn't heard anything from Betsey about joining him and her silence perplexed him. He wondered if her father had forgotten to give her the message about Harriet and toyed with the idea of going to see her. Perhaps this evening, if there was time after he'd given Ermintrude her last meal and a final inspection before the big day.

The clock on the hall stables struck two and he leapt to his feet. He'd quite forgotten the monthly Mothers in Christ meeting, and a dozen of them would be waiting impatiently in the church. He set off at a run, trying to tuck his mud-stained cravat under his chin as he went.

Ermintrude watched him go, gave a contented fart, and began to investigate the prayerbook he'd left lying on the wall.

Barnard Castle, 2.50pm

BERNARD Emmerson, court bailiff, sometime army sergeant and occasional auctioneer, was not one of Snowden's favourite people.

Bailiffs were appointed and paid to carry out court orders ranging from serving summonses and executing arrest warrants to collecting debts and seizing defaulters' money, property and chattels in lieu. Emmerson carried out his functions with a malicious enthusiasm, never happier, Snowden believed, than when he was depriving people of their possessions and taking his shilling in the pound when they were auctioned.

His premises were tucked away behind the Market Place, and Snowden stopped when he got to its heavy iron gates to decide his next move. Now that Raine was firmly connected with the theft of the candlesticks, he wondered if it was him who had sold the coat to the market trader, who in turn had sold it to Emmerson's assistant, Henderson or Anderson or whatever his name was. He had said at York that he didn't know the trader, but he must remember something about him.

Snowden's brow furrowed. There was something else about a coat he couldn't recall. Somebody, he was sure, had mentioned it among the dozens of interviews he'd done in the past few weeks, but he couldn't place it. He shook his head irritably, pushed open one of the gates and walked into the yard.

Emmerson, a tall muscular man neatly bearded and dressed in black under a tall stovepipe hat, was sitting on a tea chest beside a cart laden with furniture.

'You'll find nothing here, Snowden.' Emmerson got up. 'All legitimate seizures, court orders.'

'I'm not after goods.' Snowden looked at him steadily. 'One of your assistants, Anderson. Or it could be Henderson, I'm not sure.'

'Henderson.'

'First name?'

'Matthew. What's it to you?'

'Is he here?'

'Might be.'

Snowden sighed. 'Where is he? Don't worry, I'm not here to arrest him. Unless you think there's a reason why I should?'

Emmerson paused before giving a grudging reply. 'Far side of the yard, sorting stuff. Don't keep him long, he's busy and time's money.'

'I'll be as brief as I can.'

Snowden crossed the yard. Henderson was stacking boxes, but stopped as he approached. He was no more than eighteen, a thick-set youth with a thin wisp of a moustache and protruding ears.

'Matthew Henderson? Police.' Snowden saw a slight look of alarm cross the youth's face.

'What d'you want?'

'Just a few questions. Been working here long?'

'About a year.'

'And you were in court at York with the rest of them just after you started? When Emmerson was sued?'

'That's right.'

'Tell me about the coat.'

Henderson's eyes flickered. 'What coat?'

'The coat you had to give back to its owner. You must remember.'

'Stolen off me it was. Bastards. It cost me seven shillings and they never gave me a penny. Lovely coat, it was.'

'You remember it?'

'Course I do.'

'Where did you get it?'

'I told them, I bought it off a stall at the market.'

'Who was selling it?'

'Don't know his name. It was a long time ago.'

'It was a man, then? Tall, short, fat, thin? Anything you remember?'

'Nothing.'

'Seen him before?'

'No.'

'Or after?'

'No. I told you, I don't remember him.'

Snowden was puzzled. Henderson wasn't accused of anything, but was doing nothing to help. Perhaps he just didn't like policemen. Or perhaps, Snowden began to wonder, he had something to hide.

'But you do remember how much you paid for the coat? Seven shillings, you said in court. That's a lot of money for a young lad like you. Where did you get it?'

'Earned it.'

'Doing what, before you started here?' Henderson didn't answer. 'I can always ask Emmerson, I'm sure he'd have wanted to know before taking you on.'

'Maybe it wasn't that much, I don't remember. Five shillings, perhaps.'

'Still a lot of money.' Snowden was convinced now that the youth was concealing something. 'Good condition, was it, the coat?'

'Good enough. Wouldn't have bought it otherwise.'

'Like new?'

'Suppose so.'

'No faults, patches, lining torn, missing buttons or anything?'

Henderson hesitated. 'Might've been.'

'Might have been? Come on, lad, you just said you'd not have bought it if it wasn't fit to wear. Yes or no?'

'It was a good coat, like I said. Nothing wrong with it.'

'Never been patched up?'

Henderson wrestled for an answer. 'Not that I noticed.'

Snowden's face hardened. 'I think you're lying.'

'I told you –'

'You didn't tell me about the patch in the lining, though. You didn't know it was there, and you couldn't have missed it, neatly done though it was. I was admiring it less than an hour ago.' Snowden paused and perched himself on one of the bigger boxes, thinking hard. How could Henderson be sitting in court in a jacket he knew nothing about? Had he stolen it that day and only just put it on? Had he borrowed it from someone? Or... A light dawned and he leant forward.

'You know what I think, Henderson? I think you're making it all up. You didn't buy that coat in the market. You didn't even have it long enough to notice it had been repaired. In fact, I'm not sure you even wore it into court that day.' He paused for this to sink in. 'Now, are you going to tell me where it really came from or do I arrest you for breaking and entering, burglary, and maybe even perjuring yourself in court?'

Henderson looked horrified. 'I never did anything like that.'

Snowden sat back. 'Let me tell you a story. Once upon a time there was a man sitting in court who suddenly gets very worried. You see, he's wearing a stolen coat, and he's just seen the owner come into the room. And if the owner knows he's got it he'll be asked some very awkward questions about a lot of other things that had been stolen and who had stolen them. Are you following all this so far?'

Henderson was aghast. 'I don't know anything about stuff being stolen, honest to God.'

'So this man turns to the bright young lad next to him who's only just started working for the bailiffs and couldn't possibly have any connection with the stolen goods, and he says how would you like to swap coats for a bit? And the bright young lad says why? and the man says because if you don't, sunshine, I'm going to beat the daylights out of you afterwards. Or something like that.' Snowden smiled. 'So the lad, who perhaps isn't so bright after all, swaps coats and puts the stolen one on as quick as he can, not ever seeing the lining with the patch in it, and he tells lies when they ask him how he got it and how much it cost. Am I right?'

There was a long pause.

'He told me to say I'd got it in the market and he'd give me a pound. I just guessed at seven shillings. That's all.'

'So what's this man's name, then?'

There was another pause, even longer.

'He doesn't work here now, he left just after.'

'His name?'

'Barker. Geordie Barker.' Henderson scowled. 'Bastard still owes me the pound.'

Carlisle, 3.15pm

SOMEBODY was battering at his head with a brick. Or a flat-iron. Or something even heavier.

McQueedie fought his way to consciousness and groaned. He'd had more hangovers than hot dinners since the age of twelve, but few quite as bad as this. The fraction of his brain still functioning tried to recall the night before.

He remembered meeting his old hack-mate from Glasgow days, Sandy, now a reporter for the *Cumberland Herald*, who had managed to persuade a magistrate to release him.

He had a vague memory of being stripped, scoured and squeezed into Sandy's spare suit and the pair of them heading for the nearest bar to celebrate his new-found freedom.

He had an even vaguer memory of reminiscing about their legendary and almost successful attempt to drink a Gorbals pub dry in 1822.

The rest was blank.

The flat-iron became a steam hammer and he sank back into oblivion.

Barnard Castle, 3.25pm

SNOWDEN walked slowly back across the yard, deep in thought. Emmerson, back on his tea chest near the gate, looked up with a sneer.

'Another waste of time, superintendent?'

'Not entirely. Quite useful, in fact.' Snowden came to a halt in front of him. 'I've got one or two questions for you as a result.'

'What about?'

'The Bainbridge robbery.'

Emmerson shook his head in disbelief. 'That was last bloody year, you can't still be looking into that.'

'We never give up, Mr Emmerson. Tell me about it, the day you collected Captain Bainbridge's property.'

'Why go through it all again? I told you lot everything at the time.'

'Not me, you didn't. I wasn't there. What happened?'

Emmerson sighed in exasperation. 'You know what bloody happened. We loaded it up, took it down the Kings Head and locked it up. Then some bugger stole it.'

'How did you take it down there? In a cart?'

'One of Crabthorpe's drays from the brewery, same as usual. They've always got a few for hire.'

'What time of day was this?'

'Late afternoon. Five o'clock, maybe.'

'Open cart, was it?'

'High-sided and covered. Some of the stuff we carry is valuable, can't have it getting wet. Or nicked as it goes through town.'

'And who drove it, you?'

Emmerson looked affronted. 'I'm the court bailiff, not a bloody carrier, I don't drive wagons. One of the lads took it, I followed him down on horseback.'

'Geordie Barker, was it?'

'How d'you know that?'

'And you met him at the Kings Head?'

'I just said that. There's half a dozen stables at the back of the yard there, I've rented a couple for years to keep stuff in.'

'Till it's sold off?'

'That's where we do the auctions, the Kings Head.'

'Secure, are they, these stables?'

'Course they are. Least, I thought so till Bainbridge's stuff vanished.'

'Locked?'

'Two locks. I keep one set of keys, the other's in the hotel manager's office.'

'So you followed Barker down there, opened up one of these stables, and shifted the property from the cart inside?'

'That's right.'

'Both of you?'

'I'm not a bloody labourer, either. Barker did it.'

'And you watched him do it?'

Emmerson paused, trying to remember. 'For a bit. Then I left him to it, went into the hotel for a bite to eat till he'd finished. He brought me the keys, took the dray back and that's it. Same as we always do, done it dozens of times.'

'You checked the stable?'

'Of course. All locked up.'

'When was that?'

'Half an hour or so after we got there. Maybe a bit more.'

'And when did you discover the property had been stolen?'

'Next morning, maybe an hour before the auction was due to start. I went to check the sales list and it had gone.'

'How did they get in? Were the locks forced?'

'Just as I'd left them.'

'So how –?'

'Well, they didn't use my keys.'

Snowden looked at him narrowly. 'You're sure?'

'You don't think I took the stuff? Why would I steal my own property? I lost a small fortune when it went. They must have got hold of the manager's set, though he swore they'd never left his office.'

'Perhaps.' Snowden looked thoughtful. 'Perhaps.'

Thorpe, 4.40pm

BETSEY had been picking peas for tea and was now lying back in a wicker chair in the garden, eating handfuls and trying not feel guilty. The kittens were romping among the flowerbeds and chasing butterflies while their mother stretched asleep on the sun-dappled grass beneath an apple tree. Bees buzzed, swallows chattered on the gutters, and Betsey was almost asleep when she heard footsteps from the yard.

'Papa?' She wondered whether she could persuade him to bring her a cup of tea. 'You're early for once.'

'I'm afraid it's only me.'

She opened her eyes with a start and smiled. 'Daniel! I'm sorry, I'm being terribly lazy. I thought it was father coming home.'

'I don't want to disturb you, but I've got something for him from Darlington.'

'Darlington?'

'I've been there all day. I suppose you'll know it well, but it's the first time I've been there. I'd no idea it was so big. And the railway...' His face was alight with boyish enthusiasm. 'It's astonishing.'

'Father took me on it when it opened. I must have been about twelve, he took me with him to see my aunt and uncle near York.' She laughed. 'I was terrified. I've never been on one since, though papa uses them often.'

'I'd love to travel on a train. So fast, faster than the best of horses. It's no wonder the stage coaches are giving up.' He bent down and picked up the ginger kitten. 'She's pretty.'

'Tiger. She's a he, I think, but I'm not sure.' She stood up, faintly pink. 'Would you like a cup of tea?'

'That's very kind, but I'm already much later than I expected. I had to wait for a reply.'

'Reply?' She was disappointed he couldn't stay.

'To his message to London by the electric telegraph. I sent it at just after eight this morning, and the police in Deptford had done what he asked and sent a reply by three. It's astonishing!' He handed her an envelope. 'It's in there, can you give it to him? And there's a note from me about the Station Hotel.'

'Of course.'

'I must be off.' He put the kitten carefully back on the grass and hesitated. 'Are you going to the show tomorrow?'

'No.'

'Too busy?'

'Just not going. Papa says he's got to attend but I'd be bored silly traipsing round with him and listening to speeches. I'll stay here with the cats.'

'Ah. It was just...' He stopped.

'Yes?'

'I just wondered if you fancied going. To the show. I mean, if you had someone to take you.'

'You're going?'

'I hope so. You could come with me if you wanted, but if you don't, of course...' His voice trailed off.

She smiled, amused at his embarrassment. 'I'd love to.'

Carlisle, 5.15pm

'GOOD God, McQueedie, are you still there?' Sandy McLeod stared at the bed. 'You haven't bloody died on me, have you?'

There was a faint moan from beneath the bedclothes. 'I'm not sure. What time is it?'

'Well past five.'

'Far too early, go away.'

'In the evening.' Sandy pulled open the curtain. 'I thought you were going to catch the stage back to Greta Bridge? It left hours ago.'

McQueedie struggled to his senses. 'There'll be another one.'

'Not till Monday. They've stopped running weekends.'

'Railway, then. To Newcastle.'

'Not a chance. There's been another accident, the line's blocked at Hexham. I've spent the day chasing it for the *Gazette*.' He nodded happily. 'Four burnt to death and eighteen injured. Good story.'

'I'll just have to stay here, then.'

'That's fine.'

'But no more sessions like last night. I mean it, Sandy. I just can't take it like I used to.'

Thorpe, 6.40pm

SNOWDEN chased the last pea round his plate, forked it into his mouth and sat back. 'I suppose you'll be all right.' He looked doubtful.

'But you'll be there too.' Betsey pushed the fruit bowl towards him. 'Sorry, there's nothing else. I was going to do a pudding but it was just too hot.'

Snowden nodded. 'It can't last much longer. I wouldn't be surprised if we had a thunderstorm or two later, there's black clouds in the distance.' He picked up an apple and began slicing it carefully. 'The thing is, Betsey, I'm going to have to miss the show.'

'Miss it?'

'I'll be tied up in court in Leeds for at least a couple of days from Monday – it's a tedious embezzlement case, nothing exciting but I've got to be there, and there's the monthly county magistrates meeting to squeeze in as well – and I want to see a man in York about some blood before then, if I can find him. No trains worth speaking of on Sundays, so tomorrow's my only chance. I can get there and back in a day.'

'I suppose you must.'

He saw her face fall and came to a decision. 'I'm sure you'll be safe with Constable Craven. Tell him to wear his full uniform and take his truncheon and you'll come to no harm.' He bit into a slice of apple and grinned. 'Safer with him if there's any trouble around than with Wharton, anyway.'

'I'll be all right.' She stood up cheerfully and began clearing the dishes. 'What was in the envelope he brought? He said it was to do with our Franklands man.'

'Have a look.' He reached into his inside pocket and handed her a sheet of paper. 'Reply from the police in Deptford, as taken down by the telegraph man. It's a bit difficult to read. He had to translate lots of dots and dashes, I suppose, but most of it makes sense.'

She took it and began to read.

To: Supt R. Snowden, Grate Bridge, via Darlington
July 31 1846 2.37pm
Re yr request H Fanklands 17a Albert St Deptford Stop Have visited
premises lodging house Stop Propriater affirms HF lived there alone single
Stop Missing July 1845 not seen since Stop MPR Aug 27 Stop Owes rent
Stop Wherabouts & famly unknone if any Stop Sgt M Handley Deptford
Constably force Stop Ends Stop

Betsey sorted out the Stops and the spellings and looked up. 'What does MPR mean?'

'Missing Persons Report. The one you saw in the *Police Gazette*.'

'Oh.' She read the message again. 'So he lived alone and one day he set off to see his relatives up here without telling anyone.'

'Why should he? He wasn't married, he thought he'd be back in a few days. He got the railway to Darlington and booked into the Station Hotel.' Snowden handed her Craven's note. 'Bright lad, your young constable. He called in there today.'

She smiled as he continued. 'Next morning Frankland hired a horse, met the dreaded Mrs Mattock in Whashton, bought his pie and ended up being robbed and left dead in the tunnel.'

'You were right about the direction he was coming from.' Betsey paused. 'I wonder what happened to the horse?'

'Sold by the killer, perhaps, but that's a bit risky, too easy to trace back to him. More likely it's down a disused mineshaft somewhere on the moors. There's enough of them, you could push a dozen horses down one and nobody would ever know.'

'Well, at least we know where poor Mr Frankland is. Now all we need to do is find out who killed him.'

Snowden finished the last of his apple. 'That might be easier than finding his horse. Meanwhile, we've got to find the killer we do know about, Thomas Raine.'

'You'll find him.' Betsey headed for the kitchen. 'You've got two of them under lock and key, Breckon and Barker, you know what happened, you've got your witness Ann Humphreys, you've got –'

'Humphreys! Of course!'

Betsey halted in the doorway. 'Of course what?'

'She said something when I interviewed her, about a coat, an argument on the Sills when she was there that night. It didn't mean anything at the time, but I should have gone into it.'

'The coat you told me about at tea, the one Barker made Henderson wear? What would that have to do with the drownings?'

'I don't know. If I set off early enough tomorrow I'll have time to call by York jail and question Barker about it. And I'll see Humphreys too. She's been held there for her safety since Monday and I'm sure she'll welcome a visitor.' He got to his feet. 'I'll be back in an hour or so.'

Betsey gave an exasperated sigh. 'Now where are you off to?'

'Barney. I want a word with Sergeant Clarke, the man who knows everyone in Teesdale and how they're related.'

Barningham, 7.15pm

Wharton stood at the gate of the sty and stared in dismay. Ermintrude, who should have been waiting fat and contented for her late-night titbit, was lying on her side in the mud, eyes closed, front feet drawn up to her chin, breathing heavily and whimpering in a way he'd never heard before.

At her side lay a scrumpled scrap of paper. The rest of the prayerbook, hardboard cover, silk page-marker ribbon and even the pencil, had vanished.

Wharton rushed through the gate and fell on his knees beside her. One eye opened briefly and she gave a faint grunt of recognition.

He reached for the scrap of paper. It was a page from the Litany, and the words at the top leapt out at him. *'From pride, vainglory, and hypocrisy; from envy, hatred, and malice, and all uncharitableness, Good Lord, Deliver Us.'*

It was true. Not the hypocrisy, perhaps, and he wasn't sure he could be accused of overdoing the envy, hatred and malice, but certainly the pride, far too much pride in what he'd achieved with Ermintrude. Vainglory too, probably, though he'd have to look it up to discover exactly what that meant.

He had sinned, and the mighty wrath of the Almighty had descended upon him.

'Forgive me, Lord.' He bent to pray and tears filled his eyes, dripping onto Ermintrude's vast pink belly and trickling slowly down into the mud.

Carlisle, 7.40pm

'JUST the one.' McQueedie, dressed in Sandy's second-best and two sizes too big suit, pushed open the door of the Lowther Arms. 'We'll leave as soon as the rain clears.'

'Of course.' Sandy nodded. 'Hair of the dog, blow the cobwebs away, that sort of thing. Do you good.'

'You'll have to buy the drinks again, I'm afraid.'

'No problem. Friday night, pay night, I've plenty. Here.' Sandy sat down at an empty table and handed McQueedie a half-sovereign. 'Can't have you not buying your round. Pay me back when you can.'

McQueedie took it gratefully and made his way to the bar. A large pock-marked man with a broken nose greeted him. 'You looking for a fight?'

McQueedie stepped back in alarm. 'We're not looking for any trouble. Just a quick drink.' He smiled nervously. 'Two large Glenbuckies, if you would be so good.'

'There'll be no trouble, don't worry. It's just across the yard if you change your minds. Some good game birds in tonight.'

'Ah. Good.' McQueedie handed over the half-sovereign, collected his change and carried the drinks to the table.

Sandy took his, looking bemused. 'Game birds? What was all that about?'

McQueedie shook his head. 'I've no idea. Pheasants for sale, maybe?'

Sandy grinned. 'Or women. Knocking shop, I reckon.' Four men walked into the bar, nodded to the barman, and disappeared through a door at the back. 'Knocking shop, no doubt about it.'

Three more entered and did the same. Then two more, three on their own, and a bunch of six.

'Hell of a busy whorehouse.' As McQueedie spoke four women came noisily into the bar and headed across the room. One called to the barman as they passed. 'Any tips for tonight, Jack? We'll make it worth your while.' There were shrieks of laughter from the others as they disappeared out the back. More people, male and female, arrived and followed them.

'It's an orgy, more like.' Sandy paused halfway through draining his glass and stared at a man who scurried in holding a cage. 'Bloody hell. That one's got a flaming chicken with him.'

McQueedie's face lit up. 'Satanic rites!' The headlines flashed before his eyes. DEVIL WORSHIPPERS EXPOSED. WE REVEAL MIDNIGHT SACRIFICES TO MITHRAL. VIRGINS CLAMOUR ON ALTAR FOR —

'Don't be bloody silly.' Sandy stood up. 'It's a cockfight. Let's take a look.'

Saturday August 1ˢᵗ

Barningham, 7.15am

THE weather had broken late last night, a violent thunderstorm at first, a brief lull, and then torrential rain sweeping across the Pennines. Weeks of dust turned to mud, roads became rivers and the rocky bed of the Tees vanished under a frothing surge of peat-stained water, broken branches and the occasional drowned sheep. The Rev Wharton, soaked to the skin and red-eyed after a night on his knees beside Ermintrude, hovered miserably under an umbrella as John Coates gave his verdict.

'Constipation.' He stood up and shook his head. 'She's all blocked up with summat. What have you been feeding her?'

'Just the usual.'

'You sure?' He looked at Wharton accusingly. 'The only time I've seen anything like this before was a pig stuffed full of old carpet its damn-fool owner had given it to sleep on. They'll eat bloody anything, pigs. Worse than goats.'

'What did you do?'

'Ate it. Best bacon I ever tasted.'

Wharton looked horrified. 'I couldn't do that to Ermintrude, I'd never forgive myself.' His voice trembled. 'I mean, she's almost family.' He looked appealingly at Coates, the Barningham estate bailiff generally acknowledged to be the village expert on veterinary matters. 'There must be a dose of something that would help.'

Coates looked doubtful. 'Nothing I've come across for pigs. I suppose they might make something for humans. I'm going down to Newsham this morning and could ask Doctor Graham.'

'Please.'

'I'll call by later and let you know what he says.' He gave Ermintrude a final glance. 'You are still going to the show, I suppose, even though she can't make it?'

'I've got to.' Wharton ran a muddy hand distractedly through his sodden hair. 'I'm supposed to be taking three people and I've got a speech to make this afternoon.'

'You want to get yourself changed and dry or you'll be needing Graham yourself.'

Wharton watched Coates drive his cart off through the rain, leaving the 700 pounds of porcine passenger he'd come to collect lying supine in her sty.

Darlington, 7.30am

SNOWDEN settled himself in the corner of an empty carriage and thanked his stars he was able to afford to travel first-class. At least he had some thin cushioning on his seat, a roof over his head and windows to keep the rain out. Those in second class had wooden benches and rough shutters against the weather; third class spent their journey standing up in open trucks little better than the coal tubs waiting in sidings across the way. They fared worse, he thought, than outside passengers in the vanishing stage coaches. At least they could sit down.

He opened the rain-spattered copy of the *Yorkshire Gazette* he'd bought at the station and ran his eye down the headlines. Cholera had broken out again in London and there were questions in Parliament about what should be done. The potato crop had failed once more in Ireland. Someone had taken a pot-shot at King Louis-Phillipe in Paris and an inquest had opened on a young soldier flogged to death at Hounslow. Eton were thrashing Harrow at cricket.

He yawned and turned the page. The Newcastle and Darlington Railway had made a massive profit again and was paying a nine per cent dividend to shareholders. Perhaps he should have invested in railways after all, but it still seemed too good to be true. The town scavenger at Whitby was in trouble for leaving his cart full of dirt and ashes in the street, and Snowden grinned. They should see Briggate and be thankful they had a scavenger. He moved on to page three and the smile faded from his face.

TORIES BLAMED FOR TOWN TRAGEDY COVER-UP.

He scanned through the story. Vital clues ignored... Search abandoned... Police failing in their duty... Demand for inquiry... He screwed the paper up angrily, wondering whether to demand an apology from the *Gazette,* but then became thoughtful. Its article might stir a few more memories among witnesses, and its insistence that Yates and the girl had committed suicide would give Raine no reason to suspect he was being sought by the police. The longer he remained in the dark, Snowden decided, the better the chance of finding him.

Barningham, 8.05am

THE rectory front door was standing half-open when Sussex Milbank arrived and he stepped carefully round the pool of rainwater that had blown inside. 'Anybody at home?'

Wharton appeared from the far end of the hall, clutching an enormous jar. 'Good heavens, is it that time already?' He stared distractedly at his visitor.

'Father's away and I've borrowed the landau.' Sussex grinned. 'With luck he'll never know. I've slipped Catchpole a sov to drive us for the day. It's outside, all ready to go.'

'Go? Oh, my lord, the girls. You'll have to take them, I can't possibly go yet. Ermintrude's at death's door.'

'Ermintrude?'

'Struck down with costivation, all my fault, she ate my prayerbook.'

'Prayerbook?' Sussex stared at him. 'That great fat black one you carry around, size of our family Bible?'

'All of it, pages, binding, leather cover with the buckle, even my favourite silver pencil.' He was close to tears. 'Second prize in the divinity tripos at Cambridge and all of it gone. Mrs Avery says prunes are the answer.' He held up the jar. 'There's four pounds of them in here.'

'Prunes?' Sussex looked appalled. 'God help her.'

'Why? She says they work miracles.'

'Ermintrude, not Mrs Avery.' Sussex looked thoughtful 'My nanny used to dose us with castor oil.' He grimaced at the memory. 'Foul stuff but it did the job. Two tablespoons and we were on the privy in fifteen seconds, given a good wind behind us. Which we usually had.'

'Castor oil?'

'Must be gallons of it still at the hall. I'll nip up and get some before I collect the girls. You're sure you can't come yet?'

'I'll make my own way there later. You'll find Harriet and Charlotte at Lilac Cottage.' His face fell. 'I've no idea about Betsey. She can't be coming.'

Thorpe, 8.30am

BETSEY had spent hours working on the lacy edges round the bonnet and she gave its reflection in the mirror a nod of satisfaction. She tucked away an errant curl and went to the window. Still raining. She'd need a cape and the biggest parasol she could find.

There was a clatter of hooves in the yard and she went to the back door. It was Craven, in full uniform under a sodden greatcoat, holding the reins of a dog-cart.

Betsey stared. 'I can't ride in that, not in this weather.'

'I know.' Craven looked apologetic. 'I've tried everywhere to find a covered carriage, but there's none to be had. It's the rain, everyone wants one.'

'If you think I'm walking –'

'It's all right, I saw Sussex Milbank in Greta Bridge, in a landau on his way to the show. He says there's room for one more inside and will give you a lift. He's on his way.'

'Sussex?' She'd met him once or twice in church, a bright young man but rather too full of himself and not, she suspected, her father's first choice of a safe companion for his daughter.

'You'll be fine with him. He'd got two more young ladies going to the show.' Craven gave the reins a twitch. 'I'll meet you there.'

Betsey watched him go, passing the landau as it entered the yard. It pulled up before her and her eyes widened. It was finer than any carriage she'd ever been in, the bodywork and spokes on the four large wheels bright red, the Milbank crest in gold on the door, the horses an immaculate pair of greys, the coachman in his dark blue uniform perched miserably in front and, thank heavens, the leather roof firmly fastened to shield passengers inside from the rain. The door opened and Sussex leant out.

'In you come, Miss Snowden,' He held out a hand to help her in and pulled the door closed behind her.

Beside him sat the schoolmistress who'd replaced Betsey last year. Opposite, smiling welcomingly as she patted the space beside her, sat the girl who'd been romping in the hay with William.

Barningham, 9.35am

'STRYCHNINE?' Wharton stared at the tiny bottle. 'Are you sure?'

'Doc Graham swears by it.' John Coates nodded. 'That and a few pints of turpentine. I've got a gallon there in the cart.'

'I don't know...' Wharton shook his head doubtfully. 'Sussex came back with bottles of castor oil and syrup of figs. And then there's Mrs Avery's prunes. Which do I use?' 'If I were you I'd start with the turpentine. If that doesn't do it, try the rest one by one. Something's bound to work.'

Barnard Castle, 9.55am

SUSSEX Milbank was baffled. It wasn't the best of days to hold an open-air show, admittedly, what with the rain still teeming down and the exhibitors standing miserably on the muddy Desmesne field beside sodden groups of animals. The few spectators who had turned up so far were huddled in the central marquee, queueing for cups of tea and wondering when the beer tents would open. Sussex had left his three companions at a table in one corner and now stood in the tea queue, puzzled why two of them seemed to be having the time of their lives and the third one clearly wasn't. Betsey hadn't said a word in the landau or since, and was now sitting at a wooden bench, her back turned to the other two girls, and staring grimly the other way.

'It's such a pity about Ermintrude,' Charlotte was saying behind her. 'What d'you think is the matter with her? Sussex looked so embarrassed when I asked him to explain.'

'Something awfully internal.' Harriet lowered her voice. 'Do you suppose pigs suffer the sort of things women do? You know...'

'Oh, they can't do. Not pigs!'

'I don't see why not. That poor vicar.'

'He's a rector, Harriet, he gets tithes and things.'

'Funny sort of fellow, whatever he is. All wrapped up in his pigs and inventions and goes quite pink at the sight of a woman.'

'He comes into school every week, you know, to check the girls know their catechism and so on. He hates it.' Charlotte broke into giggles. 'You should have seen him the day they asked him about the virgin birth.'

'And that afternoon when I followed him into the hay barn and he couldn't wait to get me out again. Terrified, he was, wouldn't come near me.' Harriet looked up and stifled her laughter. 'Sssh, here comes Sussex. Now there's someone who'd have you rolling in the hay given half a chance.'

'Harriet!'

Sussex laid down the tray he was carrying and began handing out mugs of tea. He offered one to Betsey, who ignored him completely. She really was acting very strangely, staring into space with a look of dawning horror on her face.

Sussex shook his head and put the mug back on the bench. Women could be very odd sometimes.

York, 10.15am

WILLIAM Anderson, MD, FRCS & FPS, surgeon, lecturer in clinical haemotology at the York School of Medicines and medical consultant at York Castle, had one of the longest, boniest and baldest heads Snowden had ever seen, even though it was partly obscured by enormous horn-rimmed spectacles, a straggling white beard and clouds of smoke from a meerschaum clamped between his teeth.

'Come in, come in, come in!' He ushered Snowden into an armchair, reached into a desk drawer and produced a bottle of brandy. 'Drink? Good. D'you smoke?'

'Just a briar.' Snowden dug out his pipe. 'Nothing as strong as yours, I fear.'

'Parson's Old Twist, wonderful stuff.' Anderson proffered an oily rope of pungent black tobacco. 'Friend of mine in Kendal sends me four ounces every week. Try a bit.'

Snowden sniffed it, wiped tears from his eyes and handed it back. 'Stick to my usual, I think. Bit early in the day for this.'

'As you will.' Anderson sent a fresh cloud of smoke wafting towards the ceiling. 'So what does O'Neill think I can do for you?'

'It's about a murder, or at least I think it's murder. Two of them, in fact, but one will do for now, a young man found drowned in a river. He'd got head wounds which he could have received before or after he entered the water, and I wondered whether you could tell me which.' Snowden took a cautious sip of brandy. 'The inquest jury returned a verdict of misadventure. I think they were wrong.'

'Any chance of me seeing the body?'

'It happened a year ago. I had it exhumed, but far too late to find any blood. The best I can offer are statements from the inquest.' He reached into his briefcase, found a sheaf of papers and riffled through them. 'This is the only one that might help. Witness called Tenwick, a blacksmith who identified the body the day after it was pulled out of the river.'

Anderson poured himself another generous brandy and leant back. 'Go ahead.'

'I'll read you his statement. *"The body was lying in a cowhouse on some straw. I looked at his nostrils, where I observed caked blood..."*

'Nonsense.' Anderson shook his head. 'No blacksmith ever observed anything.'

'I'm sorry?' Snowden was puzzled by the interruption. 'That's what he said.'

'I suppose he had a helping hand making this statement as usual? Policemen observe things. Blacksmiths *see* them.'

Snowden gave a wry smile. 'That's probably true. But I think the meaning's clear enough.'

He resumed reading. *"I felt at the head and I found the back part was bruised and covered with caked blood. When I say the blood was caked, I mean congealed, rather harder than treacle. I put my hand to that place. I looked at my hand when I took it away and my finger was daubed with blood. It was not in lumps, but in a kind of fluid."*

Anderson nodded. 'That sounds genuine enough apart from the word congealed, unless he's a remarkably literate blacksmith. Anything else?'

'That's it, I'm afraid.'

'Well, let's see. In my experience, in the case of persons who have come by their death suddenly, the blood normally remains fluid. I would say that the coagulated blood at the back part of the head flowed from the wound before the body went into the water.'

Anderson paused, thinking for a moment. 'Any blood that flowed afterwards would have been washed away as it came out of the wound. As far as the blood in the nostrils is concerned, I should have thought that would also have been the case.'

'So why did Tenwick see liquid blood on his hand?'

'Probably just the result of changing the position of the body, rolling it over from belly to the back, perhaps. Was the man wearing a hat of any kind?'

'Not that I'm aware of.'

'Hmm. If he'd been wearing a tight cap when he went in and then received the head injuries I suppose the blood might not coagulate. Not very likely, though. Another brandy?'

'Thank you, no.'

'The bruises are interesting, of course.'

'Interesting?'

'Well, it may be possible that a blow inflicted shortly after death – whether by a human hand or just by being battered on rocks in the river – could produce discolouration, but I don't think so. I've tried the experiment on amputated limbs but never been able to produce bruises in such circumstances.'

'So it's murder?'

'Ah, I can't promise you that, Snowden.' Anderson reached for the brandy bottle. 'He could have fallen and injured himself. But however he got his head wounds, I certainly think he got them before he went into the water.'

'And you'd testify to that in court?'

'For the usual fee.' Anderson grinned though his whiskers and sent another cloud of acrid blue smoke into the air. 'A pound of Parson's Old Twist will do nicely.'

Barnard Castle, 10.45am

'THERE you are, two hundred and fifty. Bit wet, some of 'em, but they'll dry out.' The carrier from Darlington dumped the last of his five bundles of papers on the floor of the shed behind the *Gazette* office. 'Sorry they're late, floods at Gainford.'

Lancelot Fewster grabbed half a dozen copies and took the stairs to his office two at a time. Back in his chair he opened one eagerly and began to scour the pages. TORIES BLAMED FOR TRAGEDY TOWN COVER-UP, there it was, top of the page just above *Yorkshire Gazette Exclusive* by...

His face fell. *Marmaduke Hardcastle, Editor*? He stared at it in disbelief. The bastard had stolen his story. Well, McQueedie's really, of course, but that wasn't the point. It certainly wasn't Hardcastle's.

He began to read and his face fell further. Not only had the editor stolen it, he'd added and changed things. Where McQueedie's original had been carefully littered with *it is reported* and *allegations of* and *according to reliable sources,* the final version left readers in no doubt that the entire town was heartlessly scorning the memory of the dead couple, aided and abetted by a malicious conspiracy of incompetent police, self-seeking local dignitaries, deluded religious leaders and evil politicians, What's more, the *Gazette* said it could prove it.

He stood up, took a long pinch of snuff and began to worry.

Barningham, 11.20am

'THANK you so much, you've been very kind.' Betsey climbed out of the dog-cart, clutching her parasol over her drenched bonnet and cape. 'I'm so sorry about this.'

Craven helped her out, his face a picture of bewilderment, 'Are you sure you don't want to be back at Thorpe?'

'No, I'll be perfectly all right here. I just want to call in at the rectory for something.'

You go back to the show, I'm sure Sussex will be delighted if you join him and his two young ladies.' She managed a weak smile. 'Three's a crowd, you know.'

He watched her reach the rectory porch, gave a sigh and got back in the dog-cart. It was a pity, but she obviously didn't want to spend the day with him even though it did look as if the rain was dying off. And that Harriet girl looked interesting.

He gave the reins a tug and set off back to the show.

York, 11.25am

HENRY Cavendish, recently appointed deputy governor of York Jail, greeted Snowden without enthusiasm and led him into a tiny ante-room in the cell block.

'Have to make do with this, I'm afraid.' He waved a hand at the only furniture in the room, a battered table with a wooden chair on each side. 'Not the best day to come looking for prisoners, Saturday. No courts, no shifting the bastards from one place to another. We keep 'em locked up all day and most of the staff get time off.'

'They get a full two days?' Snowden sounded surprised.

'Back in tomorrow, all of them. Sunday services, compulsory for all inmates. Anglicans eight o'clock, Catholics ten, Methodists and the rest of that lot at noon. Women in the afternoon. We need every officer we've got to keep control. Not fond of religion, your average prisoner.'

'I discovered that long ago.' Snowden eyed him curiously. A tall man, mid-forties, neatly-trimmed side-whiskers, deep tan and a distinctly military air. 'You're new here, Mr Cavendish. Soldier, I believe?'

'Twenty-two years' service with the East India Company in Bengal, superintendent. And it's Colonel Cavendish.'

'Of course.' Snowden felt as if he should be standing to attention. 'Never got further than Ireland, myself.'

'Army man too, were you?'

'Just one of the rank and file, I'm afraid.' Snowden ventured a smile. 'Seven years as a fusilier was enough.'

'Hmm.' Cavendish clearly didn't agree. 'So what can I do for you?'

'I'll try not to take up much of your time, colonel. I sent details of the two people I want to see. They'll have been kept well apart, I trust?'

'Of course. No fraternising between the men and women here. Never see each other if we can help it.'

'The woman first, then, if she's ready.'

'Waiting in the guardroom. Witness, I understand, here for her own safety?'

'That's right.'

'Living in the lap of luxury, she is. Must be important.'

'Very. Double murder case.'

'I'll bring her in.'

Snowden settled himself gingerly in the chair furthest from the door and had just enough time to light his pipe before Cavendish returned, followed by Ann Humphreys.

'Miss Humphreys. Do sit down. You needn't stay, colonel, if you're busy.'

'I'll be in my office, just across the way.' Cavendish paused at the door. 'Let me know when you want the next one and I'll take you to the cells.'

Humphreys perched herself in the chair opposite him. She didn't look as if she was finding confinement luxurious, thought Snowden, but she did seem to have put on a bit of weight and lost the grey pallor he remembered. 'Are they treating you well?'

'It's all right.' She tugged nervously at a stray strand of hair. 'Have you got Thomas Raine yet?'

'Not yet, no.'

'You've got to find him, Mr Snowden. I'll be stuck in here for years if you don't, he'd kill me given half a chance.'

'We'll track him down him soon, don't worry. You've no idea where he'd be, I suppose?'

'They said he'd done a runner after some trouble in Staindrop months ago, could've gone anywhere. Left the country if he's any sense.'

Snowden sighed and hoped she was wrong. 'It's not him I came to talk to you about, it's Barker.'

'Geordie? You found him fast enough.'

'How do you know that?'

'I got a letter from Liz. She says it's all round town, him being charged with murder. Where is he?'

'Safe enough.' Snowden wasn't going to tell her that Barker was in a cell only yards away. 'Look, when I interviewed you about that night on the Sills, you said he and Yates were arguing about a coat. Can you remember any more about that?'

'Does it matter?'

'It might. What were they saying?'

Humphreys frowned as she cast her mind back. 'I dunno. We were going down the road and Barker goes up to Joe and asks him if he's going to York to speak against him about this coat.'

'What coat?'

'He didn't say.'

'Could he have meant he thought Joe was going to give evidence against him, in court here?'

'I suppose so. Joe says something like "I could do no other than go against you" as if he'd've had no choice and Barker calls him a bastard and says in that case he would never get the chance to go to York and... ' Her voice faltered.

'Go on.'

'And then he starts hitting Joe and Joe cries out "Don't knock my eyes out" and Thomas and Breckon start hitting him as well.'

'Barker hit him first?'

'I think so. I was yards away, it was dark, there were heavy blows being struck but I don't know which ones were doing it.' Tears welled in her eyes. 'Joe was crying out he was being murdered and Kate was shrieking too and Barker told us if we didn't shut up we'd be thrown in the water.' There was a sob. 'You know what happened next.'

Snowden nodded and waited while she recovered her composure. 'And that's all that was said about the coat?'

'Yes. What does it matter? They killed Joe and Kate, that's what matters, not some bloody coat.'

'But it does matter, Miss Humphreys. If we're going to convict these men for the murders, we're going to have to find a motive. They wouldn't kill him for a few shillings in his pocket, which he'd offered to spend on them anyway. There has to be some other reason why Barker wanted Yates dead. And that seems to be the coat. The question is, why?'

He sat back, tamped the tobacco down in his pipe, and tried to make sense of it all. 'I think Yates knew this coat was stolen by Barker and Barker thought he was going to say so if it ended up in court. How would Yates know that?'

'You don't think he was involved in the robbery?' Humphreys shook her head vehemently. 'Not Joe, he'd never do anything like that. He was a good lad, even if he did keep bad company sometimes, and why would he need to steal? He had a good little business going, did Joe. He wouldn't have the nerve, anyway, poor little sod.'

'He was a tailor, wasn't he?' Snowden put his pipe down suddenly. 'Of course. Patching and mending clothes for a living.'

'Good at it, he was. One of the best in town.'

A smile crept over Snowden's face. 'Thank you, Miss Humphreys, you've been very helpful. Very helpful indeed.'

Barnard Castle, 11.56am

THE first brick smashed through the first-floor window of the *Gazette*'s editorial office, bounced off Fewster's desk, missed his head by a third of an inch and made a nasty dent in the 1829 Cricket Tournament trophy on the shelf behind.

The next one followed seven seconds later, seven seconds in which Fewster had time to dive beneath the desk, crack his head on an open drawer, slice open his left forefinger on a shard of broken glass from the first brick, and discover that he'd spectacularly wet himself.

Heart thumping and trousers dripping, he crawled painfully across to the door. There was a flurry of rodent activity as he got to his feet and scuttered into the storeroom next-door, clambering over the piles of old *Gazettes* to reach the small window in the corner. One pane had been missing from time immemorial, and he peered cautiously through it at the Market Place below.

The rain had stopped, and standing among the puddles on the cobbled street was a short fat middle-aged man, a bottle in one hand and a copy of the *Gazette* in the other, surrounded by a growing crowd of spectators.

'Lying bastards!' The man reeled drunkenly towards the *Gazette* front door, took a long swig from the bottle and slung it at the building. His audience cheered. 'Have you seen what they're saying about my Katie?' He waved the newspaper wildly in the air. 'Nobody cares, they say, forgotten by heartless friends and family. Well, I haven't forgotten. She was lovely, my little girl, apple of my eye she was, lovely.' His voice cracked with emotion and the crowd growled in sympathy.

'He's right!' The cry came from a buxom yellow-haired woman Fewster vaguely remembered seeing in the Oddfellows Arms. She thrust herself forward to join the man and her voice rose to a screech of fury. 'Blonde Bombshell Barmaid he calls me! Told me he was dead, the lying sod. Well, he bloody well will be if I've got anything to do with it.'

There was a chorus of approval as the man tried to put an arm round her, staggered and missed. 'I love you, Eliza Benson.' The crowd erupted in delight. 'You know what I'm going to do? I'm going to sue them for every penny they've got.' Another cheer. 'But first I'm going to get the bugger who wrote this.' There was a roar of encouragement. 'He'll be up there now. Who's coming with me?'

'You sort him out, Bill.' One of the heftiest men Fewster had ever laid eyes on stepped forward. 'I'll give you a hand. Come on, lads, half through the front door, the rest round the back. We'll get the bastard.'

The crowd surged towards the *Gazette* and with a small squeak of terror Fewster scrambled frantically back over the old newspapers, scrunching a small rat into the floorboards as he reached the landing. The sound of angry voices rose from below and he hurtled up the stairs to the attic, home for more than a century of ancient files, broken chairs, mouldering accounts books and several tons of pigeon shit deposited by birds nesting in the rafters. Eyes watering at its pungent acidity and holding his breath as best he could, he launched into its midst and headed for the gap high in the roof at the far end through which the pigeons entered, his feet sinking into the mire until he ended up crawling across the guano quicksand on his hands and knees.

There were enough slates missing for him to be able to squeeze through onto the roof, scrabble his way over the wet tiles to the top and collapse on the ridge. Trembling with fear, he embraced the chimneystack for dear life as the mob on the floor below set fire to his office.

York, 12.10pm

'BROUGHT him down here from the main block.' Cavendish led Snowden to the holding cell and nodded to the warder outside. 'This is Superintendent Snowden, Higgs, come to see Barker. You'll not need me again?'

'I shouldn't think so.'

Cavendish scurried back down the corridor as Higgs opened a spy-hole in the cell door, glanced through, nodded and unlocked the bolts. 'We've chained him, sir, you'll be safe enough if you don't go too near. There's a chair for you, well away from him. Want me to stay with you?'

Barker was hunched on a stone slab in the far corner, shackled by a thick iron chain padlocked to a bolt in the wall. Snowden shook his head. 'I'll call when I've finished.' The door closed behind him and he sat down.

'Mr bloody Snowden.' Barker grinned and spat on the floor. 'Come to let me out?'

'Not till the court's ready for you.'

'Waste of time. No jury's going to convict us on the word of that tart Humphreys.'

'We'll see.' Snowden lent back in his chair and took out his pipe. 'I know why you did it.'

'Did what?'

'Murder Joe Yates. Nice coat, was it?'

The grin faded from Barker's face. 'Coat, Mr Snowden? I don't know anything about any coat.'

'Oh, I think you do. I've been talking to young Matthew Henderson.'

'The little bastard.' Barker leapt to his feet and grimaced as the chain brought him to a sudden halt. 'He's lying.'

'About the coat?'

'About anything he's said.'

'Bainbridge's coat, the one you couldn't resist helping yourself to when you stole it from the Kings Head. The one with the ripped lining you asked Joe Yates to repair for you.'

'I never stole it. Bought it in Barney market, how would I know it was stolen?'

'Why get Henderson to wear it if you didn't?'

'Doesn't prove anything. How could I steal stuff locked away at the Kings Head?' Barker sat down and shook his head scornfully. 'Think I nicked the manager's keys out of his safe? You must be joking.'

'But it wasn't, was it?'

'Wasn't what?'

'Locked away at the Kings Head.' Snowden blew a cloud of smoke towards the ceiling. 'You took it there, started unloading it into the stable, waited till Emmerson had gone into the hotel like he always did and then loaded it back in the dray.'

'You're making this up, Mr Snowden.' Barker gave a harsh laugh. 'Load of cobblers.'

'A load of stolen property. You gave the keys back to Emmerson and he watched you drive what he thought was an empty cart out of the yard as you'd done dozens of times before. He checks the stable is locked but doesn't look inside – why should he? – and off you go to meet Frankie Ramsden.'

'Never heard of him.'

'Oh, come on, Barker. Frankie Ramsden, your cousin up in Mickleton. My Sergeant Cooke knows all about you.' Another wave of blue smoke drifted upwards. 'Where was he, your cousin, somewhere quiet just outside the town, waiting for you with a cart of his own to take the stuff away and hide in his barn? While you take the empty dray back to the brewery?'

'You can't prove anything. Frankie won't talk.'

'I wouldn't bet on that, Barker. But I would wager that when I check the brewery records I find out that you returned the dray that night a good couple of hours after you left the Kings Head at around five-thirty. Where were you all that time? Don't tell me you got lost on the way up Gallowgate?'

'I don't know. Probably went for a drink.'

'With a horse and dray?'

'Might have. You can't prove any of this.'

'I don't think I'm going to have to. But I'm sure I can prove you knew the coat was stolen and that when you were told you were going to court about the Bainbridge robbery you thought Joe Yates was going to give evidence against you. He knew the coat was stolen, didn't he, when you asked him to repair it? Because the other thing you asked him to do was unstitch the name-tag.'

'I don't know what you're talking about.'

'You don't understand much, do you, Barker? You didn't understand when you got the order to go to court that it wasn't a criminal case about who'd done the robbery, it was a civil case to get compensation money out of Emmerson. Everyone connected with his bailiff's business was summoned to appear. No one was accused of anything. Certainly not you.'

'You're lying.'

'You jumped to the conclusion that Yates had informed on you and when you asked him if he'd testify against you he said he'd have to if he was asked. Nobody had asked him, though, or intended to. He wasn't involved at all. But you didn't know that, and that's why you beat him up and then killed him.'

'No jury's going to convict me of that robbery.'

'I'm not going to ask them to, Barker. But I'll tell them all about it when you stand trial for murder and I think they'll believe me when I tell them that was your motive for wanting Yates dead.' He paused. 'I think your mate Thomas Raines might tell us quite a bit, too.'

'Thomas? What's he got to do with it?'

'I think you went back to Frankie's place later and decided to take some of the stolen goods to sell, candlesticks for starters. Too risky to do it yourself, you being one of the bailiff lads, so you asked Thomas to do it for you.'

'Thomas won't talk.'

'We'll see.' Snowden tapped his pipe out and stood up. 'I reckon you're heading for the gallows unless you want to tell me exactly what happened that night.'

'I'll see you in hell first, Mr Snowden.' Barker aimed a gobbet of spit at his feet. 'I'm telling you nothing.'

Barningham, 2.20pm

'YOU poor old thing.' Bestey sat on an upturned bucket and stroked the back of Ermintrude's neck. The pig's ears twitched slightly. 'I do wish you'd open your eyes.'

She had been there for three hours now, ever since she'd knocked tentatively on the rectory door, found nobody in, and made her way round to the sty to find William. There had followed ten minutes of surprise, bewilderment, abject apologies, forgiveness and a few tears before she insisted that he went to the show to deliver his speech while she stayed behind to look after Ermintrude.

'Are you sure?' He'd hesitated, torn between his duty to the Teesdale Agricultural Society and the desire – which frightened him a little – to stay with this beautiful young creature who he'd never dared to dream might cry tears upon his shoulder. And then there was Ermintrude...

'Of course,' she'd said gently. 'I'll look after her until you get back.'

Duty won, and now she sat here, ankle-deep in mud, her lacy bonnet discarded, feeling very foolish but happier, so much happier, than she had been since Monday.

Above her the last of the storm clouds drifted off to the east and the sun came out.

Barnard Castle, 2.40pm

CORNELIUS Crabthorpe, brewer, property owner and widely acknowledged to be the hardest, meanest and least-loved man in Teesdale, watched as the *Gazette* roof caved in and smiled to himself. He had the building well over-insured through the Barnard Castle and District Provident Assurance Company, which he happened to own, and it would be a providential way of transferring yet more of its many gullible clients' premiums to his personal bank account. He'd have burned the place down himself if thought he could get away with it.

'What the hell was he doing up on the roof anyway?' He turned to PC Kipling, who had been lingering with Alice in her shop doorway four hundred yards away while the mob set fire to the stacks of old newspapers. They had fled long before he came on the scene.

'Had a brainstorm, sir, by all accounts.' There was a thunderous crash as the chimney collapsed. 'Some kind of religious mania. Set fire to his office and then clambered up on the roof to pray.'

'Pray?'

'When I got here he was clinging to the chimneypot and moaning my God, my God, oh my God. Kept saying he was being persecuted by a horde of devils.' Kipling shook his head doubtfully. 'That was before he jumped, of course.'

'Jumped?'

'The firemen had a blanket underneath.'

'Ah. I missed that.'

'So did he. Landed on top of a horse.'

'Dead?'

'Broken neck. Instantaneous.'

'Worse ways to go, I suppose.' Crabthorpe shrugged. 'Where's the body?'

'Knacker took it away. Be in the butcher's tomorrow.'

'Not the bloody horse, you fool. The lunatic on the roof.'

'Oh, he bounced off with just a few bruises. But completely mad, they've taken him up to the asylum. Babbling, he was.'

'Babbling?'

'And gibbering.'

Barnard Castle, 3.05pm

'WHAT'S this one been up to?' Sergeant Clarke sighed and reached for the charge book. Show day was usually one of the busiest days in the year but he'd hoped the rain would keep the villains away this time. No such luck, and he'd already got a trio of pickpockets in cell one and a horse-thief and a three-card con artist in cell two. Many more and he'd be running out of space.

'Brawling in the beer tent.' Constable McEwen pushed his prisoner forward. 'Came off worst by the look of it.'

'Never learn, do you, son?' He looked the man up and down. Jonathan Arrowsmith, he'd known him since he was a nipper. Now five-foot-six, no more, a wiry lad in his twenties. Black eye, tooth missing, blood on his jerkin, handcuffs on his wrists. 'I thought you were away working up the dale somewhere?'

'Came back this morning. Been celebrating my birthday.'

'I hope it was worth it.' Clarke picked up his pen. 'Let's sign you in. What's it to be, constable? Drunk and disorderly, breach of the peace, assault?'

'All three, I reckon.'

'Do us a favour, Sarge.' Arrowsmith wiped a dribble of blood from his mouth. 'It was just a bit of a fight, nothing serious. A quid fine for being drunk, I can't argue with that, I've had a skinful at the show. But assault, they could send me down for six months.'

'I'll think about it. Moved back into that room up the street, have you?'

'Bastard landlord's let it out, hasn't he? The bugger I shared it with's done a runner, taken all my things with him as far as I can see. You want to be looking for thieving sods like him, not arresting lads having a harmless barney at the show.'

'Harmless? You're dripping blood on my floor.' Clarke began to write. 'Jonathan Arrowsmith, no fixed abode... Who is he, this missing room-mate?'

Arrowsmith grinned. 'Thought you knew everything, Sarge.'

'Can't keep track of all you young ones, in and out of places like musical chairs. What's his name?'

'Geordie Barker.'

Clarke halted his pen in mid-air. 'Barker? Did nobody tell you?'

'Too busy getting pissed. What's he done, then?'

'He's up for murder.'

'Murder?' Arrowsmith looked thunderstruck.

'Two murders, in fact. Joe Yates and Kate Raine.'

'Them that went in the river? Jesus. Who saw him do it?'

'Half the bloody town if the number of people claiming a reward is anything to go by.'

Arrowsmith frowned. 'What reward?'

'You have been away a long time, son. There's money going for information about what went on that night.' Clarke put down his pen and looked at the young man intently. 'Were you sharing your room with him back then?'

'The night they drowned, yes. Remember it well.'

'You saw Barker?'

Arrowsmith hesitated. 'Might have done. What's it worth?'

Clarke picked up his pen again. 'How d'you spell assault, constable? One S or two?'

'Hang on, Sarge, give us a minute.' Arrowsmith wrestled with his conscience. 'You're saying Geordie killed Joe and Kate? Why would he do that?'

'I don't know, but the superintendent seems certain he did – him and a couple of others.'

'Others? Who?'

'You'll find out when we've got them all. Now, are you going to tell us about Barker or are we going to do you for assault? Could even be grievous bodily, couldn't it, constable?'

'Very easily, sir. And there's the resisting arrest, of course.'

'And assaulting an officer in the execution of. Plenty of bruises on you, constable?'

'Must be, sir. Might've worn off by the time we get to court, mind.'

'Still...' Clarke shook his head. 'Could be a twelve-month stretch, son. Anything to say before I write out the charges?'

Arrowsmith swallowed hard. 'Little Joe Yates, he was a friend of mine. And Kate was a nice lass, even if she was on the game.' There was a pause as he made up his mind. 'That bastard Barker stole my stuff while I've been away, I don't owe him any favours. How do I get the reward?'

'You don't until we've had a long chat and you convince me you know something worth knowing.'

Arrowsmith nodded thoughtfully. 'I reckon I do.'

'You'd better not be wasting our time.' Clarke returned to the charge book. 'We'll call it drunk and disorderly for now.' He frowned and looked up. 'Got a brother, haven't you? Wasn't he shacked up with the girl?'

'Charlie, yes. Buggered off somewhere before she died, never heard from him since.'

'London, I heard.'

Arrowsmith shrugged. 'We didn't get on that well. Could be anywhere.'

Clarke returned to the charge book. 'Put him in number three, constable, he's nowhere else to go. And then find a mop for the floor.'

Thorpe, 7.15pm

SNOWDEN stared at Betsey, his fork paused in mid-air. 'You spent the day nursing a *pig?*'

'I had to.' His daughter looked slightly flustered. 'It's all a bit complicated. She's not well and William had to make his speech.'

'William again, is it?' Snowden raised a quizzical eyebrow. 'I thought you and your reverend Mr Wharton weren't on good terms at the moment?'

She shook her head. 'Just a silly misunderstanding. Everything's fine now. Tell me about York and the murders. The paper's full of it.'

'I know. Rubbish, all of it. I came close to writing to the *Gazette* editor demanding an apology.'

'The *Gazette?*' Betsey looked puzzled. 'I haven't seen that yet. I meant the *Morning Post.*' She reached across the table and handed it to him. 'Didn't you get a copy ?'

'Thought I'd wait till I got back. What's it say?'

'Page six, half a column of it. They seem to know all about it.'

Snowden found the page and began to read.

DISCLOSURE OF TWO MURDERS AT
BARNARD CASTLE.

An extraordinary sensation has been produced in Barnard Castle, a small market town in the southern division of the county of Durham, in consequence of the disclosure of two murders, which until now remained veiled in mystery, by a girl named Humphreys, who states she saw them committed, and was prevented from revealing the horrible circumstances by being sworn to secrecy by the murderers. The facts are these...

Snowden looked up angrily. 'It's all there, the bodies in the river, Humphrey's accusations, Barker arrested, even something about the coat. God knows who they've been talking to.'

'I suppose it was bound to come out eventually.' Betsey regarded her father warily. 'Humphreys' friend, perhaps? The one who told you about it?'

'Maybe.' Snowden read through the rest of the story. 'Damn it, they've named Raine as well. He's not likely to turn up now, is he, knowing we're after him?' He flung the paper aside. 'Why couldn't they have got it all wrong, like the *Gazette*?'

Carlisle, 7.45pm

'IT'S been touch and go.' Dr Ambrose Hartleigh, senior physician at the Cumberland Infirmary, led Sandy down a long tiled corridor and into a small side ward. 'To be frank, I didn't think he'd a snowflake's chance in Hades of surviving.'

There were two beds in the room. One was empty, covered by a light brown blanket streaked with something darker and browner that Sandy didn't want to know about. In the other lay McQueedie, flat on his back under a slightly cleaner blanket, his eyes closed and his chest rising and falling with a faint rattling sound. His right arm was swathed in bandages, from which a length of tubing stretched to a large glass jar on the bedside table. It was half-full of a dark liquid.

'He'd lost at least five pints.' Hartleigh reached for one of McQueedie's motionless hands and began checking his pulse. 'Brachial artery was completely severed, took me two hours to stitch back together. Never done one before, or a transfusion for that matter.'

'A transfusion?' Sandy stared at the bottle. 'You mean, giving him someone else's blood?'

'That's the idea. Only ever been tried a few times, patients nearly always die for some reason or other. But it was the only possible solution.' Hartleigh nodded thoughtfully. 'Lucky the patient in the other bed died just before they brought your friend in or I'd never have found enough blood to give it a go.'

Sandy looked appalled. 'You're filling Hamish up with blood from the poor sod's dead body?'

'Warm, fresh and on the spot, too good an opportunity to miss. Otherwise I'd have had to find a pig.'

Sandy sat down suddenly on the other bed. 'Does it work?'

'Well, there may have been a few things swilling inside the body that could cause a problem. But it should work if their blood is compatible.'

'And if it isn't?'

'He'll die.'

Tears welled up in Sandy's eyes. 'What sort of things swilling about inside this other body? Where did it come from?'

'Chronic alcoholic who collapsed in the Three Tuns. Died of liver failure, I suspect. Trouble is, the blood's about fifty per cent proof and your friend's body may well reject it.'

Sandy leapt to his feet and gave a muted whoop of joy. 'Not a chance of that, doc. He'll thrive on it. Here.' He reached into his pocket and thrust a half-bottle of Glenbuckie's into the doctor's hands. 'Pour that in the jar to make sure. He'll be up and about in no time. When can he leave?'

Hartleigh shrugged. 'I've filled him full of opium till this is finished, then he can wake up. Give him two or three days and if he's careful he'll be able to move. He'll be fairly groggy for a while, though. Won't be able to walk far.'

'I'll collect him on Tuesday, carry the old bugger out if need be. Thanks, doc.'

'As you wish.' Hartleigh paused. 'Before you go, there is just one thing I wanted to ask you.'

'Fire away.'

'How did he come to be wounded like this? I've never seen anything quite like it.' Hartleigh stared at the bandages, perplexed. 'In a knife fight, was he? Fell through a window? Suicide attempt?'

Sandy shook his head and grinned. 'You're not going to believe this.'

Arkengarthdale, 11.57pm

TWO miles beneath the earth's surface a minor fault line between the carboniferous limestone and the millstone grit shifted three millimetres. The tiniest of tremors waved its way outwards and upwards.

Directly above the epicentre, a dog chained outside a shepherd's hut woke up, gave an uncertain howl, and went back to sleep.

Half a mile away a plate on the kitchen dresser at High Boggs Farm rolled sideways and fell to the floor. The sound of it smashing on the stone slabs passed unnoticed, though next morning the farmer's wife blamed it on a poltergeist her grandmother had always sworn haunted the room.

Three miles beyond at Hirst, a worm-eaten pit prop at the foot of a disused mine shaft split in two, bringing down a torrent of debris and burying forever what was left of Marigold, her saddle and harness, and a rusting six-inch knife that still carried the faintest of bloodstains on its blade.

Tuesday August 4ᵗʰ

Leeds, 9.15am

SNOWDEN settled back in his seat, opened his briefcase and hoped no other first-class passengers would decide to join him.

There was, he'd discovered, an art to getting a carriage to himself. Everyone wanted to be at the end of the train, as far away as possible from the steam, smoke, smuts and cinders pouring from the locomotive and also the safest place to be if, as happened with disturbing frequency, it hit something on the track and went off the rails. At the rear of the train there was a reasonable chance of avoiding the smoke and surviving the journey, and that was where the Leeds & Selby Railway Company placed its first-class carriages for the comfort of its directors, who travelled free, and anyone else with the money to buy cleanliness and safety. There were three first-class coaches on the 9.20am to York: the rear-most already full, the last but one half-occupied, the third from the end the one Snowden had chosen in the hope of privacy for the next hour.

Whistles blew, flags waved, two late arrivals ran down the platform and threw themselves into third-class, and Snowden's wish was granted. As the train moved out he made sure the windows were closed as tightly as possible, but a swathe of smoke and steam still managed to get in as it made its way laboriously through the half-mile-long tunnel under the black stone mills and back-to-back terraces of central Leeds.

Daylight returned and the city gave way to open countryside. He put his feet up on the leather seat opposite, dug his diary out of the briefcase, and pondered the last few entries.

SATURDAY AUGUST 1

pm Teesdale Agric Show
7.30 Railway D'ton – York
10.0 Anderson re blood
11.30 Gaol Cavenditch, Humphreys. Barker ??
5.30 Railway – D'ton
Xpnses Rail 4/2d return Luncheon 1/7d Ostler 9d

A pity he'd missed the agricultural show, but the trip to York had been more profitable than he'd expected. Anderson would testify and earn his pound of Kendal Shag, or whatever the stuff he smoked was called, and Humphreys and Barker between them seemed to have partly solved the mystery of the coat. He'd got home in good time and Betsey seemed in good spirits for a change. It was a damn nuisance about the *Post* telling the world what was going on, though. Now Raine's name was being bandied about he'd better get some wanted posters printed. Something in the *Police Gazette*, too. The man could be anywhere.

SUNDAY AUGUST 2

Must finish book index

10.0 Mng Service B'ham w Betsey?

NB Anthony C starts tomorrow – meet?

Leeds case prep

He'd spent almost the whole day on the book, skipping church. It had earned him a disapproving lecture from Betsey before she set off, clearly keen to see Wharton and his pig again.

The index was finally done, as far as it could be: an alphabetical list of everything in it but no page numbers yet, of course, as they could only be identified and inserted once the thing was in print. He wondered idly how many pages there would be. Four or five hundred, perhaps? He'd tried to work out how many words he'd written, but it proved impossible – too many additions and crossings-out, amendments and corrections, second thoughts in the margins. There must be at least two hundred thousand, though. A thousand a day for four years. He hoped it proved worth it.

MONDAY AUGUST 3

6.45 Rail to Leeds (chnge Yk 7.50)

Must post book

10.0 Abercrombie & Co fraud – all day

Hat & Feathers Inn York St

Xpnses 3/4d night & din 1/8d b/fst 6d

The book had been parcelled up and handed over to the postmaster at York while he waited for his connection to Leeds. It was running late, and he'd only got to the court a few minutes before the fraud case was due to start. It proved as tedious as he'd expected, a tortuous dispute about an exchange of shares in an obscure woollen mill that dragged on into the evening, and it had been ten o'clock before he sat down for a dubious meal of mutton and cabbage in the Hat and Feathers. He'd consoled himself with a surprisingly good bottle of marsala and the knowledge that he wouldn't be needed in court next day.

Now, on his way out of Leeds earlier than he'd expected, he could look forward to a fairly leisurely journey to Durham and with luck be back home by early evening. His eyes dropped to today's entries.

TUESDAY AUGUST 4

Leeds.

~~10.0 Abercrombie & Co fraud cont'd~~

Rail to Durham – Breckon. Ramsden?

5.0 ? Rail – D'ton Last train 6.45
Xpenses lunch ? Bucephalus 1/6d

He didn't expect to accomplish much in Durham, but it was high time Breckon was formally charged with the murders. The man might even have some idea about where Raine might be hiding, though the chances of him saying so were thin. And then there was Frankie Ramsden to have a word with. Snowden turned the page.

WEDNESDAY AUGUST 5

Whashton tunnel body found year ago this week.

He had no idea what to do about that.

Carlisle, 10.10am

McQUEEDIE sat squeezed into a wicker bath chair outside the infirmary and wondered what on earth was going on. Nobody seemed to know.

Since waking up on Sunday morning he had been tended by some sort of medical orderly who knew only that Dr Hartleigh, whoever he was, had gone to Glasgow leaving instructions that the patient, if still alive, was to be delivered to London Road railway station on Tuesday morning for collection by a Mr Alexander McLeod.

The orderly had examined his arm to check the cat-gut sutures were holding, but had no idea how he'd been wounded. McQueedie was equally baffled. All he knew was that his arm hurt like hell, trying to walk was exhausting, and the only way he was going to find Sandy at the station was by being trundled there in this three-wheeled contraption that had clearly seen very many better days.

Doing the trundling was a morose twelve-year-old boy who was being paid twopence to push him to the station. He spent the first hundred yards down the infirmary drive grumbling that it wasn't enough while McQueedie gripped the handlebar with his left hand and wrestled with the steering. He thought he'd just about got the hang of it when they reached the lodge gates, turned left and headed down the steep road towards the city centre and the Newcastle and Carlisle Railway terminus. He nodded happily. There were worse ways to travel.

Three things happened in the next ten seconds to change his mind.

The boy caught his foot on a loose cobble, tripped and let go of the bath chair.

Gravity took over.

McQueedie reached for the brake and discovered it didn't have one.

Carlisle, 10.17am

JERABOAM Cressitt, driving his farm wagon slowly along Botchergate, was whistling happily to himself until the left-hand back wheel fell off. The wagon slewed sideways, depositing its four-ton load of fairly fresh hay in a vast heap in the middle of the road.

Knacker's yard labourer Henry Upton, driving a high-sided wagon behind Cressitt, swore loudly, heaved on his reins and managed an abrupt stop just in time. Three tons of assorted rotting animal carcases, bones, hides, offal, blood and a dead cat sloshed noisily back and forth behind him.

Close behind Upton's wagon was a dog-cart carrying Eugenia Waterhouse, spinster proprietress of the Carlisle High-Class Ladieswear and Drapery Emporium, who gave a terrified screech as her pony shied, overturned the cart, spilled its owner and her latest collection of garments onto the cobbles and then bolted.

Cressitt and Upton confronted each other and started an angry dispute about who was to blame, watched by an excited crowd of passers-by. Miss Waterhouse grabbed her parasol and was about to join in when McQueedie arrived.

Estimates of the speed at which his bath chair hurtled round the corner on two wheels varied wildly, but everyone agreed it was doing at least 35 miles an hour when it ploughed into the hay and catapulted McQueedie, his face contorted in terror and screaming for help, high into the air, over Cressitt's wagon, and into the one behind.

Durham, 10.55am

SNOWDEN walked softly across the great stone slabs to the pews on the far side of the nave and sat down. He must have visited the cathedral a score of times – he rarely missed it when called to the city – but its magnificence never failed to awe him.

The first time he'd been there had been back in 1844, summoned to attend the installation of Henry Witham as high sheriff of the county. It had been a long, solemn and tedious ceremony, the cathedral packed with the great and the good on a miserably cold January morning, and although he'd greatly admired the architectural splendour of the building – the finest example of Romanesque architecture in England, they said, built high above the river Wear on the orders of William the Conqueror seven centuries and more ago – he'd thought it a cold, soulless place. But today, with the sunlight beaming down from the high celestory windows, nobody in sight and just the faint sound of a choir practising in a side chapel somewhere at the far end, it felt warm, welcoming and reassuring, a monument to enduring faith in something of far greater moment than a county sheriffdom.

Enduring faith... He leant back, drifted his eyes across the vaulted ceiling high above, and wondered a little sadly whether he would ever share the kind of unquestioning faith that had driven the builders all those years ago. His parents had been undemanding methodists in a village without a chapel and his religious instruction, such as it was, had been entrusted to the Church of England and its tiny boys' school in the corner of the graveyard. He'd happily married Suzanne in her village church and agreed that Betsey and her poor little sister should be baptised in the Anglican faith. One version of Christianity seemed as good as another.

When, he wondered, had he first had his doubts about it all? When he joined the army, perhaps, and came face to face with the suffering in Ireland and the pointless cruelty of war? Or maybe later when, serving in the preventive forces, he first encountered the bodies of rape victims and watched starving children hanged for stealing a loaf of bread. Now he wasn't certain what he believed in. Something, there had to be something, but... He smiled wryly as his mind finished the sentence. Only God knew what.

A lone cleric, gown fluttering behind him and a prayer book in his hand, scuttled down the aisle and brought Snowden back to earth. He stood up and walked towards the west door, stopping to gaze upon a small wooden crucifix in an alcove he hadn't noticed before. Christ hung from the cross, his anguished face turned to the heavens, an innocent man condemned to death for reasons Snowden had never fully understood. He, too, had sent men to their deaths in his time, and for all he knew some had been innocent. The possibility ran uncomfortably through his mind. What about Barker, Breckon and Raine? Was he sure they'd committed the murders? All of them? The only real evidence he had was Humphreys' story, after all, and was that enough to send three men to the gallows?

He shook his head irritably and turned away. Above him the cathedral struck the three-quarter hour and his thoughts turned to his next destination where, perhaps, some of his doubts might be allayed.

Carlisle, 11.55am

CONSTABLE Matthias Alsopp was not having a good day. For a start, he'd eaten something last night which had violently upset his digestive system and led to a blazing row with his wife at breakfast about the fishmonger in Denmark Street who everyone knew had always fancied her.

Then he'd gone on duty, his stomach still churning ominously, and had just arrived in Botchergate when the hay cart overturned and that lunatic in a bath chair broke the world record for speed-diving into a wagonful of offal. It had taken ages trying to sort that out, and he'd be there still if that reporter fellow hadn't turned up and persuaded the owner of the wagon to drive it, still containing the bath chair lunatic, to the station.

And then this demented woman whose dog-cart had spilled a load of ladies' clothing into the road said the reporter had stolen some of it and demanded he was arrested immediately or she'd be having words with the wife of the Carlisle chief superintendent of police who was one of her best customers, the wife, that was, not the bloody chief superintendent, and why wasn't he, Constable Alsopp, highfooting it after the clothes-thief instead of standing there gawping at a pile of hay?

Grateful for an excuse to leave the chaos behind, he'd got as far as the station when the combination of last night's fish and the offal wagon stench sent him in urgent search of the Gentlemen's Waiting Room & Ablutions on platform four.

Carlisle, 11.56am

AMELIA Gosford, the lone occupant of the Ladies' Waiting Room next door, finished reading the *Cumberland Gazette's* report of the Cumbrian Primitive Methodist gathering and nodded approvingly. She stood up, adjusted her bonnet before the looking-glass, inspected a notice informing her that if she was caught expectorating on the premises she would be liable to a fine of five shillings, sniffed and wandered across to the window.

Her noon train to Newcastle had been standing outside for the past five minutes, but ever since that dreadful journey when she'd found herself travelling with three inebriated horse-dealers she'd waited until the last minute before selecting a carriage, watching carefully to see where other passengers installed themselves. So far only a handful had joined the train, and she was just telling herself confidently that she would have no trouble finding a compartment to herself when the two men came into view.

The tallish man with the sack and the grubby carpet bag looked moderately normal, though he was clearly no gentlemen – his check jacket alone was evidence enough of that. But his companion trudging behind was a disgrace, covered from head to foot in mud or, Amelia realised with disgust as they passed the window and a reek of rotting flesh wafted into the room, something much worse. A tramp of the lowest possible kind, certainly not the kind of creature with whom to share a carriage, and she gave a sniff of relief as the pair carried on beyond the waiting train to the end of the platform some thirty yards away. Not passengers after all, Amelia concluded, but railway workers of some kind.

She relaxed and watched idly as they halted beside a tall metal structure on top of which was one of those giant water tanks which she had seen locomotives use to fill their boilers. The tall man climbed a ladder on one side, got to the top and must have turned a tap on because water began pouring down onto the platform. How odd.

What happened next haunted her dreams for months.

Carlisle, 11.58am

'STAND still, for God's sake, Hamish, or we'll never get you clean.' Sandy gave the water tap another turn. 'Our train's due to leave in two minutes.'

'It's bloody freezing!' McQueedie writhed under the deluge. 'And what do you mean, *our* train?'

'I'm coming with you, I'll explain later. Just stop dancing around or we'll both be in the shit.'

Sandy's words were drowned by a sudden whistle and a blast of steam from the locomotive and he turned the tap off. 'That'll have to do. Let's get on the train.'

'On the train?' McQueedie shivered violently as Sandy scrambled down the ladder. 'I can't go anywhere like this.'

'Put this on and get going.'

McQueedie stared in dismay at the garment thrust into his hand. 'Don't be ridiculous, Sandy. I can't wear this.'

'You'll have to, Hamish, best I could do. I grabbed a sack of stuff lying in the street where I found you and you can have the rest later. But put this on for now, fast as you can or we'll miss the train.'

Carlisle, 11.59am

AMELIA dragged her eyes from the window, seized her basket and cautiously opened the door. As she stepped out she saw the two men running back down the platform towards her, one of them wearing nothing but a flimsy lady's nightgown through she could clearly see –

She let out a piercing scream and fainted gently to the ground outside the Gentlemen's Waiting Room and Ablutions.

Constable Alsopp, sitting inside with his trousers round his ankles, shot to his feet, gashed his right hand badly on the nail suspending torn-up scraps of the *Cumberland Gazette* provided for the convenience of Gentlemen Abluters, and watched the notebook in which he had been recording the morning's misfortunes fall into the fetid depths of the earth closet. He really, really wasn't having a good day.

As the policeman tried to staunch the blood with bits of the *Gazette,* Sandy reached the first carriage, saw it was empty, threw in his luggage and hauled McQueedie inside just as the train started to move.

Durham, 12.01pm

HORATIO Mitten greeted Snowden like the old friend he was, with a broad smile, warm handshake and a glass of brandy. They had first met as twelve-year-olds, boy recruits with the Northumberland Fifth, Mitten a drummer boy and Snowden a fifer. Neither had proved to have much musical ability and were soon transferred to more military duties, ending up as fusiliers. They had kept in desultory touch after leaving the army, Snowden joining the preventive forces and Mitten the prison service, in which he'd risen rapidly to become one of the youngest deputy governors of a jail in England.

'Still keeping us in business, I see, Ralph.' Mitten settled back in his office chair. 'This fellow Breckon you want to see, what's that about? He can't have done much wrong recently unless he's been slipping in and out of his cell without us noticing.'

'Double murder a year ago, before he got sent down. I'm ready to charge him and see what he's got to say.'

'Hmm.' Mitten looked doubtful. 'I wish you luck. My officers think you'll be lucky to get a word out of him.' He glanced at the clock above the fireplace. 'What do you say to seeing him now and then the pair of us having lunch together? The Dun Cow does an excellent beef pie.'

'Why not?'

'I'll get one of the lads to take you over to him.'

Snowden rose. 'On his own, is he, Bracken? He might be more ready to talk if no one else is around.'

'Normally he'd be sharing with a couple of others, but one's just been released and the other's in the kiss and tell.'

'Kiss and tell?'

Mitten grinned. 'Rhyming slang. They're hanging him tomorrow.'

Somewhere east of Carlisle, 12.13pm

'A CHICKEN?' McQueedie stopped drying himself with a long woollen shawl Sandy had produced from his sack of stolen clothing and stared at him in disbelief. 'You're telling me that I've come within inches of death, lost days of my life, nearly forfeited an arm, ended up in a cartload of god-only-knows-what and been half-drowned in freezing water all because of a bloody *chicken*?'

'That's more or less it.' Sandy nodded. 'Except that it was a cockerel, not a chicken. You really don't remember?'

McQueedie racked his memory of the previous Friday night. 'I remember going to that cockpit at the back of the pub.' He paused, thinking hard. 'You put a florin at three to one on the black bird in the first fight. I told you it hadn't a chance and it was dead in two minutes. '

'And then you said you could do better and stuck six shillings – six shillings of my money, mind, money I'd subbed you for the evening – at twenty to one on a bird called Pride of Eden in the next fight.'

'Pride of Eden, yes, that rings a bell. Had a couple of the finest silver spurs I've ever seen.'

'I thought you'd gone mad – twenty to one, Hamish, on a scraggy-looking cock with one eye and half its tail-feathers missing.'

McQueedie grinned for the first time in several days. 'That was why, Sandy. That bird was never going to give up, come what may. Bit like me, come to think of it.'

'And the bloody thing won.'

'I remember that. But from then on it's blank.'

'You leapt to your feet, shouted "Oh you little beauty!" and cracked your head on a roof beam – it was in the cellar, you must remember that, six foot floor to ceiling at most –'

'Ah.' McQueedie felt the top of his head. 'That explains the bump.'

'– and landed unconscious on top of the Pride of Eden which lashed out with its spurs and sliced open your arm. You wouldn't believe how much blood there was.'

McQueedie ran his fingers across his scalp again and produced a fragment of dead cat. 'I think I've got to the stage when I could believe anything. Then what?'

'We lashed your arm up with your tie and you were carried off to the infirmary. You're lucky to be alive.'

'It really was that bad?'

'It could have been worse. The owner of the Pride of Eden wanted to kill you on the spot for injuring his prize cockerel. I had to fork out two pounds compensation before he let them move you.'

'Two pounds? That's downright robbery!'

'He was a big lad. Anyway, you could afford it. I took it out of your winnings.'

McQueedie did some rapid calculations. 'Where's the other four pounds?'

'Two pounds infirmary fee. Ten shillings to bribe the offal carter to bring you to the station. Two rail tickets, second class, sorry about the wooden bench. Five bob to the locomotive driver for turning a blind eye to us wasting railway company water. Oh, and the half-sovereign I lent you on Friday.' Sandy totted it up. 'You owe me half a crown. Have you finished with that shawl yet?'

'More or less.'

'Hang it out of the window to dry, then, and we'll get you dressed.' Sandy began rummaging in his sack of clothes.

'That tie you bound my arm up with, I wondered where that had got to.' McQueedie turned back from the window. 'It was my Old Harrovian, very useful sometimes. You haven't got it, I suppose?'

'Don't be ridiculous, Hamish. It wouldn't go with what I've got in here, anyway.' Sandy held out McQueedie's new outfit. 'There you are. Should be a good fit.'

Carlisle, 12.25pm

'UNCLOTHED?' Constable Alsopp, his right hand heavily bandaged and his insides still fighting among themselves, stared at Amelia across the tea-stained table in the porters' rest room. 'You mean, he'd taken his jacket off?'

'And everything else.' Amelia quivered with outrage.

'Everything?' Alsopp's mouth fell open. 'You mean, even his trousers?'

'I mean everything. He had nothing on.'

'Nothing at all?'

'Not a stitch.'

'You mean he was –?' Alsopp's jaw dropped further.

'I keep telling you, constable, the man was *naked*. Completely naked.' Her eyes bulged at the memory. 'Dancing around in the water at the end of the platform wearing no more than the day he was born. It was revolting.'

Alsopp shook his head disbelievingly. 'You're quite sure of this, Mrs –?'

'*Miss*, if you don't mind. Miss Amelia Gosford. Of course I'm sure, you fool. I know a naked man when I see one.'

There was a long pause.

'You did say *Miss*, miss?'

Amelia felt her face redden. 'There's statues in the museum. Roman ones, quite disgusting.'

Alsopp eyed her uncertainly. When he'd found her lying senseless on the platform and half-dragged her back to the porters' room to come round he'd wondered whether to arrest her for being drunk in a public place, vagrancy or perhaps even soliciting, though he had to admit they didn't get a lot of fifty-year-old tarts in Carlisle. Now he wasn't sure what to believe. He'd heard of women getting some very funny ideas at her age, and there was that aunt of his in Cockermouth convinced a man was hiding under her bed every night.

'Well?' Amelia glared at him. 'What are you going to do about it? You should be out looking for those repulsive brutes, not sitting there. They'll be miles away by now.'

'Perhaps you'd better give me a description of this man to start with.' He sighed, reached for his notebook and remembered where he'd last seen it. He'd just have to memorise what she said. 'What did he look like?'

'Short, a bit fat.'

'Hair, beard, moustache?'

'I don't know, I didn't notice his face.'

Alsopp gave her a long stare. 'You didn't notice his face? What *did* you notice?'

'More than enough, constable, I assure you.'

'So you'd recognise the rest of him if we held an identification trial?'

'You mean, pick him out from a row of men?'

'Of course. A bit difficult if you didn't see his face, but I'm sure there's something you'd recognise to tell which one was guilty.'

Amelia blanched. 'Are you suggesting –?'

'I can't see how else we could do it.'

'All of them? In a parade in front of me?'

'I suppose they'd have to be.'

There was a long pause.

'I don't suppose you know when the next train leaves for Newcastle?'

Durham, 1.05pm

'MY favourite table.' Mitten led Snowden across the Dun Cow diningroom to a place by the window. 'Hangman's Corner, they call it.'

Snowden seated himself and contemplated the view of the jail across the road. Half a dozen workmen were busy erecting a tall wooden platform against the wall and he realised what it was for just as his friend returned. 'The gallows?'

'Always in the same spot. There'll be thousands out there tomorrow to watch the hanging. First one for months. Every room on this side of the inn will be packed. There's even a special balcony three floors up for those who can afford it.'

'Good view of it from here, I imagine.'

Mitten nodded. 'Hence Hangman's Corner. Calcraft always sits here watching till they're ready for him. He'll be on his way up from London now, always stays here.'

Snowden knew the name. William Calcraft, England's best-known public executioner, a favourite with the crowds not least because he favoured short-drop hangings which meant the condemned man – or woman – endured a slow and agonising death by strangling instead of an instantaneous snap of the neck. 'I saw him in action years ago, in Newcastle, hanging a highwayman. It took five minutes for the poor bastard to die, and in the end Calcraft had to climb on his shoulders and jump to break his neck. Dreadful business.'

'I'll have to be there tomorrow. Not looking forward to it.' Mitten paused as the claret and beef pie arrived. 'This man you've just been to see, Breckon, is he going to end up on the end of a noose? Double murder, I think you said.'

Snowden frowned. 'I'm not sure. He's one of three involved, and I'm still not certain who did what. Or even whether they did it at all.'

'What did he have to say about it?'

'Nothing. I read the charges to him, he told me what I could do with them, and that was that. Wouldn't say another word.'

Mitten hesitated. 'I don't want to waste any more of your time, and it's probably not worth mentioning. But while you were seeing Breckon I dropped down to see the man they're hanging tomorrow and he asked to see you.'

'See *me*?' Snowden looked puzzled. 'Do I know him?'

'Name of Knowles, Archibald Knowles.'

'Never heard of him. Where's he from?'

'Chester-le-Street, I think. Convicted of robbery and wounding. Nasty case, victim almost died.'

Snowden shook his head. 'Don't hang many these days for much less than murder.'

'Swore he had nothing to do with it, but don't they all? Anyway, the judge wasn't in a merciful mood and had the black cap out before the jury came back with their verdict.' Mitten looked pensive. 'I wasn't convinced. Funny little fellow he is.'

'What's he want to see me for, anyway?'

'Says he knows something about Breckon, something you'd want to know, but wouldn't tell me what. Probably nothing.'

Snowden frowned. 'Maybe. But if they've been sharing a cell Breckon might have left something slip.' His curiosity wrestled with the attraction of an early return home. 'I'd better see him just in case.'

Somewhere west of Newcastle, 1.15pm

'YOU look lovely, Mrs McQueedie.' Sandy grinned approvingly. 'There's a big straw bonnet in here to go with it, and you can wrap the shawl round you when it's dried off.'

'Stop bloody laughing and lace me up. I don't know how women manage to get in and out of these things.'

'Just be grateful I didn't find any corsets.'

'And it's bloody cold up my legs. These drawers don't even have a crotch. Aren't there any better ones in there? Preferably not pink?'

'You'll just have to keep your legs together, dear. And keep your feet out of sight, that dress is long enough to hide them if you're careful. Just shuffle when you walk.'

'Walk? I can hardly breathe in this thing and my arm's killing me. This is all your fault, Sandy, you and your bloody cockpits.'

'My fault? Who squashed the damn cockerel?'

'I'd never have gone near it if you hadn't started laying bets.' McQueedie sat down angrily on the bench and winced. 'Bloody hell, this dress is thin, I'll be full of splinters if I'm not careful. What am I going to do when we get to Newcastle and I'm on my own? I'll never make it back to Barney.'

'You won't be on your own, Hamish. I'm coming with you.'

'All the way?'

'All the way.'

'Oh.' McQueedie's anger subsided. 'Well, that's very good of you, Sandy.'

'The least I can do.'

'I'm very grateful.'

'Anything for an old friend, Hamish.'

'Of course.... By the way, I'm not Hamish these days. It's Angus.'

'Angus?' Sandy looked doubtful. 'You don't look like an Angus.' He grinned. 'More like a bloody Agnes at the moment.'

'It's a long story, but Hamish is supposed to be dead. Just remember if we meet anybody. I do appreciate this, Sandy.'

'What are friends for, Hamish?'

'Angus.'

'Angus, yes. And anyway, I've been sacked, nowhere else to go.'

'*Sacked?*' McQueedie stared at him. 'Whatever for?'

'It's all your fault, if you must know.'

'*My* fault?'

'Getting yourself injured like that.' Sandy dug into a pocket and produced a copy of the *Cumberland Gazette*. 'I don't suppose you've seen this?'

McQueedie took it and scanned the front page. Advertisements for forthcoming events, auctions and patent medicines lined each side, but the centre was occupied by two long columns of tightly-printed text, the main story of the week. It was headlined

THRONG ACCLAIM INSPIRED SPEAKER.

under which, in slightly smaller type, came

UPLIFTING ADDRESS AT CUMBRIAN PRIMITIVES' GATHERING.
MINISTER'S ROUSING WORDS.
'SUFFER ME TO COME UNTO THEE'.

McQueedie looked up, puzzled. 'You wrote this?'

'All of it.'

'Not the most exciting story, I suppose, but nothing to be ashamed of. Just the sort of thing to keep the faithful of Carlisle on their toes. What's the matter with it?'

Sandy sighed. 'After you'd been hauled off to the infirmary on Friday night I needed a pint or two, naturally, just to get over the shock –'

'Naturally.'

'– and then I stuck around to watch the rest of the fights.'

McQueedie looked highly affronted. 'They never carried on while I was lying at death's door? The callous bastards.'

'They were a lot more worried about the Pride of Eden than you, Hamish. Anyway, it went on well into the early hours and what with one thing and another I didn't get home till six. Never got to bed. I was absolutely knackered.'

McQueedie gave an unsympathetic grunt. 'Not as much as I was.'

'I was supposed to be on duty all weekend. You know what it's like in August. I had four flower shows, a church fête, two weddings, an exhibition of appalling pictures by some colour-blind artist from Wigton, a boat race, a cycle rally and a pageant to cover on Saturday, and then I went up to the infirmary to see if you were still in the land of the living. After all that I was too bloody tired to go back to the office. I went home, fell asleep and didn't wake up till two on Sunday afternoon. By then it was too late.'

'Too late for what?'

'To find a note in the office from the editor saying his brother-in-law was addressing the Cumbrian Primitive Methodist gathering that morning and I was to fill the front page with a glowing report, that's what.'

McQueedie stared at him, then at the *Gazette* front page, and back again. 'So what did you do?'

'What else could I do? The paper was going to press overnight. I've done dozens of these reports, they're all the same, long rambling religious speeches, lots of applause, praise all round, a few hearty hymns and then back home for Sunday dinner. I made it up, handed it over to the printers just in time and went for a drink.'

'Exactly what I'd have done.' McQueedie scanned through the report. 'Nobody will ever know, Sandy. You've done a great job. I love the bit about them writhing in ecstasy when he describes what awaits the ungodly in hell, and the drunkard father repenting and whipping himself is genius.' He shook his head in admiration. 'Maybe you went a bit far with the cripple throwing away his crutches and starting to dance, but I can't see what you're worrying about. Your editor and his brother-in-law must have loved every word.'

'They would have done.'

'Would have done?'

'If the bloody brother-in-law hadn't had a fit as he mounted the podium and dropped down dead. The whole affair was cancelled as a mark of respect. How was I to know he'd do a damn-fool thing like that?'

'Ah.' McQueedie read the headlines again. 'Yes, that does make things a bit difficult.'

Carlisle, 1.20pm

SEVENTEEN-year-old Joseph Bertram Binksley, his acne-pitted face pinker than usual, sat down in a corner of the Railway Hotel, opened his notebook and wondered excitedly where to start.

He'd only been a proper reporter since eleven o'clock that morning, when he'd been plucked from the ranks of *Cumberland Gazette* editorial trainees – two of them, trained to make tea, fill inkpots and place bets for the sub-editors – and told he was replacing Mr McLeod who had left so suddenly. Mr McLeod! His hero, the man who could spin a thousand sparkling words from a meeting of the council Ways and Means Committee, the man who could winkle a story out of a deaf mute, the man who had regaled him with the secrets of successful reporting over many a pint in the Printers' Arms. Glowing with pride, Binksley had vowed to prove himself a worthy successor to so great a man and set off eagerly on his first assignment.

So far it had proved jolly exciting. The editor had sent him to Botchergate to investigate a major traffic incident, though by the time he'd got there all that remained was a broken-down wagon, a pile of hay, the remnants of some sort of wheelchair and a very irate woman loading muddy clothes into a dog-cart. When he asked her what had happened she said some very rude things about a policeman who had gone to the railway station to arrest someone and never come back, and what the *Cumberland Gazette* should be doing was exposing the stupidity of the local constabulary instead of standing there staring at respectable ladies' underwear.

Undaunted, Binksley had headed for the station. There was no sign of policemen, but he'd found an aged porter who said he'd been questioned by a constable about men dancing naked in the station. Within half an hour Binksley had interviewed seven waiting passengers, three people in the street outside the station, a passing vicar, two taxi-cab drivers, the landlady of the Railway Arms and four of her customers. All said it was appalling.

Now all he had to do was write it up. He could see it now.

DRUG-FUELLED DANCERS IN RAILWAY REVELS.
NAKED ORGY ON PLATFORM FOUR.
PASSENGERS FLEE IN TERROR.

EXCLUSIVE BY B. J. BINKSLEY, GAZETTE REPORTER.

Binksley glowed. Mr McLeod would have been proud of him.

Durham, 2.05pm

OVER the years Snowden had seen perhaps a dozen convicted felons awaiting the gallows. Most had been in a state of obvious fear, ranging from trembling protestations of innocence to wide-eyed terror; a few, determined to go bravely their deaths, had put on a show of bravado; one had gone completely insane.

Archibald Knowles looked supremely happy.

'The Lord is with me.' He was a small man in his mid-twenties, his dark hair already thinning, with surprisingly blue eyes that lit up as his visitors walked in. 'He knows I bear no guilt in my soul and will welcome me into paradise tomorrow. I have nothing to fear.'

Snowden looked at Mitten in surprise. 'Is he always like this?'

'So I'm told.'

'Well, I suppose it makes things a lot easier for all of us.' He turned back to the condemned man. 'I'm Superintendent Snowden. I'm told you want to talk to me.'

'Indeed I do.' Knowles beamed. 'I cannot enter the Kingdom of Heaven bearing secrets of earthly evil, can I?'

'Probably not a good idea. Suppose you tell me what it's all about?'

'You've been to see Breckon, haven't you? He told me you were coming, he said so yesterday before they brought me down here.'

'That's right.'

'About a murder.'

'Perhaps.'

'Well, he did it. He said so.'

Snowden stared at him. 'He admitted it?'

'About the blood and everything.'

'The blood?'

'By the river.' Knowles leant back happily. 'I thought you would want to know.'

'I most certainly do.' Snowden nodded firmly. 'And you'd be prepared to swear to this in court?'

'Of course. It won't be in this world, of course, but I shall certainly testify in the next one if the Lord demands it.' Knowles shook his head vehemently. 'An evil man, Breckon, there's no place for him with me in our Father's house.'

'I think testimony on this earth would be rather more helpful. A statement from beyond the grave isn't going to carry much weight.'

'Can't be done, Mr Snowden.' He grinned. 'They're hanging me in the morning.'

Snowden turned to Mitten. 'Any chance of a temporary reprieve for him?'

Knowles looked aghast. 'You wouldn't do that?'

'Impossible. I don't have that sort of power.' Mitten shook his head. 'Even if I had I couldn't do it. There's thousands coming to watch tomorrow, I'd be lynched.'

'Thank the Lord!' Knowles gave a sigh of relief. 'He's expecting me, you know, I couldn't possibly be late.'

Snowden's hopes sank. It wasn't unusual for gallows-bound prisoners to claim knowledge of a cellmate's crime, hoping that by turning Queen's evidence they'd earn a reprieve in return. Usually they were lying, but that clearly wasn't the case with Knowles. Not only was he anxious to meet his maker, but his mention of the blood proved he knew things about the murders that had never been made public. Breckon must have told him.

'I don't think evidence from a dead man is going to get me very far, but I suppose it's worth a try.' Snowden sighed and dug out his notebook. 'Let's have a statement. When did Breckon tell you all this?'

Knowles looked at him in surprise. 'Tell me, Mr Snowden? Oh, he never told me.'

Snowden stood up angrily. 'I hope Mr Calcraft takes his time stretching your neck tomorrow, Knowles. At least a minute for every minute of my time you've been wasting here.'

'No, no, you've got it all wrong, Mr Snowden.' Knowles stared up at him anxiously. 'It was the other fellow he told it to.'

'The other fellow?'

'Cruddace they called him, the one they released last week. He told me all about it the day he left.'

Somewhere north of Durham, 3.30pm

SANDY gazed out of the carriage window, listening to McQueedie snoring in the corner, and wondered what he was going to do next to earn a living. He'd spent the past half-hour making a mental list of everything he was any good at and so far all that he'd come up with was writing, drinking, persuading barmaids to give him credit, playing the bagpipes and being able to flip nineteen playing-cards left-handed. Well, eighteen if he was honest. And he'd only managed that once.

He sighed. He'd hoped they would come up with some plan for working together on the *Yorkshire Gazette*, but that was before Hamish confessed that nobody from the paper had any idea where he'd been for the past seven days and the odds were he was out of a job too. They'd toyed briefly with the idea of running a pub together, agreed sadly that they'd drink it dry in a week, and that was that.

The train slowed down, shuddered to a halt, released a loud blast of steam, and McQueedie woke up.

'Belmont.' Sandy peered out of the window. 'More collieries. Must have been pretty round here till they found coal.'

McQueedie grunted and scratched an armpit. 'What's it stopped for? Not another bloody cow on the line?'

'It's a junction. There's a line goes off to Durham, I suppose it's picking up passengers from there.'

'No sign of a waitingroom, is there? I'm bursting.'

'Ladies or gents?' Sandy grinned. 'Which do you prefer – being arrested as a gent going into the ladies or vice versa?'

'Bugger, I hadn't thought of that.'

'You'll have to wait till we get moving again and then go out of the window. Might not appreciate it next-door, though.'

McQueedie scowled. 'I'll be all right so long as nobody else comes in here. No chance of that, is there?'

Sandy scanned the platform. 'Just one bloke heading this way and he looks like first class.' The train gave a sudden lurch forward. 'He's going to miss it if he doesn't get a move on.'

'I don't know how on earth women manage on these long journeys. Do you know, Sandy –'

'Sod it. Get your bonnet and shawl back on, fast as you can, and curl up in the far corner. I think the bugger's coming in here.'

Durham, 3.34pm

'HE'S got *what*?' Mitten stared at the landlord of the Dun Cow in dismay.

'Hayfever, sir. Sneezing all over the place. Ordered a bottle of brandy and went straight to bed. Thought I should let you know.'

'Hayfever? Hangmen don't get bloody hayfever!'

'This one does, sir. Says he's a martyr to it. Could be laid up for days.'

'But what about tomorrow?'

'Still going ahead, sir, his deputy's standing in.'

'Not that damned George Smith? Young fellow, big exponent of the long drop?'

'That's him, sir. One-Twitch Smith, I think they call him. All over in a second."

'Dear God. Bad enough having a villain who's looking forward to being hanged without the bloody hangman making it easy for him.'

'Crowd's not going to like it, sir.' The landlord shook his head sadly. 'Not going to like it at all. Takes all the fun out of it.'

Belmont, 3.35pm

SNOWDEN abandoned hopes of a first-class seat and clambered into the nearest carriage as the train began to move out of the station. Second-class. He supposed it could have been worse.

He gave the other two occupants a brief glance. Fair-haired man in his early fifties, thin on top, no beard but obviously hadn't shaved for a day or two, check jacket with well-worn cuffs, bit of a drinker, mud all over his shoes, looking worried. Folded newspaper beside him. Probably bought a third-class ticket and was wondering whether he'd get away with it.

The woman sitting opposite him was odd. Huddled in the corner in an appallingly shapeless dress, her bonnet pulled down above a pair of remarkably bushy eyebrows, she was clutching a shawl over her mouth and staring at him with what looked almost like horror. Very odd, but it took all sorts.

He dug out his pipe, lit it, and began rummaging through his briefcase. Yesterday's trial notes, hotel bill, his diary, a copy of his book index, the warrant for Breckon's arraignment for murder, a sheaf of wanted notices for Raine that he'd had printed in Leeds, a couple of bills he'd forgotten to post, yesterday's *Morning Post*, a copy of the 1843 Act for the Control of Fisheries in Scotland (what on earth was he doing with *that*?), two battered law books, half a letter from his brother John... where the devil were his notes from this afternoon's encounter with Knowles? He sighed and took everything out, piling it all on the seat beside him until he found them, tucked inside the trial notes.

Matthew Cruddace, 29, quarry worker from Ferryhill, sentenced in May to two months' hard labour for assault. Previous convictions for similar offences. He shouldn't be too hard to track down, Snowden decided, and nodded to himself. A job for Anthony Coulthard tomorrow, perhaps.

He sat back, sent a cloud of blue smoke towards the roof, and was about to start refilling his briefcase when the train rattled over a set of points and sent his pile of papers slithering to the floor. With a silent curse he bent to gather them up. Some had drifted into the corner under the woman's seat and he paused, uncertain how to reach them without affronting her.

'Want a hand?' The man in the checked shirt knelt down to retrieve them and his companion shifted to one side, revealing bare feet and the hairiest legs Snowden had ever seen on a woman.

Except once.

He wrestled with his memory for a moment, refused to believe it, tried again, came to the same conclusion and decided there was only one way to find out.

'Your wife, sir?'

The man emerged from beneath the seat and stared at him uncertainly. 'Yes. I mean, no. My sister. Aunt. Aunt Hagnes.'

The woman gave a strangled squawk.

Snowden raised an amused eyebrow. 'I could be wrong, but I think we may have met before.'

Greta Bridge, 3.50pm

'YOUR father's not back yet, then?' Anthony Coulthard followed Betsey into the kitchen and sat down at the table. Four enormous iron pans sat on the range, bubbling furiously and filling the room with a rich fruity aroma. 'Making jam?'

'Stewing prunes.'

'Can't stand them myself. Ralph fond of them, is he?'

'I don't think he likes them much either.' Betsey spooned one of the fruit out of its pan and examined it doubtfully. 'They're for the rector's pig. It's got problems.'

'Problems?'

'Inside.' Betsey looked faintly embarrassed. 'We've tried everything else but nothing seems to work. We're giving her these tomorrow. If they're no good...' Her voice faltered as she dropped the prune back into the boiling water. 'She's going to have to be put down. It's very sad.'

'Fond of it, is he, the rector?'

'Very. He'll be heartbroken.'

'Haven't met the fellow yet. Good man, I'm told.'

'Yes.' She turned her back, clearly upset, and Coulthard decided to change the subject.

'Any idea when he'll be home? Your father, I mean?'

'Sometime this evening, he said. Is it important?'

'I've been talking to someone in Barney about the river murders. Young lad, name of Arrowsmith. I think the superintendent might be interested.' Coulthard dug an envelope out of his pocket. 'There's a report here for him. Can you make sure he sees it when he returns?'

'Of course.' She gave one of the pans a stir. 'Do you think these will work? I don't know what else we can do.' There was a catch in her voice and Coulthard stood up uncomfortably, uncertain what to say. She was a kind-hearted girl, he knew, but crying over a pig seemed a bit extreme.

'Worth a try, Betsey.' He tried to sound encouraging. 'Tomorrow, you said?'

'I'm taking them up at mid-day. It's her last chance.'

'It's time I met your rector. Suppose I go up to Barningham with you? I could give you a hand and be introduced.'

'He might not be at his best... but yes, that would be very kind.'

'I'll pick you up in the dog-cart.' Coulthard nodded thoughtfully. 'I may have something that might help.'

North of Darlington, 4.15pm

SANDY wiped the tears from his eyes and tried to stop laughing. 'You never told me you made a habit of this sort of thing. The Newgate Flasher! You'll be the death of me, Hamish.'

'I will be if you don't stop.' McQueedie scowled. 'It's not funny, Sandy. It was only Mr Snowden here who saved me from going to jail. And for God's sake remember I'm Angus.'

Snowden intervened as Sandy dissolved into laughter again. 'Perhaps when you've decided whether you're Hamish, Angus or Agnes – and I really don't mind which it is, I've had a long day – you'd like to explain?'

McQueedie did his best. 'It's all above board, Mr Snowden.' He glanced uncertainly at Sandy and then hurried on. 'Mr McLeod and me, we're working undercover. Major investigation, big story, exclusive. Special assignment.'

'Ah.' Snowden sounded sceptical. 'Anything I should know about?'

'Oh, no, nothing like that. Big society scandal, titled family's story of shame, that sort of thing. Nothing criminal.'

Snowden contemplated him with mock severity. 'You do realize that I could have you arrested for vagrancy, soliciting, indecent exposure, going abroad in disguise for an immoral purpose and anything else that occurs to me. I might even be able to do the pair of you under the Unnatural Offences Act.'

McQueedie gaped at him. 'You wouldn't do that, Superintendent?'

'As I said, I've had a long day already.' Snowden consulted his pocket watch. 'Should be in Darlington in a few minutes, I suppose if you want to tour the country dressed as Aunt Agnes it's hardly a police matter. Just don't go loitering around street corners at night.' He put his recovered documents back in the briefcase and looked round to make sure he hadn't missed any. 'There's something still down there, if you'd be so kind.'

McQueedie hitched up his dress, scrabbled under the seat and produced a sheet of paper. He held it out for Snowden, glanced at it and stopped.

'Wanted?'

'That's what it says.'

'For murder?'

'Two murders. You must know about them, it's been in all the papers.' He smiled. 'Except the *Yorkshire Gazette*, I believe. Somehow it seems to have missed it. You can keep that if you like.'

McQueedie was still clutching the paper. 'Thomas Raine, aged twenty or thereabouts, six-foot-two, dark-haired, black beard, brown eyes, scar on left cheek...' His voice rose with excitement. 'Last seen in... Anyone giving information will be... Bloody hell, Sandy, there's a £100 reward!' He leapt to his feet. 'We're rich!'

Snowden stared at him. 'You know this man?'

'The bastard threatened to stick my head down his slop bucket!' McQueedie shuddered at the memory. 'Great hairy bloke, you'll remember him, Sandy, he was in court the day you found me. Beat up a landlord in Gretna or somewhere.'

Sandy nodded. 'Nasty piece of work. Fined £5 if I remember, paid up on the spot. He's right, Mr Snowden.'

'When was that?'

'Thursday last week. Carlisle.'

'You're sure it was him?'

'Has to be.' McQueedie nodded firmly. 'But you've got his name wrong. He's calling himself Routledge, Thomas Routledge.'

'That's him.' Snowden almost gave a whoop of joy. 'Thomas Routledge Raine.'

'And I know where he'll be now.' McQueedie grinned. 'When do I get the reward?'

Barnard Castle, 7.10pm

THE chaise pulled up outside the Three Horsehoes at the foot of Gallowgate and McQueedie clambered out as Sandy paid the fare.

'They must have given you a good pay-off when they sacked you.' McQueedie looked at his friend, a puzzled frown on his face. 'Set of clothes for me – secondhand and not much of a fit, but they must have cost you a bob or two in Darlington – postchaise all the way here, another half-sovereign if it was a penny. I thought you said we were broke?'

Sandy grinned. 'You are. I've still got my winnings.'

'Winnings?'

'From the cockfight.'

'You lost. I saw you.'

'First time, yes. But after you'd had your little accident and been hauled off to the infirmary I put everything I had on the Pride of Eden in its next fight. Twelve to one, nobody thought it had a chance after you fell on it, but the bugger was raring to go. Got a taste for blood, I reckon.'

'Blood?'

'Yours. Flew at the other bird like a bat out of hell, ripped its throat out in ten seconds. Wonderful, you should have seen it.'

'You callous bastard! I was at death's door.'

'Be grateful. It's going to buy your drinks until you start earning again or get your reward from Snowden. Come on, we'll have the first in here.'

They made their way through the narrow front room of the Three Horseshoes and settled into a corner of the bar at the far end.

'Evening, Mr McQueedie.' The barman reached for the Glenbuckie's. 'The usual, is it?'

'Two large ones, Joe.'

'Haven't seen you for a bit. Been away?'

'Over Carlisle way for a week. Have I missed much?'

'Let's see...' Joe pondered as he poured the drinks. 'Lot of talk about the murders, but you'll know all about that of course.'

McQueedie winced. 'Of course.'

'Another arrest expected, they say. Not a lot else. The show was a bit of a washout, but I did all right. Came first with my chrysanthemums.' He took the half-crown Sandy had put down on the bar. 'You've heard about the pigs, I suppose?'

'Pigs?'

'That vicar fellow from Barningham who's won fattest in show the past three years didn't enter. They say his pig was nobbled.'

'Nobbled?'

Joe lowered his voice conspiratorially. 'Somebody slipped something into its feed, by all accounts. Hasn't moved since. You lads should be investigating.'

McQueedie's eyes lit up. 'PARSON'S PORKER POISONING PROBE... What do you think, Sandy?

'RIVAL RAIDERS ROCK RECTOR...'

'VICAR VICTIM OF VILE VENDETTA VOWS VENGEANCE...'

'It'll write itself. That and the murders, we'll fill the front page.'

'We'll be onto it first thing tomorrow, Joe. Two more Glenbuckie's, and one for yourself.' McQueedie turned to Sandy. 'That should stop Fewster complaining about me being away for a week. I can walk into the *Gazette* office without any worries about being fired.'

Joe chuckled as he refilled their glasses. 'That's a good one, that is. You gentlemen of the press do have a way with words.'

McQueedie looked puzzled. 'I'm sorry?'

'Being fired. Given what happened last Saturday and everything.'

'Last Saturday?'

'You know...' Joe stared at him. 'Bloody hell. You don't, do you?'

'Last Saturday I was in an infirmary swapping blood with a dead drunk.' McQueedie shuddered at the memory. 'Go on, surprise me. What don't I know?'

Thorpe, 7.35pm

'AN excellent day.' Snowden mopped up the last of his gravy with a chunk of bread and sat back happily. 'Excellent.'

'I still can't believe it about – what's his name? McReedy?' Betsey giggled. 'I'd love to have seen him.'

'McQueedie. I'm still not sure if he's Hamish or Angus.'

'Or Agnes.' Betsey giggled again.

'Well, I'm glad we met, whichever he is. With a bit of luck we'll have Raine locked up in a couple of days.'

'A couple of days?'

'At the most. I'm off first thing tomorrow.' He reached for his pipe. 'I promised McQueedie he'd be the first to know, and he'll get some of the reward money, too. He must be a very happy man tonight.'

Barnard Castle, 7.37pm

'THIS is terrible.' McQueedie stared across the Market Place cobbles in horror. 'I go away for seven days and that bastard Fewster burns the place down. What the hell am I going to do, Sandy?'

'Celebrate.'

'*Celebrate?* No office, no job, no money and you want me to *celebrate?*'

'Best thing that could have happened. Fewster's out of the way, you're acting editor, you need a new reporter and you're standing next to him.' Sandy clapped him on the shoulder. 'We're laughing, Hamish.'

'You think so?'

'Certain of it. They're not going to sack you, not with the murder story about to break. First thing tomorrow you get a message to York saying you've taken over, everything's in control, you've got a new office and a world-beating exclusive on the murders for Saturday's paper. Two exclusives if the pig story stands up.'

McQueedie shook his head doubtfully. 'What new office?'

'Name your pub. We'll book a couple of rooms, move in, and work the rest out later. Good God, Hamish, with the reward money coming your way we can set up a bloody news agency if we have to. Start a newspaper of our own, even. The *Teesdale Intelligencer*, Born and Read in the Dale.'

'*Intelligencer?* What kind of title is that?'

'*Despatch*, then.'

'*Courier.*'

'*Herald.*'

'*Messenger.*'

'Whatever you like. Come on, we need a drink to celebrate.'

'You really think this could work?'

'No doubt about it. Trust me, I'm a journalist.'

Wednesday August 5th

Barningham, 11.55am

WHARTON stared helplessly at Ermintrude as she lay spread-eagled on a pile of straw, her legs aimed at the sky, eyes closed and her vast belly gently rising and falling. 'Are you sure she'll be all right, doctor?'

'If it's good enough for Her Majesty when she's adding heirs to the throne, it's good enough for your pig.' Matthew Graham gave a satisfied nod. 'She's got enough chloroform to keep her quiet for fifteen minutes or so.'

'I just wish there was something I could do.' Wharton wrung his hands. 'Do you think it would help if I held her trotter?'

'Just wedge that funnel between her teeth, as far down her throat as you can, and hold it still.' Graham turned to Betsey and Coulthard, watching anxiously from across the sty. 'We're all agreed, then? Everything we've tried so far plus the prunes, all in one dose?'

'It seems to be the only hope.' Betsey choked back the tears. 'Poor Ermintrude.'

'Kill or cure, then.' Graham reached for a bucket. 'Let's get on with it. What's first? Castor oil?'

'Castor oil.' Betsey passed him the bottle.

'She may as well have the lot.' He poured it into the bucket. 'Turpentine?'

'Turpentine.'

'Syrup of figs?'

'Syrup of figs.'

'Strychnine? No, I've got that.' He pulled a phial from his pocket. 'Gave her half a grain last time, let's double that. Prunes?'

'Prunes.' Betsey passed over a jug. 'Stewed last night.'

'In they go.' Graham gave the bucket a stir. 'Is that everything?'

'I don't know whether this might help.' Coulthard produced a battered tin. 'My father brought it back from India. Some sort of spice mixture they add to stews out there.' He examined the label. 'No idea what's in it, but he said he tried it once and spent the next week on the – well, he didn't go out a lot.'

Graham took the lid off the tin, sniffed the contents gingerly, sneezed and swallowed hard. 'India, you say?'

'Twenty years with the Punjabis.'

'I'm not surprised.' He wiped the tears from his eyes. 'Well, it can't do any harm, I suppose.' He emptied the tin into the bucket and gave it another stir. 'Let's see if it works.'

There was a clatter of hooves and a trap came to a noisy halt at the yard gate. Two figures sprang out and ran across.

'McQueedie and McLeod, *Yorkshire Gazette*.' McQueedie stared at Ermintrude for a moment and dropped his voice to sepulchral. 'Too late, Mr McLeod, too late I fear. The poor creature has already departed to the great sty in the sky.' He turned to Wharton. 'May we offer our deepest condolences, your reverence?'

'Condolences?' The rector looked confused.

McQueedie put on his most mournful death-knock face. 'We have no wish to intrude at this time of grief, but perhaps you would give us a few words so that we might pay due tribute to Eglantine in our columns? We find that it can be such a comfort to the bereaved, don't we, Mr McLeod?'

'Indeed, indeed. To know that the memory of one's departed loved one lives on in our pages –'

'A testimony to their love and devotion.' McQueedie dug out his notebook. 'Did she perhaps have any last words... or grunts, or anything? A message of hope, perhaps, from the world beyond?'

'It's Ermintrude.'

'I'm sorry?'

'She's called Ermintrude. And she's not dead yet.'

'Are you sure?' McQueedie moved over to the pig, disappointed. 'She doesn't look very alive to me.'

Graham picked up the bucket. 'She certainly won't be alive much longer if we don't get this down her. I've only knocked her out for quarter of an hour.'

'Knocked her out?' McQueedie's eyes lit up. 'You mean she put up a fight? POISONED PORKER'S LAST BATTLE, FRANTIC FISTICUFFS, DEATH-BED DRAMA, that sort of thing?'

'Don't be ridiculous. Now, if you wouldn't mind moving away from this end... Thank you. Just hold the funnel steady, rector, and I'll pour it in.'

'There must be more I can do.' Wharton looked at Betsey despairingly. 'If she was human I could give her absolution or something, but there doesn't seem to be anything in the prayer book to cover pigs. I'm not even sure they can commit sins.'

'I'm sure she'll come through, William.' Betsey took his arm as the doctor up-ended the bucket and watched its contents gargle down the funnel and disappear.

Nothing happened.

McQueedie drew Sandy away to Ermintrude's tail-end and whispered urgently in his ear. 'We've got to know one way or the other, Sandy. Dead or alive, we've got a story. Hovering on the brink's no good.' His brow furrowed and then lit up. 'Have you got that half-bottle of Glenbuckie's in your pocket?'

'Good idea. I could do with one.'

'Not for us, you fool. Go and pour it down that funnel. It saved my life last week and if it can save me it must do something for a pig. Think about it. GAZETTE SAVES STRICKEN SOW, REPORTERS HAILED AS HEROES.'

'And if it dies?'

'It'll die happy. Go on, I'll wait here.'

There was a faint rumble from within the pig and McQueedie gave its rump an encouraging pat. 'Come on, old girl, you can do it!' He bent nearer in excited anticipation. It was, he admitted later, probably one of the most foolish things he'd ever done.

Alston, 12.15pm

'I'M getting too old for this, Snowden.' Superintendent Browne eased himself out of the saddle and winced. 'Long time since I rode this far in one go.'

'Do you good.' Snowden grinned. 'Highest town in England, they say, all downhill to Carlisle from now on. Come on, we'll get the horses sorted out and see what the inn's got in the way of lunch for us.'

They made their way into the Angel, ordered food and drinks, and settled into a corner beside the hearth.

'Bit different to when I was last in here.' Browne nodded at the empty grate. 'Back in February. Roaring fire going then, and we needed it. Foot of snow or more outside.'

'Bit outside your patch, isn't it?'

'Came to see an old friend who lives in the town. Oddly enough, I got involved in a murder inquiry while I was here.'

'Murder, in Alston?' Snowden's brow furrowed. 'Can't remember hearing about it.'

'Just down the road, village called Garrigill. Involved a leadminer called...' Browne searched his memory. 'Winskill or some such. Anyway, his wife, young woman in her thirties, died after a long illness and word went round that her husband had poisoned her. Neighbours reported that he had a medicine chest full of drugs – fifty or sixty bottles of them, most of them poisonous.'

'Good lord. Police were called in, I suppose?'

'They were looking for him when he turned up demanding a post mortem to prove his innocence. I was here and said I thought it a good idea. They stopped the funeral, surgeon cut her open and found she'd died of a diseased heart, had it for years. Inquest next day, verdict of natural causes, and the coroner told the gossiping neighbours they should be ashamed of themselves.'

'What about the medicine chest, or didn't it exist?'

'Oh, it existed all right. It turned out that Winskill was fascinated by science and studying chemistry in his spare time. Clever fellow, hoped to better himself.'

'Lucky, too.' Snowden looked thoughtful. 'What do you suppose would have happened if he hadn't asked for the postmortem?'

'Probably been arrested and sent for trial. By the time they got round to a post mortem, if ever they did, the wife would have been long buried, too late to identify a heart problem.'

'Likely they'd have hanged him.' Snowden shook his head. 'Wouldn't have been the first innocent man to go to the gallows.'

'Or the last.' Browne gave him a quizzical look. 'No doubts about your man Raine, I hope?'

'Well, we've got a witness who says she saw him do it and another who says she saw him at the scene of the crime next day trying to get rid of bloodstains.'

'Sounds cut and dried.'

'We've got to catch him first.'

Barningham, 12.45pm

McQUEEDIE hauled himself out of the rectory yard horse trough and shivered. 'I don't think I'm ever going to feel clean again. I'll go to my grave reeking of prunes and turps and the rest of it.'

'Just make sure you've shifted the worst of it.' Sandy handed him a towel. 'The rector's got an enormous copper tub full of hot water waiting for you inside. Soap, scrubbing brushes, pumices, the lot.'

'Then what? I can't go back to Barney like this.' McQueedie fished something he didn't want to know about from his left ear. 'I'm not walking up the Market Place wrapped in a wet towel.'

'No problem. I asked the rector if he had anything you could borrow.'

'He ought to be offering me his best suit after what I've been through to save his bloody pig.' McQueedie scowled. 'It did bloody live, I hope?'

'Bouncing around like a baby. The rector's over the moon.'

'So he should be. What's he come up with, then? Shirt, trousers, jacket?'

'Well....' Sandy hesitated. 'He is six inches taller than you, Hamish, and not nearly as... well, broad, so there wasn't much choice. Just this.'

McQueedie stared at the garment in Sandy's hand. 'What is it, another bloody nightdress? I can't wear that.'

'Not a nightdress, Hamish.'

'A shroud? That's even worse.'

'Not a shroud either. It's perfectly acceptable garb for a budding St Francis like you. Found it in the vestry, been there for years.' Sandy handed it over with a grin. 'Surplice to requirements, you might say. Come on, your reverence, it's bath-time. And then we've got stories to write.'

Saturday August 8ᵗʰ

Thorpe, 12.40pm

'MRS Eeles sent her regards and one of those apple pies you're so find of.' Betsey untied her bonnet and regarded her father with mock disapproval. 'I thought you were going to have a work-free weekend. I don't suppose you've moved an inch since I went out this morning?'

'Too much paperwork.' Snowden leant back at his desk and stretched. 'Bane of my life and I've got a week's worth to catch up on.' He waved a hand at the pile in front of him. 'Interview records from York and Durham, reports on the arrest, transcripts of yesterday's committal, bail applications, a dozen fresh cases for review before next week's magistrates hearings, expenses...'

'Come and have some lunch. There's a ham salad waiting in the kitchen and a bowl of raspberries I picked yesterday that can go with the apple pie.' She made her way out of the study. 'And I picked up the paper at Greta Bridge.'

Snowden followed her, sat down at the kitchen table and looked despondent. 'I haven't even done July's crime statistics yet.' He picked up the *Yorkshire Gazette* and turned to the main news page. 'Cholera's spreading in London, more questions in the Lords about what the government's going to do about it.'

'*Is* there anything they can do?'

'Clear up the slums, for a start. The latest theory is that it's caused by foul vapours from rotting flesh and vegetation, carried through the air, but nobody knows for certain. Let's just hope it doesn't re-appear up here.' He turned the page. 'Extraordinary. There's two – no, three – columns reporting a lecture in Wakefield on the use of guano on turnip fields.'

'Guano?'

'Bird manure. Apparently the best comes from Peru.' He folded the paper, passed it over to Betsey and started helping himself to cold ham. 'Show it to your Mr Wharton, he'll be fascinated. How is he, anyway?'

'Much happier since Ermintrude recovered.' She picked up the *Gazette*. 'I wonder if there's anything in here about his speech last week? They usually report the show. I can't see anything...' She turned the page and stopped suddenly. 'But there is a whole column on your murders.'

'Just one column?' He smiled. 'Not as important as Peruvian bird-droppings, evidently.'

'Look.' Betsey held up the page. 'THE BARNARD CASTLE MURDERS: THREE SENT FOR TRIAL. COURT TOLD OF THRILLING POLICE PURSUIT. EXCLUSIVE REPORT BY OUR TEESDALE CORRESPONDENTS.'

'That's McQueedie and his colleague. They spent all yesterday scribbling away at the committal hearing.'

'It's got the whole story...' She began to read it avidly. 'All about the bodies in the river, that woman Humphreys finally revealing her secret, Barker being arrested...'

'I don't suppose there's much there we don't know already.'

'...and then it's about you catching Raine.' Betsey looked at her father reproachfully. 'You haven't told me all this.'

'I suppose McQueedie's made the most of his exclusive interview with me. Go on, tell me what he says as I finish this salad and I'll tell you what he's got wrong.'

Betsey began to read aloud.

> *'Mr Snowden, armed with a warrant, commenced a pursuit Thursday morning last, proceeding to Newcastle, Carlisle, Gretna Green, Kirtle Bridge, and to the works on the Caledonian railway, which is near one hundred miles length. This was most hazardous undertaking – a mere handful of officers venturing amongst so many hundreds of navvies.'*

Betsey broke off. 'How many were with you, papa?'

'Superintendent Browne from Bishop Auckland. And a couple of others we picked up in Carlisle.'

'Against hundreds?' Betsey looked aghast.

'It was enough. Go on.'

> *'Mr Snowden, arriving at Carlisle, took a post chaise for the line near Kirtle Bridge, taking along with him Mr Sabbage, the superintendent of the Carlisle police force, a police sergeant also from that place, and Superintendent Brown of the Durham force. The whole were well armed with truncheons, and Mr Snowden carried loaded pistols.'*

Betsey stopped again. 'Just you?'

'Just me what?'

'Armed with pistols.'

'Well, McQueedie's got that wrong, for a start. I only had one.' Snowden frowned. 'Couldn't find the other, the lord knows where it's got to.'

'Just you, with one pistol? But... how many bullets does it have?'

'Just the one. It's a bit out of date, I'm afraid. But I had some spare cartridges in my pockets just in case.'

'Oh, papa...' Betsey shook her head in disbelief. 'Anything could have happened to you.'

'The others had their truncheons, of course.' He shook his head. 'Didn't want bullets flying all over the place. What's next?'

> *'On arriving at Kirtle Bridge, Mr Snowden obtained a clue to the whereabouts of Raine from a person who had seen him the day before. Mr Snowden immediately placed Superintendent Brown and the sergeant at this person's door; and Mr Sabbage and himself took the chaise four miles further to Eccle Feckum, a small town near the line of the railway in Scotland.'*

'They've got that wrong, too. Ecclefechan, one word.' Snowden sighed. 'I do wish reporters would check their spellings.'

'I've never heard of it. What's it like?'

'Not much more than a village, really, a staging post on the road to Glasgow. A church dedicated to St Fechan, whoever he was, a couple of inns and that's about it. But over-run at the moment with navvies building the railway nearby.'

Betsey frowned. 'Why did you leave Browne and the sergeant behind?'

'Raine had said he'd be coming back there within a few days and I wanted someone waiting for him if we couldn't find him at Ecclefechan. I had to leave Browne, he knew what Raine looked like. Sabbage had never heard of him.'

'I see.' Betsey nodded and continued reading.

> *'At this place they ascertained that Raine was in lodgings, and by a stratagem they succeeded in obtaining entrance into the house about four o'clock in the morning. Mr Snowden immediately rushed upstairs followed closely by Mr Sabbage. They entered a room in which were four navvies. Mr Snowden immediately recognised Raine, who was in bed but refused to get up, but he was immediately seized by both officers. Mr Snowden then read the warrant over to him, which charged him with the murder of the two people already named.'*

'It was a bit more complicated than that, Betsey, but carry on.'

> *'Prisoner said "Me?" The officer said "Yes, you, are you not Thomas Routledge Raine, from Barnard Castle?" Prisoner said "Yes." On being taken into custody, he said "if they had not got him in bed, blood would have been shed before they got him." He never spoke after this, and being made secure, he appeared in an excited state of mind, and was conveyed by Mr Snowden to Greta Bridge, and remanded for a fortnight to Northallerton gaol.'*

'That's it.' Betsey laid down the paper. 'What did you mean, it was a bit more complicated than that?'

'Well...' Snowden hesitated. 'There were a few details I didn't think it wise to mention to Mr McQueedie.'

'Details? What sort of details?'

'About the arrest.'

'The arrest? But it sounds quite straightforward. In you all went, pistol in your hand, he's in bed, you tell him who you are and that's it.'

'Not quite.' Snowden helped himself to another slice of ham. 'Sabbage and I had no problem finding the lodging house, a ramshackle building on the outskirts of the village. There were dozens of them, thrown up by the railway company to accommodate navvies. We got the site foreman out of bed – he was staying in the village inn, no draughty lodging shed for him – and persuaded him it would be worth his while to tell us where we'd find Raine.'

'McQueedie says you got in by a stratagem, whatever that means.'

Snowden smiled. 'It means a couple of sovereigns from the reward money and the threat of arrest for obstructing the police if he didn't help.'

Betsey looked disappointed. 'Then what happened?'

'He took us to the building where Raine was asleep and said there were three other navvies in there with him. Sabbage went round the back in case Raine tried to get out that way, I made sure my pistol was loaded, and in I went, quiet as I could.'

'The paper says you both rushed upstairs straight away.'

'I wouldn't be surprised if Mr McQueedie had me leading a cavalry charge. No, just me, and no upstairs. One room, and it was just getting light enough to make out the shapes of the four men, lying on the floor on mattresses with their belongings piled beside them. Fast asleep, all snoring away. The foreman had told me their names were chalked on the wall above them, so all I had to do was look for Routledge, the name he was going under. Except...'

'Except what?'

'Except he didn't tell me one of them had a dog. Damn great thing, tethered to a table on one side, thank God, or it would have had my throat out in an instant. As it was it made enough noise to wake all four navvies and probably everyone else within a hundred yards.'

Betsey stared at him. 'So what did you do?'

'Guessed which one was Raine, pointed my pistol at him, and told him that if he moved an inch I'd blow his brains out. Sabbage come in to see what all the row was about and had him handcuffed in no time.'

'But how did you know which was Raine?'

Snowden paused to fork the last morsel of ham into his mouth. 'Imagine you're a navvy, sleeping in a place like that and never knowing whether one of them might decide to rob you in the night. What would you do?'

'Hide anything valuable, I suppose. Under the mattress, probably.'

'Anything else?'

'Have something to protect myself with, a cudgel or a knife perhaps.'

'And where would that be?'

'Right beside me, where I could grab it if I needed it.'

'That's what I thought. So when all four of them reached out for a weapon – and they did – I knew which to go for.'

Betsey shook her head. 'I don't understand.'

'Three of them reached to their right. And I remembered that you told me a couple of weeks ago that the only thing you knew about Raine was that he was left-handed. If he had a weapon, that's the side he'd keep it. As soon as he began to move left, I decided it had to be him.'

Betsey stared at him. 'But what if one of the others was left-handed, too?'

'Odds were against it, but I didn't have time to worry about that. Good job he was the only one, or I might not be here.'

'He had a weapon?'

Snowden nodded. 'Beside his bed, a foot from his hand.'

'A knife?'

'A pistol. Loaded.' He pushed the empty plate aside. 'Now, where's that apple pie?'

PART THREE

December 1846 - January 1847

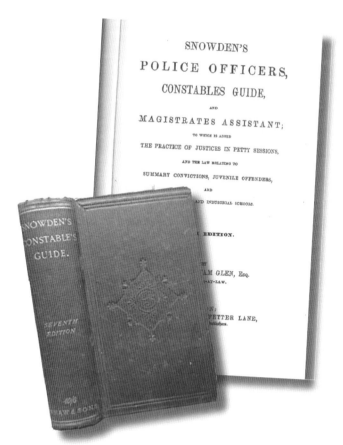

Snowden's book, first published in late 1846

Saturday December 12ᵗʰ

Thorpe, 12.20pm

' I 'M really going to miss you, Tommy.' Betsey gave the cat's left ear an affectionate scratch and got up from the kitchen table. 'But it's the only answer, I'm afraid. I can't take you with me, and papa won't be able to look after you here.'

She hung her apron behind the kitchen door and delved into the pantry for the remnants of a chicken from the previous night. 'I don't think he ever fed himself properly when I was living in Barningham last year, and he'll never remember to look after you when I'm gone.' She put the carcase on the floor and watched the cat sniff at it cautiously before picking out a remnant of skin. 'Make the most of it, Tommy. I'm not sure you'll get chicken very often with Mrs Eeles, but she'll feed you well enough.'

She sat down again and gave a sigh. 'I'll miss her, of course, too. But York's not that far away and I'll be back at Easter.' She gazed out of the window and wondered if it was going to snow again. There had already been a couple of light showers turning the garden white overnight, and she hoped there would be no more until after she and papa had travelled south.

The cat finished eating, jumped up on the table and began licking its paws. 'You'll be all right, won't you, Tommy? I've told Mrs Eeles I'll take you up to Barningham in the morning, before church.' She began stroking the cat absent-mindedly. 'Papa's off to York tomorrow, where he's going to be very busy with this murder trial, and on Monday I'm going to Nunnington to stay with Uncle John and Aunt Jane for Christmas. Which reminds me, I must write to her this afternoon... And then it'll be the new year and I'll be in York learning to be a teacher.' She felt half excited, half apprehensive at the prospect. 'It's all in here, look.'

She reached across the table for a large brochure among the pile of books she had gathered to pack. 'It sounds terribly grand, Tommy. It's brand new and called the York and Ripon Diocesan Institution for the Training of Mistresses of Parochial Schools and there's going to be twenty of us starting in January.' She turned to the first page. 'We've got ever so much to learn. Lots of church stuff, of course – holy scripture, catechism and liturgy and so on, which all sounds a bit boring, but there'll be writing and reading and arithmetic – do stop yawning like that, Tommy, it's all very important – history and geography, music and needlework, and all about the theory and practice of teaching, of course.' She smiled. 'A year there and maybe I'll be able to come back and take that horrible Miss Walton's job in Barningham.'

The cat jumped down, wondered if there was anything left of the chicken and went to have a look.

'All gone, I'm afraid, Tommy, and do leave those little bones alone, you know they're not good for you.' Betsey rose and moved the carcase out of reach. 'And in any case you've had quite enough to eat.' She picked up the cat and frowned. 'In fact, you've been putting on weight recently and are getting disgracefully fat. Far too much food. Unless, of course...'

The cat squirmed out of her arms and sauntered out of the room. Betsey watched it go and shook her head. 'Oh, Tommy, how could you?'

She picked up the brochure and put it back among the books. 'I do hope Mrs Eeles likes kittens.'

Greta Bridge, 2.45pm

SNOWDEN ran his finger down the list. 'Wilkinson, Wrightson, Wright, Young... That makes thirty-nine, I think.'

Coulthard nodded. 'Must be some sort of record. There can't have been many cases with that number of prosecution witnesses.' He pushed the last file to the back of the police office desk. 'Let's just hope they turn up.'

'They've all had subpoenas ordering them to attend. They know they'll be arrested and probably jailed if they don't, and anyway it's a couple of days off work, free meals, accommodation paid for, threepence a mile travel expenses – worth well over a pound for some of them. They'll be there.'

'They say there's a dozen or more for the defence, too. A coachload booked to go down tomorrow, friends and neighbours ready to swear our trio wouldn't hurt a fly.'

'Wouldn't have thought Breckon, Barker and Raine would have a dozen friends between them.' Snowden looked at his list again. 'There must be enough here to convince a jury, whoever the defence call on. We've got a couple of dozen witnesses to testify those three were there when the murders took place, and another dozen to prove they had the motives for murder.'

'Hmm.' Coulthard looked unconvinced. 'Only one who actually saw the killings, though, or says she did. You're sure the Humphreys girl will stand up to cross-examination?'

Snowden nodded. 'Our prosecuting barristers think so. I spent half a day down in York last week discussing how we'd handle all these witnesses and they're confident we'll win.'

'Well, I hope they're right.' Coulthard stood up. 'Fancy a cuppa? Young Craven keeps us well-stocked with tea.'

'Good idea.' Snowden leant back and rested his eyes on the ceiling. 'How's he shaping, that lad?'

Coulthard added a shovel-full of coals to the fire, moved the hob across and put the kettle on. 'Pretty well. Bright, efficient, keen enough. I reckon he's read your book right through at least twice.' He chuckled. 'Keeps quoting bits of it to me and I have to pretend I know what he's talking about. I've sent him up to Helwith to investigate some missing sheep, which should keep him quiet for a while.'

'I wonder...' Snowden reached for his pipe. 'You're happy to come down to York with me tomorrow to lend a hand?'

'If you need me, of course.' Coulthard hesitated. 'I have to confess it's not gone down well at home. Ann had me lined up to paint the back bedroom this week. Why?'

'Maybe it's time Craven saw the inside of a proper court. He's watched the magistrates in action often enough, but there's a world of difference between ticking off poachers and seeing men on trial for their lives at the county assizes. He could take your place – all I need is someone to run errands and keep the files in order.'

Coulthard nodded, pleased. 'Good idea. I could live without the painting, but Ann will be delighted.' He found a couple of mugs, spooned in tea-leaves from a battered caddy on the fireside shelf, and added hot water. 'I'll find some milk. Craven keeps it cool in the back room, though it's hardly likely to go off in this weather.'

Snowden picked up the day's *Yorkshire Gazette* from the desk and wondered how the assizes had gone so far. They were held at York Castle three times a year to hear the most serious cases – larcenies, highway robberies, rapes, murders and the rest – presided over by judges from London; this winter's assizes had begun a week ago and, Snowden discovered, had already dealt with several dozen trials that filled more than two tightly-packed pages of the *Gazette*. He was frowning over the judge's opening address the previous Monday when Coulthard returned.

'Have you read this?'

'Haven't had a chance yet. Why?'

'We may have a problem with the judge.' Snowden passed the paper across. 'Read that bit, where he's talking about the cases to be dealt with.'

'I wish draw the jury's attention to a charge of the blackest description — a charge of murder – in fact, two charges of murder, one the murder of young man, and the other the murder of a young woman, the same night. The depositions returned to me are numerous, but a great many of them do not present any facts of importance, and the case seems, so far as the depositions are laid before me, to depend upon the evidence of an eyewitness – a young woman, who some time after made a communication respecting the facts, and who alleges that she was present with the party, and saw the transaction. If you find her evidence to be credible, of course, there is an end of the case...'

Coulthard looked up. 'He doesn't sound very convinced, I agree. Who is this judge?'

'Mr Justice Cresswell Cresswell.'

'Cresswell Cresswell?'

'Not blessed with very imaginative parents, obviously, but they own a large chunk of Northumberland.' Snowden smiled grimly. 'The barristers in York were telling me about him. Went to Cambridge, received the lowest marks in the honours list of the entire university but still managed to get called to the bar. Had a brief spell as a Tory MP, crawled up Peel's backside and was made a judge a few years ago.' He shook his head angrily. 'It's amazing what money can do.'

'Not on our side, you think?'

'Not likely to give much credence to a seventeen-year-old part-time whore with a drink problem.'

'Good job there's a jury, then.'

Snowden picked up the paper. 'Have you seen who they've sworn in as the grand jury? Foreman, the Honorable Edwin Lascelles, MP. Fellow jurors, the Honorable Octavius Duncombe, Sir Joseph William Copley, Sir John Vanden Johnstone, William Maudaunt Edward Milner, Esquire... it goes on and on, twenty-three to pick from and not one without at least an Esquire after his name.'

'But at least they only decide beforehand whether there's a case to answer. The trial juries can't be all gentry, surely?'

'Not much better.' Snowden scoured the page. 'No names, but there's a clockmaker, two drapers, farmers, a maltster, a butcher... all well-to-do. I shouldn't think one of them has the faintest idea what life's like in the back-alley slums of Barnard Castle..'

'Careful, Ralph. You're starting to sound like one of those revolutionary Chartists.' Coulthard poured milk into the mugs and handed one over. 'You wouldn't have ordinary workingmen on a jury, surely? Most of them can hardly read their own names.'

'They'd understand why somebody might steal food even if it meant risking the gallows, though.' Snowden took a sip of tea and grimaced. 'Any idea where young Craven keeps the sugar?'

Thorpe, 3.15pm

Thorpe Grange
Saturday

Dearest Aunt Jane,

This must be the briefest of letters, as I wish to catch the evening post so you receive it before I arrive. I shall be travelling on Monday. and with an early start should be there by mid-day. I cannot wait to see Sarah Jane and baby William – though I suppose he cannot be a baby any longer! – and the rest of you, of course.

I'll keep most of my news until we meet. I am greatly looking forward to going to the training college in York, a bit frightened by the thought of living in a big city but papa says I will soon have plenty of friends among the other girls. He is very busy as usual, and delighted that his book has been so well received. Did you see the notices in the press? I have them all pasted into my scrapbook – the Law Times called it "the most perspicacious and complete treatise upon its subject we have ever seen" and the Justice of the Peace journal said it was "far more practically useful than any other work"!

Papa says he will do his best to join us for Christmas and a rest will do him good, as he is looking quite weary sometimes these days and I worry about his health.

My parsnip wine has proved very successful this year – better than last summer – and I have made some quite palatable elderberry, too. I shall bring a bottle of each with me to celebrate on Christmas Day – if it lasts that long!

~~The Reverend Wharton~~ No, I will tell you all about that when we meet, I must stop writing now and post this.

All my love to you all,

Your loving niece, Betsey

Greta Bridge, 5.15pm

COULTHARD looked up as Constable Craven came into the office and hung his hat on a peg beside the door. 'Any luck with those sheep?'

'Waste of time, Sarge. Farm was miles from anywhere in the middle of the moors, took me ages to find it.' He dug out his notebook. 'Fellow by the name of Peacock, reckons one of his neighbours is helping himself to his ewes. No proof, but the daft old bugger wanted me to go up and count 'em all to show some were missing. I told him we had better things to do. There must be bloody hundreds of them up there.'

Coulthard nodded. 'Not much love lost among some of those families up there, always accusing each other of one thing nor another.'

'I reckon they're all a bit odd. We were up that way last summer, me and Mr Snowden, at Hirst, and there was his old woman wanted to marry him. Mad as a hatter, thought he was her husband-to-be. You should have seen the super's face.'

Coulthard grinned. 'What were you doing up there? Not chasing lost sheep, I'll wager, if he got involved.'

'The Whashton murder, that body in the tunnel. Long before you came, Sarge, but you'll have heard about it.' Craven frowned. 'Never found who did it, nor ever will after all this time, I reckon. There was an inquest, first one I ever went to, which ended up with an open verdict.' He picked up one of the mugs on the desk. 'Had a visitor?'

'Mr Snowden. We've been talking about the trial next week. Which reminds me, he wants you to go to York, see how it all works.'

'Me?' Craven's face lit up. 'I thought you were going.'

'Work to do here, son. You'd better mug up on what's been going on so far.' He pushed the *Gazette* across. 'Have a read of this. You'll learn more there about how the courts work than in all your law books put together.'

Thorpe, 6.20pm

'HAVE you read this, papa?' Betsey looked up from the *Gazette*. 'There's pages about the assizes and it mentions your trial coming up. The judge says –'

'I've read it.' Snowden grunted irritably. 'He was as good as telling the grand jury to throw the case out straight away. The man's a fool.'

'They didn't though, did they?'

'No, thanks heavens.' He dripped a little more brandy onto the cloth in his hand and turned back to his jacket, spread across his knees. 'My mother swore spirits of wine would get rid of wax stains, but this is proving damnably stubborn. I can't appear in court with candle grease on my cuffs.'

'Do they often do that?'

'Do what?'

'Go against the judge's advice.'

'Not often, but they don't want him to think he can always get his own way. There were other cases he thought shouldn't go ahead, and I think you'll find they agreed with him on most of them.'

Betsey turned back to the paper. 'You're right. There were five cases of rape or assault on young girls due to be heard and he said none of them should go on because they depended upon the evidence of a single eye-witness, the victim. It's appalling.'

'There's a lot needs changing, Betsey.' Snowden shook his head, laid down his cloth and examined the jacket. 'I think that's about the best I can do. A waste of good brandy.'

'It wouldn't happen if women got to be judges. Or barristers. Or even allowed to study law.'

'Maybe.' He was surprised at the bitterness in her voice. 'They'd still be hard-pressed to know how to deal with cases like that, when it's one person's word against another. I'm not sure they'll ever find a solution.'

'I'd like to try.' She went back to the paper and giggled suddenly. 'I know it's not really at all funny, but there's a case here about a man who started a fight outside a public house and the other man bit his nose off.' Her eyes widened. 'The one who did it was charged with wounding but the judge said the case shouldn't go ahead because you have to use a weapon to wound someone. That's ridiculous.'

'He was right, though.' Snowden smiled, glad her outrage had evaporated. 'There was a case in 1837, I think it was, when a woman bit off half the nose of a man she said tried to kiss her. The courts ruled that teeth weren't a weapon in the eyes of the law and acquitted her of wounding him.'

'Quite right, too.'

'You don't think the girl should have been punished?'

'Of course not. She was the one who was assaulted.'

'So she said. Her word against his.'

'They should have charged the man, not her.'

'Sent to jail for a stolen kiss on top of losing half his nose? Don't you think that would be a trifle harsh?'

'Well, perhaps...' Betsey frowned. 'I don't know. It's all very difficult.'

Sunday December 13ᵗʰ

Barningham, 11.24am

'AN excellent sermon, rector. Rather too long, perhaps, as usual, but I'm sure your message about the true meaning of the Nativity will have touched the hearts of all who were fortunate to hear it this morning.' Lady Augusta Milbank, blocking the doorway out of church, nodded emphatically. 'A pity there were not more in attendance.'

'One does one's best, your ladyship.' Wharton glanced surreptitiously over her shoulder at the rest of his flock piling up behind her. He'd seen Betsey and her father among the worshippers and didn't want to miss them coming out. 'I hope for a better turn-out this evening, though the weather may prove a problem. They say it may well snow again later.'

'That's no excuse.' Augusta sniffed the cold air outside. 'I fear I shall be unable to attend, however. We leave for Thorp Perrow tomorrow and I have so much to do.'

'Of course.'

She looked at him sharply. 'I wanted to have a word with you before I leave. I've been talking with your mother.'

'Mother?' Wharton stepped hurriedly away from the porch. 'Perhaps we could move somewhere a little more private?'

'If you insist.' She followed him a few yards into the graveyard and made way for the rest of the congregation to escape. 'I met her last weekend and she tells me they rarely see you. She is perturbed about your relationship with the Snowden girl.'

'Betsey?' He stared at her, baffled.

'Is that her name? A contraction of Elizabeth, I presume?'

'Just Betsey, I believe.' He'd never thought about it before. 'I rather like it.'

'I see.' Lady Augusta pursed her lips. 'How common. Well, whatever her name is, I understand her to be a somewhat forthright young lady. Not very *sound*.'

'Sound?'

'Doctrinally, among other things. She left the village school, did she not, after a dispute about the authenticity of the Scriptures, and holds very radical ideas about the Creation?'

Wharton retreated backwards a couple of steps. 'Well, she does have opinions of her own, of course, but –' He stopped and winced as his back came into sudden contact with one of the gravestones.

'Not at all suitable a choice for a rector's wife, in fact. I told your mother so. And the bishop.'

'Wife?' Wharton goggled at her and dropped his hymn book. 'The bishop??'

'He was most interested in my views.' She looked him squarely in the eyes. 'Especially as he was wondering whether you might be a suitable choice to be our next rural dean.'

'Rural dean?'

'Do stop repeating everything, rector. It's bad enough in your sermons without wasting my time out here.' The clock on the hall stables chimed the half-hour as she spoke. 'You will be well aware that the Anglican Church does not regard celibacy among its clergy with the same enthusiasm as the Papists, for very good reasons which I have no intention of going into. Suffice it to say that it will do your prospects no harm to get married before much longer – to a suitable partner, of course.'

'Suitable?'

'*Sound*. And that does not include the young lady whose eye you were so blatantly attempting to catch during the second lesson this morning. Now I must be on my way.' She turned to go. 'I assured the bishop, and your mother, that your connection with Miss Snowden was merely that of a conscientious clergyman and an enthusiastic parishioner, and I trust that will continue to be the case.'

'But –'

'Should you desire to enter matrimony, I have a distant great-niece of excellent family who would suit you admirably. Her father is an archdeacon.'

Wharton watched her make a stately departure down the path towards the hall, his mind in a whirl. Married? He was far too young and there was so much to do. He had a sudden vision of being dragged down the aisle by his mother, Lady Augusta and the bishop, his arm gripped by some appalling archdeacon's daughter, and shuddered. Dear God, what was he to do?

He turned round and came face to face with the monument that had impeded his retreat.

Here Lyeth y *Mortall Remaines of My Beloved Wyfe*
HANNAH THOMSON
who d. 25th Feby 1793 ag^d 83 yrs
Also
JOSHUA THOMSON
Devoted Husband of *y* above
d. 17th May 1793 ag^d 84 yrs
Together in Death as in Life

They'd probably had sixty happy years together, reflected Wharton, no mothers and bishops forcing *them* into wedlock. He bent down to recover his hymnbook and saw more words, half-hidden by grass at the foot of the stone.

Hede Not This Worlde, but Followe Heart's Intente
For Life is Shorte, Too Soon our Chance is Spente

Wharton stood up, took a deep breath, and decided. He would find Betsey and talk to her. He scurried back to the church, found it empty, and then to the rectory. It, too, was deserted and his heart sank. Surely she wouldn't have left without saying goodbye? He wondered for a moment whether she intended to return for the evening service, but realised that she wouldn't travel in the dark. He would just have to go down to Thorpe this afternoon and hope to find her there.

He changed hurriedly from his ecclesiastical garb, pondered what he would say to her and realised he had no idea how to go about it. His confidence diminishing by the minute, he stood in front of his bedroom mirror practising possible openings.

'Mother and Lady M say I can't marry you, but I think it's a jolly good idea. Not just yet, of course, but one of these days. How about it?' Somehow he didn't think that struck quite the right romantic note. Betsey was a sensible, practical sort of girl, but she'd expect better than that. Something lyrical from the heart, perhaps. He got down on one knee and addressed his reflection.

'Betsey, my dear, you cannot know how much I yearn for you. I dream of nothing but your golden hair, those eyes like limpid pools on a sunlit evening...' It was hopeless. She'd have burst out laughing by now.

Somewhere, he remembered suddenly, he had a book that might help. He found it in his study, buried under a pile of old dictionaries. *The Gentleman's Letter-Writer, A Guide to Correspondence on All Subjects.* He wasn't planning to write, but it must have some useful advice. He flicked through the index and found *A Letter from a Gentleman to a Lady of whom he is Enamoured.* That should do it.

> *'Dear Miss —*
>
> *I venture to assure you that my happiness greatly depends upon the reply with which you may deign to favour me. The income which I can place at your disposal is not large, but I promise you ever the most tender and affectionate attention...'*

Wharton wasn't sure he'd be able to remember all this, but it seemed promising stuff. He read on.

> *'Should you not reject me, the only study of my future days shall be to render your life as happy as you deservedly merit it should be.'*

Wharton paused. He wasn't quite sure he could promise Betsey to abandon absolutely everything else in his life. There was Ermintrude, for a start. He frowned and went on.

> *'My mother (to whom I have confided my secret) is rejoiced at the hope of having you for a daughter...'*

Wharton threw the book aside. Whoever wrote the wretched thing obviously had no idea about real life. He'd just have to make it up as he went along.

Ermintrude. He'd quite forgotten her lunchtime feed and it was almost twelve. Grabbing his hat, he hurried guiltily out towards her sty.

Greta Bridge, 11.52am

'SORRY to intrude on you at home, Sarge, but...' Craven waited at the cottage garden gate while Coulthard sorted through a fork-full of potatoes and dropped half a dozen into a bucket. 'I wondered what the arrangements were for me tomorrow. I've tried to find Mr Snowden but he must have gone already.'

'Ah, yes.' Coulthard wiped the sweat off his brow, replacing it with a smear of mud.

'He called by this morning on his way to church, said he was looking for you.' He gave the constable a quizzical look. 'Thought you were on duty today?'

'I am, Sarge. I'd gone over to the Morritt's, bit of bother there last night.'

'Bother?'

'Nothing to worry about, just old Zeb Pinkney in his cups again. I'll have a word with him when he sobers up.'

'You'll probably find his missus has done that already. Anything else happening?'

'All quiet, Sarge. I've been looking through the murder files, checking up on what to expect in York.' He frowned. 'Some unanswered questions, if you ask me.'

'Solved them all, have you?' Coulthard smiled. 'Anything in particular you think the superintendent's overlooked?'

Craven looked embarrassed. 'I didn't mean that, Sarge. But...' He hesitated. 'Well, for instance, the girl who was drowned. She'd been living with some pimp and walked out on him not long before she died. They'd had a fight, as far as I can gather. Couldn't he have done her in? Seen her out on the town touting for business a few nights later, had a row, and chucked her in the river?'

'I think you'll discover that he'd left town some time before the murders. Nobody saw him that night. Or ever again, for that matter.'

Craven's eyes widened. 'Well, if he didn't do it, maybe he was killed as well, chucked in the Tees and his body never found?'

'So how does yates fit into it?' Coulthard picked up his bucket and shook his head. 'If I were you, son, I'd concentrate on sorting out old Zeb Pinkney and leave solving murders to Mr Snowden. Now, do you want me to tell you what you're doing tomorrow or are you going to work that out as well?'

Barningham, 12.05pm

THE cat stretched out on the mat in front of the Lilac Cottage fire and drifted back to sleep. Betsey sighed and got up from her chair. 'I'm going to have to leave you now, Tommy. You behave yourself while I'm away.'

Mrs Eeles' face fell. 'Must you go yet?'

'Papa said he'd only be half an hour up at the hall seeing Sir Mark, and it has be more than that now.' Betsey glanced at the grandfather clock in the corner. 'And I must say goodbye to William. He can't still be in the churchyard with Lady Augusta.'

'Still keen on you, is he?' Mrs Eeles raised a speculative eyebrow and Betsey blushed.

'Don't be silly, Mrs Eeles. We're just good friends.'

'You could do a lot worse than him, my dear. Make sure you promise to keep in touch.'

'I will.' She bade the cat a final farewell, gave Mrs Eeles an affectionate embrace and made her way to the porch. 'Take care of Tommy for me. And tell papa he'll find me at the rectory.'

She made her way up the street and along the curved drive to the rectory front door. There was no answer to her knock and she paused for a moment before realising where he must be and smiled. She could say farewell to Ermintrude as well.

Wharton's eyes lit up as she came round the corner of the yard and he leapt to his feet to greet her. 'I thought you'd gone home.'

'Papa had to see Sir Mark before they all left for Thorp Perrow, something about poachers in the woods. And I couldn't go without saying goodbye.'

'You're sure you won't be back before Christmas?'

'Maybe not until Easter.'

'Easter?' His face fell. 'That's a long time.'

'Yes.'

'Months.'

'Yes.'

'Till Easter.'

'Yes.'

'An awfully long time.'

'Yes.'

There was a long pause, broken by Betsey. 'We'll have to keep in touch.'

'I could write to you, I suppose.'

'Yes, that would be nice.'

'Letters and so on. Telling you about my latest inventions, that sort of thing. I've got a really interesting idea for a revolving turnip harrow.'

'A turnip harrow?' Her voice sounded strangely flat. 'Yes, I suppose I'd look forward to that.'

'And you could write back.'

'Of course.'

'Yes.'

Wharton felt this wasn't going quite as well as he'd hoped. There was another long silence while he summoned up his courage and then reached out suddenly for her hand. 'You'll be greatly missed, you know, Betsey.'

She gave him an encouraging smile. 'Oh, I'm sure you'll manage without me.'

'No, really. I mean, there's Ermintrude for a start. You know how much she looks forward to seeing you.'

'Ermintrude?' She frowned.

'And your father, Mrs Eeles and – well, everyone.'

'Everyone?'

'Of course.'

'Of course.' She drew back her hand, looking thoughtful.

Wharton swallowed, looked her deep in the eyes and tried again. 'Betsey, there's something I wanted to ask you before you went. Something important.'

'Important?'

'Yes, terribly important. I wondered...' He hesitated.

But Followe Heart's Intente
For Life is Shorte, Too Soon our Chance is Spente

He took a deep breath and plunged in. 'I wondered –'

There was a rattle of hooves in the yard as Snowden arrived. 'Afternoon, rector.' The trap came to a halt beside them. 'Sorry to take so long, Betsey, Sir Mark just went on and on. Jump in, I've just got time to drop you off at home before I leave for York.'

'One moment, papa.' She studied Wharton's face intently. 'What did you wonder, William?'

He stared at her in desperation, then at her father. 'Oh, nothing. Just –'

'Yes?'

'Just, well...' He sought wildly for an answer. 'Are you really called Betsey?'

'Of course I am.' She shook her head, baffled. 'What on earth are you asking that for?'

'I just wondered.'

'I'll have to go.' She gave him a sad smile. 'Goodbye, William. Take care of Ermintrude till I come back.'

'Yes, of course.'

He watched her climb into the trap, wave a hand and vanish out of the yard. For a moment he stood staring at the empty gateway and then walked slowly back to the sty to sit beside the pig, his head in his hands and his mind reeling before a vision of life with the archdeacon's daughter.

Thorpe, 12.30pm

SNOWDEN hauled himself into the saddle and checked his bags. 'That's everything, I think. If the weather holds I should be in Ripon not too long after dark. A night at the Unicorn, early start in the morning and York in time for court.'

He looked down at his daughter and frowned. 'What was all that about up at the rectory, Wharton asking if you were really called Betsey?'

'I've no idea.' She shook her head. 'It *is* my name, isn't it?'

'Of course it is. I saw you christened.' He smiled at the memory. 'You were supposed to be Elizabeth after my mother, but by the time we got you christened everyone called you Betsey and we stuck with it. Mind you, the vicar still got it wrong.'

'Wrong?'

'It was supposed to be Betsy without an E and nobody noticed till too late. But Betsy or Betsey, it makes no difference. I still spell it both ways, you must have noticed.'

Betsey nodded. 'I had wondered about that.'

'You can tell your William when you write to him.' He smiled again. 'You are going to write to him, I presume?'

'I think so.' Betsey gave Bucephalus a farewell pat. 'You'd better be on your way, papa. I hope it all goes well in York.'

'And you have a good journey tomorrow.' He leaned over to give her a farewell kiss. 'I've ordered the chaise to pick you up here at seven sharp and you'll be in Thirsk by lunchtime. Your uncle John will be waiting there to take you over to Nunnington. Give him and the family my best wishes and say I'll be there at Christmas if I can.' He took up the reins. 'If there's any problem, Anthony will sort you out. He's in charge while I'm away.'

'Mr Coulthard?' She looked puzzled. 'I thought he was coming with me and then going on to York?'

'Change of plan. You've got young Craven for company. Hope you don't mind.'

'Constable Craven?' Her face brightened. 'Not at all.'

Monday December 14ᵗʰ

York, 9.45am

'NOT a bad life, being a judge.' McQueedie settled back in his seat in the Dun Cow back bar and took an appreciative sip of Glenbuckie. 'Suite of rooms in your own lodgings, two-hour breakfast, into your robes and wander off to court at ten-thirty. Nice work if you can get it.'

Sandy nodded. 'An hour or so for lunch, call it a day when you get fed up and then it's back to your rooms for a slap-up dinner. No idea what it's like having to work hard for a living like the rest of us.'

McQueedie finished his drink and stood up. 'Time for another one?'

'Why not?' Sandy pondered the day ahead until his partner returned. 'Any idea where young Binksley's got to? We're going to need him to run our stuff to the London trains.' He glanced at the ornate clock on the mantelpiece. 'He should have been here by now. Probably still in bed after last night's session.'

'Not at all.' McQueedie sat down. 'He was up with the lark and kicking his heels in the hall when I came down for breakfast. I told him if he'd nothing better to do he could try a quick vox pop and off he went. Keen as mustard.'

'Vox pop? Anything in particular?'

'The old RATS INVASION TERROR story. Never fails.' McQueedie nodded thoughtfully. 'I wasn't sure it was a good idea taking him on when he wrote asking you for a job, but he's turned out well. Did an excellent piece last week on that tenement fire in Briggate.'

'With the family screaming from the top windows and the daughter running back into the inferno to save her dog?'

'That's the one. Seems to be lucky with fires, Binksley, always on the spot at the right moment, long before the fire brigade arrive. Uncanny.'

'No idea how it started, have they?'

'Not a clue, Binksley says. Talk of the devil, here he is. How d'you get on?'

Binksley looked dispirited. 'Nothing. Must have asked twenty people and none of them had seen a rat in days.'

McQueedie looked baffled. 'What did you ask them?'

'Well, if they'd seen one, of course.'

'Seen one?' McQueedie shook his head. 'You don't ask them if they've actually seen one, son.'

'Then what –?

'Look, I'll interview Mr McLeod here, show you how it works. All right, Sandy?' Sandy nodded.

McQueedie put on his best professional voice and began. 'Good morning, madam, I wonder if you could spare me a minute? I'm doing a survey for the *Gazette* about this latest rat invasion.'

'Rat invasion?'

'You haven't heard about it?'

'No.'

'Ah, well, they're trying to keep it quiet, of course. You know what these Board of Guardians health officials are like. I imagine you think they should be doing something about it before it reaches this part of town?'

Sandy nodded. 'Well, if it's true—'

'I'm sure you're right, madam.' McQueedie opened his notebook, found a pencil and pretended to make a brief note. 'Terrible things, rats. Get everywhere before you know about it, up through the drains and into your house – married with children, are you, madam? Three boys and a girl, lovely – gnawing away at your children's feet as they sleep. You'd think they'd have the rat-catchers round, but have you seen one? No, of course not.'

He consulted his notebook. 'Just one last question. Would you describe this as (a) good (b) bad or (c) a total disgrace that demands immediate action before upright citizens and taxpayers like yourself get eaten alive in their beds?' He put down his notebook and smiled. 'There you are, young Binksley. Ten of those and away you go. FRANTIC FAMILIES LIVING IN FEAR. NINE OUT OF TEN DEMAND ACTION ON RATS HORROR.'

Binksley stared at him, open-mouthed with admiration. 'Only nine out of ten?'

'Makes it sound more believable. Then all you need to do is ask the health board what they're doing about it and you've got RATS? WHAT RATS? SAY GORMLESS GUARDIANS AS RODENTS RUN RIOT.'

Sandy grinned. 'I did the rats once in Paisley and a mob stormed the town hall. And do you remember the Loch Ness Monster Terror, Angus? Oh, those were the days.'

York, 10.27am

MR Justice Cresswell Cresswell stood before the mirror in the judges' changing room and decided he was definitely beginning to look his age. More than his age, certainly more than fifty-two. What little hair he had left was distinctly grey, his face gaunt, the bags under his eyes no longer hidden behind his half-rimmed spectacles, the lines each side of his nose now stretching almost to his chin.

He lifted his new wig out of its box, put it on and wondered whether it was a good idea. It looked smart enough, dazzling white, neatly turned and reaching a good nine inches below his shoulders, but it wasn't the tight fit he'd got used to with the old one. He tilted his head and the wig slid slightly to one side. No, he couldn't risk it. One vigorous shake in the middle of his summing-up and the whole damned thing might fall off. He'd be a laughing-stock.

'Take this back to Grantley's and get it tightened up, Timson.' He thrust the wig angrily into his dresser's hands. 'Paid nearly thirty pounds and it doesn't even fit. A disgrace. Where's the old one?'

Timson delved into a cupboard. 'Are you sure, my lord? This one has certainly seen better days.' He handed it over reluctantly. 'I think the moth has been at it again.'

'It'll have to do.' Cresswell put it on, nodded approvingly to himself in the mirror, straightened his cravat and turned round as the church clock across the square sounded the half-hour. 'Time to go, I think.'

'Will you be needing the cap and gloves, my lord?'

'Ah, yes,' Cresswell took the small square of black felt and the matching gloves. 'I doubt I'll be wearing them today if the case goes on as long as I fear, but I'll take them with me, all the same. The sight of them before me in court can concentrate a defendant's mind wonderfully.'

He made his way along the short corridor to the courtroom, nodded to the usher guarding the door, summoned his thoughts and went in.

'All rise!' There was a scraping of chairs and shuffling of feet as he made his way to the bench, another as he settled gingerly into the huge ornate wooden seat and surveyed the scene before him.

Just below the bench, almost out of view, were the court clerks, a dozen or more arrayed at desks piled high with lawbooks and ribboned documents, and a pair of note-takers with inkwells and pens at the ready, Beyond them on the left, the prosecution. He recognised the three counsel from previous visits: portly Mr Bliss, with his ridiculously long side-whiskers and plummy voice; Mr Pulleine, tall and thin, beginning to go to seed; Mr Overend, no more than forty and youngest of the trio, wispy-haired and rather too fond of himself. He also recognised the police officer sitting just behind them and frowned. Snowden, the fellow who'd been pursuing this case for eighteen months and getting himself headlines in the press. He'd just written a book which had been widely acclaimed in the press but was causing judges no end of irritation as constables and magistrates started quoting it to them about their rights and duties and what the laws of the land were. Cresswell shook his head. If the man started telling this court how to behave there'd be trouble.

He shifted his eyes across to the defence team on the right. Three counsel there, too, none of whom he recalled seeing before though that didn't surprise him. Although the law had been changed recently to allow defence barristers to take a full part in the proceedings, few defendants could afford them and only in capital cases like this one, when the accused faced a possible death sentence, did the state offer any financial help. Even then it was unlikely to attract lawyers of any standing: defending common criminals was not why one entered the bar.

Cresswell viewed the three before him with faint disapproval and turned his attention elsewhere. Further back on the left sat the jury, twelve well-to-do men in their best suits, one looking suspiciously as if he'd already fallen asleep. On the right stood the empty witness box and beyond it a press bench with just enough room to accommodate a handful of reporters. In the centre was the dock, raised six feet above the rest, guarded with spiked railings and accessible only from the cells deep below. At the back of the court a small high gallery was packed with members of the public, the usual motley rabble of criminal associates, anxious families and sensation-seekers already loudly discussing the day's prospects. Well, he'd put a stop to that for a start.

He reached for his gavel and rapped loudly on his desk. 'Members of the public will be silent in court!' He glared at them across the room. 'This is not a bear-garden. Any further noise and I will have the gallery cleared.' There was silence and he nodded, satisfied. 'Very well. The proceedings may commence. Bring the prisoners up.'

Barker, Breckon and Raine, manacled and guarded by two hefty officers, were summoned from below and ushered into the dock. Cresswell studied them for a moment. One was dressed in prison garb, an habitual offender, obviously. The other two, the tall one with the scar on his face and the short one with the sly look, had found decent clothing from somewhere, probably stolen it. He wouldn't trust any of them for a moment.

'The Startforth murders case, your lordship.' The clerk turned to address the accused. 'George Barker, John Breckon and Thomas Routledge Raine, you are charged that on the tenth of August 1845 you did beat, strike, and kick one Joseph Yates, giving him several mortal wounds; that you did push, cast, and throw the said Joseph Yates against the ground and against certain stones, thereby giving him several mortal contusions; that you did push, cast, and throw the said Joseph Yates over a certain wall into the river Tees; and that you did twist and tie a neckcloth about his throat, and thereby strangle him; and that you did feloniously, maliciously, and of malice aforethought murder the said Joseph Yates. How do you plead?'

'Not guilty.'

'Not guilty.'

'Not guilty.'

'Mr Bliss, Mr Pulleine, and Mr Overend appear as counsel for the prosecution, my lord. Mr Matthews and Mr Blanshard appear on behalf of Barker and Raine, and Mr Pickering acts for Breckon.'

Cresswell frowned. 'I understood this was a trial for two murders, this Yates fellow and some girl. Have I been misled?'

Bliss stood up with an ingratiating smile. 'If I might elucidate, my lord? The prosecution believes a conclusion to these proceedings will be reached more readily if only the Yates murder is deal with at this stage.'

'Speed things up, you mean? We'd get away earlier?'

'Indeed, my lord.'

'Very well. Continue.'

'I'm obliged to you, my lord.' He turned to face the jury box. 'Gentlemen of the jury, the duty which you are now about to discharge is one of the most responsible and arduous you could ever be called upon to pay to society. You are called upon to inquire into the death of a fellow creature said to be murdered, and into the guilt of three persons charged with that murder.' He waved a hand towards the dock. 'This is not a case which depends upon what is called circumstantial evidence. It depends on the testimony of an eye-witness, who was present the time the crime was committed. Yet a good deal of circumstantial evidence will be offered and brought before you, not as creating a case of itself, but as affording reasons from which you may think that it will be safe for you to trust the testimony of the principal witness. The name of that witness, gentlemen, is Ann Humphreys...'

At the far end of the press box, McQueedie stopped scribbling and turned to Sandy, squeezed in beside him. 'Here you are, the first thousand words.' He spoke in as low a whisper as he could manage. 'Two copies. Binksley's waiting for them outside, make sure he knows what to do. And then you can take over for a bit, I've done my first stint.'

Sandy took the notes, waited until the judge was looking the other way and crept out of the room. He found Binksley among the throng of lawyers, court officials, witnesses and hangers-on milling around the entrance hall and led him to a quiet corner. 'Here you are, laddie. Two copies – wonderful stuff, carbon paper – one for the *Gazette* office, make sure it goes straight to the printers. Then fast as you can to the railway station with the other copy, it's got to be on the eleven-thirty to London. Give it to the guard – here's a shilling to make sure he looks after it, tell him he'll get another from our man who'll be waiting for it at the Regents Park terminus. Then you come back here for the next instalment. Any questions?'

'Just...' Binksley took the sheets of paper and stared at them. 'I don't understand. How did he write all this so fast? The court's only been going half an hour.'

Sandy grinned. 'All done in advance, laddie, just a paragraph or two added at the top about today's guilty pleas. All the rest is the prosecution opening speech outlining the case, which Mr McQueedie and I reported at the committal hearing months ago. We spent yesterday afternoon copying it out. It'll be just the same, word for word. Always is.'

'You mean –'

'We're hours ahead of the other reporters in there who are hearing it for the first time. And first with the news gets paid. What you've got in your hands will be in papers all over the country tomorrow morning – unless you hang about here much longer and miss the train. Off you go, laddie, and make sure the *Gazette* doesn't know about the London copy. They think they're getting it exclusive.'

Binksley scurried off and Sandy made his way back to McQueedie in the press box. 'How's it going?'

'Nothing new so far.' McQueedie, his voice no more than a whisper, pushed across a sheet of paper. 'List of what he's covered so far. Description of Barney and Startforth, who Yates was, a bit about him and Barker in dispute about the coat, funny business that... then onto the night of the murder with Yates and the girl being seen together and being joined by Barker, Breckon and Raine – and Humphreys, of course. He's just got to them all arguing by the river. Over to you, Sandy, I'm off for a pint. See you in half an hour.'

Sandy watched him go and switched his attention to Bliss. The man was in full flow. 'Gentlemen of the jury, Ann Humphreys will tell you that Barker then struck Yates and all the three prisoners gathered round him. Catherine Raine cried out, the shrieks were many and loud, until she was silenced, and Ann Humphreys also, by threats which were made by the prisoners, who said the females should be thrown over the wall or into the river if they were not quiet.'

There was a faint gasp from the public gallery and Cresswell looked up with a warning frown. 'They then left Yates leaning against the wall, a distance of fifty or sixty yards from the bridge. Ann Humphreys then saw the prisoners dividing or counting money as Yates lay against the wall groaning. The prisoners again gathered round him – the night was dark, and what was done she could not see that moment – but she heard a splash in the river, and she saw no more of Joseph Yates.'

Bliss paused for dramatic effect. 'Gentlemen, after this was done, Barker asked Ann Humphreys if she would tell. She said she would not. They asked Catherine Raine if she would tell, and she said she would tell the moment she got into the town. We are not inquiring today into the death of anyone except the death of Joseph Yates but it is necessary, however, to account for Catherine Raine not being here, and therefore is necessary to show that Catherine Raine is dead; she did not die by accident, and she died before she had opportunity of getting to the town. Therefore, I propose to prove the fact of her death, and that the bodies of both were found in the water some time after.'

'The bastards killed her too!' The cry came from a woman in the gallery. 'They want hanging, the three of them.'

Cresswell reacted with fury. 'Seize that woman and take her down!' He hammered his gavel on the desk. 'Seven days for gross contempt of court. And I shall not be so lenient with anyone else who ventures to interrupt the proceedings of this court.'

She was led out, still shouting, and Sandy made a note to find out later who she was. A distraught relative, Anguished Aunt Demands Justice, perhaps, or even a Sobbing Sister Sent To Cells.

'You may continue, Mr Bliss.'

'Thank you, my lord.' Bliss tried to remember where he'd got to. 'Bodies in the water, members of the jury. The time this took place, shrieks were heard by people who live at the other side of the river, three of whom will be called before you, and to the character they give of those cries it will be necessary that you should pay particular attention. You will hear that on the following morning a Mrs Galland, who resides at Startforth, and goes to Barnard Castle to church, went, according to her custom, along this road to the bridge, and when she got to the place which I have mentioned, about nine o'clock that morning, she saw blood upon the ground, and also on the stones of the wall...'

Snowden, to whom all this was very familiar, stifled a yawn and let his mind drift away from the proceedings. Betsey would be well on her way by now, he imagined, and no doubt young Craven would take good care of her. He smiled to himself, remembering how her eyes had lit up when she heard the constable would be accompanying her to Nunnington. A livelier companion than the rector, no doubt, good fellow though he was. Not likely to spend the whole journey extolling the virtues of pigs, anyway, or get lost on the way.

Nunnington. He'd grown up in the tiny village beside the Rye, his father the local blacksmith who, widowed these past three years, still lived there with Snowden's youngest brother John and his family. It must be two years since they all last met, he reflected with a twinge of guilt. They'd been so good to him, taking in Betsey after Susannah and the baby died. God knows what he'd have done without them.

A vision of Susannah's face came before him, and with it the usual pang of sorrow. He could still see her eyes, her hair, the freckles on her shoulders inherited by Betsey, but he was grieved that he could no longer recall her voice. He shut out the image and went back to his brother. Twelve years his junior, John had been tempted by Snowden's success to follow a similar career path and had just been made up to full sergeant with the county constabulary. Snowden wondered idly whether they would ever work together, decided it was unlikely, and returned his attention to Mr Bliss. The barrister had somehow wound his way tortuously back to Ann Humphreys.

'As I said before, gentlemen of the jury, the case against the prisoners depends upon whether or not you give credit to this witness. My learned friends for the defence will probably suggest either that the tale she tells is pure fiction, or that it is pure delusion.' He shook his head sadly at the idea that anyone could possibly make so ludicrous a suggestion. 'I am not aware what reason there is to suppose that that statement is a pure wilful fiction. And I apprehend if the other alternative is resorted to, such a state of mind must have manifested itself on some previous occasion. What I wish to call your attention particularly to is this, whether the statement could have been concocted, with so peculiar a set of circumstances, will be proved by other independent witnesses, and that will be a strong reason and test to come to a decision one way or the other. Gentlemen, I believe I have now discharged my duty, and that I have nothing more to add.'

Bliss sat down, looking pleased with himself. The jury looked totally bewildered. Mr Justice Cresswell Cresswell looked at the clock, decided he'd had enough for one morning, and declared it was time to adjourn for luncheon.

York, 12.55pm

SANDY found McQueedie in the Dun Cow and took a grateful draught from the pint awaiting him. 'Good drop of ale, Sam Smith's. Beats Crabthorpe's any day.'

McQueedie nodded. 'It's the water, you know. They get it from a well under the brewery, full of all the right chemicals and so on. Crabthorpe gets his from the Tees at the back of Briggate, and you've seen what goes into that.'

Sandy thought about it, wished he hadn't and changed the subject. 'So what did you think of this morning? Went on a bit, that Bliss. Thought he'd never end.'

'Don't complain, Sandy. We're getting a ha'penny a line, the more the better. We'll have made at least a couple of pounds by tonight if it goes on like this. Young Binksley's got the second part off to London all right, I hope?'

'Should have caught the twelve-thirty without any trouble.'

'Good. Did you get anywhere with that woman who shouted out in court?'

Sandy shook his head. 'Nothing to do with the case. Apparently she's a regular in the public gallery and does it all the time. Just out after a month's hard labour for telling a judge he was a miserable old fart who should be put out to grass, but it doesn't seem to have stopped her.'

'Worth a couple of paragraphs, all the same.' McQueedie drained his glass. 'Your round, Sandy.'

York, 1.25pm

ACROSS the hall in the inn's diningroom, Snowden picked at the day's lunchtime special without enthusiasm. He'd never been fond of stewed pig's trotters.

'Prefer 'em roasted myself.' Bliss plucked a gobbet of gristle from his plate. 'Better flavour altogether.'

Snowden put down his knife and fork and sat back to view the three prosecution barristers who shared his table. He'd not been greatly impressed by any of them when they'd met the previous week to discuss the trial, and what he'd seen today had not been encouraging. Maybe Pulleine and Overend would do a better job than Bliss had managed so far, but he wouldn't put money on it.

'Case is looking good, Snowden.' Bliss pushed the greasy remnants of his trotter aside, wiped his mouth with a sleeve and beamed. 'Judge seems to be on our side, saw him eyeing up the three in the dock and could tell he didn't think much of 'em. Jury seems sound, what d'you say, Pulleine?'

'Seen worse, Mr Bliss, seen worse.'

'All down to the witnesses now. Happy to start off with the first one this afternoon, are you? I'll take over the tricky bits and Mr Overend can round off with the leftovers.'

'As you wish, Mr Bliss, as you wish.'

Snowden was tempted to suggest that the three of them shared things out a bit more evenly rather than let Bliss run the show, but as he was wondering how to put this tactfully one of the court ushers appeared beside them.

'Excuse me, gentlemen, but I have a message from his lordship. He wants to see you in his chambers before the court resumes. Ten to two at the latest.'

'All of us?' Bliss looked longingly at the cheese tray awaiting them on the sideboard.

'I'm afraid so, sir. The three prosecuting counsel and Mr Snowden, he said.'

'If we must.' Snowden stood up. 'Any idea what it's about?'

'None at all, sir. But he does appear to be a little agitated.'

York, 1.40pm

McQUEEDIE returned from the Dun Cow to find Binksley sitting in the press box, admiring the initials carved into its desktop by generations of bored reporters. 'Do you think I could sit in for a bit and see what's going on?'

McQueedie shook his head firmly. 'Not a chance. There's only room for six in here and it cost a small fortune in bribes to get two of us in. You'll just have to follow it from outside as best you can.'

Binksley's face fell. 'Well, at least give me some idea what I'll be missing.'

'It's not going to be that exciting. They'll be hearing the prosecution witnesses one by one, most of them saying nothing we haven't heard before from Bliss but you never know what might come up in cross-examination. Tell you what, I'll mark the best bits and you can glance though them while you wait at the station.'

He dug into his pocket and found a couple of coins. 'Here's another two bob for the guards. There's trains at four, six-thirty and the over-night at eleven, though God forbid it goes on that long.'

York, 1.50pm

'WAIT!' Cresswell abandoned the search for suspected livestock in his wig, put it carefully back on his head and adopted his most severe expression. 'Enter!'

The prosecution team filed in and stood before his desk, giving Snowden a momentary flashback to schoolday appearances before an irate headmaster. All Cresswell needed was a cane.

'I've summoned you here, gentlemen, to discuss the inordinate number of witnesses you propose to inflict on the court. There are some forty of them on this list before me and I cannot believe they are all necessary. Can you not dispense with some, Mr Snowden?'

'It is a very complex case, my lord. We have three defendants whose motives for murder have to be demonstrated, witnesses who will attest to their movements and those of the victims, evidence of alleged confessions to the crime...'

'It seems perfectly straightforward to me. Did this woman Humphreys see them do it? If so, they're guilty. If she's lying, they walk free.' He jabbed a finger at the list of witnesses. 'I see no need for all this discussion about stolen coats and bloodstains on walls and whether the dead man had half a crown or so in his pocket. I was told this case would be over by Wednesday at the latest, but it could go on all week.'

'I'm sorry, my lord, but –'

'I have to warn you that I am booked on the first train back to London on Thursday morning and I have no intention of missing it. If the case is not resolved by then it may have to be abandoned and a new trial ordered for the spring assizes.' He pushed the list towards Snowden. 'Your enthusiasm for explaining matters in the finest detail may be appreciated when composing textbooks but it has no place in my court. I'd be obliged if you would bear that very carefully in mind.'

'As your lordship pleases.' Snowden gritted his teeth and took the list. He'd rather have had the cane.

'And Mr Bliss, I presume you are being receiving the full statutory fee for undertaking this brief?'

'Indeed, my lord.'

'I am glad to hear it. Your loquacity this morning had led me to suspect you might have joined the ranks of the gutter press and were being paid by the word. You have been given a brief, Mr Bliss. Kindly keep it so in future.'

York, 3.45pm

BINKSLEY found a bench on platform four, sat down to await the four o'clock for London, and opened the envelope containing McQueedie and Sandy's latest despatches.

MONDAY AFTERNOON. – The court resumed at two o'clock and the following witnesses were then called:

Thomas Scrafton, examined by Mr. Pulleine: 'I reside Stainton, near Barnard Castle. I married the sister of Joseph Yates; and I last saw him on August the ninth last year. He was then residing the same house with his father...'

Binksley turned to the next page and the first of McQueedie's asterisks.

Thomas Oliver, examined by Mr. Bliss: 'I am a master nailer, at Barnard Castle. I know Barker and Yates.

'I went with Barker to see Yates five or six days before the assizes at York last year in the summer and found Yates at Briggate-end, and Barker said "Joseph, thou hast been saying I told thee I got that coat at Cotherstone." Yates said "Thou knows very well what thou said." I asked Yates if he made a report that Captain Bainbridge's name was in the coat. He said he had not, and it never was.

'Yates and Pratt then left us. Barker then said he had a good mind to strike off half the side of Yates's face or some words to that effect. When we came to my house, Barker said to me he believed he would have knocked Yates's head

off, he was that vexed, if it had not been for me."

'After the York Assizes I saw Barker and Jonathan Arrowsmith together, before Yates's death. I heard Barker say he thought Yates "deserved a good thrashing for telling such a story of me."

Binksley nodded. He wasn't sure how the coat came into it all, but it was clear that Barker had a grudge against the dead man.

Matthew Pratt, examined by Mr. Overend, corroborated the preceding witness as to the conversation about the coat, and added: 'I recollect being in Briggate on the night Yates was missing, about twelve o'clock. I saw Sarah Proctor taking Catherine Raine out of a porch in Greenacre's lonning, and take her into her house. I then saw Breckon following them. We all went into Sarah Proctor's house and Catherine Raine started to call Breckon about going with her sister. She called Breckon "pot eye" and also said before she would go with such a pot eye as him, she would fling herself into the Tees." Breckon and her then quarrelled...'

She would fling herself into the Tees... Binksley's eyes widened as Murder Victim Foretold Her Own Death flashed through his mind. But maybe she wasn't murdered after all, maybe she just rejected Breckon's advances up on the bridge and leapt into the river rather than suffer a fate worse than death. No, that couldn't be right. It was Raine who was supposed to have killed her, and anyway all the evidence was that she was on the game and not that bothered about...

Binksley moved on, his eyes skipping over evidence from a string of witnesses telling the court what a wild and stormy night it had been and how they'd seen the three accused and their victims in various drinking dens in Briggate. William Graham, Francis Cooper, John Robinson, George Dobson, John Stockdale... Half the town seemed to have been out that night, despite the weather. He reached the third page and the testimony of Ann Humphreys.

There was a distant rumble and he looked up to see the London train approaching. Two minutes to read the rest of the story so far. He skimmed through it.

'Going over the sills... demands for money... cries for help... a big splash in the water... they said God would strike me dead if I told...'

Binksley had seen it all before in the committal reports, but it still made dramatic reading. The train pulled into the station and he reluctantly thrust the pages back into their envelope, found one of McQueedie's shillings, and went in search of the guard.

York, 4pm

CRESSWELL'S bladder had been bothering him for the past half-hour and as soon as Humphreys' story ended he ordered a ten-minute adjournment and scuttled off to his chambers.

'She came through that rather well, I thought.' Bliss rejoined his colleagues on the prosecution bench. 'Nearly two hours and hardly put a foot wrong.'

Snowden nodded, reluctantly admitting to himself that the man had done a good job guiding Humphreys through her evidence. 'She looks exhausted. She may not fare so well when the defence are let loose on her after the break.' He looked across at the team of lawyers on the opposing bench. 'Know anything about those three?'

'The well-rounded one with the red face is Matthews, been around for a while. He'll take the lead. The thin one with the monocle is Blanshard, getting past it, I'm told, and going deaf though he won't admit it. Pickering, the young fellow representing Breckon, is a new one on me. Comes from Durham way, I assume, and got the brief because his client's in jail up there.'

Snowden studied the three for a while and then turned his attention to Humphreys. She was still standing in the witness box, a tiny figure clutching the rail, and he wondered why nobody had thought to offer her a seat. It was probably forbidden, he decided, to encourage witnesses to get their evidence over with as soon as possible. He, on the other hand, was beginning to feel numb after hours on a wooden seat and was just getting up to stretch his legs when Craven appeared.

'Sorry I'm a bit late, sir.' The constable looked somewhat dishevelled. 'Chaise hit a dog on the turnpike just outside York, had to sort it out.'

'Everything go all right at Nunnington?'

'Delivered your daughter to your brother, Mr Snowden, safe and sound. Didn't know he was with the police as well. Just made sergeant, he told me.' He shivered. 'Cold out there, snow on the way, I reckon.'

'Not much warmer here in court, I'm afraid. But get your great-coat off and join us.'

'Case going well, sir, I hope?'

'Could be better, Craven. Sit down and I'll bring you up to date.'

He had just finished outlining the day's proceedings when Cresswell returned, made himself comfortable and looked expectantly at the defence bench. 'Do you have any questions for this witness, Mr Matthews?'

'One or two, my lord.' Matthews gazed at Humphreys for a few moments in silence, and then began his cross-examination. 'Miss Humphreys, you told the court earlier that you reside in Barnard Castle.'

'That's right, your worship. In Briggate.'

'I am not your worship, Miss Humphreys. A mere Sir will suffice.'

'I'm sorry, your – ' She stopped, confused. 'Yes, sir.'

'In Briggate, you say. And you have come from there to be at this court?'

'Yes, sir.'

'When was that? Yesterday? The day before?'

'I don't know for sure, sir.'

Matthews sounded astonished. 'You don't know?'

'No, sir. It would be about ten weeks come Saturday.'

'So where have you been these past ten weeks?'

'Here, sir, in York. In the prison.'

'In the prison?'

'Yes, sir. I was taken to the magistrates to swear my evidence and then I was brought here and kept in custody from that time till now.'

'Did you object to that?'

'No, sir. I had rather come than stop at Barnard Castle.'

'Comfortable here, is it?'

'For a prison, yes, sir.'

'Better than others you have known?'

'Yes, sir.'

'I see.' Matthews gave the jury a knowing look. 'This time it was not as a punishment, I understand.'

'No, sir. I believe it was in order that they might be sure of having me here today.'

'They thought you might run away?'

'I don't know, sir.'

'Or might be persuaded not to testify?'

'I don't know, sir.'

'Or perhaps even persuaded to tell the truth, that your story is a pack of lies and inventions?'

'No, sir. It's true, all of it.'

'We shall soon see whether the jury here believes you.' He paused and changed tack. 'You knew Joseph Yates well, I believe?'

'Yes, sir. He was a good man.'

'And the girl Catherine Raine?'

'My best friend.'

'Their deaths must have been very painful for you.'

'Yes, sir. I miss them both very much.'

'It still distresses you?'

'A great deal, sir.'

'Of course. Tell me, do you recall meeting a constable called Pearson in Barnard Castle last summer?'

Humphreys looked surprised at the question and nodded. 'Mr Pearson? Yes, sir, several times. He's one of our locals, I've known him all my life.'

'And did you speak to him?'

'Yes, sir.'

'What about?'

Humphreys hesitated and looked towards the judge. 'Do I have to talk about that, sir, I mean, my lordship?'

Cresswell didn't look up. 'Answer the question, girl.'

'I told him about Constable Elliott.'

'What about him?'

'About... the assault, sir, by him. On me.'

Cresswell looked up sharply. 'Are you claiming a constable assaulted you?'

'He did, sir.'

'I find that hard to believe. What manner of assault are you alleging?'

'I don't want to speak about it, my lord.'

'You may not want to, but you will, Miss Humphreys. How did he assault you?'

'He tried to rape me in my own bed, sir.'

'In your own bed? What was he doing there?'

'Trying to rape me, my lord.'

'Yes, yes.' Cresswell shook his head irritably. 'This is a very serious allegation, very serious. Was it brought before the magistrates?'

'Yes, sir –'

'And did they believe you?'

Humphreys shook her head. 'No, sir.'

Matthews intervened. 'My lord, this was not the line of questioning I intended to raise today. I proposed asking the witness about ghosts –'

'Ghosts, Mr Matthews?'

'Yes, my lord.'

'They will have to wait. Were you aware that the witness had made these unfounded allegations about Constable Elliott?'

'No, my lord.'

'I would have thought them very pertinent to your cross-examination which is, I presume, intended to demonstrate that this witness is either subject to wild flights of fancy, accustomed to lying in court, or both? Perhaps you would like to pursue it?'

'As your lordship pleases.' Matthews returned his attention to Humphreys. 'Why did the magistrates not believe your claims?'

'Constable Elliott told them he saw me visiting a beerhouse in Briggate and suspected me of... acting unlawfully, sir.'

'Unlawfully? You mean soliciting?'

'It wasn't true, sir.'

'You were not in the beerhouse?'

'I was, sir, but –'

'Are you a frequent visitor to such places? Remember you are on oath.'

'I like a drink sometimes, yes, sir.'

'Gin, is it?'

'Usually, sir.'

'So you went to this beerhouse in search of gin and perhaps somebody who might buy it for you?'

'Not that night, sir –'

'Not that night. But some nights that was the case?'

'I went out that night because of the bairn.'

'Bairn?'

'My child, sir. It was unwell.'

'Your child. You are single, are you not?'

'Yes, sir.'

'You do not cohabit with the father of this child?'

'Live with him, you mean, sir?'

'Indeed.'

'No, sir.'

'No.' Matthews paused. 'Let us return to Constable Pearson. Did you tell him on another occasion that you had seen Yates and Catherine alive and well – a year after both had been found drowned?'

Humphreys' voice dropped to little more than a whisper. 'I don't remember, sir.'

'Come along, Miss Humphreys, you are hardly likely to forget so remarkable an encounter. Did you tell him or not?'

'Yes, sir.'

'And did you say –' Matthews consulted his notes – 'did you say that Catherine smelled strongly of brimstone and asked if you had told anyone how they died?'

'I may have done, sir.'

'And you told your friend Mrs Sutcliffe the same?'

'Yes, sir.'

'And other people you knew?'

'One or two, yes.'

'And was it true?'

'No, sir.'

'A pack of lies and inventions, like everything else you've said? Like the story about Constable Elliott?'

'No, sir, I thought it was true at the time but it must have been a dream.'

'It must have been a dream... You were living in Briggate in August last year?'

'With my father and sister and my child, yes. I haven't a mother.'

'You slept alone?'

'With my sister and my child, in one bed. My father was in the other.'

'Do you frequently get up in the night and go outside, as you say you did on the night Yates disappeared?'

'Not frequently, sir, no.'

'How often, then?'

'I don't know. I can't say I ever did it before.'

'You told this court a few minutes ago that you were out one night and suspected of soliciting for an immoral purpose. Was that why you left the house the night Yates disappeared, to find what I believe ladies of night call a punter?''

'No, sir, that's not true.'

'Then why go out into the street in the early hours, on a foul and stormy night? Hardly for a breath of fresh air, surely? Or have the environs of Briggate acquired a reputation as a health resort?' There was a ripple of laughter from the public gallery and Cresswell rapped the desk with his gavel.

'Silence!' The laughter subsided. 'Answer the question, Miss Humphreys.'

'Which one, sir?'

'Not sir, girl. My lord, if you please.'

'Yes, sir, my lord, if you please. I don't know.'

'You don't know what?'

'About Briggate, sir.'

Cresswell slammed down his gavel in exasperation. 'Repeat the question, Mr Matthews, or we shall be here all night.'

'Indeed, my lord.' Matthews turned back to the witness box. 'Tell the court why you left home that night.'

'I don't know. I couldn't rest in bed, I don't know why. My sister and child were asleep, I didn't wake them. I got up, and put on my clothes and went down to the door that opens onto Briggate.'

'And how long were you away?'

'I can't say, I don't know what time I went out.'

'You then met Yates and the others and the dreadful events you have already described to this court took place?'

'Yes, sir.'

'And then you came home and went back to bed?'

'Yes, sir.'

'Miss Humphreys, is it not the truth that this nocturnal expedition of yours was, like the vision of the dead couple, really a dream? A nightmare, in fact, concocted by your fevered imagination? You were very confused, were you not, last summer?'

'I had a lot of problems, sir. I'd just lost my bairn –' Humphreys broke off and began to cry.

'You had just lost your child, you had lost two of your best friends, you had taken to drink and were so distressed that you were almost out of your mind, were you not? So much so that you didn't know what was real and what was the figment of your distraught imagination, and told people you'd seen ghosts beside the river.'

'I was upset, I didn't know what I was saying –'

'And I put it to you that you also didn't know what you were saying when you made up your preposterous story about these three innocent young men committing murder?'

'No, sir, that's all true, I swear it.'

'You are asking this jury to believe that you got up in the middle of the night, for reasons you cannot explain, went wandering around Briggate for an hour or so, saw not one but two foul murders being committed and then went back to bed as if nothing had happened? And then said not a word about it for almost a year?' Matthews shook his head in disbelief.

'I was frightened, sir.' She was fighting back the tears. 'I did not tell because I thought the three boys would not care what they might do to me if I did tell. And I didn't think I would be believed if I did tell.'

'And can you give the gentlemen of the jury a single reason why they should believe you now?'

She shook her head in despair. 'No, sir.'

'No further questions, my lord.'

Snowden watched grimly as Humphreys, still sobbing, was led out of the courtroom. He didn't like admitting it, but Matthews was good, very good. In less than an hour he'd deftly given the jury a portrait of a deluded woman of dubious character, mother of a bastard child, an habitual drinker and a self-confessed fantasist and liar who the prosecution was so unsure about that it had locked her up in jail. It couldn't have been much worse.

He sat through the next forty minutes, pondering events so far, while a succession of Humphreys' neighbours gave evidence about what they had heard on the night of the murders. James Lincoln, who lived in a room above Humphreys, swore that he'd seen her in the house around eleven-thirty and a little later heard someone going downstairs. He'd mentioned it to his wife, Hannah, who followed him into the witness box and confirmed it. The woman in the room below, Elizabeth Hall, told the jury she had heard the Humphreys' door shut after midnight and footsteps going out. They sounded as if the person was barefoot, or wearing very soft shoes, but she didn't know who it was.

'Is there much more of this, Mr Bliss?' Cresswell was becoming increasingly impatient. 'You appear to be producing a string of witnesses who haven't witnessed anything.'

'Forgive me, my lord, but the prosecution is attempting to prove that Miss Humphreys did, as she says, leave the house that night. It was occupied by three families, two of whom have just stated in evidence that they did not go out, but heard someone else do so. With your lordship's indulgence, I propose next to call upon Miss Humphreys' father and sister who will tell the jury that neither of them left their beds that night. The only person it can have been was Miss Humphreys herself.'

Cresswell grunted, unconvinced. 'If you must, Mr Bliss, but make it as brief as possible.'

'I am obliged, my lord. Call Mr John Humphreys.'

York, 6.22pm

BINKSLEY thrust the latest despatch into the hands of the *Gazette* head printer, ignored his surly complaints about it being late, and set off at a run down High Ousegate towards the station. It was dark, it was snowing steadily, and he had eight minutes to make the six-thirty for London.

He skidded into Bridge Street, over the Ouse and into Micklegate. The last time he'd done the trip he'd turned right up Hudson Street to the station, but he was sure he could save at least two minutes if he went further on and took a short cut down the back alleys. He hurried on till he found one. There were no gas lamps but he could see a glimmer of light at the far end that must be the back of the station. Then all he had to do was nip over the wall and across to the platforms.

He set off into the darkness, his shoes squelching in what he hoped was nothing worse than a mixture of mud and snow. Well, there were worse things than wet feet.

Thirty seconds later he came face to face with one of them.

York, 7.10pm

HENRY Pulleine, barrister at law, rose to his feet as Jane Humphreys took her place in the witness box. It was the first time he had been allowed to take part in the proceedings, and that was only because Bliss's feet were beginning to play up.

'You are Jane Humphreys, eldest daughter of the last witness?'

'Yes, sir.'

'Do you recall the night of August the ninth last year?'

'Yes, sir.'

'You went to bed early, I believe? And were joined later by your sister Ann and her child?'

'Yes, sir. But I was asleep by then.'

'You were not aware of their presence? They didn't awake you?'

'No, sir. I never felt her get out of bed during the night. I didn't awake or get up at any time. I'm a hard sleeper. '

'A hard sleeper. So your sister might well have arisen and gone out for a while, as she claims, without you knowing?'

'She could have, sir.'

'Well, you didn't leave the room that night. Your father has given evidence that he did not either. There was nobody else there apart from the child, who can hardly have been our mysterious midnight walker. It must have been your sister who was heard opening the door of your room and going downstairs, must it not?'

'I suppose so.'

'Thank you.' Pulleine sat down, looking pleased with himself, and Matthews took over.

'Miss Humphreys, is it not remarkable, when neighbours above and below your room say they heard the door of your room shut and someone walking down the stairs, that nobody actually in that room, not even you sharing a bed with your sister, heard a thing?'

'Perhaps they're mistaken, sir.'

'Perhaps they are, indeed.' Matthews nodded. 'Perhaps they are.'

Craven turned to Snowden, puzzled, as Jane Humphreys left the witness box. 'That didn't help us much, sir. Which side is she on?'

'I'm not sure.' He had wondered whether it was wise to subject Ann Humphrey's father and sister to cross-examination.

'Who's next?'

Snowden consulted his list. 'More evidence about who heard what that night and the morning after. I'm hoping we fare a bit better with this.'

York, 7.25pm

WILLIAM Burland pulled his boots on, lit a lantern and stomped angrily to his back door. 'The bloody thing's loose again, Martha, out there making one hell of a racket. I'll have to go and find it.'

'I keep telling you to mend that yard gate. Poor thing's on its last legs and half-blind, you can't blame it for wandering out into the alley.'

'I should have had it put down years ago.' Burland picked up a length of rope, opened the door and cursed before hunching his shoulders against the snow and setting off across the yard. There were plenty of footprints there, slowly vanishing beneath fresh snow, and he followed them out into the alley and beyond towards Micklegate.

He found his quarry thirty yards further on, hopping from foot to foot and snuffling eagerly at the door of a neighbour's privy. 'Come on, you daft old bugger.' He spoke fondly despite himself, reached up and slipped the rope round its neck. 'Time your dancing days were over. Let's get you home.'

Binksley, trembling with terror in the pitch-dark privy, heard them depart and wondered dismally what he had done to deserve this.

York, 8.15pm

'I KNOW what I saw and heard, sir. I'll remember those shrieks for the rest of my days.' Her eyes widened at the memory. 'Awful, they were.'

'Thank you, Mrs Dalkin.' Pulleine turned to face the judge. 'No more questions, my lord.'

'I'm pleased to hear it.' Cresswell looked pointedly at the clock. 'I think it is high time these proceedings were adjourned until tomorrow, and I am sure the jury will agree.'

'My lord...' Matthews rose to his feet. 'I wonder if I might have a word with you on a matter of some urgency?'

'Urgency?'

'Indeed, my lord, A point of law which I believe it wise to bring to your lordship's attention.'

'If you must, Mr Matthews. Make it brief.'

'In chambers, if you would be so good, my lord. It is a matter which you may well feel it is not in the interests of justice to be discussed in the presence of the jury. Or the press and public.'

'This is most inconvenient, Mr Matthews.'

'A matter relating to a possible appeal, my lord, if not resolved at this stage.'

'An appeal?' Cresswell looked appalled. 'Very well. In my chambers in five minutes. The court will adjourn until our return.'

McQueedie laid down his pen. 'What's all that about, then, Sandy?'

'No idea.' His partner shrugged. 'I thought we'd finished for the night. Waste of good drinking time.'

McQueedie handed over his latest notes. 'Here's the last session for you to run an eye over before Binksley takes them away. Where is he, anyway? Should have been back long ago.'

'In a pub, probably.'

'Lucky little bugger. Wish I was with him, wherever he is.'

Sandy began to read.

> *Margaret Walker, examined by Mr Pulleine:*
> *'I am a widow and live in the middle of Briggate. My house faces the water.'*
> *'Do you recall the night Yates went missing?'*
> *'I do. Whilst I was sitting up in bed late that night I heard an awful shriek from the middle of the Sills.'*
> *'A shriek?'*
> *'Three altogether. I got up and opened the window. It was wet, windy and the water was very rough.'*
> *'And what did you see?'*
> *'Nothing, sir.'*
> *'Nothing?'*
> *'But I heard a man's voice. The first cry was "Oh dear, oh dear, oh dear me." From the last voice it appeared as if the person was choking.'*
> *'And how long did this go on for?'*
> *'From first to last, I think a quarter of an hour.'*
> *Cross-examined by Mr Matthews:*
> *'How long have you lived in that house?'*
> *'Seven years, sir.'*

'And have you heard shrieks on other occasions?'

'Oh, yes, sir, many a time.'

'So this was nothing unusual?'

'Oh, it was, sir. They was never so awful as they were that night.'

Mary Hall, examined by Mr Bliss:

'I am a milliner at Barnard Castle. I live next-door to Mrs Walker on the side nearer the bridge.'

'And did you hear anything on the night in question?'

'I had the candle burning and was at work when I heard shrieking, sir, from the opposite side of the river.'

'At what hour?'

'It would have been between one and two in the morning. The shriek was a shrill one and loud, and I didn't think at the beginning it was a man's voice.'

'Was that all?'

'No, sir, the shrieks began again louder than before and I heard a voice say "Oh dear!" Then the cries grew weaker and weaker.'

'Did you know the deceased, Joseph Yates?'

'Yes, sir. He was only a small man, he had a very soft voice.'

'Like a woman?'

'I suppose so, yes, sir.'

'But you believe it was him who was crying out?'

'I do so, sir.'

Cross-examined by Mr Matthews:

'You have heard shouts and screams from across the water on many occasions, I imagine?'

'Quite often, sir.'

'Shrieks like this are commonplace, in fact?'

'Not like that, sir. They were different from anything I had ever heard before.'

'You clearly remember the events well, Mrs Hall.'

'Very well, sir. I wouldn't forget a night like that.'

'A stormy night, was it not? The weather wild, the wind howling outside, the rain beating upon your window and the river in full spate?'

'It was very high, sir, going down at a tremendous rush.'

'Very loud, I presume.'

'Yes, sir.'

'Your window was closed against the rain, I assume?'

'I did open it the once to look out, sir.'

'You heard nothing when it was open?'

'No, sir. Then I closed it again.'

'And yet you were then able to hear across the river – a distance of some fifty yards if not more – the weak cries of a man having what you described only a few minutes ago as a very soft voice?'

'I know what I heard, sir.'

Mary Ann Dalkin, examined by Mr Overend:
'I am a widow and in August 1845 I lived in Briggate. I was sitting by my fireside, it was between one and two in the morning, and I heard the shrieking of women's voices from the other side of the river.'

'From the Sills?'

'Towards the end of the tram-wall, sir.'

'Did you see anything?'

'Not then, sir. But next morning I looked out in that direction and noticed three young men at about the spot I supposed the shrieks came from.'

'And did you see what they were doing?'

'They were moving about and looking over the wall, sir. I noticed them for a considerable time, for perhaps near an hour.'

Cross-examined by Mr Matthews:

'These three figures, Mrs Dalkin... Did you recognise any of them?'

'I couldn't make out their faces, sir, no.'

'But you could tell they were all young men?'

'Oh, yes, sir.'

'How could you tell that?'

'I don't rightly know sir, they just looked like they were.'

'They could have been middle-aged or even old men?'

'I suppose so, sir, but I thought –'

'Or women, even?'

'Well, I thought they were young men.'

'This was a Sunday morning, Mrs Dalkin. Do you not often see men and women, young and old, walking along the Sills on such a morning?'

'Sometimes, sir, yes.'

'On their way to church, perhaps, enjoying a walk on their day of rest, or just idly waiting for one of the local hostelries to open? It is, in fact, a popular place for people to gather?'

'I suppose so, sir.'

'Mrs Dalkin, it is quite apparent that there is no reason for you to suppose that the three people you saw – if indeed you saw any – had anything at all to do with the shrieks you claim to have heard the night before. I put it to you that you, and the two preceding witnesses, saw and heard nothing at all that night.'

'That's not so, sir.'

'Gentlemen of the jury, you may think it instructive that none of these three so-called witnesses said anything to the appropriate authorities until almost a year later – when they connived together to concoct this parcel of lies about shrieks and people by the river to claim a share of the reward money. Is that not the truth of the matter, Mrs Dalkin?'

'I know what I saw and heard, sir. I'll remember those shrieks for the rest of my days. Awful, they were.'

'No more questions, my lord.'

'It all looks fine to me.' Sandy handed the notes back to McQueedie and looked across at the jury. 'They're getting restless over there. I wonder what's keeping Matthews and the judge?'

York, 8.25pm

MATTHEWS had been kept waiting for ten minutes before Cresswell called him into his chambers. He was offered no explanation or apology for the delay, but suspected the judge had been fortifying himself from the decanter on the table. He didn't blame him. It had been a long day.

'Now, Mr Matthews, what's this all about?'

'My lord, it is in regard to the evidence given during cross-examination by the witness Humphreys.'

'Case is full of Humphreys. Which one?'

'Ann, my lord. You will recall she made allegations of a serious sexual assault by a Constable Elliott.'

'What of them?'

'Well, my lord, apart from the possibility that Elliott might consider an action for slander or libel–'

'Nonsense, Matthews. Allegations were made in open court, thrown out by magistrates. Said so yourself. Privileged material, perfectly legitimate to repeat it here.'

'With all due respect, my lord, that may not be the case. It has been brought to my attention that these allegations were made during a private disciplinary meeting at which the magistrates were not acting in a judicial capacity. Mr Snowden tells me he was there and I have no reason to disbelieve him. He says the allegations have never been aired before in public.'

'And?'

'My lord, it is conceivable that Elliott may be somewhat unhappy if these allegations are repeated in press reports of the case. Were that to be the case, he may institute proceedings against those involved.'

'I am not here to protect the press, Mr Matthews. If they wish to print defamatory statements that is their problem.'

'Not just the press, my lord. As you are of course aware, the laws of defamation are complex and uncertain. Any proceedings might well require evidence from myself, my fellow counsel, and even your lordship. They would, I fear, prove both irksome and time-consuming.'

Cresswell eyed him doubtfully. 'I see no reason why I should be called to account for the shortcomings of the defence, Mr Matthews.'

'There is a further problem with Elliott, my lord.' Matthews shifted his feet uncomfortably. 'Mr Snowden also informs me that the man is no longer a constable.'

'I can't see that makes any difference, Mr Matthews.'

'It may, my lord. He is currently serving a three-year sentence in the jail behind us for...' He consulted a sheet of paper in his hand. 'For larceny, fraud, deception, obtaining goods by menaces and conduct unbecoming a police officer.'

'Disgraceful.'

'Oh, and attempted grievous bodily harm upon his wife.'

'He didn't succeed?'

'Apparently she broke his jaw, my lord. It's a long story, but suffice it to say Elliott is hardly a reliable source of information. It may well be that the witness Humphreys was telling the truth about the assault upon her.'

'Ah.'

'Were we to win the case, my lord, it could be argued that the defence had been remiss in making public his unsubstantiated allegations and then unfairly discrediting the witness in cross-examination.'

'Argued? By whom?'

'Well, my lord... by the prosecution, perhaps, should it wish to appeal the verdict and request a re-trial. Mr Snowden is understandably concerned that his witness has been grossly misrepresented.'

Cresswell looked appalled. 'A re-trial? You mean go through all this again? God forbid.'

'That might be the case, my lord.'

'It would be extremely regrettable.' Cresswell paused. 'You *were* excessively hard on her, Mr Matthews.'

'At your lordship's insistence, as I recall.'

'I can hardly be blamed for the defence's ineptitude.'

'I hope the appeal court agrees with you, my lord. There is, of course, one course of action that would relieve both of us of any possible embarrassment.'

'Very well, Mr Matthews.' Cresswell narrowed his eyes. 'I do not, of course, accept any responsibility for this sorry state of affairs, but I have no wish to add to the appeal court's heavy burden. We will return to court.'

York, 8.35pm

McQUEEDIE slid a fresh nib onto his pen, examined the old one and shook his head. 'They don't seem to last five minutes, these steel nibs. This one's rusting already.'

'I blame the ink.' Sandy inspected his own pen without enthusiasm. 'They put the cheapest they can get in the press box, not much better than water.'

'Never happened with the old quills.' McQueedie sighed nostalgically. 'You could sharpen them down to a stump and they kept on going. I still carry my penknife round with me, comes in handy for all sorts of things.'

'I seem to get more blots with these steel ones, too.' Sandy frowned. 'I wonder why that is?'

'Couldn't be your hands shaking more these days, could it?' McQueedie gave a grin. 'On your feet, Sandy, all rise. His lordship's coming back.'

Cresswell settled into his seat and waited for the court to subside before addressing the jury. 'You will be pleased to learn, gentlemen, that you will shortly be relieved of your duties until tomorrow.' There was a murmur of relief from the jury box. 'In a case like this it is essential that you do not communicate with witnesses or the public, and it is therefore necessary for you to remain within the walls of the castle. I have given instructions that provision should be made for your comfort.'

'Poor buggers.' McQueedie watched the jury's faces fall. 'I bet they thought they'd be going home.'

Sandy nodded. 'Or living it up in the Dun Cow.'

Cresswell waited for the mutters of disappointment to die down before continuing. 'Before you leave, however, I need to instruct you regarding certain evidence you have heard here today. For legal reasons which do not concern you, you are to disregard that part of the proceedings in which the witness Ann Humphreys was questioned about allegations of an assault by a constable. It will be struck from the record and you must cast it from your minds. Is that understood? Very well, you may depart.'

He watched as an usher guided them out of the room and then turned to the press box. 'The same applies to the gentlemen of the press. There will be no report of this episode nor mention of the constable in question. Any contravention of these instructions will be regarded as a gross contempt of court and I shall deal with it with the utmost severity.' He rose to leave. 'This court is adjourned until nine o'clock tomorrow morning.'

'That's terrible.' McQueedie looked aghast.

'Nine o'clock?' Sandy nodded. 'It won't even be light by then. The man's a sadist.'

'Not the time, you fool. The reporting ban.'

'Bloody hell.' Sandy stared at his partner. 'The *Gazette*'s no problem – they don't go to print till Friday, we've plenty of time to change things for them – but the London copy...'

'It'll be halfway there by now.'

'Utmost severity, he said.'

'What do you suppose you get for gross contempt of court?'

'I think he can lock us up for as long as he feels like it. Could be years.'

'I don't suppose we could lay the blame on young Binksley? Say he was in charge, nothing to do with us?'

'Bit rough on the lad, but it might be worth a try. We could make him editor-in-chief or something. He'd want a pay rise, mind.'

'Better than five years in the nick. Where is he, anyway?'

'Waiting outside, I suppose. Let's see.'

They found him huddled in a corner of the court entrance, staring wide-eyed into the night and muttering to himself. Sandy clapped him on the shoulder and he gave a terrified shriek.

'Mr McLeod! I thought you were one of them.'

'Them?'

'The bears. Great big black ones, roaming the streets.'

'No bears here, laddie.' Sandy stared at him. 'Rats, maybe, though I'm not too sure about that.'

'Bears, I tell you. I've seen them.'

'Must be the drink.' McQueedie shook his head sadly. 'I've seen it before, but not in one so young. It's usually pink elephants, not black bears.'

'They're not going to believe he's our editor-in-chief, Hamish. Not if he goes on like this.' Sandy surveyed Binksley's bedraggled figure dispassionately. 'Come on, let's get him to bed. We can do the midnight train delivery afterwards. Not that there seems much point now, thinking about it.'

'Wait!' Binksley grabbed his arm. 'There's something I've got to tell you.'
'We know, there's bears everywhere. We'll make sure they don't get you.'
'Not bears. The copy for the six-thirty train.'
'What about it?'
Binksley dug into his inside pocket and produced the notes. 'I missed the train.'
'You did what?'
'I was late, and then this bear –'
'Sod the bear, you mean you didn't send the story?'
Binksley shook his head miserably. 'I'm sorry, Mr McLeod. I suppose you'll want to fire me.'
'Fire you?' Sandy grabbed the notes and to Binksley's astonishment gave a whoop of delight. 'Nonsense. How would you like to be promoted to –'
McQueedie broke in rapidly. 'Deputy assistant editor, we thought, didn't we, Sandy?'
'That's right, third in command. What do you say, Binksley?'
'Do I get a pay rise?'
McQueedie frowned. 'Don't push your luck, laddie. But we might buy you a drink or two.'

York, 9.35pm

HEZEKIAH Elsopp, elected foreman of the jury mainly because he was the only one with a pencil, looked dispiritedly round their sleeping quarters. The usher who had brought them down there had announced cheerfully that it was a former dungeon that in its time had housed recusants awaiting the stake, Scottish prisoners of war and a colony of lepers, as well as generations of transient convicts. All of them seemed to have spent their time scratching names, dates and favourite obscenities on the walls. It smelled of damp, drains and despair, and Elsopp wouldn't be surprised if there were rats watching him as he perched gingerly on the nearest iron bed. The blankets felt damp, too.

He wondered if the role of foreman included saying something to encourage the rest of his companions-in-law, who were also surveying their surroundings with dismay, and decided that it probably did. So far they'd hardly spoken to each other: the judge had clearly disapproved of conversation in the jury box and the meal they'd just consumed had been so bad – he'd never seen grey soup before or wrestled with such overdone mutton – that it had been endured in silence apart from the occasional mutters of disbelief, disgust, or both. He took a deep breath and stood up.

'Gentlemen, I wondered if it might be a good idea to introduce ourselves before we retire?' There was an unenthusiastic turning of heads in his direction. 'I'm Elsopp, Hezekiah Elsopp. You may have seen my shop just off Walmgate, I make clocks, mend them and so on. Plenty of time on my hands, you know, ha-ha.'

Nobody smiled.

'Perhaps we could go round the room and I'll just make a note of who's who.' He found his pencil and notebook and looked expectantly at the first man to his left.

'If you must. Henry Babbington, butcher.' Elsopp made a note. *Large, well-fed, big moustache.*

'Francis Culbeck, maltster.' *Bald, sixty-ish*

'Dipple, John Dipple. Brick-maker.' *Squint, hairy hands.*
'Joshua Chatterway, farmer, Copmanthorpe.' *Small, wiry.*
'Richard Fisher, farmer.' *Red hair, beard.*
'William Dart, blacksmith.' *Big.*
'Crowl.'
'First name, Mr Crowl?' Elsopp paused his pencil.
'I prefer that to remain my business, Mr Aslop.'
'Elsopp. As you wish, sir, as you wish.' *Name??* 'Next?'
'Will Astwood, baker.' *Youngish, high voice.*
'William Field, draper.' *Black wig.*
'John Buckerfield, grocer.' *Eyeglasses.*
'William Edwards, cordwainer and bootmaker.' *Sideburns, nervous.*

Elsopp counted the names, looked puzzled, remembered he hadn't included himself and gave an embarrassed laugh. 'Forgot myself there.'

Nobody looked amused.

'Well, here we all are. I know it's a little early in the proceedings but it might be useful to know what you thought of it all so far. Does anybody want to say anything?'

'I do.' The red-headed one – Fisher was it? – responded with a scowl. 'It's bloody cold in here. Bloody freezing.'

One of the Williams, the one with the wig, nodded vigorously. 'And that food was inedible.'

The butcher's moustache bristled. 'Probably all be dead of food poisoning by morning. I hope you're going to do something about it.'

'Do something?' Elsopp looked at him uncertainly. 'You mean me?'

'You're the bloody foreman, aren't you? You want to be telling them.'

'Yes, well, I'm not sure it's really part of my role. I was more interested in what you thought of the trial, actually.'

'Trial? Guilty, the three of them, no doubt about it.' There was a murmur of agreement from most of the others. 'Don't know why we're hanging about to hear any more.'

'You don't think we should –'

'Hang the buggers now and get it over with. You can tell them that and all.'

Tuesday December 15th

'DO I have to, Mr McQueedie?' Binksley was horrified. 'I might never come back. Anything could happen.' He shuddered. 'I could die.'

'Nonsense, laddie. Duty calls. Get out there and face it before your nerve goes for ever.' McQueedie nodded firmly. 'You think you saw a bear last night, you go out and find it. It's a lovely sunny morning, the snow's nearly gone, and bears don't come out in the daytime.'

'Are you sure?'

'Everyone knows that.'

'Supposing the bears don't?'

'You owe it to yourself and your public, quite apart from Sandy and me who think there may be a bob or two to be made out of it. Off you go. Back by eleven with five hundred words of BERSERK BEARS ON RAMPAGE – CITY IN URSINE TERROR, eight hundred if they actually kill someone.'

'A GREAT pool of blood by the wall.' Mrs Galland was in full flow and, Snowden suspected, greatly enjoying her chance to be in the spotlight. 'There was more blood on the top, too, and some had run down the side. I walked on and saw marks of a violent struggle, such as much trampling, and as if they had been on their knees.'

Bliss nodded encouragingly. 'This was on your way to church, around nine o'clock that Sunday morning?'

'Yes, sir. And on the way back I saw all the blood was covered over and there was mud and dirt on the wall. The spots of blood there were scratched off, as with the toe of a shoe.'

'And this young man you have told us you saw there earlier, was he still there?'

'No, sir.'

'Did you recognise him?'

'No, sir, not then.'

'Not then? Do you mean you have seen him again, on a later occasion?'

'This summer, sir, when I went to see the prisoners being examined before the magistrates at Greta Bridge. After I had seen the prisoner Raine it came powerfully to my mind that he bore a strong resemblance to the young man I had seen that morning.'

'Thank you, Mrs Galland. Stay there while Mr Matthews asks you some questions, if he has any.'

'Just a few.' Matthews eased to his feet. 'Is there not a smith's shop close to the place where you saw the blood?'

'There is, sir, more's the pity.'

'You have complained from time to time about horses being bled there?'

'I have, sir. It's a disgrace.'

'So that may be how blood came to be by the wall that morning?'

'Well, there was not the print of a horse's foot as far as I saw. There had been much rain that night and the roads were very muddy.'

'But it is possible?'

'I suppose so.'

'Let us turn to this young man you say you saw. What did he look like?'

'Well...' She frowned. 'Like a young man, like they all do.'

'One's much like another, you mean?'

'Well, they are, aren't they?'

'Are they, Mrs Galland? Tell me what you remember about this one. Was he particularly tall or short? Dark or fair? Wearing a beard or clean-shaven?'

'Well, now...' She paused, searching her memory. 'Quite tall, I fancy, dark-haired. With a beard.'

'And do you see this man in court today?'

She peered round the room, her gazing ending up on the trio in the dock. 'He's one of them up there, sir.'

'Which one?'

'With the beard, sir.'

'There are two with beards, Mrs Galland, are there not? Both tall and dark-haired? Which is the one you saw that morning and again at Greta Bridge?'

There was a lengthy pause. 'The one on the right, I think, sir.'

'You think?'

'That's him, sir.'

'Mrs Galland, when you attended the proceedings at Greta Bridge, how many of the defendants were present?'

'Just two, sir.'

'Indeed, Barker and Raine. I have the records before me should his lordship or the jury wish to see them. Breckon was not required to attend.'

'I wouldn't know about that, sir. But I never saw the three altogether till now.'

'Now that you have seen Breckon, would you not agree that he and Raine look much alike?'

'I suppose they do, sir, yes.'

'So much alike that a few moments ago you identified Breckon as the man you saw that Sunday morning and later at Greta Bridge?'

'Well, he looks like him, sir.'

'It could have been him?'

'I don't think –'

'It could have been him?'

'Yes, sir, it's possible.'

'Or it could have been any one of hundreds of tall, dark, bearded young men living in Barnard Castle or thereabouts? As you said earlier on, one young man looks much the same as another.'

'I'm sure it was him, sir. Or one of them two.'

Snowden sighed. Thank God he'd found other witnesses who might do better.

York, 10.05am

BINKSLEY stood halfway along Micklegate and peered cautiously down yet another alley. They all looked alike and he had no idea which one he'd ended up in last night. He'd explored five so far, his heart in his mouth, ready to turn and flee at the first sight of anything remotely like a bear. He hadn't found one yet, but had come close to cardiac arrest when a tramp stumbled out in front of him a few minutes ago.

He took a deep breath and ventured forth, examining each doorway he came to. Thirty yards along he found last night's privy. He had no doubt it was the right one. There were deep scratches down the door's flaking paintwork, made by the beast as it tried to find him.

He stepped forward to examine them and froze.

He could hear something inside.

Something alive.

His first instinct was to run, but the thought of the derision and contempt that would greet him if he returned to McQueedie empty-handed rooted him to the spot, staring at the door. Halfway down there was a tiny knothole. The least he could do was see what was inside.

He bent down very slowly onto his hands and knees and peered through.

'Well, well, well, what have we here?' The voice from the alley behind sent Binksley's face crashing into the door. 'The Micklegate Peeping Tom, caught in the act. We've been looking for you, sunshine.'

York, 10.40am

BELLA Clarkson left the witness box, faintly disappointed that her tale of discovering Yates' body in the river was over. Standing up there in front of all those people had been the most exciting thing she'd ever done or, she suspected, ever would do. She could hardly wait to see her name in the papers.

'Next witness.' Emmanuel Tenwick came forward, took the oath and waited until Bliss was ready to question him.

'On the thirteenth of August last year, did you identify the body of Joseph Yates?'

'I did, sir. It was lying in a cowhouse on some straw.'

'Did you examine it for injuries?'

'Yes, sir. I looked at his nostrils, and saw caked blood...'

In the press box McQueedie turned to whisper to Sandy. 'Where the hell is Binksley? If he's not back in five minutes we'll miss the eleven-thirty.'

'Perhaps the bears have got him.' Sandy grinned. 'If he's not outside I'll run the copy to the station myself and then go looking for him. Enjoy the blood.'

York, 11.10am

'CAUGHT him red-handed, Sarge.' Constable William Wintergreen rubbed his hands gleefully. 'On his hands and knees, he was, peering through a netty knothole. Dirty little sod. I've put him in the far cell till his nose stops bleeding.'

Sergeant Tom Hoskins frowned. 'If he gets blood on the floor I'll do him for damaging police property. What's he got to say for himself?'

'Good as confessed, sarge, keeps going on about wanting to see something big and black and bare. Not much chance of that down the back of Micklegate.' He chuckled. 'You should have seen old Ma Pollitt's face when he smashed the door open. Sitting there with her unmentionables round her ankles, she was. Screamed her bloody head off.'

'I don't know what gets into these perverts, constable. Nobody went peeking into privies in search of naked darkies in the old days. Or anything else, for that matter. '

'I blame the missionaries myself, Sarge. Coming back from Africa with pictures of them natives running round with nothing on. It's not natural.'

York, 12.01pm

SNOWDEN turned to Craven as the court rose for lunch. 'Back at one. Cresswell seems determined to get this over with as fast as possible.'

'There can't be many more of them.' Craven ticked off names on the list before him. 'We've had Clarkson, Tenwick, Anderson – I thought he did us proud, sir, when he was cross-examined about whether Yates was injured before he went into the water. All that about blood congealing and so on, he really knew what he was talking about.'

'It's cost me a pound of Parson's Old Twist, but worth every penny.' Snowden stood up and stretched. 'Come on, constable, we'll get something to eat before we call the last of our witnesses.'

Craven looked puzzled. 'More of them, sir? I've no more names here.'

'Just a couple.' Snowden gave a grim smile. 'I've kept them up my sleeve till now, but I think we could do with them this afternoon.'

York, 1.15pm

MATTHEW Hornsey, landlord of the Bell and Bucket in Micklegate, shook his head. 'Haven't seen anyone like that. What's he done?'

'Disappeared.' Sandy put down his glass. 'Said he was coming down this way to find a bear and not been seen since.'

'A bear?'

'Daft bugger reckoned he'd seen one last night.'

'That'll be Bill Burland's, always getting loose, it is. Bloody nuisance. '

Sandy looked astonished. 'A real bear?'

'Dirty great thing, stinks to high heaven. Bill used to make money out of it, bear-baiting all over the place till they banned it, what, ten years ago? Then he taught it to dance and took it round the pubs. Same again, is it?' Sandy nodded. 'Poor bloody thing's well past it now, mind. Drives his missus mad.'

'Bloody hell. It scared the shit out of our lad last night.'

Hornsey laughed and pulled another pint. 'Soft as butter, it is, wouldn't hurt a fly. Bill says he hasn't the heart to have it put down, but there's plenty round here would be glad to see the back of it, for all that.'

Sandy looked thoughtful and reached for his notebook.

CRESSWELL was not amused. '*More* witnesses, Mr Bliss? Are we to have the entire population of Barnard Castle giving evidence before the prosecution is satisfied?'

'I'm sorry, my lord, but I am instructed that these are essential if we are properly to present the court with the full case against the accused. I am sure your lordship would not wish to deprive the jury of all the facts.'

Cresswell frowned, recognising a hint of a possible appeal when he heard one, and decided to retreat. 'Very well, if you must.'

'Thank you, my lord.'

Jonathan Arrowsmith, examined by Mr Bliss:
'I am a labourer. In August 1845 the prisoner Barker lodged with me in Briggate. We slept in the same bed.'

'Do you recall a conversation with him about Joseph Yates on August the ninth?'

'Yes, sir. He asked me if I would go with him to give Yates a severe beating for taking a false oath about a coat. I denied him. He had told me another time that he would punch the b——r's bloody guts out, forgive my language, sir, but those were his words. That would be a week before Yates' death.'

'And where were you on the night of the ninth, the night that Yates disappeared?'

'I went to bed, between ten and eleven.'

'Alone?'

'Yes, sir. I heard one o'clock strike when I was in bed and Barker had not come to bed at that time. After that I fell asleep.'

'Did he eventually join you?'

'Yes, when he came in, he awoke me and spoke to me.'

'What time was this?'

'I don't know, sir.'

'Well after one o'clock?'

'I think I had been asleep some time, sir.'

'Well after one o'clock... And did you speak to him next day?'

'I walked with him in the evening, between six and seven.'

'Did you know then that Yates was missing?'

'No, sir. But Barker told me "Yates, the b——r, was gone." Three or four months later he told me never to mention those words.'

Cross-examined by Mr Matthews:
'Was Barker not bigger than Yates and quite capable of beating him very well on his own?'

'I suppose so, sir.'

'Did you not later fight with Barker about some tobacco and threaten to stab him?'

'That's not true, sir, not about threatening to stab him. We did have a bit of a fight but we made it up and he lodged with me for five months.'

'I put it you, Mr Arrowsmith, that you still harbour resentment against Barker, that you believe he stole goods from you while you were away from your shared lodgings, and that you have made up this testimony of yours to exact revenge upon him?'

'I do believe he stole from me, sir, but everything I've said is true.'

'No further questions.'

Matthew Cruddace, examined by Mr Overend:

'Mr Cruddace, you have been brought here from Durham jail, where you are a prisoner, I believe. You were there last spring?'

'Yes, sir.'

'Did you share a cell with anyone?'

'Yes, sir. Breckon, him there in the dock, and later a man called Knowles.'

'And did Breckon tell you why he was in jail?'

'Yes, sir. The first night we shared a cell he said he had been at Wycliffe getting examined before a magistrate on a charge of murder. I said I doubted it would be a bad charge for him.'

'Did he say anything else?'

'He swore that if ever he had the chance he would kill the girl.'

'Which girl?'

'The one who had told the police about it, I don't know her name. He said there was blood, as fresh the next morning for all it had been such a steeping rain, and he would tell me all about it, the murder.'

'And did he?'

'No, sir. The turnkey was coming in just at the time, and we were obliged to hold our tongues. Breckon did not speak of the murder to me again.'

'Did you tell the prison officers of this conversation?'

'No, sir, I'd not dare to. But I spoke to Knowles about it, sir, when he joined us in the cell and Breckon was not near.'

'Thank you, Mr Cruddace.'

Cross-examined by Mr Matthews:

'This man Knowles, he will corroborate your story?'

'He'll have a job, sir. They hanged him just after.'

The public gallery erupted in laughter and Cresswell hammered on his desk. 'If there is another such outbreak I shall have the court cleared.' The noise subsided. 'Continue, Mr Matthews.'

'Why were you in prison at the time, Mr Cruddace?'

'Assault, sir.'

'On a police officer?'

'Yes, sir. Two months I got.'

'And you were released shortly after these alleged conversations with Breckon and Knowles?'

'Yes, sir.'

'But back inside again now. What for this time?'

'Assault, sir.'

'Also on a police officer?'

'Yes, sir. Different one, though.'

There was another wave of laughter and Cresswell finally lost his temper. 'I will not tolerate this behaviour any longer. Ushers, clear the gallery.' He waited for the chorus of complaints from spectators to fade away as they were led out of the courtroom. 'Mr Matthews, I presume your questioning is intended to acquaint the jury with the witness's criminal record?'

'Indeed, sir.'

'And suggest that the testimony of someone who makes a habit of assaulting officers of the law might be less than reliable?'

'Your lordship's grasp of the case is admirable, as always.'

'You might also have proposed to remind members of the jury that it is not unknown for convicted prisoners to concoct alleged confessions from their fellows in the hope of receiving beneficial treatment from their guardians?'

'It had been in my mind, my lord.'

'Then let us take it as read. That is the end of your cross-examination, I hope?' He glanced at the clock. 'Half-past two. Let's get on with the defence.'

York, 4.35pm

McQUEEDIE stopped writing and looked up enquiringly at Sandy as he slid into the press box. 'Found Binksley yet?'

'Not a sign of him, but I've tracked down his bear. Nice little story,' He frowned. 'Can't decide whether to do BANISH BRUTAL BEAST SAYS SCARED CITY or SAVE OUR BRUIN BEG BEAR-LOVERS. What do you think?'

'Go for the heart-strings. WE LOVE TEDDY SAY SOBBING SISTERS, that sort of stuff. Can't fail with a cuddly animal story.'

'Cuddly? You should see the bugger.' Sandy surveyed the courtroom. 'What's going on?'

'Ten-minute adjournment after Matthews and Pickering ended their opening addresses for the defence. Went on for nearly two hours, I could have done with you being here instead of chasing bears.'

'They'll earn us a few bob. You've coped without me, I'm sure.'

'Well, I've taken it all down. The usual stuff – jury to disregard what they'd read in the press beforehand, prosecution witnesses all mistaken or lying, no credible evidence of any motive, quite obvious Yates and the girl threw themselves in the river or fell in drunk, only possible verdict not guilty.' He sighed. 'I can't believe anyone will want to read it all, but I'm not complaining at a ha'penny a line. There must be a couple of pounds' worth here at least.' He pushed his notes across. 'Have a look through, then you can take over for the next session. I need a break.'

Sandy skimmed through the report. 'Matthews had a real go at the Humphreys girl, didn't he?'

'I do not say, members of the jury, that a woman who becomes the mother of an illegitimate child is never to be believed upon her oath, but I cannot help

suggesting that those who are regardless of some great point of morality could never be very strict about others... This girl claims that she got up from her bed, went out, saw a double murder being committed and then went back to bed and to sleep without one troubling thought or one pang of conscience. I do not say such things are impossible, gentlemen, but they draw upon the utmost credibility of the human understanding...'

'Pass it over, Sandy, I need to get it on the four o'clock train. I'll look out for Binksley on my way back.'

Sandy cast him a disbelieving glance. 'Don't have too many. It looks like being a long night and I'll need you sober.'

York, 4.40pm

SNOWDEN ticked off another name and nodded thoughtfully. Two defence witnesses so far: tailor Thomas Gunson, who said Yates had spoken to him at five o'clock on the night he disappeared, showing him six shillings and sixpence which he said was all he possessed; and Ann Minikin, a pawnbroker, who recalled that not long afterwards she refused to give Yates a shilling for a handkerchief he tried to pledge. Blanshard, counsel for Barker and Raine, had reminded the jury that Yates had spent the rest of the evening drinking in Briggate; it was obvious, he declared, that Yates would have little or nothing left by midnight and to suggest that his clients would risk the gallows for the sake of a few pence was frankly preposterous.

'He's got a point.' Craven looked at Snowden doubtfully. 'He wouldn't have been worth robbing.'

'Humphreys said he had ten shillings or more. He must have got it from somewhere.' Snowden shook his head. 'I wish I'd been able to find out where.'

'Who's next, sir?'

Snowden glanced at his list. 'Jane Parkin, lives with her mother in the house where Barker was lodging. I went there to interview Thomas Oliver who gave evidence for us yesterday. Parkin's got the ground floor, the Olivers live above her, Barker and Arrowsmith shared the attic. She wasn't helpful when I met her, not surprised she's helping the defence. Let's see what she says.'

> *Jane Parkin, examined by Mr Matthews:*
> *'I remember the night when Yates and Catherine Raine were drowned. My mother and I were up late.'*
> *'Did you see Barker that night?'*
> *'I remember him coming home. There is a passage and our door opens onto it. He went past our door and up the stairs into the Olivers' room.'*

Snowden looked grim. 'Oliver never mentioned that to me.'

> *'How long was he there?'*
> *'Not more than ten minutes, then he went to the attic.'*
> *'And what time was this?'*
> *'There is a clock in the Olivers' and I heard it strike one while Barker was there. We were getting some tea when he came along the passage and we might*

perhaps go to bed half an hour after.'
'You don't have a clock of your own?'
'No, sir.'
'Did you hear Barker again that night?'
'No, sir.'

Cross-examined by Mr Bliss:
'You say Barker went past your door on his way to the Olivers' room. How was he dressed?'
'Dressed, sir?'
'Yes.'
'Well, I don't know, sir.'
'You can't remember?'
'I didn't actually see him, sir.'
'Did you in fact see Barker at all that night?'
'Not see him, sir, no.'
'You just heard him. It could have been anybody, then?'
'I heard him talking upstairs, sir. I knew it was his voice.'

Ann Parkin, examined by Mr Matthews:
'You are the mother of the previous witness?'
'I am, sir.'
'Do you confirm her account?'
'I do, sir, every word.'

Cross-examined by Mr Bliss:
'Do you always hear Barker when he goes upstairs?'
'Not always, sir, no.'
'Why is that?'
'Well, sir, usually he takes his boots off before going upstairs.'
'But that night you heard them?'
'Yes, sir.'
'Do they have some particularly unusual noise, these boots, so that they knew they were his?'
'No, sir.'
'They just sounded like any other boots?'
'Yes, sir.'
'Boots that could well have belonged to somebody else?'
'Yes, sir, I suppose they could.'

Snowden shook his head. 'I don't think Bliss is going to get very far trying to argue it was anybody else. There's no dispute that Barker went home at some stage, the question is when. We should be asking about the clock and exactly when everything happened.' He scribbled a note and handed it to Craven. 'Just slip over to Bliss and give him this.'

Ann Oliver, examined by Mr Matthews:
'Barker came home that night a few minutes before one o'clock. He came

into my room and sat down and got his pipe.'

'How did he appear to you?'

'He was in very high spirits, sir.'

'And did he stay long?'

'Just a few minutes, sir. Then he went upstairs to where he slept and I heard him lock his door. I heard him put his shoes off and fling them on the floor.'

'That would be just after one o'clock?'

'When I locked the door I looked at the clock and it was five minutes past one. I went to bed near about two o'clock. I never heard anyone come downstairs again that night.'

<u>Cross-examined by Mr Bliss:</u>

'You say that Barker was in high spirits. What do you mean by that?'

'He seemed as if he had got a sup of drink and wanted to make a disturbance. He tried to pull the bedclothes off my husband but I pushed him out.'

'Had he ever done anything like that before, Mrs Oliver?'

'He sometimes came in of a night when he returned home, but I never saw him so much concerned in liquor before and I thought that made him agitated.'

'Do you suppose he might have been acting so unusually to ensure that you and your husband recalled him coming home at that hour?'

'I don't know, sir.'

'You spoke of a clock, Mrs Oliver. Tell me about it.'

'It's a clock without a case, sir, on the wall by the door.'

'You can see it from where you sit?'

'If I turn round, sir. My chair faces the fire, on the other side.'

'The clock is high up on the wall?'

'No, sir, at eye-level.'

'So you can reach it easily?'

'Yes, sir.'

'To re-wind it, adjust the hands and so forth?'

'Yes, sir.'

'And it is reliable, this clock?'

'It's good enough, sir, for the likes of us. We've little need to be right to the minute, so if it runs fast it's no matter.'

'It runs fast, does it? How fast would that be?'

'Well, it is often half an hour faster than the church clock.'

'And was it running that fast on the night in question?'

'It may have been, sir, I don't know.'

'You didn't look at it that night until after Barker left?'

'I don't remember doing so, sir.'

'Does it strike just upon the hour?'

'And the half-hour, sir.'

'A single chime?'

'Yes, sir.'

'Did you hear it strike a few minutes after Barker arrived?'

'Not that I recall, sir. I think I didn't hear it strike twelve, one or two either, but I am so used to it striking that I rarely notice it.'

'We have been told by your neighbour downstairs, Jane Parkin, that she heard it strike one while Barker was with you.'

'She may have done, sir, I can't say.'

'So you really had no idea when he arrived what time it was?'

'Not at the time he came in, sir, no.'

'When he entered the room, your husband was asleep in bed and you were sitting in your chair. What were you doing?'

'Nothing, sir, just sitting by the fire.'

'Perhaps dozing off from time to time?'

'I might have done, sir.'

'Did you hear Barker coming up the stairs?'

'No, sir.'

'No sound of boots, no knock on the door?'

'No, sir, he just came in.'

'So there you were, dozing by the fire, and the first you knew was that he was in the room?'

'I suppose that might be so, sir.'

'Did you notice if the clock was showing the correct time next morning?'

'I don't recall doing so, no, sir.'

'How often do you check it against the church clock?'

'Only when it's stopped and needs re-winding. Perhaps every two or three days.'

'When you wouldn't know if it had been fast or slow when it stopped?'

'No, sir, I don't suppose so.'

'Do you recall re-winding it the next day?'

'I might have done, sir, I cannot remember. But my husband might have done.'

'Thank you, Mrs Oliver. You may go.'

'Well done, Mr Bliss.' Snowden gave Craven a broad smile. 'Now let's see him put it all together.'

Bliss turned to the jury. 'Gentlemen, is this not the truth of the matter? We have heard witnesses swearing that they heard the murders being committed between one and two that morning. I suggest that Barker returned home not just before one o'clock but in fact an hour later – long after his fellow lodger Mr Arrowsmith had heard the church clock strike one and fallen asleep on his own. Barker, anxious to create an alibi, went upstairs, entered the Olivers' room, and saw Mrs Oliver asleep by the fire. He also saw the clock, which, if it was running fast as she has just testified it usually did, would be showing sometime after two o'clock. He realised he had a way of making out that it was much earlier than in fact it was, and before waking her he turned the hands on the clock back to show five to one.'

Bliss paused for a moment to allow the jury to digest this before continuing. 'Barker then wakes Mrs Oliver and behaves in an extraordinary manner to ensure they do not forget his visit, during which time the clock strikes once, as her neighbour Mrs Parkin has told us. But if the Olivers' clock is like any I have ever known, moving the hands back does not change the order in which it strikes the hours. What Mrs Parkin heard, members of the jury, was not the clock striking one o'clock, but the single chime of half-past two.'

Bliss paused again as the jury worked it out. 'A few minutes later Mrs Oliver sends Barker on his way, locks the door and sees the clock showing five past one. Barker goes up to his room and wakes Arrowsmith, by which time – the real time, gentlemen – is sometime well after two o'clock. He has his alibi, and before anyone can notice the clock is wrong it stops, later to be re-wound and re-timed.'

'Do you think that is what happened, sir?' Craven looked at his superintendent doubtfully.

'I don't know, lad. But it's possible, and I'm hoping the jury might think so too.'

York, 5.45pm

ELIJAH Button, twelve-year-old son of the pie shop owner round the corner, put his basket down on the floor of Micklegate police office and dug out two paper-wrapped parcels. 'One special with extra carrots, one scrag-end, no gravy.' He dumped them on the desk. 'Ma says that'll be fourpence-ha'penny.'

'Daylight robbery.' Sergeant Hoskins handed over the money with bad grace and began unwrapping the larger parcel. 'They'd better be warm.'

'Straight out of the oven, sir.'

'You can save my legs and give the other one to that bugger in the cells.' He took a bite out of the pie and nodded appreciatively. 'Don't know why we feed him, mind, dirty little sod should be left to starve.'

'What's he done, then?'

'Raging sex maniac, he is, lad.' Hoskins wiped a dribble of gravy from his chin. 'Mind you keep well away from him.'

Elijah's eyes lit up. He'd delivered food to other prisoners in his time, but they'd all been drunks or pickpockets and the like. A real live sex maniac would be worth seeing, a great big hairy brute, no doubt, slavering with lust and his evil eyes aglitter.

Scrag-end pie in his hand, Elijah scurried off round down the corridor.

He was about to be very disappointed.

York, 7.45pm

SANDY sidled his way back into the courtroom, avoided the judge's eye and tiptoed into the press box. 'How far have they got?'

'Just had a string of witnesses saying they'd seen Yates out drinking that night. Trying to prove he was pissed and quite capable of falling into the river, I suppose.' McQueedie glanced across the room. 'Here's another one, I think.'

> <u>*Douthwaite Stephenson, examined by Mr Blanshard:*</u>
> *'I am a shoemaker and live on The Bank in Barnard Castle.'*
> *'Do you recollect the night Joseph Yates was missed?'*
> *'I do, sir.'*

'Where were you?'

'I was in Ellery's public-house, off Briggate, and left it between eleven and twelve.'

'And who did you see?'

'When I came out I saw Catherine Raine. John Walker and Thomas Nelson were with her. She was crying.'

'Crying?'

'Yes, sir, she seemed to be in great distress.'

'For what reason?'

'I don't know, sir.'

'And did you see her again?'

'No, sir. Never.'

<u>*John Walker, examined by Mr Blanshard:*</u>

'You are a carpet weaver, residing in Briggate?'

'Yes, sir.'

'You were in Ellery's public house, as stated by the previous witness?'

'Yes, sir, with Thomas Nelson.'

'Did you see Catherine Raine there?'

'I recollect Nelson going out with her. I went after them and I saw she was crying.'

'Did you leave here there?'

'No, sir, I brought her along Briggate. After I left her, I turned about and saw Breckon and some more follow her down, in the direction of Sarah Proctor's.'

'What time was that?'

'I think it would be about twelve then.'

'You knew Miss Raine well, I believe.'

'Yes, sir. I was sweet-hearting her at that time.'

McQueedie gave Sandy a nudge. 'See if you can catch that lad on his way out. Sorrowing Weaver Still Weeps For Sweetheart, Tees Tragedy Lover Tells Of Torment. Got to be worth half a column in the Sundays.' He turned his attention back to the witness box.

<u>*Sarah Proctor, examined by Mr Matthews:*</u>

'I live down Greenacre Lane, off Briggate. Catherine Raine was in my house on the night before she went missing.'

'What time was that?'

'I don't know, sir.'

'After midnight?'

'Probably, sir, yes.'

'What state was the girl in?'

'She was in liquor, sir.'

'And who else was there?'

'There were seven young men, sir, as I recall.'

'And was John Breckon, one of the accused, among them?'

'He was, sir. He and Catherine scolded one another very much.'
'You mean they were arguing? What about?'
'I don't know, sir, but she was very much put about.'
'Did they remain there?'
'The men went, sir, but she stayed for a time before leaving.'
'Thank you, Mrs Proctor. You may go.'

Craven looked puzzled. 'What's all that about?'

'They want to prove that the girl was full of gin and in a highly emotional state after having a row with Raine.' Snowden thought back over the past twenty-four hours. 'You'll remember one of our prosecution witnesses – Pratt, was it? – said they were arguing about Raine going with her sister.'

Craven nodded. 'Didn't she say she'd rather throw herself in the river?'

'That's what the defence want the jury to think she did.'

'Maybe Yates jumped in after her, tried to save her and got swept away as well?'

Snowden frowned. 'Keep your voice down, son, or Mr Matthews will be asking if you want his job.'

York, 8.15pm

MRS Pollitt sat in her favourite corner of the Bell and Bucket, cup of gin in her hand and the centre of rapt attention.

'I knew there was something odd about him first time I saw him, last night when it was snowing. Nasty shifty-looking little beggar, came sneaking out of the you-know-what just as I was on my way to use it.'

'Still got the same old problem, then, Millie?'

'Gets no better, Ada. You should see them.'

'None of us getting any younger, dear. So what did he do?'

'Took one look at me, gave a sort of shriek and then shot off towards Micklegate fast as his legs could carry him. Well, I thought it was just some man caught short, like they do, but this morning...' She took another sip of gin and lowered her voice. 'He came back *while I was in there.*'

'Ee, the cheeky devil.'

'I heard him outside and then all of a sudden he crashes the door open and flings himself at me feet.'

'Eee, Millie, it don't bear thinking about.'

'Thought I was going to die, I did, and me with my second-best pink lacies round my ankles.'

'Them frilly ones with the holes in? Eeee, Millie, the shame of it.'

'Terrified, I was, Ada, I thought my hour had come. Then that dozy constable Wintergreen grabs him and leads him away.' She finished off her cup with a shudder. 'I'll not sleep tonight thinking about it.'

'Have another gin, dear, and I'll tell you about my legs.'

York, 8.25pm

CRESSWELL'S eyelids began to droop again and he stifled a yawn. For a moment there he had almost fallen asleep, something he'd only done once in his career and that in a case of such stupendous tedium that nobody had noticed. He'd woken up ten minutes later to find it going on quite satisfactorily without him, a discovery that left him feeling profoundly depressed for weeks. He shook his head irritably at the memory and became suddenly wide awake as something fell onto the desk and scuttled to safety under the legal tomes piled beside him. Timson was right about the wig. It would have to go.

He dragged his attention back to the witness under examination. Thomas Routledge, farmer, living in Gallowgate, Barnard Castle. Rough-looking fellow, in his sixties maybe. Matthews was questioning him.

'You are related to one of the accused?'

'I am, sir. Grandfather to the prisoner Raine.'

'Does he live with you?'

'Until his arrest, sir, yes. He's lived with me a good many years, on and off.'

'Was he living with you on Sunday the tenth of August last year?'

'No, sir. At that time he was working for the blacksmiths at Etherley and living with his master there.'

'Etherley?'

'About fifteen miles from Barnard Castle, sir.'

'Did you see him that day?'

'Yes, sir. He came to my house at half-past eight that morning and I was with him till after ten.'

'And then?'

'I left him in my house when I went to chapel with my daughter. I attend the Wesleyan chapel, and the bells start ringing at ten. I stayed at home a good while after, before I went to chapel.'

'So he could not possibly have been by the Sills walls at nine o'clock as has been claimed?'

'No, sir. He was with me.'

'Thank you. Stay there, if you please. Mr Bliss may want a word with you.'

'Just a brief one, Mr Routledge.' Bliss pondered him for a few moments. 'Did your grandson visit you every Sunday morning while he was staying over at...' He consulted his notes. '... at Etherley?'

'Not every week, sir. But often enough.'

'Had he been the week before, for example?'

Routledge shook his head. 'I'm not sure, sir. He may have done.'

'Can you tell us any other Sunday on which he was with you that summer?'

'He was at our house a fortnight before, I think, sir.'

'You're not sure?'

'Well, sometimes he was, sometimes he wasn't.'

'So what makes you remember this particular Sunday with such certainty?'

'Well, I don't know, sir.'

'And neither do I, Mr Routledge, neither do I.' Bliss turned to the jury with a flourish. 'Gentlemen, is it not quite clear that this witness has no idea whether his grandson was with him on the day after Yates and the girl disappeared, or whether it was one of the many other Sundays he can't recall?'

There as a rumble of agreement from the jury box, and Bliss sat down with a satisfied nod.

Cresswell glanced at the clock. 'Is that the end of your queue of defence witnesses, Mr Matthews? We cannot try the jury's patience forever.'

'Just one more, my lord.'

'Indeed? I have no more on my list.'

'With your lordship's indulgence, I would like to add one additional name.' Matthews glanced at Snowden, a faintly malicious smile on his face. 'I would remind your lordship that you allowed a similar request by the prosecution this afternoon.'

Cresswell gave an exasperated sigh. 'Is this really necessary, Mr Matthews?'

'I believe so, my lord. Her testimony will cast doubt on the veracity of one of the main prosecution witnesses.'

Cresswell nodded reluctantly. 'Very well. Who is this additional witness?'

'A Miss Dorothy Drover, my lord.'

'Bring her in.'

Snowden looked up sharply. Drover? He racked his memory. Sometime during his investigations, it must have been last year, he'd interviewed a woman of that name. A sharp-faced woman in her early twenties, living in Briggate and working at Longstaff's carpet factory. She had told him nothing useful and he'd dismissed her from his inquiries, like all the others he'd spoken to who knew nothing – or said they knew nothing – about the murders.

He turned to Craven as Drover entered the room. 'Have you read my notes on Ann Humphreys' examination yesterday?'

'Yes, sir.'

'Do you remember her saying where she worked?'

'She was a weaver, I think, sir. Longstaff's, wasn't it?'

'That's what I thought. She must have known this Drover woman.' He frowned. 'Matthews has spent most of his time trying to find alibis for his defendants, but he must know his best chance is to convince the jury Humphreys was lying – or at least deluded. My guess is he's been saving that till last, and that's where Drover comes in.'

'What do you think she's going to say, sir?'

'I've no idea, but it won't be good. It would probably help if we knew something about her.'

'I wonder...' Craven hesitated. 'There was someone I noticed in the gallery, before it was cleared, who might have information. I'm not sure of his name, but I remember facing him last summer.'

'Facing him? In court, do you mean?'

'No, sir, I was playing cricket for Barningham. He's a tidy left-hand bowler, plays for Eggleston and had me out first ball. I got talking to him afterwards and he said he worked at Longstaff's.'

Snowden looked doubtful. 'Worth a try, I suppose. See if you can find him – he'll probably be outside waiting somewhere – and see what he says.'

'Right, sir.' Craven quietly made his way out as Drover stepped into the witness box.

<u>Dorothy Drover, examined by Mr Matthews:</u>
'You are acquainted with the witness Humphreys, I believe?'
'I worked with her, sir, at Longstaff's.'
'And did you have conversation with her on or about July the eighth this year?'
'I did, sir, about three weeks before she was taken to York.'
'And what did she tell you?'
'She said she had met Joe Yates and Kate Raine. I asked her where and she said down the Sills. I said I could not believe that but she said she had and she was to meet them again on the Saturday evening. She told me they said she had to tell about the murder.'
'Their murder?'
'Yes, sir. She said Kate smelt that strong of brimstone that she flinched from her, but she, Kate I mean, sir, told her not to be afraid. The next day she told me the same over again.'
'Did you believe her?'
'Of course not, sir. I thought she was mad.'

<u>Cross-examined by Mr Bliss:</u>
'Where were you when she first told you all this?'
'At Mark Sweeting's, sir.'
'That is a public house, is it not?'
'Yes, sir.'
'And you had been drinking?'
'Well, yes, sir. '
'How much?'
'We had three pots of rum, as I remember.'
'Three pots of rum? Each?'
'No, sir, between us. And there was George Burrill with us.'
'You were all drunk, in fact?'
'I was not drunk, sir.'
'Have you ever been taken up by the police for drunkenness, Miss Drover?'
'I've never been taken to court, no, sir.'
'I see. Thank you. No more questions for this witness, my lord.'

– The court was adjourned for five minutes while the judge heard an application by Mr Bliss to introduce a further witness.

<u>James Knapton, examined by Mr Bliss:</u>
'You are employed at Longstaff's flax mill in Barnard Castle?'
'That's so, sir. I am the factory overlooker.'
'In charge of the weavers?'
'Yes, sir.'
'And you know the previous witness, Dorothy Drover?'
'I do, sir. I've known her some twelve or thirteen years.'

'She is a reliable worker?'
'I couldn't say that, sir.'
'Honest?'
'Well, sir...'
'Do you think she was telling the truth just now?'
'From what I know of her, sir, I should not believe her on her oath.'
'Thank you, Mr Knapton.'

Mr Justice Cresswell then said:
'Gentlemen of the jury, I am sure you will agree with me that after sitting thirteen hours and a half all our strength and vigilance must be pretty well expended. We will therefore adjourn until nine o'clock in the morning. I am sorry again to inconvenience you, but it must be so.'

– The court rose at about ten o'clock.

'Well done, Craven.' Snowden smiled to see the constable flush with pride. 'Worth being bowled out for a duck. Come on, I'll buy you a drink and you can tell me about your more successful exploits with the bat.'

York, 10.10pm

McQUEEDIE scribbled the last few words of his report and stuck his pen back in the inkpot. 'That's it, Sandy. We'll get this to the station and then have a few in the Railway Arms.'

As they walked out into the street a tiny ragged figure came out of the shadows and accosted them nervously. 'Either of you two gents Merkweedy or Merclowd?'

'McLeod, laddie, and it's Mister McLeod to the likes of you. What're you after, an autograph?'

'Got a message for you, sir. From a Mr Binksley.'

'Binksley? Spotty-faced lad with hair all over the place?'

'That's him, sir.'

'Spit it out, then. What's the message?'

'Said you'd give me sixpence if I found you, sir.'

'Sixpence?' Sandy frowned.

Elijah Button eyed him thoughtfully and decided to chance it. 'Each, sir.'

'A *shilling*?'

'Come on, gents, I've been waiting here in the cold since eight o'clock and my ma's going to kill me when I get home. Course, if you don't want the message...'

Sandy dug reluctantly into his pocket. 'There you are. Now, then, what's the daft bugger been up to?'

Elijah grinned. 'Sergeant says he's a dangerous pervert, sir, but he don't look much like one to me.'

York, 10.25pm

ELSOPP prodded dismally at the rissole lurking amid a mound of cold mashed potato on his plate and vowed he'd never complain about his wife's cooking again. At least her rissoles had never turned green.

'Fat lot of good you are as a foreman.' Babbington scowled from across the table. 'I thought you were going to get this food sorted.'

'Well, I did mention it, but –'

'I've given better to my pigs.'

'Yes, well, we won't have to be here much longer.' Elsopp abandoned his rissole and pushed it back under the potato. 'Just a final speech from the prosecution man tomorrow and the judge's summing-up. Then all we've got to do is reach a verdict and we can all go home.'

'We don't need any more bloody speeches.' Babbington picked a green strand out of his moustache, examined it and stuck it back in his mouth. 'Let's take a vote now and save time.'

'I'm not sure we can do that.' Elsopp looked nervously round at the other jurors. 'What does anyone else think?'

'Sounds a good idea to me.' The one with the squint and hairy hands – Dabble, was it? Dibble? something like that – thrust his plate aside and leant forward. 'They're guilty, the three of them. That's my verdict.'

'No doubt about it.' Fisher, the red-haired one, nodded firmly. 'Come on, let's hear the rest of you.'

'Do it properly, Elsopp.' Babbington swallowed the last of his rissole and belched. 'Call the names out, alphabetical, if you can manage that. You do know your ABC, I suppose?''

Elsopp ignored the jibe and dug out his notebook. 'If that's what you all want... Alphabetical, let's see...' He consulted his list of names. 'That's interesting. Had you noticed we're all near the top of the alphabet?' Nobody responded and he moved on quickly. 'They must have just picked the first dozen in their list. Pity we're not all called Youngman or Zissler, isn't it?' He tried a laugh, thought better of it and turned it into a cough.

'Get on with it, man.' The Babbington bristles quivered angrily. 'Who's first?'

'It seems to be Mr Astwood.'

'Guilty.'

'I think we know where you stand, Mr Babbington. Mr Buckerfield?'

'Guilty.'

'Mr Chatterway?'

'The same.'

'Mr Crowl?'

'I'll tell you when we've heard everything tomorrow.'

'As you please... Mr Culbeck?'

'Guilty.'

'Mr Dart?'

'Not sure. Probably guilty.'

'Mr Dribble? I think you said guilty a few moments ago?'

'It's Dipple. Yes, of course they are, it's obvious.'

'Mr Edwards?'

'I haven't decided yet, I'm sorry.'

'Then there's me...' Elsopp hesitated. 'I think I'll wait till tomorrow, if it's all the same with you.'

'For God's sake!' Babbington erupted. 'What is there to wait for? It's an open-and-shut case.'

'I just want to hear everything before I decide... Mr Field?'

'I feel the same as you, Elsopp. I'll wait.'

'And Mr Fisher?'

'No doubts. They're guilty.'

Elsopp did some rapid arithmetic. 'That's seven guilty, one probably, three unsure, one no answer.'

Babbington glared round the table. 'You five who aren't saying guilty yet had better make your minds up soon, or you'll have me to answer to.'

Elsopp wondered momentarily whether making threats to fellow jurors was something he should report to the authorities, flinched as Babbington gave the table an angry thump, and decided it wasn't.

York, 10.50pm

McQUEEDIE led Binksley out of the police office and into Micklegate. 'Sandy's taken the latest stuff up to the station. He said he'll meet us in the Bell and Bucket up the road. Come on, I'm gasping for a drink.'

'I still don't know how you got me out.' Binksley scurried alongside him. 'What was all that shaking the sergeant's hand and showing him your ankles and whispering about buffaloes?'

'I'll tell you sometime, it can be very useful. That and slipping him five bob.'

They arrived at the pub door. 'After you, laddie.' He looked around the bar for a vacant table. 'Settle yourself over there by the old biddy in the corner and I'll get a round in.'

Mrs Pollitt's shriek of terror as Binksley walked towards her set dogs howling three streets away.

Wednesday December 16ᵗʰ

Nunnington, 8.20am

BETSEY dried the last of the breakfast plates, sat down at the kitchen table and wondered how to spend the day. There was a shriek of laughter as three-year-old William raced into the room, followed by his sister Sarah Ann. The pair chased round the table and out again, narrowly avoiding their mother approaching in the passage outside.

'I don't know how you cope.' Betsey shook her head as Aunt Jane entered. 'They never stop.'

'You get used to it.' Her aunt sat down heavily. 'At least the baby's gone back to sleep. I was up half the night with him.'

'I'll make you a cup of tea.' Betsey got up and busied herself with the kettle. 'Uncle John said he'd be late back, something about a burglary at Stonegrave. I haven't seen grandfather yet, though.'

'He'll have been out down the smithy long before you woke up, love. Sixty-seven this year but he's still going strong.' She looked pensive. 'He's hardly ever in the house now, since Lizzie died.'

Betsey nodded sympathetically. Aunt Jane's parents had both died young, and she'd come to work for the Snowdens as a maid when she was barely twelve, becoming part of the family and eventually, of course, marrying their youngest son John. Had to, in fact, as she'd once cheerfully confessed to Betsey: Sarah Ann had been well on the way and they'd only just made it to the altar in time.

'I miss grandma, too.' Betsey poured the tea and handed Aunt Jane a cup. 'She wasn't local, was she, like grandfather?'

'Came from Whorlton, I think.'

Betsey's eyes widened. 'That's just near us. I never knew that.'

'Not that Whorlton, the one up near Stokesley, fifteen or so miles away. They were married there, of course. Your grandfather told me he drove her back over the moors in a snowstorm – it was a January – and they nearly didn't make it.'

'I wonder how they met?' Betsey frowned. 'You know, I don't know much about my family. Well, bits about papa's side, you and John and so on, but nothing much about my mother. I don't remember her – I was, what? only two or three when she died – and papa never talks about her.'

'She came from Slingsby, not far away. Harper, her surname was. That's where they got wed, I was one of their bridesmaids, and you were born there, of course. Your mother came back down from Tyneside or wherever they were living at the time to give birth. She did the same when...' Aunt Jane hesitated. 'When your sister was due.'

'And they died.'

'Yes. It was awful.' She fell silent, lost in the past.

There was a wail in the distance and she stood up with a sigh. 'I knew it wouldn't last. Look, if you've nothing better to do today, I'll find the family scrapbooks and you can browse through them. They're full of bits and pieces from down the years.' She smiled. 'You could update them for me if you like. There's all sorts waiting to be pasted in.'

York, 8.55am

SANDY arrived to find McQueedie already in the press box, head bent over a newspaper. 'One of yesterday's London papers, picked it up at that stationer's down the road. It's got most of our Monday report in.' He handed it over.

'*The Express?*' Sandy looked at it dubiously. 'Haven't heard of that one before.'

'Only been coming out a few months. Shouldn't think it'll last long.' McQueedie looked round. 'Seen Binksley yet this morning?'

'He staggered downstairs just as I was leaving. Still looks a bit rough.'

'I'm not surprised. That old woman in the pub gave him one devil of a clout on the head with that stick of hers.' He chuckled. 'You should have seen it, enough to fell an ox. You wouldn't think she had it in her.'

'I told him to be here as usual for the morning run. Might be his last one, too, as I reckon it could be all over by lunchtime.' There was a rustle of activity round the court room as the lawyers trooped in. 'Here we go, Hamish. You do the first bit, I'll take the judge.'

'Don't bother doing it all verbatim, nobody's going to read what they already know. It's the verdict that's important.' McQueedie grinned. 'And with a bit of luck, the judge sending them off to the gallows. There's nothing the readers like more.'

Mr Bliss summed up for the prosecution, with particular reference to the time at which the accused Barker was said to have gone home. He had done so in an unusual manner as if desirous of exciting the attention of the inmates and in such a fashion as he might have turned back the hands of the clock.

As to the claim that Ann Humphreys was influenced by delusion, he contended that the testimony of Drover ought to have been corroborated by other witnesses, it having been shown that she was not to be believed upon oath. If there had been any proof of Humphreys' insanity, why had the defence not called natives of Barnard Castle, a person employed at her factory, or the surgeon of York Castle who had observed her many times, who could all have produced abundant proof of such a fact?

The defence had not done so; and it was for the jury to judge why this was so, and whether a woman could be so wicked and perjured as the counsel for the defence would have them believe.

'That should do nicely,' Sandy picked up his pen. 'Now for the judge.'

Mr Justice Cresswell then summed up the facts of the case. He stated the charge as it appeared on the face of the indictment, and hoped that the jury had come from a part of the country where they had not read or heard any of the details of this charge before they entered the jury box. If they had, they must discard them from their minds, because they would know how vague they

*were, and how little they resembled those which had been presented to them
during the course of this trial.*

'He's not fond of the press, is he?' McQueedie muttered. 'Fat chance of the jury not
having read about it. They'd have to have been living in the bloody Hebrides to have
missed it.'

*The Judge said the charge against the prisoners was the highest that one
subject could commit against another – the murder of Joseph Yates. The jury
had been told by counsel and told very truly that in all cases the presumption
was in favour of innocence, that the prosecutor had to make out to the
satisfaction of the jury the charge which he laid against any individual brought
to trial, and unless that was made out to the satisfaction of the jury, if it was
left in any doubt, the accused was entitled to be acquitted.*

Snowden grimaced. He hadn't expected Cresswell to give the prosecution an easy
ride, and he'd been right. He glanced across at the jury, and was encouraged to see at
least some of them looking unconvinced by the suggestion that acquittal was a possibility.

*His Lordship then went through the evidence of the several witnesses. First,
he remarked on the evidence of motive: as to Barker, a desire to prevent an
apprehended evil; as to Raine, to obtain the deceased's money; as to Breckon,
no motive had been alleged, or even been suggested. The jury would
recollect that evidence was presented to them in the following form. First, to
trace the prisoners, the deceased, and the principal witness Humphreys to the
spot where the crime is said to have been committed, then to show by that
eye-witness the fact that the crime was committed, and then to confirm her
testimony by collateral circumstances observed by others.*

Craven turned to Snowden and whispered. 'I'm sorry, sir, but I don't know what
collateral means.'

'Neither does the jury.' Snowden gave an exasperated shrug. 'I sometimes wonder
if they appoint judges on their ability to talk convoluted English.'

'Convoluted, sir?'

'Sorry, Craven, he's got me at it now. Complicated. Difficult to understand.'

'Convoluted. I'll remember that.'

'Good. Just don't say it.'

*If Ann Humphreys' story was believed, his Lordship continued, he would
present no alternative; no struggle or fight which could present a case of
manslaughter. If her story was true, the prisoners were guilty of murder; if it
was not, there was no proof that a murder had been committed, and the case
fell to the ground. Then the jury must acquit the prisoners, because whatever
noises might have been heard, whatever appearances might have been
presented at the spot where the murder was committed, there would be no
proof that the prisoners had been guilty of the awful crime with which they
were charged.*

The jury would see how far she was corroborated. Her evidence, certainly, needed to be confirmed; for, though she was not strictly in the light of an accomplice, yet, having been present at the commission of a heinous crime, she concealed it for a whole year. If the jury believed her wilfully false to any of the details, it would be very dangerous, in such a case, to rely on her in the other parts, for where were they to stop?

When the body of Yates was found, the learned Judge added, it was unfortunate that no medical man saw him directly, as he might have been able to have said whether the wounds had been inflicted before his death, or had been caused, as the counsel for the defence had said, by coming in contact with the rocks as his body was carried down from the place where the murder was supposed to have been committed, to that where his body was discovered.

'I thought our blood man Anderson had sorted all that out.' Snowden shook his head irritably. 'Judges hate expert witnesses.'

'Why's that sir?'

'They know what they're talking about. Puts judges at a distinct disadvantage.'

His Lordship said the jury should now retire and consider, first, whether the death of Joseph Yates was produced by violence or not. If they were of opinion that he had been murdered, then they would be so good as consider if it was by blows before he was thrown into the water, or by blows and drowning conjointly, or lastly, by drowning alone. If they were of opinion that he came to his death in any of those methods, then they would consider whether the prisoners, or any of them, did that deed.

If they were satisfied that they did, they would find a verdict of Guilty; but if they were not satisfied of it, if, from the circumstances of the case itself, or the circumstance of the deed being so long concealed, their minds should be left in doubt, they would give the prisoners the benefit of that doubt, and acquit them.

The summing concluded at a quarter to two o'clock, when the jury retired to consider their verdict.

'Three bloody hours that took. I thought I was going to run out of ink.' Sandy handed over his copy to McQueedie. 'All yours. I'm off to the Dun Cow.'

Nunnington, 1.50pm

BETSEY dipped her brush in the pot of flour-and-water glue, spread a little of the sticky mixture on the back of the cutting and positioned it carefully on the page.

Aunt Jane had produced four scrapbooks, passed down through her husband's family. The first had started life as a notebook in 1742, recording the finances of a William Snowden who Betsey calculated must have been her great-great-grandfather. There were lists of outgoings for iron, nails, implements and coal, payments of rent and parish dues, wages for a labourer, the purchase of a new bellows; running alongside were columns detailing income for shoeing, harness-making, the construction of cartwheels, gates and other fabrications. After a couple of years entries began to appear in another, neater hand which Betsey guessed was that of William's wife Margaret: notes on household management, recipes, cures for common ailments, and then the first of many similar entries down the years: *Thomas Snowden born this daye 1747.*

Betsey followed the family's story to the end of the book and into the next, by which time the first newspaper cuttings had appeared. The earliest were from the *Leeds Intelligencer* which, Betsey surmised, was probably the only local newspaper available in those days. A Mrs Elizabeth Snowden, silk mercer in Leeds, advertised all her stock for sale in 1756 and over the next two decades the wife of a William Snowden dropped dead in the street, a bay gelding owned by a Mr Snowden won him a small fortune at Scarborough races and a Miss Snowden of Hurworth went to the altar. Betsey had no idea who any of these were or how they were related, if at all.

She passed on to the third scrapbook and on the second page found people she did know: *Marryed 17 Aprill 1779, Thomas Snowden & Martha Holton* and then, after a recipe for oxtail soup and tips for treating dog bites, *George Holton Snowden born 3rd September 1784*. George, her grandfather. She'd had no idea he had a middle name.

From then on the names came thick and fast. George's brothers and sisters, his marriage in January 1805 to Elizabeth Leconby, new handwriting as she took over to list their children: Sarah in 1807, Jane two years later, then Elizabeth, Mary, George and finally Uncle John in 1817. Betsey frowned and went back, searching for her father's name. He was the eldest but there was no mention of him. How odd. She'd have to ask Aunt Jane about the omission, or maybe grandfather could explain.

She carried on through the book, now with cuttings from almost every month and many from the *York Herald* which, she saw, proudly proclaimed on its front page that it had been founded in 1790. It seemed to have been the Snowdens' choice of newspaper ever since.

One by one the older Snowden children went to the altar, and her father's name finally appeared on the last page but two. *Ralph married to Susannah Harper.* There was no date, but it was tucked among cuttings for 1827 and then, on the final page, came *Betsie Snowden baptised 2nd Sept 1828*. A week after her birthday. She smiled, recalling papa's words about confusion over how to spell her name, and moved on to the fourth and final scrapbook. A report of a cricket match in which her grandfather scored 36 not out, a village wedding of people she'd never heard of, the obituary of a neighbouring vicar, and *Sarah Snowden born this day Jany 16th 1831*. Betsey paused. Her sister who... *Buried March 18th, Sarah Snowden*. There was no record of her mother's death. The next entry was more than a year later, *Mary S married, April 14th 1832*, followed by a recipe for rosehip jelly.

Betsey skimmed through the pages to the end of the decade, halting at a line about Uncle John marrying Jane Huglie in 1837. Her aunt must have no more than sixteen at the time, Betsey reflected, younger than I am now. How young to be taking such a big step in life... She moved on, reached 1839, and found a small cutting recording a meeting that year of the Gilling West General Association for the Protection of Property and the Prevention of Crime in which, underlined, was a sentence noting the appointment of R. L Snowden as superintendent of the Greta Bridge Constabulary.

Papa's name appeared after that with increasing frequency. There were cuttings about the poacher who'd shot at him in Hartforth, a child murder he'd investigated at Forcett, the riots at Barnard Castle a couple of years ago and a host of lesser cases. And then, of course, the Startforth drownings that had led to the trial now going on in York.

The last story snipped and pasted into the scrapbook told of Raine's arrest last summer, and Aunt Jane had produced a small pile of more recent newspapers with stories she wanted to preserve ringed in red pencil.

Betsey had set to work and now only two papers remained. The first was a *Yorkshire Gazette* containing a report of September's Cleveland Agricultural Show at Stokesley, chosen because it recorded grandfather George Snowden's second prize in the draught horse harness section. She ran her eye down the tightly-printed paragraphs and was bemused and slightly horrified to find halfway down the column a passing reference to a gasometer at the site exploding during the proceedings, hurtling four people through the air. The recovery of one, the report said before moving swiftly on to list the cattle awards, was extremely doubtful.

She cut it out, pasted it in and turned to the last paper, a four-week-old *York Herald* which she scoured in vain for red pencil. She stood up and went to find her aunt.

'On the inside back page, I think, dear.' Aunt Jane looked up from feeding the baby. 'It's about your father chasing someone round Westmorland.'

'I wondered what he'd been up to. He came back looking exhausted and I never got round to asking him about it.' Betsey found the page and ran her eyes down the columns. 'This must be it.'

GALLANT CHASE AND CAPTURE OF
NOTORIOUS OFFENDER

Thomas Newton, a notorious sheep stealer, has for some time been a terror to the peaceable inhabitants of Westmorland and was strongly suspected of stealing twenty-one sheep from Mr Wilson of Spanham in Yorkshire.

Application was made for the services of Mr Superintendent Snowdon of Greta Bridge, who commenced pursuit and after travelling more than four hundred miles in search of the fugitive found himself at Alston in Cumberland, where the delinquent had been roosting at the home of his sister, a Mrs Dixon, who said he had left to visit a brother at Brampton, 22 miles further.

There the officer proceeded but no brother could be found. Mr S. was not, however, to be done so coolly, and immediately made up a letter containing three farthings to imitate three sovereigns, and addressed it to Thos. Newton, at Dixon's, Alston, the very parties who had put the officer on the wrong scent. A person was selected to convey the letter and he entered the house of Dixon, stating there was a money letter for Thomas Newton.

Mrs Dixon said he had left "but you may leave the letter." "No, I can't do that, it contains money." "Can it be sent to him?" inquired the sister. "Oh yes!" stated the wily postman, "if you alter the direction," which she altered to Thomas Newton, Little Asby. Mr. Snowden immediately dispatched a police officer to Asby, where the offender was found in bed. He was immediately captured and afterwards committed to Appleby Jail for trial.

'Four hundred miles!' Betsey shook her head. 'No wonder he was tired out. But how clever of him!'

'He's a very clever man, your father.' Aunt Jane stood up and hoisted the baby onto her shoulder. 'If you turn out half as clever as your namesake, young Ralph Leconby Snowden, you'll do all right.'

York, 2.35pm

SNOWDEN stood at the court entrance, pipe in hand, and wondered if he'd been mistaken. He rarely had doubts about the wisdom of his prosecutions or the guilt of those he accused. This case was no different: he was convinced the three on trial had committed the murders and deserved to be in the dock. But he had a nagging feeling that Bliss and his colleagues could have done better, given all the evidence he had produced for them. The case against Raine and Breckon hadn't been made out as well as he'd hoped. Perhaps he should have dropped the charge to manslaughter, or just accused Barker of Yates' murder and done the other two for conspiracy to murder or simply aiding and abetting? But then none of them would have been tried for the girl's murder, and he was sure Raine at least was guilty of that... It might have been better if he'd fought to have both killings dealt with together, as he'd intended, instead of bowing to the lawyers' and Cresswell's desire to get through it as fast as possible.

He knocked his pipe out irritably on one of the stone pillars guarding the doorway and went back inside. In the end, as the judge had said in his summing-up, it came down to whether the jury believed Ann Humphreys, and Snowden wasn't sure they did.

York, 2.50pm

ELSOPP watched nervously as the rest of the jury took their places at the table. The usher made sure they were all there, checked the bucket in the alcove was empty and left, closing the door firmly behind him.

'Well, get on with it, foreman.' Babbington's growl broke the silence. 'You all heard what the man said. Nobody gets out of here until we've reached a verdict. Let's take a vote and get it over with.'

'You don't think –'

'You know what I think. Guilty. Ask the rest of them, they'll all agree.'

Elsopp capitulated. 'Alphabetically, then. Mr Astwood?'

'Guilty.'

'Mr Buckerfield?'

'Guilty.'

'Mr Chatterway?'

'Guilty.'

'Mr Crowl?'

'Probably guilty.'

'What do you mean, *probably*?' Babbington thumped a heavy fist on the table. 'What's there to be probable about, for God's sake? Anyone in their right mind can see they're guilty.'

'Are you suggesting I'm out of my senses, Mr Babbington?' Crowl spoke calmly, but with a hint of menace in his voice. 'You may bully the rest of them, but I'd like a little discussion before we reach a verdict.'

'Discussion? About what?'

'About how reliable that young strumpet's testimony might be, for a start.'

'Of course it's reliable. She described it all, start to finish. People heard the shrieks, like she said, there was the blood at the scene. She couldn't make all that up.'

'Perhaps, perhaps.'

Elstopp intervened.'Shall we just hear what the others think before we start arguing? Mr Culbeck?'

'Babbington's right. Guilty.'

'Mr Dart?'

'Well... She did say she'd seen ghosts, remember. Apart from that, I'd say guilty.'

'Mr Dipple?'

'Definitely guilty.'

'Mr Edwards?'

'I'd like to say guilty, but... ' Edwards hesitated. 'I need to think about it.'

'As you wish.' Elsopp consulted his list of names. 'I'm next, I think. I say guilty. Mr Field?'

'I'm sure about Barker, but all three of them? It's a pity we're not trying them for the girl's murder as well. I'm convinced they did that. But, yes, guilty, I suppose.'

'Mr Fisher?'

'No doubt. They killed them, Yates and the girl.'

Elsopp did a quick calculation. 'Ten guilty, one probable, Mr Edwards uncertain.' He sighed. 'Let's go over the evidence bit by bit and see if we can convince him.'

York, 5.45pm

McQUEEDIE yawned and gave Binksley, dozing on the press bench beside him, a sharp nudge in the ribs. 'You're snoring again, laddie.'

Binksley came reluctantly to the surface. 'Are the jury back yet?'

'No sign of them. If we don't get a verdict soon we'll miss the six-thirty.' McQueedie shook his head. 'I don't know how you can sleep like that. You'll end up in the cells again if you're not careful.'

'I hardly got a wink last night.' Binksley shuddered. 'Chased by bears, banged up as a sex maniac, beaten half to death by that manic old witch in the pub. I bet nothing like that's ever happened to you.'

McQueedie grinned. 'You'd be surprised, laddie. All part of the job, you might as well get used to it.'

Binksley grunted, unconvinced. 'Where's Mr McLeod?'

'Up in the public gallery interviewing people about their reaction to the verdict.'

'The verdict? But we haven't got one yet.'

'We can't wait for the jury, Binksley. Sandy'll find half a dozen who think these lads are guilty and ask how they'll feel if they're cleared. Then he'll ask another half-dozen who think they're innocent how they feel about them being convicted. Doesn't matter what the verdict is, we'll have good quotes from six people saying it's a disgrace. All we have to do is drop them into the story. Which we've already written, of course.'

Binksley blinked. 'I don't understand. How can you –?'

McQueedie looked at him in despair. 'I sometimes wonder if you're cut out for this, laddie.' He picked up a couple of sheets of paper from the desktop. 'We've done two stories, one if they're guilty, one if they're not. All we need now is the verdict so we know which version you're going to be running up to the station with.'

'You mean –'

'Let's have a little training session, stop you falling asleep again. Suppose they're found guilty, how would you start your story?'

'Well...' Binksley's brow furrowed. '*The jury in the Barnard Castle murders case last night returned a verdict of –*'

'No, no, far too early. You need to set the scene – the rising tension as the court waits for the result, the atmosphere of impending doom, the defendants trembling fearfully in the dock, excitement in the public gallery and then the sudden silence as the jury walk back in. Then – well, listen to Sandy's version.' He picked up one of the stories and began to read. '*The eyes of all in the courtroom, from the learned judge in his wig and gown to the lowest spectator peering from the public gallery, were resolutely fixed on the foreman as he solemnly carried out his solemn duty and pronounced that awful word the accused had dreaded to hear, the word that would condemn them to the gallows and face a yet mightier judgement in the world beyond – Guilty!*' McQueedie paused a moment for effect. 'And then you've got the shrieks from the gallery, the looks of terror on the faces of the accused – with a bit of luck one will collapse and have to be hauled back up – the judge donning his black cap and the bit about being taken to a place of execution and being hanged from the neck until they're dead. Add the condemned men being dragged off to their awful fate and Sandy's interviews and you've got a column and a half at least.'

Binksley nodded. 'And if it's not guilty, I suppose it's much the same, but without the black cap?'

'Well, perhaps, but not nearly as good a story without death at the end of it. What else do you think you could you do?'

Binksley pondered. 'Well, if they're not guilty, somebody else must have done it.'

'So...?'

The youngster's eyes brightened. 'You mean MURDERER COULD STRIKE AGAIN, WARN POLICE – JURY DECLARES DANGEROUS DOUBLE KILLER STILL ON LOOSE?'

McQueedie gave a nod of approval. 'A bit wordy, but that's the right idea. Sandy went for TERROR STALKS TOWN AFTER ACCUSED TRIO WALK FREE.' He grinned. 'There'll be a few worried prosecution witnesses in Barney if they hear Barker and his crew are back home.'

Nunnington, 7.40pm

UNCLE John threw another log on the parlour fire and went back to polishing his boots. His father had disappeared in the direction of the Royal Oak, the children had at last gone to bed, and Aunt Jane was at the table trying to explain the mysteries of crochet-work to Betsey.

'Round this finger, make a slipknot, hook it like this and away you go.' Betsey looked dubious and Aunt Jane gave her a reassuring smile. 'You'll soon pick it up.'

Uncle John looked up from his polishing. 'Your mother did some fine crochet lace work. I remember her sitting there making little dresses for you when you were a baby.' He paused for a moment. 'I think there's some in that box in the attic, Jane, with all the other things.'

'I'd love to see them.' Betsey turned to him, curious. 'What other things?'

'Well...' Uncle John looked uncertainly at his wife. 'I suppose you ought to have them, really. Just bit and pieces she left behind when she died. Ralph couldn't bear to see them at the time and your grandmother put them away in the attic. They've been there ever since.' He put down his boots and stood up. 'I'll find them if you like.'

York, 7.50pm

'WE'RE agreed, then?' Bliss looked at Snowden for confirmation. 'Whatever the verdict, we don't go any further with the other charge.'

'If they're found guilty I agree there's no point in going through all this again.' Snowden nodded reluctantly. 'They can only hang once. And if they're acquitted of Yates' murder it would be damn near impossible to prove they killed the girl.'

'I wouldn't like to try it.' Bliss shook his head. 'Humphreys would be totally discredited as a witness. It's a pity we've only her word that they were responsible, but there it is.'

A door banged across the courtroom and they looked round. An usher had come in from the corridor leading to the jury room and was heading towards them. Snowden greeted him hopefully.

'Verdict at last?'

'Afraid not, sir. The jury foreman's given me a message with questions for the judge and I think you and Mr Bliss will want to be there when I deliver it. Mr Matthews as well, I suppose.'

'Questions? What sort of questions?'

Bliss stood up. 'Probably just asking if they're ever going to get fed.'

'No, sir. They're asking if the judge will accept a majority verdict of guilty, eleven to one, for a start.'

'That's good news.' Snowden's face brightened. 'He won't let them, of course, but it shows we're on the brink of victory. What else do they want to know?'

'Whether the charge could be dropped to manslaughter.'

'No chance of that.' Snowden shook his head firmly. 'This was murder. Come on, Mr Bliss, let's get Matthews and watch Cresswell lose his temper again.'

Nunnington, 8.10pm

BETSEY undid the brass clasp on the small wooden box and lifted the lid. Inside, carefully folded, lay an exquisitely-crafted lace shawl. She lifted it out carefully to reveal more items below: a baby's dress, miniature mittens and socks, the tiniest of bonnets.

'They're beautiful.' Her eyes prickled as she laid them out on the table. 'She made these for Sarah?'

'Yes.' Aunt Jane nodded sadly. 'I don't think they were ever worn.'

Betsey looked at them wonderingly. 'It must have taken her ages.' She delved back into the box and took out the rest of its contents piece by piece. A laced handkerchief, a pair of gloves, a wooden bodkin, a thimble, half a dozen buttons, a battered prayerbook, a curiously-shaped ring, a locket on a chain, a piece of paper folded to form an envelope and tied round with pink ribbon. Inside was a lock of fair hair.

'The baby's?' Betsey looked inquiringly at Aunt Jane.

'I don't think she lived long enough to have hair like that. It could be yours.'

'Or my mother's.'

'Perhaps. She had fine fair hair, just like you.'

'I wish I'd known her. I can't remember her at all.' Betsey fell silent, staring at the jumble of objects on the tabletop.

'You were very young at the time.' Uncle John broke gently into her thoughts. 'No more than two, I suppose.'

'What happened? Papa's never really talked about her and all I know is that she and the baby died. Sarah's burial is in the scrapbooks, I saw it, but there's nothing about my mother.'

'No.' Uncle John glanced at his wife for guidance. 'I think you should ask your father about that.'

'Why?' Betsey looked puzzled. 'I'd like to go and find her grave. Was she buried in the churchyard here, like the baby?'

'She's not there, Betsey.'

'So where is she?'

There was a long silence, broken eventually by Aunt Jane. 'I think you'd better tell her, John. Somebody has to.'

'Tell me what?'

Uncle John hesitated, wondering where to begin. 'You probably know that your father was working up on Tyneside after coming out of the army?'

'Yes, he'd told me a bit about that. With the crime prevention people.'

'He used to come back home occasionally to see us, and that's how he met your mother. They fell for each other straight away. Six months later they were married and she went up north to live with him. Then you came along.'

'I thought I was born here, in Nunnington?'

'You were. Your father was all over the place – just like now, away for days on end – and she didn't want to be alone when she had you. So she came to stay here.'

'What about her family in Slingsby?'

'As far as I remember, her father died not long after their wedding and her mother moved away, somewhere down south. There were a couple of other children, but they'd grown up and long gone. This was the obvious place to be, and she was very welcome. We were all very fond of her.'

'So I was born in this house?'

'Yes. I'd be about twenty then. I wasn't best pleased, mind. I was turned out of my bedroom to make room for you both and ended up sleeping in the hayloft.'

'And then she went back to papa?'

'That's right, till she was expecting your sister. Then she returned here and...' He paused. 'Well, she had a hard time with the baby, a difficult birth and little Sarah wasn't expected to survive. They baptised her the day after she was born, thinking she'd not last long, but the poor little mite struggled on for a few weeks. And then...'

'She died.' Bestey nodded sadly. 'In March, I saw it in the scrapbooks. Poor, poor mama.' She realised she'd never called her that before, but mother sounded so cold. 'She must have been desolated.'

'We all were.' He shook his head. 'She'd not been right since the birth, almost a different person, and when the baby died she seemed to give up completely. She just sat there beside the crib, not saying a word, not even to you. And then next morning she'd gone.'

'She died, too, there by the baby?'

'Well, no...' Uncle John looked at his wife for support. 'This isn't easy, Betsey. We don't know what happened to her.'

Betsey stared at him. 'You don't know?'

'Nobody does. Sometime during the night she walked out of the front door and vanished. We searched for her high and low, most of the village were out looking for her for days, but there wasn't a sign. Nobody saw her then or ever since.'

Betsey was stunned. 'You mean she might still be alive?'

'No, there's no chance of that. It was a bad winter, it was snowing hard that night and she went out in her nightdress, barefoot as far as anyone could tell. God knows was going on in her mind. She couldn't have got far in that weather.'

'But where could she just disappear like that?'

'Up in the hills, perhaps, she often went walking up there and there's plenty of places a body could lie for years without anyone finding it, old quarries and mineworks. Or down to the river, maybe. The Rye would have been in full spate, high enough to take her down to the Derwent if she fell in.'

'And out to sea?'

'It's possible.'

'But what was papa doing? Why didn't he stop her going?'

'He wasn't here, Betsey. He was chasing villains up in Northumberland somewhere and it was almost a week before he came back and learned what had happened. He was in a terrible state.'

Betsey was silent for a while, trying to imagine what he'd gone through. 'I wish he'd told me.'

'I think he nearly went out of his mind as well, blaming himself for not being here when she needed him. He spent weeks searching for her, long after everyone else knew she must have died, before he gave up and went back to work.'

'Leaving me here.' Betsey picked up the lock of hair again and nodded sadly. 'What else could he do? He couldn't cope with a two-year-old child on his own.'

'He came to see you as often as possible.' Aunt Jane got up and put an arm round her shoulders. 'And he took you to live with him as soon as he could.'

'Yes.' A tear trickled down Betsey's cheek. 'Poor papa. He didn't deserve to lose any of us.'

York, 10.25pm

McQUEEDIE grinned as he reached the end of his tale. 'So I wrote up the story about everyone backing the idea of holding civic dances at the town hall and in it went on the front page. They'd printed about five hundred copies when the editor came hurtling in shouting Stop the Presses! and demanding a new headline on my story. You'll never guess what the sub-editor had written.'

'Go on.' Binksley's eyes shone with anticipation. 'What did it say?'

'BIG PUBLIC SUPPORT FOR MAYOR'S NEW BALLS.'

Binksley erupted in laughter. 'What did he change it to?'

'Well, he just told the printers to get rid of any reference to balls. They cocked it up, as usual.' McQueedie paused. 'There it was next day on a thousand breakfast tables, MAYOR GETS PUBIC SUPPORT FOR DANCING. There was all hell on.'

Binksley was still giggling five minutes later when there was a sudden flurry of activity in the courtroom. Barristers returned to their places, the dozen or so spectators still in the public gallery leaned forward, and the distant clang of gates being opened in the cells below the court heralded the reappearance of the three defendants.

'Here we go at last.' The jury filed in and McQueedie studied their faces in vain for any hint of what they had decided. 'What d'you reckon, Sandy?'

'That bookie in the Dun Cow was offering three to one they'll hang before Christmas.' Sandy nodded at the jury. 'I can't see that lot recommending mercy.'

'Or the judge taking any notice if they do.' McQueedie shook his head. 'Well, we'll soon know. Here he comes.'

Cresswell had been slumbering in front of his chambers fire, a half-empty glass of claret beside him, when the usher came to find him. He awoke in an ill temper, exacerbated by the discovery that his wig had dropped off into the coal bucket as he slept, and arrived in the courtroom in unmerciful mood. He glared at the defendants and the jury with equal displeasure, sat down and ordered the usher to get on with it.

'Foreman of the jury, have you reached a unanimous verdict in this case?'

Elsopp stood up. 'We have, sir.'

'And do you find the accused guilty or not guilty of the murder of Joseph Yates?'

McQueedie picked up both versions of his story and wondered which one he'd be discarding. The three defendants tightened their grip on the rail of the dock. Cresswell fingered his black cap and prepared to place it over the sooty patch on his wig. Elsopp swallowed nervously.

'Not guilty.'

Saturday January 2ⁿᵈ

Barnard Castle, 2.15pm

BARKER drained his glass and put it down on the Oddfellows Bar. 'Fill us up, Tom. And another pint for my friend Mr Raine here as well.'

'Still celebrating, I see, Geordie.' Marwood turned to the barrel behind him. 'What is it this time – Christmas, New Year or still making up for time spent in York jail?'

'New Year at the moment, I reckon. Thomas and me are waiting for Breckon to join us before we celebrate winning the Yates case properly.'

'Out soon, is he, Breckon?'

'Won't be long, his six months are nearly up. Then the three of us will be visiting a few friends, won't we, Thomas?'

Raine grinned malevolently. 'That's right. Friends who turned up in court to tell a lot of lies about us. We're going to show them just how grateful we are.' He glanced round the room. There were half a dozen others on the far side, four men engrossed in a card game, a fifth watching them, the sixth a young lad reading the day's *Gazette*. 'Thought we might find one or two in here.' He sounded disappointed.

Marwood handed Barker the fresh pint and began pulling a second for Raine. 'You want to be careful, lads. You start going round beating up witnesses, you'll end up back in York.'

'Beating them up?' Barker looked pained. 'Wouldn't dream of it, Tom. Just a quiet word or two, maybe a few broken windows, a bit of persuading them to put a bob or two into our defence fund.'

Marwood looked unconvinced. 'They said in the papers that your mate Breckon threatened to kill the Humphreys girl if he got the chance.' He handed Raine his refilled glass. 'You lot may have beaten two murder charges but I wouldn't put money on you getting away with it a third time.'

'There won't be anybody to see us next time, if there is a next time –' Raine halted and eyed him intently. 'You saying we killed Yates and the girl?'

'No, no.' Marwood backed away. 'Just offering a bit of friendly advice.'

'We wouldn't murder anyone for ten bob, would we, Geordie? Have to be worth at least a guinea apiece before we topped 'em.' Raine gave a mirthless grin. 'You want to watch what you're saying, Tom Marwood. Be a pity if anything happened in here.' He picked up his pint and surveyed the room again. 'Remember the last fight we had in here, Geordie? Made a right mess of the place as I recall.'

'I'm not after any trouble, lads.' Marwood gave a weak smile. 'Have those pints on the house, eh?'

'Don't mind if we do.' Raine downed his pint in two swallows, leant over the bar and dropped the glass on the stone floor below. Marwood jumped backwards as it shattered. 'Sorry about that, hand must have slipped.' Raine turned back to his companion. 'Sup up, Geordie, we've got a few more pubs to visit this afternoon. We'll leave Mr Marwood in peace... for now.'

Barker drained his pint and the pair walked to the door.

In the corner Binksley lowered his newspaper and watched thoughtfully as they disappeared, slamming the door behind them.

Thorpe, 4.30pm

BETSEY laid down her pen, dabbed her signature with a corner of blotting paper and began to read what she'd written.

> *Thorpe Grange*
> *Saturday*
>
> *Dearest Aunt Jane,*
>
> *I write to you with a very heavy heart to tell you what I have decided I must do. When I cut my visit to you short and returned here to Thorpe with papa on Boxing Day I intended it to be just for a few days, thinking he would soon overcome the melancholy that has afflicted him since the trial at York, but he is unchanged. He spends his days brooding about his failure to secure a conviction, though heaven knows it was not his fault, and I fear for him were he to remain here alone. It is all I can do even to persuade him to eat.*
>
> *It has not helped that the local magistrates who encouraged him to pursue the case with such vigour are now pressing him to resume his investigations, they believing, as he does, that the three accused were guilty. Papa is at a loss to know what to do and I cannot help except to be here to ease his life as best I can.*
>
> *So, dearest aunt, I have concluded that I must forego my teacher training, for the time being at least. I have written to Miss Cruse in York to explain and ask if I might perhaps be allowed to start next year. It grieves me to do this, but I could not bear to think of poor papa here alone while he is subject to such unhappiness. I am sure you will understand.*
>
> *Please give my love to Uncle John and the children.*
>
> *Your loving niece,*
> *Betsey*

She frowned. It sounded such an unhappy letter and there must be something she could say that would bring at least a glimpse of a smile to Aunt Jane's face. She picked up her pen and scribbled another sentence.

> *P.S. There is one good thing about all this – I shall be able to have Tommy back!*

That should do it. She double-folded the letter to create an envelope, wrote Aunt Jane's address on one side, sealed it with a splash of glue and added a penny stamp. The last post collection at the Morritt Arms on a Saturday was at five o'clock, and she'd have to hurry to make it.

Donning her cloak, scarf and gloves she set off, clutching the letter and the one she'd written earlier to Miss Cruse.

Barnard Castle, 6.40pm

'IT'S high time you Sassenachs learned how to celebrate the new year properly.' McQueedie drained his pint and stared morosely round the Golden Lion bar. 'Look at this place, 1847 still wet behind its ears and there's hardly a soul to be seen.' He pushed his empty glass across the table. 'Couple of pints on New Year's Eve and that's it for most of them. No wonder you lot never got much further than Hadrian's Wall.'

'Bit different up in Scotland, is it?' Binksley took a sip from his own drink, wondering how long he would manage to keep up with his companion. 'New Year, I mean.'

'Goes on for days.' McQueedie shook his head sadly. 'I remember one year when I was about your age it lasted till Burns' Night and I didn't sober up till February. Proper Hogmanay, that was.'

'Hogmanay?'

McQueedie stared at him in disbelief. 'I don't suppose you even know what Burns' Night is?'

'Scottish Bonfire Night?'

'God help us. Go and get the drinks in, laddie, and you can tell me what you've been up to today while I've been slaving over the workhouse guardians' annual report.' He gazed gloomily round the room again and wondered how Sandy was getting on in York. He was due back tomorrow and it wouldn't be a moment too soon.

York, 6.55pm

SANDY strode along Monkgate, gritting his teeth against the bitter north-east wind and wondering what McQueedie was doing in Barnard Castle. Probably having the time of his life in a pub, while he, Sandy, traipsed round freezing York. Thank God he was going back tomorrow. It wouldn't be a moment too soon.

He shivered, turned into a side street and stopped under a gas light to check the address on his list. Number 86. He found it, a small shop halfway along on the left, wedged between a dye works and a builder's yard. Above the shop window a faded sign carried the words Henry Babbington ~ Family Butcher & Purveyor of Fine Meats. It was, as Sandy had expected, closed and shuttered but there was a dim light behind the first-floor curtain and he knocked loudly on the shop door.

A window above opened and a small head leaned out. 'Mam says she told you before you're not coming back in till you're sober so you're to bugger off.' The window slammed shut.

Sandy sighed. He'd had the same lack of success at the previous eleven places he'd called over the past two days. Eight occupants had flatly refused to talk to him at all, one had died on Christmas Eve, two had threatened to call the police and the eleventh set a dog on him. Babbington was the last on the list of names and addresses he'd managed to bribe out of the court usher, and the Purveyor of Fine Meats, clearly in the domestic doghouse, could be anywhere.

Well, maybe not. Sandy cast his mind back to his own short-lived marriage, wondered where he'd have gone in similar circumstances, and set off to find the nearest pub.

Barnard Castle, 7.15pm

'RAINE actually said that?' McQueedie sat back and stared at Binksley. 'You took a note of it, I hope?'

'Word for word. Well, almost. Here, look. *There won't be anybody to see us next time, if there is a next time.*'

'Had a few by then, had he?'

'Both of them, I reckon, they didn't seem to care much what they said. Didn't actually admit in so many words that they'd done it, of course, but...' Binksley looked doubtful. 'I've been all over town today, talking to people like you told me, and almost everyone thinks they were guilty. Not that they'll say so to their faces, of course. He's a big lad, that Raine, I wouldn't want to cross him.'

'No.' McQueedie shook his head. 'I can't see what we can do with that. We need a follow-up story to the trial, but we can hardly go into print saying they've got away with murder. We'd have every libel lawyer in the north on our doorstep.'

'But if we know it's true...'

'You've a lot to learn, laddie. Knowing it's true's just the start. You need to be able to prove it in court, and even then it doesn't always work. Look at what happened to Mr Snowden there. He was sure they were guilty, wasn't he?'

'Must have been.'

'And he had plenty of proof – even an eye-witness to swear to it – but the jury took no notice. Funny things, juries, you just can't trust 'em.'

York, 7.25pm

BABBINGTON was sitting in a corner of the Mason's Arms, the only occupant of the back bar, staring blearily at an almost-empty pint mug. It was the third pub Sandy had tried and without doubt the most dismal. Thin gaslight flickered through the gloom, paint peeled from the walls and a bare trickle of smoke rose from a fire well into its death throes. Just the place for a man drowning his sorrows after his wife had barred the door to him.

Sandy ordered a large whisky from the landlord, who proved no more welcoming than the rest of the pub, and eyed his quarry thoughtfully. A big beefy-looking man, every inch a butcher, whose wife must be a formidable woman if she ruled the roost with him around. Not someone to antagonise, Sandy told himself as he pondered the best way to approach him. So far in this quest he'd attempted honesty, bribery, threats, appeals to civic duty and even abject pleading, and all had failed dismally. He'd rather hoped to find Babbington sobbing over his beer, ready to pour out his troubles to a friendly stranger, but that didn't look likely. He'd just have to rely on the well-trained professional journalist's traditional standbys of cunning and duplicity. He picked up his glass, crossed the room and parked himself on a bench near the fireplace.

'Evening. Bloody cold out there.' There was no response and Sandy picked up a battered poker by the hearth, gave the fire a poke and watched the final wisp of smoke die out. A coal bucket stood to one side, empty but for a couple of sticks and a crumpled copy of the *Yorkshire Gazette*. Two weeks old, the December 19th issue with the full trial report in it. Inspiration dawned.

Sandy picked it up, smoothed the pages, and turned to page two. MURDERS AT START-FORTH began halfway down the first column and continued for eleven packed columns to the not-guilty verdict on the far side of page three. It was just what he needed, and he settled down to read.

He gave it two minutes and then looked up in astonishment. 'Not guilty? I can't believe it!' He bent his head over the page again for a moment. 'I'd have put my life savings on an acquittal. Well, well, well, I'll be damned.' He flung the paper down, sat back and was gratified to find Babbington staring at him. 'Forgive my outburst, but I've been away these past couple of weeks and only just caught up the news. You'll have read this, of course? About the murder trial and those three young villains getting away with it? Astonishing!'

Babbington dropped his stare and said nothing, but it was a start. At least he hadn't walked out or, even worse, sunk into a drunken stupor. Sandy persevered.

'You never know what these juries get up to, mind.' He leant confidentially across the bench towards Babbington and dropped his voice. 'My brother Duncan was on a jury back in Glasgow and says they agreed their verdict in the first five minutes but decided to hang on for a bit to get a full day's expenses. Someone got a pack of cards out and they ran a poker game for the next two days before anyone twigged.' He sat back. 'I don't imagine that happened here, mind. There's only one explanation. I'd wager they were bribed, the lot of them.'

'You'd lose your money, then.' Babbington's growl was slurred but music to Sandy's ears.

'Nonsense, it's obvious. Someone slipped them a few bob apiece to vote not guilty, you mark my words. I'll offer ten to one to anyone who can prove me wrong.'

'Would you now?' Babbington swallowed the last of his pint, banged the empty glass down and turned towards the bar. 'Silas!'

The landlord reappeared at the bar. 'Another pint, is it?'

'Bring it over, I want a word with you.' He dug a handful of coins out of a pocket and dumped them on the bench top as his drink arrived. 'Don't go yet. This fellow here wants to place a bet and I need you as a witness.' He turned to Sandy. 'Ten to one, you said?'

'If you can prove it.'

'You heard that, Silas?' Babbington inspected the rest of his coins, selected four pennies and pushed them forward. 'That's for the beer. The rest...' He did a laborious calculation. 'Shilling, a threepenny bit and another ninepence in coppers. Two shillings, I make it.'

Silas nodded. 'Looks right enough.'

'That's my stake.' Babbington sat back. 'Now, Mr clever bloody Scotsman, time to put your money where your mouth is. A pound you're going to owe me.'

Sandy gave a confident smile and laid two half-sovereigns on the bench. 'This'll be the quickest two bob I ever made. You can't possibly prove those men weren't bribed.'

'We'll see. Where was I the week before Christmas, Silas?'

'That'd be the week you missed the darts finals, first time you hadn't been in on a Tuesday for years. Down at the courts, weren't you, sitting on a jury?'

Sandy managed to look astounded. 'You never told me that!'

'Never asked, did you?' Babbington grinned. 'Here's your proof.' He dug into a jacket pocket and produced a crumpled letter. 'Jury service order – Mr Henry Babbington. That's me, see? I was on that jury and I know whether we were bribed or not.'

Sandy took the letter and stared at it. 'That's not proof. You'll have to do better than that if you want my pound, Mr Babbington."

'You calling me a liar?'

Sandy shook his head hastily as Babbington leant menacingly forward. 'No, no, of course not. But if you weren't bribed, I think the least you could do is explain what really happened.'

Babbington eyed the two half-sovereigns speculatively. 'Sworn to secrecy, weren't we? They could do me for telling you what went on.'

'I'm not going to go round boasting how you made a fool of me, am I? But if you're too frightened –'

'Calling me a coward now?' Babbington stood up, fists clenched.

'Calm down, Henry.' Silas stepped forward. 'You know the rules, no fighting in the bar until after closing time.' He waited for Babbington to subside. 'Now, it seems only fair the gentleman knows the truth before he loses his pound, and I'd be interested to know too.' He picked up the coins. 'I'll guard your winnings, Henry, while you tell us about that verdict.'

Babbington hesitated. 'You'll not say I told you?'

Sandy shook his head and crossed his fingers. 'Word of honour. Go on then, what happened in the jury room?'

'Edwards, that's what happened. Mr William bloody Edwards.'

Monday January 4ᵗʰ

Thorpe, 11.15am

'WHO?' Snowden stared blankly at the pair standing before his desk. 'I've never heard of him.'

'You'd recognise him, sir. One of the jurors at the trial.' McQueedie turned to Sandy for confirmation. 'Third from the left in the back row of the jury box as I recall.'

Sandy nodded. 'Weedy-looking fellow in a brown suit. Didn't look as if he'd say boo to a goose but it was him that swung it.'

'Are you telling me all the others wanted a guilty verdict but this man Edwards managed to change their minds?' Snowden shook his head. 'I don't believe it.'

'Not change their minds, Mr Snowden, just their verdict. All twelve of them thought Breckon and the others had done the murders, but Edwards flatly refused to say they were guilty.'

'Why in God's name would he do that?'

'Because it might send three men to the gallows. Against all his religious principles, he said, and he wouldn't budge.'

'Religious principles?'

'He's a Quaker.' Sandy dug out his notebook. 'I went looking for him yesterday morning at their meeting house and it seems he's one of their elders, a sort of minister as far as I could gather. I didn't tell him why I wanted to know, of course, made out I was interested in joining them and wanted to know what they stood for. Abolition of capital punishment comes high on their list.'

Snowden still looked baffled. 'But the verdict –?'

'It's quite simple. The jury had been locked up in the castle for three long days and were determined they wouldn't spend another night there. The judge said they had to stay there till they were unanimous. So when Edwards stuck to his guns, the other eleven finally decided that if they couldn't beat him they'd join him. Not guilty all round, and off they went home.'

'So you didn't lose the case after all, papa!' Betsey, who had been listening intently from her desk across the room, clapped her hands in delight. 'I knew you were right all along.'

'I'm not sure this makes any difference.' Snowden picked up his pipe and began filling it thoughtfully. 'They reached a verdict, for whatever reason, and that verdict will stand.'

Betsey's face fell. 'Can't you appeal?'

'Not a chance. They can't be tried again once they've been acquitted, however wrong that may be.'

'That's not fair!' Betsey looked appalled.

'It's the law, and has been for centuries. It's called the rule against double jeopardy. Otherwise we could just re-arrest everyone who's found not guilty and keep on prosecuting them until we won.' Snowden gave a wry smile. 'It would make my life a lot easier, but it wouldn't be good for justice, believe me.'

'Not even if there's fresh evidence?'

'Not even if there's a confession.'

'We've been wasting our time, then.' Sandy closed his notebook. 'We thought we might help you get both of those.'

Snowdon raised an eyebrow. 'And how might you do that?'

'Well, young Binksley – '

'Binksley?'

'Our junior reporter, you'll have seen him in court, spotty-faced lad but quite promising. He was in a pub in town on Saturday afternoon when Barker and Raine came in and as good as told everyone they'd done the murders.' Sandy dug out his notebook again. 'The lad had the sense to take notes, I've got a copy of them here...'

Snowden read them in silence. 'As I said, even a confession isn't going to change the verdict. But thanks for trying.'

'I wondered... that bit about not worth killing again for just ten bob. Mr McQueedie and I sat through the whole trial but we can't recall any evidence about how much money Yates really had on him at the end. Did we miss that?'

Snowden frowned. 'He did have about ten shillings at the end of his night out, that's true. I'd planned to bring forward evidence about that – people who'd paid Yates money, landlord of the last beerhouse he visited, two girls who saw Yates with money just before he met Barker, Raine and Breckon – but then the judge decided I was bringing too many witnesses and I left them out. They didn't seem important, and we weren't doing Barker and his mates for robbery, just the murders.'

'So how did Raine know how much Yates had unless he'd stolen it?'

'A good question. A pity we didn't ask it at the trial.'

Sandy took the notebook back. 'Binksley's been talking to a lot of people in town over the weekend. According to him, Barker was broke the night before the murders but had money next morning. And there's a girl who claims Raine admitted having some of Yates' money.'

Snowden shook his head. 'That still wouldn't be enough to prove they killed the lad. They've been acquitted of murder, and it's all too late now.'

'Is it?' Betsey looked unconvinced. 'Too late to convict them of murder, perhaps, but I can't believe they can get away with all this scot-free.'

'So what would you do?'

'Put them on trial again, this time for robbery. They wouldn't face the gallows for that, but at least they'd be severely punished. No religious principles to get in the jury's way. Why not?'

Snowden stared at her for a moment. 'You know, Betsey, that's not a bad idea. Why not indeed? I'll have to get the magistrates' approval, but that shouldn't be difficult – they're as keen to see those three put away as I am. And I'll have to talk to these witnesses again.' He turned to McQueedie. 'If I do this, I don't want Barker and his crew alerted. Not a word in print till I know I can go ahead.'

'Then we get it exclusively? In time for Saturday's *Gazette*?'

'I'll do my best.' Snowden gave a grim smile. 'I can't wait to see their faces when we re-arrest them.'

Saturday January 9th

Barnard Castle, 10.50am

TOM Marwood poured a third gallon of water carefully into the new barrel, wondered whether to add another and decided regretfully that he probably wouldn't get away with it. Any more and customers would start wondering why the colour of the Oddfellows' Arms best bitter was looking as pale as horse-piss as well as tasting like it. He put down the bucket and was tapping the bung back into place when a shriek came from Eliza on the floor above.

'Mr Marwood! Have you seen this?'

He sighed. Another dead mouse in the kitchen, probably, or fresh graffiti in the gents. You'd think she'd be used to it by now. He made his way up the cellar steps, paused for breath at the top, and found her in the bar.

'Look at this! I can't believe it!' She waved a newspaper at him excitedly. 'Today's *Gazette*, just arrived.' She thrust it into his hands. 'Read it!'

THE BARNARD CASTLE MURDERS

Exclusive by Our Teesdale Correspondent

THE verdicts in these cases were so great a surprise to those entrusted with the prosecutions that they have determined to make a further investigation, which has been conducted with great vigilance by Mr Snowden.

The result is that evidence further corroborative of the statement of Ann Humphreys, the principal witness, has been obtained, and other facts have come to light, which we are not at liberty further to disclose at the present time.

The magistrates of the division have however determined that the case shall undergo a legal investigation, and under the requisite authority Barker and Raine were yesterday re-apprehended and committed to Northallerton House of Correction on a remand for further investigation. The charge preferred against them will be that of robbery with violence to the person of Yates, for whose murder they have already been acquitted after much difference of opinion on the part of the jury who tried the case.

We feel that the public are deeply indebted to the magistrates and those acting under their authority for their pains-taking exertions and inquiries which they have made.

'Bloody hell.' Tom stared at the page. 'So that's where they are. I wondered why they didn't turn up last night.'

'What about Breckon?' Eliza looked puzzled. 'They don't mention him.'

'He's still in Durham jail for that assault, remember? Due for release this coming week, I think, but they'll not be letting him out now.'

Northallerton, 12.05pm

JOSAPHAT Garbutt had never forgiven his mother and father. He could have been Jacob, Joatham, Ezekias or any of the other forty-odd perfectly acceptable names listed on the family bible page his parents chose at random to stick a pin in. Even Zorobabel would have done at a pinch. Half an inch higher up the page he'd have been Roboam, Robbo for short, now there was a name for a man to be proud of.

But the pin came down on the eighth verse of the first chapter of the Gospel according to St Matthew, landed on Josaphat, begat by Asa and begetter of Joram, and from the day he went to school the world called him Fat Joe.

By now, forty-one years later, Robbo Garbutt would have been tall, strong and a leader of men. Fat Joe Garbutt was short, overweight and earned his living as an orderly in the House of Correction. He'd spent the morning swabbing floors and peeling potatoes, and now they had him carting pailfuls of gruel round the cells. It just wasn't good enough.

Simmering with resentment, he turned into the next corridor and halted outside the first cell. It had been empty yesterday, but two fresh names had been chalked on the slate beside the door. Barker and Raine. He frowned, wondering where he'd heard that combination of names before, put the bucket of gruel on the floor and slid back the cover on the cell door peephole. One of the occupants was asleep on his bed – a proper cot with a blanket, one of the perks accorded to remand prisoners along with three meals a day instead of two and the right to lie around all day instead of keeping the treadmill busy like convicted men. It was all right for some, Fat Joe reflected bitterly, life of bloody Riley.

There was no sign of the second occupant and he moved closer to the peephole to squint inside. It wasn't, he realised a second later, the wisest thing to do. A bearded mouth appeared before him, a gobbet of well-aimed saliva shot into his eye and he staggered back in alarm. His left foot hit the bucket, the bucket went flying, Joe fell over and two gallons of gruel poured across the floor.

There was a howl of laughter from inside and another as he struggled to his feet, skidded on the gruel and fell down again.

'Well, well, well!' More of the bearded face appeared beyond the peephole. 'If it isn't Fat Joe! Remember me, Joe? Tommy Raine, spent six months in here for assault a couple of years back.'

Raine. From somewhere Barnard Castle way, if Joe remembered rightly, and he suddenly realised who the newcomers must be. Raine and Barker, two of those murdering bastards who'd managed to escape the gallows at York.

'Lost your tongue, Joe?' There was a hint of menace as Raine continued. 'That would be a pity, because you and I have things to discuss.'

'Discuss?' Joe finally managed to get upright. 'Like what?'

'Like me giving you a letter to post for me when I was last in here, and that letter never getting posted. Pocket the money, did you, Joe?'

'Must have got lost on the way.' Joe edged further away from the door. 'Or delivered to the wrong address by accident. Happens all the time.'

'How very true, Joe. You had any accidents recently – apart from kicking that bucket over?'

'Accidents?'

'Just wondered, Joe. I have a feeling that maybe you should be very, very careful in future.' Raine grinned. 'Just remind me, are you still living over that shop in Zetland Street?'

Joe's heart sank. 'Why d'you want to know that?'

'Maybe Geordie here and me will pay you a little visit when we're out of this place. Teach you how to post a letter, perhaps.' Raine's face turned from the peephole. 'Geordie, there's someone here who's going to make sure our stay here is as comfortable as possible.' The face reappeared. 'That's right, isn't it, Joe?'

Joe nodded dumbly and Raine grinned again. 'It won't be for long, we'll be out in a few days. Meanwhile, you can make a start by finding us something worth eating instead of that slop you've spilled outside.'

Robbo Garbutt would have laughed in his face and told him to get stuffed. Fat Joe picked up his bucket and stumbled miserably off towards the kitchens.

Barker swung his legs off the cot. 'You're sure about that, us getting out of here soon?'

'I told you, they can't do us twice for the same thing. We'll be home in no time.'

Barnard Castle, 2.15pm

McQUEEDIE drained the last of his pint and pushed the empty tankard across the table. 'Your turn, I think, laddie.' He frowned. 'You've hardly touched yours. Something the matter?'

Binksley laid down the *Gazette* and shook his head. 'Not really. It's just...' He hesitated. 'Your story in the paper, it's not your usual style. I expected something a bit more dramatic.'

'Dramatic?'

'You know, RESIDENTS ROCKED BY RETRIAL REVELATION AS DEATH ROW DODGERS ARE DRAGGED BACK TO DOCK, that sort of thing. And more of it.'

'Think I'm losing my touch?' McQueedie chuckled. 'I was lucky to get anything in, seeing Snowden only told me on Thursday, just before the *Gazette*'s deadline for this week. And I wrote it that way to keep him happy – he's not a great one for racy headlines – and I've high hopes of more revelations from him soon.'

'Oh.' Binksley nodded uncertainly. 'It seems a shame you couldn't get more in.'

McQueedie looked at him pityingly. 'You've a lot to learn, laddie. Why give them more than we have to? The *Gazette* got its exclusive, and we'll get paid. The rest we'll spread out over the next week.' He counted the days off on his fingers as he continued. 'Tomorrow the Sundays lift the *Gazette* story and we'll claim off them, too. Monday we give them the local reaction – town in shock, cheers and fears and so on. Tuesday they get a scene-setter for the committal taking place next day – mounting excitement, crowds expected in court, police on guard in case there's an escape attempt –'

'Escape?'

'POLICE FOIL BREAK-OUT BID, always worth a few pars, laddie. Then, Wednesday they get the actual committal report, stern words from the magistrates, prisoners stunned as they're shipped off to York to await the next assizes, weeping women and children if we can find any. Thursday will be more reaction – with a bit of luck we'll find a lawyer to say it's all illegal because they've already been acquitted. Friday it'll be interviews with the prisoners declaring their innocence –'

'Interviews? How will you manage that?'

'No need to see them, you know what they'll say without all the bother of going to York and they're hardly likely to complain about a piece giving their side of the story. Not that anybody would listen to them if they did.' McQueedie delved into his pocket and produced a sheaf of papers. 'I knocked it out last night. You can read it if you like.'

'And then?'

'For Saturday we'll do a comprehensive round-up of everything so far for the weeklies which come out that day. Just a re-write job really.'

Binksley's face brightened. 'Not much for me to do, then?'

'We'll need something completely new to follow this lot, something to keep you busy next week. There's a cow up the dale just given birth to a calf with two heads and six legs. Or two calves joined together, depending how you look at it. Like those Siamese twins in America who were in all the papers last year.'

Binksley looked doubtful. 'I can't seeing that making much of a tale.'

'Oh, it will, laddie, by the time you've finished with it. Get yourself up there and find someone who thinks it's a sign from God, divine punishment for the sins of the locals.'

'Sins? What sort of sins?'

'Bound to be something. Satanic rituals on the moors, midnight sacrifices in the churchyard, drinking after hours, whatever you like. Leave a decapitated cockerel on a gravestone somewhere and they'll be all over you in no time.'

Greta Bridge, 4.35pm

SNOWDEN laid down his pen and looked up at the young man across the police office desk. 'Why didn't you tell me about this before?'

Jonathan Arrowsmith gave an apologetic shrug. 'Nobody asked me about it at the trial and I just didn't think it was important.'

'Well, I think it could be very useful at the next one.'

'You mean, I'll have to go to court again?'

'Almost certainly. Is that a problem?'

Arrowsmith twisted his hands nervously. 'When I gave evidence last time I thought they'd be convicted. Then when they got off, word went round that they were looking for me. And you know what that means, Mr Snowden. God knows what they'd do if they found me. I've been hiding from them ever since, over on my uncle's farm in Bowes. I thought I'd be safe for a while.'

'So why come to see me now?'

'I saw in the paper today that you've arrested them again and I don't want them set free a second time. I thought what I've been telling you today might help you stop that happening.'

'I'm sure it might.' Snowden nodded thoughtfully. 'They won't go away forever, mind.'

'No, but it'll give me time to.' Arrowsmith leant forward. 'I've a cousin who went out to Africa three years ago and he's doing very well by all accounts. He's working for the Cape Colony police and reckons I could do the same.'

'Police?' Snowden's eyebrows rose. 'With your record?'

'Nothing serious, Mr Snowden, just fighting after a few beers. I've never done anything you'd call really criminal.'

'Well, I wish you luck with that.'

Arrowsmith was silent for a moment before replying. 'You could do a bit more, sir. I need a reference saying I'm from an honest God-fearing family, got no known criminal connections, always happy to help the forces of law and order, that sort of stuff. Like me being in court as a witness and telling you everything.'

'No known criminal connections? What about Barker? You shared a room with him.'

'You don't get much choice when you're lodging in Briggate. I didn't know he was a wrong 'un, Mr Snowden, honest. Well, not as bad as he turned out to be.'

'And what about this God-fearing family of yours?'

'My dad was a quarryman, died in a stone-fall when I was just a kid. He was never in trouble, ask your Sergeant Clarke in Briggate, he's known me all my life. My mam's gone, too. There's only me and my brother, and God knows where he is.'

'Charlie, isn't it? Lived with the girl who died?'

'Haven't heard of him since summer before last. He's got more sense than me, never got himself arrested.'

'Deserved to be, from what I heard. I went looking for him.'

'I don't know about that, sir. But he was never in court.'

'Hmm.' Snowden eyed him speculatively. 'You're not thinking of disappearing yet, I hope? Not before the new trial, anyway?'

'Wouldn't dream of it, sir. Not if I knew I'd be safely on my way to the Cape when it was over, with a good reference in my pocket from a top-ranking policeman like yourself.'

Snowden frowned. 'I'll not lie for you, Arrowsmith, but I may be prepared to say you've been very helpful to us in our inquiries. Come and see me when the trial's over and I'll think about it.'

PART FOUR

March 1847

*The entrance to York jail, built in 1835 and demolished a century later.
Within its walls lay the castle, which still houses the
city's crown court today.*

Tuesday March 16ᵗʰ

York, 11.40am

ROBERT Monsey Rolfe, Puisne Baron of the Exchequer and Northern circuit judge, eased his meagre frame into the thinly-padded seat and waited for the court to settle down before announcing his decision.

'I have given lengthy consideration to Mr Matthews' arguments this morning on behalf of his clients Raine and Barker, who appear before these assizes accused, along with the third defendant Breckon, of feloniously assaulting Joseph Yates and stealing from his person the sum of ten shillings in silver.' He turned to the jury. 'Mr Matthews' plea is one of *entrefois acquit*, which, for the benefit of those of you unfamiliar with such legal terminology, means that the accused have already been tried with having pushed, cast, struck and thrown Yates to the ground, that upon such indictment they were acquitted, and that the stealing with they now stand indicted was the same identical pushing, casting, striking and throwing upon the ground, and that therefore their liberty could not again be imperilled. In short, they should not be tried for the same offence twice.'

Rolfe paused for effect before slowly shaking his head. 'I am, however, of the opinion that this is a bad plea. The accused were acquitted of murder, but not of assault or robbery. I therefore override Mr Matthews' submission, and order this trial to go ahead. Take the prisoners' pleas, and the court will then hear counsel for the prosecution.'

'First round to Mr Snowden.' McQueedie leant across the press box to exchange whispers with Binksley. 'He told me he was confident he'd win this *entrefois* business, but you never know what to expect with some judges.'

'This one looks as if he knows what he's doing.'

'I've come across him before. Miserable old bugger, you wouldn't think he was related to Nelson, but a fair judge.'

'Nelson?' Binksley looked baffled.

'Second cousin twice removed or something.'

'Oh, that Nelson. The sailor at Waterloo.'

McQueedie sighed. 'Here's my report on this morning's proceedings. Make sure it catches the twelve-thirty to London, and find Sandy who's coming down from Darlington by the same train. Don't let him near a pub until he's delivered this afternoon's story to me here.'

'This afternoon's? How can –?'

'Look, laddie, the next few hours are going to be a repeat of the prosecution evidence we heard back in December. Sandy's written it up again from our files and all we have to do this afternoon is make sure nothing important's changed. No point in doing the same job twice.' McQueedie glanced across the court. 'Prosecution's about to start.

Off you go before Mr Bliss takes the floor.'

York, 3.25pm

SNOWDEN watched Ann Humphreys leave the witness box and sat back with a satis-fied smile. 'She did well, better than last time. Congratulations, Mr Bliss. Nobody on this jury's going to think she made it all up.'

'I hope we do as well with the new witnesses.' Bliss shuffled through his papers. 'We've got a ten-minute adjournment, could we just run through them again, the ones showing Yates had money on the night he died?'

Snowden nodded and found his list. 'First up is a tailor called John Kaye, who paid Yates seven shillings around five o'clock that evening. Next we've got Ann Rutherford, who was visiting Yates' father a couple of hours later when Yates came in and asked his sister to change a sovereign for him. He gave his father two half-crowns, his sister two shillings, and put the rest in his pocket.'

'Leaving him thirteen shillings, plus the seven Kaye had paid him – a pound?'

'Unless he'd spent some of Kaye's payment already, of course. Next witness is a shoemaker, Joseph Brown, who met Yates between eight and nine and paid him five shillings. Yates was obviously having a lucky night.' Snowden gave a brief smile as he read his notes. 'Brown says he remembers wishing next day, when Yates was reported missing, that he hadn't paid him.'

'So we can show that Yates set off for a night's drinking with well over a pound to spend?'

'I think so. We've got a carter called George Sparrow who saw Yates around nine o'oclock in a pub where he pulled a handful of silver from his pocket – about a pound's worth, Sparrow says. At ten o'clock Yates was in another pub, where a plumber called Bowron saw him with at least sixteen shillings, all in silver.' Snowden paused. 'I've got more witnesses tracking Yates round various ale houses, spending money on drink, but I don't think we need call them all. The next important one is Ann Braithwaite, who was with a friend called Hannah Todd when they met Yates by the county bridge at about one in the morning. He tried to persuade them to go with him for a drink – not many pubs in Briggate obey the licensing laws, I'm afraid – and showed her he still had plenty of money, about ten shillings, she thought. They refused, and Yates walked off.'

'The next person he met, of course, was Catherine Raine, and then they were joined by Barker, Raine and Breckon.'

Snowden nodded. 'And Yates' lucky night came to a sudden end.'

'Indeed. Well, that all seems enough to convince the jury that he had money to be stolen. Where do we go from there?'

'We've already had Humphreys' account of what happened next. That leaves two more people I want to put in the witness box –'

Snowden broke off as the door behind the judge's chair opened. 'Rolfe's back. We'll talk about the others later.'

York, 5.40pm

'PLENTY of new faces among that lot, Sandy.' McQueedie grinned. 'Meant re-writing your re-write, has it?'

Sandy continued scribbling. 'I thought you said it would all be the same as last time? Bloody Snowden. Eight fresh witnesses so far and more to come... Which one was the plumber, Sparrow or Bowron?'

'Sparrow, I think.'

'Sparrow it is.' Sandy laid down his pen. 'Time you took over. I'll give this to Binksley for the six-thirty train and see you in the pub.'

McQueedie opened his notebook and began to take notes.

John Headlam, examined by Mr Bliss

'You are Mr John Headlam, curate, son of the Very Rev Headlam, Rector of Wycliffe and archdeacon of Richmond?'

'I am, sir.'

'You were present, I believe, when the body of Joseph Yates, a tailor, was recovered from the river Tees on the evening of August the twelfth 1845?'

'That is correct. It was trapped between rocks in the middle of the river where it runs past the rectory. I assisted two of our servants to bring it from the water.'

'And did you examine the body?

'I did.'

'And the clothing?'

'Yes.'

'Did you find anything in the man's pockets?'

'A number of items, yes. As I recall, a knife, a thimble, a bodkin and a packet containing some small needles.'

'The tools of a tailor's trade, in fact?'

'Yes, sir.'

'This pocket... was it a long one?'

'I suppose it was, sir. I remember having to reach deep into it to recover the items.'

'It would have been difficult for anything to have fallen out?'

'They were right at the bottom, sir. I can't see how they could have.'

'There were no holes or tears in the pocket?'

'No, sir.'

'And you found nothing else? No coins, for example?'

'None, sir.'

'So if this man had had a handful of silver coins in this pocket when he fell into the river, you would expect to have found them?'

'Certainly, sir. They would have been heavier than the other items, apart perhaps from the knife. If they remained in the pocket, I can't see how coins would have been lost.'

'Nor can I, Mr Headlam, nor can I, and I am sure the gentlemen of the jury will be equally baffled. We have heard that he had money – plenty of it, twelve shillings or more in halfcrowns, shillings, sixpences and doubtless coppers as well – when he met the three defendants on that fateful night. Minutes later he was in the river without a single coin. It is, I suppose, possible that moments

before he died he threw all his wealth away into the swirling Tees to placate Prowling Peg, whom I'm told haunts those waters –'

(laughter in court)

'– but I suggest that a far more likely explanation for its disappearance is that Yates was robbed and went penniless to his death, and those responsible, members of the jury, stand before you today in the dock.'

'Don't over-do it, Mr Bliss.' The judge cast him a warning look. 'You'll have nothing left for your closing address, and I am anxious to conclude the prosecution case this evening. Have you finished with this witness?'

'Yes, my lord.'

'Many more?'

'Just three, my lord. They will be brief.'

McQueedie frowned as the next witness was directed to the witness box and gave the oath. Jonathan Arrowsmith, who'd given evidence at the first trial and disputed the time Barker came home on the night of the murders. Odd that Snowden should bring him back at this stage.

Jonathan Arrowsmith, examined by Mr Bliss

'Am I right, Mr Arrowsmith, in believing that you are a friend of the defendant Barker?'

'I know him, sir, yes.'

'In fact, you shared a room with him in August 1845?'

'Yes, sir.'

'Cast your mind back to the evening Joseph Yates disappeared. Do you recall a conversation with Barker in which he said he was short of money?'

'I do, sir. He said he had found no work that day and had but a shilling to his name.'

'But he went out that evening and was gone until the early hours?'

'Yes, sir. Two o'clock or later.'

'And next morning who rose first?'

'I did, sir. Barker was still asleep.'

'Can you tell the jury what happened when you got dressed?'

'I picked up the wrong trousers by mistake, sir, Barker's instead of my own, and money fell out of the pocket.'

'How much money?

'At least three or four shillings, sir. Silver coins, I didn't count it.'

'And have you any notion where Barker had obtained such wealth?'

'I've a good idea, sir.'

'So have I, Mr Arrowsmith. That will be all.'

Mary Alderson, examined by Mr Bliss

'You live in Thorngate, Barnard Castle?'

'That's right.'

'And you are acquainted with the prisoner Thomas Raine?'

'I've met him from time to time, yes.'

'*Do you remember meeting him near the county bridge on the evening of December the twenty-ninth last?*'

'*Yes, sir. It was late and he'd been drinking, he asked me to lend him a shilling but I didn't have one.*'

'*And did you discuss anything else?*'

'*We got talking about the trial, how he'd got off the murder charge and that. I said I thought it was an awful thing, little Joe Yates being killed for nothing.*'

'*And did he comment on that?*'

'*He said it wasn't for nothing and he'd had some of Joe's money in his pocket the day after.*'

'*Thank you, Miss Alderson.*'

<u>*Thomas Marwood, examined by Mr Bliss*</u>

'*You are a publican, I believe?*'

'*Landlord of the Oddfellows Arms in Briggate, sir.*'

'*Where the three accused are regular customers?*'

'*They come in fairly often, yes, sir, when they can.*'

'*Were any of them in your establishment on the afternoon of January the second this year?*'

'*Barker and Raine came in, yes.*'

'*And did you have some conversation with them?*'

'*They were talking about the trial, sir.*'

'*Boasting about getting away with murder?*'

'*Sort of, sir. They were celebrating being set free.*'

'*They were not aware that their words were being recorded by someone else in the room?*'

'*Of course not, sir. They'd no idea, any more than I did.*'

'*I have discussed that record with his lordship, who has agreed that it comes from a reliable source – which is not to be made public – and can be accepted as admissible evidence in this court. Can you confirm that in this discussion of the events of August the ninth 1845, Raine said "There won't be anybody to see us next time"?*'

'*I believe he did, sir.*'

'*And that they wouldn't murder anybody "for just ten bob"?*'

'*Yes, sir.*'

'*Did he offer any explanation as to how he knew almost exactly the amount of money Yates had that night – information which had not been released during his trial?*'

'*No, sir.*'

'*Because there is only one explanation, isn't there? They'd robbed him.*'

York, 7.45pm

'BY then it was just gone seven, and Rolfe adjourned until tomorrow.' Snowden paused, lit his pipe and blew a tentative shimmer of blue smoke towards the Dun Cow ceiling.

'All in all, Anthony, a good day.'

'You certainly covered a lot of ground.' Coulthard poured them both a second glass of wine. 'It sounds to me as if the defence were just going through the motions.'

'Apart from Matthews' initial plea for the whole case to be dismissed, yes. There was hardly any attempt to cross-examine, and when they did it was half-hearted. I think all them, Matthews, Blanshard and Pickering, knew they were fighting a lost cause.' Snowden took a sip from his refilled glass and nodded appreciatively. 'And of course we didn't have to go through all the evidence about the murders, which saved a lot of time. With luck it'll all be over tomorrow.' He savoured another mouthful of claret. 'How was the journey from Darlington?'

'Uneventful, except I shared a carriage with a couple of reporters from Newcastle who lured me into a game of cards to kill the time.' Coulthard shook his head ruefully. 'Cost me three shillings.'

Snowden smiled. 'I'm sure you'll find a way of hiding it among your expenses.'

'I'm not sure playing seven-card brag counts as hospitality.'

'Well, I'm sorry if dragging you down here means you're out of pocket, but if this case goes on into a third day I'll need you to wrap things up while I'm in Leeds for Thursday's magistrates' meeting. Did you bring the crime files with you? I'll get started on the monthly report tonight.'

'They're here.' Coulthard dug them out of his bag. 'I brought the post as well.'

'Anything interesting?

'Routine stuff mainly. There's one addressed to you personally that I haven't opened and another I'm not quite sure what to do with.' He handed them over, drained his glass and stood up. 'Unless you need me any further, I'll go and get changed before we eat. Back in a few minutes.'

Snowden watched him go before switching his attention to the two letters. The first was in a pristine white envelope, the Penny Red positioned precisely in the top right-hand corner, the address written in extravagant copperplate flourishes that had become familiar to him over the past year. They came from the pen of his publisher Henry Shaw, and Snowden broke the wax seal on the back hoping it brought news of how his book was selling. It had received very gratifying reviews when it was published back in November, but kind words didn't pay the bills.

He pulled out the letter and began to read.

Fetter Lane, London
March 12ᵗʰ '47

My Dear Mr Snowden,

 I trust you are well and continue to enjoy success in your battle to uphold the law in those distant parts.

 I am sure you will be greatly encouraged to learn that the first print run of your book has sold out, and that we are proposing a reprint within the next few days. Demand for copies has exceeded all our expectations, with enquiries from all corners of the civilized world, and I am told several constabularies in this country have already pronounced it mandatory reading for all their officers.

*A full account of sales and a first payment of royalties will be
forwarded to you shortly.*

*May I offer my sincere congratulations and our gratitude for entrusting
this matter to our establishment.*

I remain, Sir,

Your Obedient Servant,

Henry Shaw

Sold out! Reprinted! All those long nights scribbling away in the candlelight had been worth it after all. Snowden sat back and allowed himself a faint glow of pride to go with the last of the claret. And royalties! The book sold at seven shillings and sixpence a copy and he was promised fifteen percent which was... he juggled the figures in his mind... just over a shilling a copy. That meant –

He realised he had no idea how many copies had been printed so far. Could it be as many as 500? That would bring him about £25, six weeks' salary. But he must have spent three hours a day on average for two years putting the book together, perhaps two thousand hours in all, and that worked out at...

Threepence an hour.

He grinned to himself, wondered briefly how even Dickens made a living, and tucked the letter away in his pocket.

The second one was very different, a small grimy parcel made up of several sheets of rough paper tightly folded together, tied with a piece of twine and untidily addressed to *The Chief of Police, Great Abbridge, York County, England.* In place of a stamp were scribbled letters and numbers recording what had clearly been a lengthy passage through the postal system before someone finally deduced it was intended for him.

It took him five minutes and a broken fingernail to undo the knotted twine and unfold the letter inside.

Doomesburg, Ohio

November 9 1846

Sir,

> *I aint sure this mail will find you but your name and address is as I was told and I done my best as promised and pray the Good Lord guides it to you.*

> *Why I write you is last night I was called to a prisoner in the town gaol wanting to confess of his sins afore they hanged him today which they did God rest his soul. He swore on the Holy Book he was innercent of the killing what he was being hanged for but he was sore troubled about a crime he done back in England where he came from and asked me to send this letter, him being not able to write too well even afore he'd gotten a bullet thru his arm when the posse caught him.*

> *He told me that summer afore last he came across a lone horse by the roadside in your part of the world and was cutting loose the saddel bag for to steal what was in it only the owner appeard of a sudden and there was a fight and he knifed him, not meaning to kill him or so he said but he died.*

He hid the body down some kind of cavern where it might still be and he wanted you to go find it and give it a Christian burial and not blame any innercent man for a murder he didnt do like he was being hanged for here. I hope I've told all that right.

This man called hisself Charley but he never told no-one his full name, he would be age 25 or thereabouts, on the short side and spoke English real odd I couldnt understand all he said.

Anyways, that's all I can tell you and I hope you can find this body and lay the poor mans soul to rest.

Yours in the Lord,

Rev Joshua Peacehorn

Pastor, Doomesburg Church of the Second Coming

Snowden laid down the letter, uncertain whether to feel pleased he no longer had a killer on the loose or disappointed because he would never know exactly what happened, and was still wondering when Coulthard returned.

Snowden handed him the letter. 'They've hanged our Whashton killer.'

'Hanged him?' Coulthard looked startled. 'I didn't even know we'd caught him.'

'We didn't. Read it, you'll see.' He waited for Coulthard to absorb the Reverend Peacehorn's message. 'You'll remember me telling you about it all, the body in the tunnel, Mrs Mattock's pies, the mad old aunt up at Hirst.'

'Of course. This Charley, any idea who he was?'

'A strong suspicion, but nothing I could prove.'

'Didn't mean to kill him, it says. I wonder what really happened.'

'My guess is that Frankland set off with his pie, got a few hundred yards up the road towards Richmond and decided he had to nip behind the bushes for, well, the obvious reasons.'

'Mrs Mattock's pie upset his stomach, perhaps?'

'It'd be a brave man who faced her with that accusation. Whatever the reason, he tethers his horse to a tree and disappears. Along comes Charley boy, on foot I imagine, and he's cutting open the saddlebag when Frankland comes back, tries to stop him and ends up dead. Charley hauls him down the tunnel, takes the horse – heaven knows where it is now – sells off whatever he's stolen and then gets away as far as he can from the chance of getting caught.'

'America.'

'So it would seem.' Snowden took back the letter. The Whashton case could be quietly closed with a note saying '*Murderer unidentified but believed deceased*'. If any of Henry Frankland's relatives could be found, apart from that demented woman up at Hirst, they could be assured that the killer had ended his days swinging from a hangman's rope. And, Snowden realised with a wry smile to himself, Jonathan Arrowsmith could have a reference declaring that he had no proven criminal connections. Not live ones at least. 'It's not the perfect solution I'd hoped for, but it could have been worse.'

He put the letter in his pocket and stood up. 'Come on, time we ate.'

Wednesday March 17ᵗʰ

York, 10.04am

HENRY Beaumont Matthews, barrister-at-law, adjusted his wig and rose wearily to his feet. Long ago, fresh out of Lincoln's Inn, he had dreamed of becoming one of the country's leading counsel, famed for his oratory, a member of parliament with a place in government, attorney-general perhaps or even lord chancellor. It had not happened. Instead here he was at yet another assizes, one of a handful of unfulfilled advocates appointed by the court to defend the usually indefensible.

Only recently had defendants facing a charge of felony been allowed the luxury of a defence lawyer, and Matthews would be the first to admit that it did few of them much good. Acquittals were still uncommon, owing more to prosecution deficiency than incisive cross-examination and passionate speeches from the defence, and he had begun to wonder whether it was all a waste of his time. He'd hoped that his success in December proved otherwise, but then came rumours about the jury only voting for acquittal to get the trial over with... and now this retrial had all the makings of a disaster. Everyone from the judge to the jury knew the defendants had been unaccountably cleared of murder. Half his defence witnesses, the ones who'd sworn the defendants were nowhere near the murder scene, had failed to turn up; the ones who had come to court seemed far less convinced about their evidence.

'When you're ready, Mr Matthews.' Rolfe's voice brought him back to earth.

'I'm obliged to you, my lord.' He'd do his best, though he didn't hold out much hope, and at least he'd get his three guineas a day plus expenses, win or lose. Grasping the lapels of his gown, he turned to the jury box and began.

'Gentlemen of the jury, when standing in this very place three months ago I felt it necessary to caution the jury then sitting against any prejudice that they might have imbibed, to take care that their minds should not be biased with anything they might have heard or read respecting this robbery. It is my duty to repeat that caution to you today.' He nodded gravely and paused for a moment, as if hoping for some response, before continuing.

'When the prisoners were last tried, their lives were in danger, but there is a principle involved in the present trial that is of higher and greater importance than that. You well know – it cannot be concealed, it is a matter of record – that the previous jury have already inquired into this case, that they deliberated for a considerable time on the evidence before them, and that they acquitted the prisoners. Yet you are being asked by my learned friends for the prosecution to say that the former jury gave a verdict that they should not have given. It should be remembered that there were at least twelve witnesses at the last trial who have not been called now, and in the absence of their testimony how can the prosecution say you might not reach the same conclusion as the previous jury?' Matthews' voice rose in outraged disbelief. 'To reverse their verdict when you have not had the same evidence would surely place the lives and liberties of the public in danger, a course of proceedings that would shake the foundations of one of the most valuable institutions which our country can boast – trial by jury, founded by the blood of our ancestors and upheld by their blood against the evils of star chambers and secret courts –'

'Mr Matthews?'

'My lord?'

'Loathe though I am to deprive the jury of your impassioned oratory, I feel obliged to remind you that I have already ruled that this and the previous proceedings are two different trials and this jury must consider only such evidence as is brought before this court.'

'My lord –'

'And I cannot be alone in wondering why at the commencement of your address you urged members of the jury to clear their minds of the previous hearing, and yet you now ask them to compare it with the current proceedings.' Rolfe shook his head. 'You really can't have it both ways, Mr Matthews. Please restrict your remarks to the case before us.'

'As your lordship pleases.' Matthews subsided. 'In that case, let us turn to the witnesses we *have* heard. Foremost among their testimony is that of Ann Humphreys, upon which the whole prosecution case depends. If you disbelieve her statement, the prisoners are entitled to an acquittal, and I propose to examine her statement closely and bring forward witnesses to show that she is a person not to be trusted, either on the ground of her moral character or her mental soundness...'

In the press box McQueedie laid down his pen, leant over and spoke as softly as he could. 'Your turn, Sandy. Should be straightforward from now on.' He handed over a sheet of paper. 'Here's the list of defence witnesses. Got it from Matthews, said I wanted to check spellings.'

'Same ones he produced back in December?'

'Some of them. Plus a new one, last on the list. Recognise him?'

Sandy ran his eye down the names. 'If that's who I think it is, Matthews must be really desperate. Do you suppose Snowden knows about him?'

'I'll ask him when we break for lunch.' McQueedie glanced across at Matthews, still in full flow. 'If our learned defence counsel ever stops talking, that is.'

York, 1.45pm

'PURVIS?' Snowden stopped halfway through forking a dismal-looking roast potato from his plate and stared at McQueedie. '*Alexander* Purvis?'

'That's the name on the list, Mr Snowden. Constable Alexander Purvis.'

'The little bastard.' Snowden abandoned the potato. 'That comment's not for publication, Mr McQueedie.'

'Of course not, sir. We assume it's the Constable Purvis stationed in Barney.'

'Oh, it will be.' Snowden eyed the reporter cautiously. 'You've come across him?'

'Well known among the beer-houses of Briggate, sir.' McQueedie hesitated. 'I don't suppose you can explain why he's appearing for the defence?'

'You suppose correctly, Mr McQueedie. You'll have to wait for him to give his evidence, but thank you for warning me.'

'Always happy to assist the constabulary, sir.' McQueedie grinned. 'One good turn, you know...'

Snowden watched him disappear across the room and turned to his dining companion. 'You know this Constable Purvis, Anthony?'

'Of course.' Coulthard nodded. 'Not one of the most active officers, I'm afraid, except when wielding a tankard.'

'He was on duty in Briggate the night Yates disappeared. Or supposed to be. I interviewed him a few days later and it was quite clear he'd spent the evening wandering from beer-house to beer-house and never saw or heard a thing.'

'I understand he's been warned about drinking on duty. No use as a prosecution witness for you, then?'

'He'd have been a complete embarrassment. A serving police officer at the scene of a double murder, shrieks and screams all around and he doesn't notice a damn thing? I don't control the Barnard Castle constables, though I work closely with them as you know, or I'd have thrown him out of the force. As it was I tore a strip off him and told him to keep his mouth shut.'

'You think he offered his services to Matthews?'

'Probably. I'm sure he'd be delighted to see me lose this case.' Snowden looked thoughtful, pushed his plate aside and stood up. 'I must have a word with Bliss. If anybody's going to be embarrassed by Purvis appearing in the witness-box I want to make sure it's him, not me.'

York, 5.40pm

SANDY scribbled a last sentence, sat back and stretched his arms. 'That'll have to do for the six-thirty. Nothing much new apart from Purvis at the end. Give it a quick once-through, Hamish, and then Binksley can run it up to the station.'

McQueedie picked up the sheets of paper, selected the last one and began.

Alexander Purvis, examined by Mr Matthews:
'You are a constable in Barnard Castle?'
'That's right, sir.'
'Were you on duty on the night of August the ninth, 1845, the night Joseph Yates and Catherine Raine were missed?'
'I was, sir. I went on duty in Briggate from nine to twelve and then went on the higher part of the town.'
'And did you return to Briggate later?'
'I did, sir, a little after one o'clock, and remained there about till half-past three.'
'And did you see the prosecution witness Ann Humphreys, who claims to have been out and about in that area in the early hours of that morning?'
'I did not, sir.'
'Or any of three young men she claims to have met?'
'Them in the dock, sir? No, none of them.'

'*Or Yates or the girl Raine?*'

'*Never saw Yates, sir. I believe I did see the girl, though, at around half-past one.*'

'*Where was that?*'

'*She was walking along Briggate towards the bridge, as I recall.*'

'*Alone?*'

'*Yes, sir.*'

'*So you are telling the jury that although you were on duty throughout that night, you saw no sign of the accused, the man they are alleged to have robbed or the witness Humphreys who claims to have seen the crime?*'

'*None at all, sir.*'

'*In fact, you have no reason to believe they were ever in the area?*'

'*None, sir.*'

'*And what do you conclude from that?*'

'*That Humpheys is lying, sir, or deluded.*'

'*Thank you, constable.*'

Cross-examined by Mr Bliss:

'*Tell me, constable, did you see anyone at all that night?*'

'*Of course I did, sir. Plenty of them.*'

'*We have heard evidence from upwards of twenty prosecution witnesses who have sworn that they saw one or more of Humphreys, Yates, Raine and the three accused in Briggate that night. Did you see any of these witnesses during your patrol?*'

'*Only two or three of them, sir.*'

'*And are they, and all the others, lying or deluded?*'

'*I believe they may be mistaken, sir, yes.*'

'*And you heard none of these screams other witnesses have told us about?*'

'*I heard some shouting, yes, sir, between eleven and twelve, but they weren't the screams of persons in distress.*'

'*Nothing later?*'

'*No, sir.*'

'*I see... You say you saw plenty of people. Where were they? On the street?*'

'*Some of them, sir.*'

'*And the others?*'

'*I don't know, sir. I was in some of the passages during the night, there must be a dozen of them.*'

'*All with ale-houses?*'

'*Most of them, sir.*'

'*Busy, were they?*'

'*It was a Saturday night, sir, always busy.*'

'*You would know that because your patrol duty includes checking all such premises?*'

'*Yes, sir.*'

'*And how many did you visit that night? All of them?*'

'Yes, sir. Well, most of them.'
'All of them anxious, I imagine, to keep on the right side of the law?'
'They don't want any trouble, sir, if that's what you mean.'
'Not averse to offering the occasional gratuitous beverage to visiting constables?'
'I'm sorry, sir, I don't understand –'
'How many free drinks did you get during your patrol, constable? Remember you are on oath and I am sure we can if necessary produce evidence to corroborate or contradict what you say.'
'Well, perhaps the one.'
'Or two? Half a dozen? More?'
'I don't recall, sir.'
'Just as you don't recall seeing witnesses, hearing screams or indeed anything else about that fateful night. You spent most of it drunkenly staggering from alehouse to alehouse, is that not the truth of it?'
'I was not staggering, sir –'
'Gentlemen of the jury, you may be wondering why the defence brought this man here to testify today when his evidence is so patently worthless. I can only suggest that their case is so lacking in credibility that they have been reduced, as no doubt Constable Purvis has been in his time, to scraping the very bottom of the barrel. No further questions, my lord.'

York, 6.50pm

'TOOK your time, laddie.' McQueedie grinned at the youngster as he squeezed back into the press box. 'Been looking for bears again?'

'Don't.' Binksley shuddered. 'I still keep looking over my shoulder every time I go down Micklegate. No, I got talking to the man in the telegraph office. He reckons it won't be long before everybody gets connected to it. Can you imagine, being able to send a message to anyone in the country?'

'I don't think so. For a start, everyone would have to learn that tap-tap-tap dot-and-dash code they use.'

'They could teach it in schools. More use than Latin and Greek and stuff.'

'And you'd have to have wires going from every house to every other house, millions of them.' McQueedie chuckled. 'Easier to teach pigs to fly messages around. Not a chance, laddie, not a chance.'

Binksley looked affronted. 'Well, I think it could work. Then I wouldn't have to keep running up to the station all the time. It's bloody cold out there, I reckon we're in for more snow.' He shivered and gazed round the court. 'Having a break, are they?'

'We needed one after Matthews and Bliss had finished their final speeches to the jury. They went on for ages.'

'Anything interesting?'

'Just what you'd expect. Matthews said all the prosecution witnesses were rubbish and Bliss said the defence didn't know what it was doing.'

'So what's next?'

'The judge will come back and spend half an hour telling the jury it's up to them to reach a verdict based on what they'd heard over the past two days. And then they'll go off to talk about it.' He glanced at the clock. 'If it's anything like the last trial we could be in for a long night.'

York, 7.55pm

THE jury filed out of the courtroom, Rolfe disappeared towards his chamber and Snowden stood up. 'Time I got some fresh air. Back in a few minutes.'

He made his way out, crossed the foyer and halted to light his pipe beside one of the stone columns protecting the doorway. He was not surprised to discover that it was snowing outside, thick flakes floating down through the gaslight and already an inch or so deep on the steps. It had been a hard winter, the worst he could remember since...

Fifteen years ago, almost to the day. Arriving back knowing nothing of what had happened, the baby already buried, Susannah God knows where, the long days trudging the snow-drifted hills and valleys, refusing to believe it.

He shook his head in a vain attempt to clear the memories and was still there, gazing sightlessly at the past through the falling snow, when Coulthard came to find him.

'You'd better come back in. Something's happening.'

York, 8.05pm

'HAVE you reached a verdict upon which all of you are agreed?'

'We have, my lord.'

'On the charge of feloniously assaulting Joseph Yates and stealing from his person the sum of ten shillings in silver, how do you find the prisoner Barker, guilty or not guilty?'

'Guilty, my lord.'

'And on the same charge, the prisoner Breckon?'

'Guilty.'

'And Raine?'

'Guilty.'

There was a ripple of applause and an excited buzz of voices from the public gallery. Rolfe waited patiently for it to subside before turning a grim face towards the convicted men.

'Prisoners in the dock, it is impossible for anyone who has witnessed these proceedings not to feel that you have been guilty of two of the most atrocious murders that perhaps the annals of crime ever furnished. You have succeeded undoubtedly in defeating the ends of justice hitherto, for I am perfectly certain that any jury who has heard what has been detailed on this occasion could not have the remotest doubt but that you barbarously – and not merely, I suspect, for objects of plunder but for some motives of revenge – murdered Joseph Yates, and you followed that up with equal barbarity in murdering the young woman. I also see enough to convince me that you formed the deliberate plan of murdering Ann Humphreys as well.'

Rolfe picked up the black cap lying on the desk before him and a gasp went round the room. 'I feel somewhat ashamed that the law is not able to reach you further than it is. But this I will say, that whether your lives shall, by the pleasure of God, be determined early or be protracted late, you will live the objects of abhorrence and detestation even among the guilty associates amongst whom you will be placed, who will be ashamed and contaminated at being with you.'

He paused and pondered the black cap for a moment before regretfully laying it back down on the desk. 'The severest sentence that the law allows me I shall pass upon you, and that is that you be severally transported beyond the seas, to such place as her Majesty shall direct, for the space of fifteen years. Take them down.'

PART FIVE

May 1847

An aerial view of the Barnard Castle grounds today. They weren't that tidy in McQueedie's time.

Below on the right is the County Bridge, from which Kate Raine was thrown to her death.

Saturday May 15th

Thorpe, 7.20pm

BETSEY dumped a pile of newspapers on the kitchen table and began rummaging in a drawer in search of scissors. 'I've been meaning to do this for ages, Tommy.' The cat looked up from its bowl in the corner, wondered if the papers were worth investigating and decided food was more important. 'I'm making a scrapbook for papa. I've collected every story about the murders since it all began and all I've got to do now is cut them out and stick them in. I'll tell you all about them as we go along.'

She found the scissors, sat down and picked up the first paper. 'I'm not quite sure what order to put them in. Papa would know.' She frowned. 'I wonder where he's got to? He went out this morning to chase horse thieves or something but said he'd be home in time for tea. I hope he's not much longer, I need his advice about Friday.'

Tommy finished eating, ran a tongue round the bowl to make sure she hadn't missed anything, and strolled across to the table. Betsey gave her an affectionate stroke. 'I'm sure you'd love to help, but I'm not sure you'd understand. You see, William's giving a talk at the Teesdale Agricultural Society dinner on Friday about his latest invention, something to do with harrows, and I more or less promised to be there to give him support. He gets ever so nervous about speeches, you know. I sometimes wonder how he gets through his sermons.'

The cat nuzzled her hand as she continued. 'The problem is, there's a band concert at the Temperance Hall the same night and Daniel's invited me to go. He plays the bugle, you know, ever so well, and that sounds a lot more fun.' She gave a sigh. 'I'm very fond of both of them and I just don't know what to do. What do you think, Tommy?'

The cat thought there might be something left in the bowl after all and wandered off to investigate.

'You're not being much help, Tommy. I just hope papa will know what's best.' Betsey returned to her newspapers. 'He must be back soon.'

Barnard Castle, 9.28pm

BINKSLEY squelched into the front bar of the Golden Lion, spotted Sandy nursing an almost-empty glass in the corner and went to join him. 'Bloody wet out there but at least it's stopped raining. Half the street's flooded.' He sat down and began examining his left shoe. 'I knew I should have got this mended. My foot's soaking.'

'Been out on the town?'

'Listening to an emergency meeting of the Sanitation Committee arguing about who's to blame for the drains overflowing, that's where I've been.'

'I thought you were on a night off?'

'So did I till Mr McQueedie collared me a couple of hours ago. Five hundred words of TERRIFIED TOWN SWAMPED BY SEWAGE he wants, plus at least one interview with a mother who's rescued children from a cess-pit.' He sighed. 'I'll probably have to push one in myself to keep him happy.'

'Shitty evening.' Sandy nodded sympathetically. 'I'll get you a drink.'

Binksley was still brooding over his problems when Sandy returned with two pints. 'I wouldn't mind so much, but I was on the track of a really good tale when Mr McQueedie stepped in and took it over. He said I could do the drains instead.'

Sandy looked dubious. 'What's this really good tale, then?'

'Well...' Binksley hesitated. 'You remember back in January when he had me chasing all over the dale in search of satanic rituals?'

Sandy grinned. 'Good stuff. You got three page leads out of that if I remember right. Midnight grave-robbers, wasn't it, vampires loose on the moors and witches flying over Cockfield Fell? There wasn't a virgin between here and High Force who didn't expect the devil to leap out at her at any moment.'

'Yes, well, it wasn't all true, of course. I didn't actually find any grave-robbers or witches. Or virgins, come to that.'

'Well, you wouldn't, not up Teesdale.'

'I was just reporting what I was told.'

'Of course. You did a good job, lad.'

'Didn't get any bylines, mind.' Binksley looked morosely into his glass. 'It just seemed to take off. I'm still getting stories about cats being sacrificed and there's a woman up in Eggleston swears Beelzebub lives in her wardrobe. It sounds daft, I know, but I've started wondering whether there really might be something going on. And then this message arrived.'

'What message?'

'This one.' Binksley produced a crumpled sheet of paper from his pocket. 'No name on it or anything. It was in the post this morning, look.'

Sandy straightened it out. '*Let he who seeketh the Prince of Darkness in our midst be in the castle an hour after sunset tonight and the truth shall be revealed.*' He laughed. 'Someone's playing games with you, lad. You weren't really going to take any notice of this?'

Binksley looked affronted. 'You never know, perhaps one of the devil worshippers wants to spill the beans. Mr McQueedie said even if it was just a hoax it was high time we did a story about the castle. HEADLESS HORROR ROAMS RUINS, BLOODTHIRSTY BEAST ON THE BATTLEMENTS, that sort of thing. I'm surprised he's never thought of it before.'

'Well, I suppose we could do with something lively for next week's papers. The only stories in sight so far are your drains and the latest cholera outbreak, all a bit depressing.' Sandy examined the note again. 'When's sunset?'

'Half-past eight, maybe? Not that you'd be able to tell on a night like this.'

Sandy consulted his watch. 'He'll be on his way, then, the daft sod.' He drained his glass. 'Put your shoe back on, lad, and see if it'll get you as far as the bar. It's your round.'

Thorpe, 9.45pm

BETSEY snipped the last cutting from the paper, pasted it carefully into the scrapbook and sat back with a satisfied smile. 'That's it, Tommy. All done.'

The cat opened one eye, yawned and went back to sleep.

'You could at least give me a purr of appreciation.' Betsey shook her head reproachfully. 'I've spent hours putting all this together and you haven't paid any attention. I'll tell you about the latest ones all the same.' She turned back a few pages. 'There's a really good comment in the *Yorkshire Gazette* praising papa, listen. *"The result of Mr Snowden's energy and persistence has been the conviction of a gang of desperate characters."* I suppose three's a gang, Tommy, if they're desperate enough. Then there's a letter in the *York Herald* from someone in Richmond demanding that papa be given a public testimonial *"for his indefatigable exertions in searching out and bringing to light the dark and horrible crimes of the Barnard Castle murderers."* Indefatigable means not wearing out, I think, Tommy, though papa seemed terribly wearied by it all.'

The cat slept on.

'Not everybody was happy, though. Here's another letter in the *Herald*, from someone who signs himself *A Political Economist*, whatever that is. He says the two trials plus police expenses cost a total of thirteen hundred and nine pounds, six shillings and sevenpence – I wonder how on earth he worked that out? – and wants *"a searching inquiry and deep investigation inquiry into why taxpayers should be expected to pay for such lavish expense."* It does sound an awful lot of money.'

She turned the page. 'Did I tell you that the murders were even talked about in the House of Commons? There's a column here from the *London Evening News* about Mr Bright – he's the member of parliament for Durham and very important – asking the Home Secretary, no less, if he knew juries were more and more reluctant to return guilty verdicts on people who might be hanged? Some people are saying jurors who don't believe in capital punishment shouldn't be allowed, and some say verdicts shouldn't have to be unanimous, and there are even some saying juries should be abolished altogether, though I think I'd much rather be tried for my life by twelve ordinary people than one judge, if what papa says about judges is true.'

She moved on to the next cutting. '*The Times* thinks so, too, Tommy. Would you believe it devoted a whole editorial to the murders? Ever so cleverly written, I don't know how they do it. *"Justice was left behind on the high road, but she succeeded at length in overtaking the fugitives by a by-path"*. You don't get writing like that in the *Yorkshire Gazette*.'

The cat re-surfaced and started ferreting for imaginary fleas in its under-fur. Betsey gave up and closed the scrapbook. 'There's lots more, Tommy, but you're obviously not very interested. I sometimes wonder why I persuaded Mrs Eeles to let you come home.'

The cat stopped ferreting, gave her a long cold stare and stalked off to her basket. The clock in the hall struck ten.

'You're right, it's getting late.' Betsey stood up. 'I wonder where on earth papa's got to. He said he'd be back hours ago.'

Barnard Castle, 10.05pm

THE storm clouds that had drenched Teesdale over the past twenty-four hours were disappearing at last, and the sky was still just light enough for McQueedie to see his way through the arched north gate in the curtain wall of the castle. He stopped in the open space beyond and peered into the dusk, wishing he'd had the foresight to bring a lantern. There was no sign of anyone. The ground before him was overgrown, a tangle of long grass, bushes and the occasional stunted tree, but he could make out two paths leading into the night. One to his right led to the silhouetted ruins of the great Round Tower, in the depths of which a hermit had lived for many years. McQueedie decided he was unlikely to be the mystery satanist, even though mothers were said to warn children venturing too near the castle that he ate infants for breakfast, and chose the path to his left.

It led him past what was left of a smaller tower built into the curtain wall. Only the ground floor remained, a vaulted room disappearing into the darkness, and he paused at the entrance.

What happened next surprised him more than anything he could remember since the Gorbals barmaid he was seducing at the age of seventeen turned out to be a transvestite drum major in the Black Watch. Hands from nowhere gripped his arms, a noose was thrown round his neck and he was thrust into the room.

A door at the end opened as he stumbled forward onto his knees and a blazing torch appeared, held aloft by a figure in a black hooded cloak swirling with signs and symbols McQueedie didn't recognise. Half a dozen more figures emerged from the shadows as the invisible hands behind him bound rope round his legs, trussing him up like a chicken for slaughter.

McQueedie wondered if he'd wet himself.

'You are the man who has been seeking the mysteries of our order?'

It was a deep male voice, cultured and oddly familiar, and McQueedie breathed a sigh of relief. He wasn't in the hands of a gang of murderous robbers as he'd feared but on the verge of a tremendous scoop. Headlines flashed through his mind. DARING DALES REPORTER REVEALS DEVIL'S DISCIPLES' DEN – WORLD EXCLUSIVE BY OUR MAN McQUEEDIE. There might even be SEX SECRETS OF SATANIC SISTERHOOD. He nodded eagerly. It had been his idea in the first place, after all, and he wasn't going to let a snotty little seventeen-year-old like Binksley share the credit.

'I am, sir. Angus McQueedie, reporter, at your service. Or any other sort of ceremonies you'd like to show me, for that matter.'

'You appear to have come very close to seeing them already, Mr McQueedie.'

'Ah, yes.' McQueedie gave a nervous laugh. 'Good old-fashioned investigative journalism, you know, you can't beat it.'

'Very close indeed. The Brethren would like to congratulate you on your persistence.'

'That's very kind of you.' McQueedie's hopes rose. 'Anything you can do to help will be much appreciated.'

'We certainly wish to bring your involvement in our affairs to an end as soon as possible. Perhaps you would care to participate in one of our rituals? We have a ceremony at midnight at which we make sacrifice to His Satanic Majesty. You would be most welcome to attend.'

'Sacrifice?'

'Yes.'

'Chickens, I suppose?'

'Usually. There are special occasions when we offer larger creatures. Tonight may be one.'

Somewhere deep within McQueedie's brain a tiny bell began to ring. 'What would I have to do?'

'Just... be there.'

The bell got louder. 'Nothing else?'

'You would have a very central role in the proceedings, I promise you.'

The bell went into a campanological frenzy and McQueedie suddenly wondered if stealing Binksley's glory had been a terrible mistake. 'Perhaps another night, something a bit less sacrificial. I've got this terrible blood phobia, you know, pass out at the sight of it. I'd completely spoil your evening.'

'The Lord Lucifer would be most disappointed.'

'No, no, I don't think so.' McQueedie scrabbled for an escape. 'I mean, isn't the point of a sacrifice that you're offering him something you value – like a chicken or a lamb or, I don't know, a virgin?'

'Of course. Though where you think we'd find –'

'I really don't think I qualify. As something you value, I mean, quite apart from definitely not being virgo intacta within living memory.' McQueedie shook his head and the noose tautened, reducing his voice to a desperate gurgle. 'It's up to you, of course, but if I was your friend Lucifer I'd think being offered someone worthless just because you want to get rid of him would be a bit of an insult. I'd probably cremate you all on the spot.'

There was a long silence before the figure responded. 'You will remain here while I confer with my fellow brethren.' The figure withdrew to the far end of the room, followed by the others.

McQueedie waited on his knees to learn his fate. He couldn't recall the last time he'd knelt in prayer. It was unlikely the Almighty would give high priority to a plea for help from someone in a room full of demonic antichrists, but he muttered a few despairing words all the same. If he came out of this alive he'd change his life, be nice to everyone, give up the drink or at least cut down a bit... He gave a muted sob of despair. The future looked hellish whatever happened.

The cloaks stopped conferring and their leader returned. McQueedie looked up, heart in his mouth, to hear their decision.

'I'm afraid, Mr McQueedie, that your arguments have not impressed us, though your thoughts on the nature of sacrifice did raise some interesting theodemonological issues.' McQueedie's heart sank back. 'However, we are agreed that you are not a suitable offering at the moment for the Prince of Darkness. He has quite enough on his plate, what with the methodists and the baptists and this appalling temperance movement sweeping the country, to have to deal with the likes of you.' McQueedie's heart did a double somersault. 'We're also persuaded that your continued presence on this earth is unlikely to do his cause any harm. You're probably one of his more valuable assets, in fact.'

McQueedie wasn't sure he agreed, but this was no time to argue. 'You mean I can go?'

'Be patient, Mr McQueedie. We still have to decide some alternative way to prevent you bringing yet more of our activities to the attention of the public. We have a great deal to consider.'

'A deal?' McQueedie relaxed and sat back on his heels. 'No problem. Have you ever thought of appointing a public relations officer? You could do with someone to sort your image out – frankly, it's not so hot right now – and I've got all the contacts.'

'That's not quite what we had in mind. Is there anything else we could offer you?'

'Well, to start with I could do with a drink.' After what he'd been through he deserved one. Several, if possible. He'd start cutting down tomorrow.

'Of course. We produce a passable wine to accompany our more convivial rituals.' One of the dark shapes in the background came forward with a salver bearing two silver goblets sprouting devil's horns as handles and invited McQueedie to choose one before handing the other to his leader.

McQueedie sniffed the contents of his goblet cautiously. The wine, a deep blood red, had a rich aroma he'd never come across before.

'Let us toast our future together, Mr McQueedie, though I shall have to turn my back on you lest you see my face.' He turned around, lifted his hood and emptied the goblet.

McQueedie raised his drink to his lips and took a long swig. It was the best thing he'd ever tasted, better even than Glenbuckie's finest oak-casked malt, and so strong his eyes began to water.

The first thing he saw when they'd cleared was the black-hooded figure walking towards him.

The second was a large blood-red stain on the front of the man's cloak.

The third was the knife in his hand.

Then the room started spinning. McQueedie gave a burble of horror as the noose was pulled taut, jerking his body back until his neck pointed invitingly upwards. All he could see was a giant shadow on the ceiling above, the shadow of a hand holding a knife. He gave a final terrified whimper, the room spun faster and the knife plunged towards him.

Sunday May 16th

Thorpe, 1.05am

ASLEEP beside the dying embers of the kitchen fire, Betsey was lost in an endless forest where, no matter which path she took, she always ended up at the same crossroads. It didn't help that she had no idea where she wanted to be, or what if anything she was looking for. In her hand was a tiny casket which she couldn't open though she knew it was terribly important, and dancing around her feet was a small furry creature which vanished whenever she bent down to examine it. She had no idea what to do.

There was a violent crash behind her and she spun round in alarm. Something impossibly enormous was coming through the trees and she tried to run, but her feet refused to move. She gave a scream and woke up, trembling with fear.

The kitchen door was open, banging in the wind, and her father was slumped across the table.

She stared at him in horror. His head was bare and spattered with mud, his coat sodden, one outstretched hand covered in blood. For a moment she thought he was dead.

'Papa!'

'I'll be all right.' He let out a long gasping breath and tried to sit up. 'I need to get dry, fresh clothes and hot water. Bandages for my arm, though I don't think it's as bad as it looks. Nothing broken as far as I can tell, but I've twisted a knee. It hurts like the devil.' He shivered violently. 'God, I'm cold.'

'Don't try to move.' She ran for towels and blankets, helped him out of his soaked clothes and stoked up the fire. 'Hot water as soon as this gets going. You can clean off the mud and blood and I'll make some tea.'

'I'd rather have brandy.' He tried to stand up, winced and subsided back into the chair. 'Make it both.'

'In a minute. First tell me what happened.'

'I honestly don't know, Betsey.' He gave another long shiver as he wrapped himself in a blanket. 'I was up on the moors, miles away. One moment I was riding back through the rain, the next thing I remember I was lying half-submerged in a beck.' He shook his head and winced again. 'I must have been there for ages, it was pitch black when I came to. Bucephalus was still there, bless him, but I couldn't get into the saddle because of my knee.' He gave a grim smile. 'Try it sometime, it's damn near impossible with one leg out of action. I hobbled back holding onto his reins.'

'Do you think he stumbled and threw you?'

'No, I'd remember. I just can't recall anything.' He looked almost guilty. 'I think I must have fainted. Lucky I didn't get a foot caught in a stirrup when I came off or I wouldn't be here.'

'Oh, papa!' She looked aghast. 'Suppose it happens again?'

'It won't.'

'It mustn't. I'll find the brandy, then it's bed for you and a good night's rest. I'll get the doctor first thing tomorrow.'

Monday May 17ᵗʰ

Unknown, 10.30am

MCQUEEDIE drifted into consciousness and groaned. His head was thumping, his stomach churning, his throat felt like sandpaper and although the room had stopped spinning it was now lurching up and down alarmingly.

He tried to recall the night before. The noose round his neck, the shadow above him, the knife coming down and slicing through the rope, the wonderful realisation that they weren't going to sacrifice him after all even though the room continued to spin faster and faster until... he'd no idea what happened next. He must have passed out, drugged by something in the wine. McQueedie groaned again as he realised his satanic adversary, back turned, had simply tipped his own drink down his cloak.

Cursing his stupidity, he managed to open one eye. He was in total darkness. He'd never gone blind before, no matter what he'd drunk, and he lay panic-stricken for a moment before reaching out a hand. It met wood on both sides and above him. None of it would move.

He was locked in a box, a man-sized box.

A coffin.

He was told later that his screams could be heard a good hundred yards away. Within a minute that felt like an age McQueedie heard voices, the sound of metal on wood, and the lid was prised open. A large weather-beaten face behind an enormous black beard loomed over him.

'Bugger me. They said you wouldn't wake up till Thursday.'

'Thursday?'

'Friday, even.' A large hairy hand helped McQueedie clamber out of the coffin. 'Welcome aboard. I'm Paine, Captain John Paine.'

'Captain?' McQueedie staggered as the floor lurched away from him and he stared about in disbelief. 'Dear God. I'm on a bloody ship.'

'Course you are. Sixteen hours out from Hartlepool, well on your way. They said you knew all about it.'

'They?' McQueedie gave up trying to cope with the see-sawing deck and sat down on the edge of the coffin. 'Who's they?'

'Your mates in the revolutionary anarchists brigade who brought you aboard. Hell of a send-off they must have given you. Vodka, was it?'

'This is ridiculous.' McQueedie heard his voice rising hysterically. 'I'm not supposed to be sailing from Hartlepool. Or anywhere.'

'Got to be better than the death cell, comrade.' Paine dropped his voice conspiratorially. 'They told us all about you going on the run after trying to blow up them politicians, deserve all they get if you ask me. Your secret's safe with us.' He grinned.

'Bloody clever idea, hiding in a coffin like that, police at the docks let it straight through. Don't need it now, though, do you? I'll find you a bunk with the rest of the lads you'll be working with.'

McQueedie goggled at him. 'Working?'

'That was the deal.' Paine surveyed him critically. 'Can't see you being much use up the rigging but we can always use an extra hand clearing the bilges. You'll get used to it after the first few weeks.'

'*Weeks?*' McQueedie's eyes bulged. 'Where the hell are we going?'

'Newcastle, non-stop.'

'That can't take weeks.'

'Newcastle, New South Wales. I've got a load of convicts from the last assizes to deliver. You'll be safe enough out there and from what I hear you can blow up politicians to your heart's content. Beer's not much good, mind.'

McQueedie sank his head in his hands and began to sob.

Tuesday May 18th

Thorpe, 4.20pm

THERE was no answer to Wharton's knock on the Grange front door and no sign of anyone when he walked round the back to peer through the kitchen window. He was wondering what to do next when Betsey appeared from the garden, her arms full of rhubarb.

'William!' She greeted him with a smile. 'You don't want any of this, do you? There seems to be more every year.'

He looked at it doubtfully. 'I'm not really all that fond of rhubarb.'

'It's supposed to be very good for you. I'm going to stew some for papa.'

'Ah, yes, I heard he wasn't well. Recovering, I hope?'

'Not really.' Betsey shook her head. 'He's not a very good patient, I'm afraid. Dr Graham ordered him to rest for the week but he insisted on getting up yesterday and spent most of it buried in paperwork in his office. Heaven knows what he was doing, but today he seems even worse than before and he's back in bed.'

Wharton's face fell. 'That's a pity. I came over especially to ask his advice about patents, you see.'

Betsey looked blank. 'Patents?'

'There's a man in Norfolk advertising a turnip harrow that looks exactly like the one I invented last year. I want to know what I can do about it. There's really no chance I could see your father, just for a minute or two? It's really important.'

'So is getting him well again.' Betsey shook her head firmly. 'No visitors. You'll have to wait, I'm afraid.'

'It's most inconvenient.' Wharton frowned. 'Maybe somebody at the dinner on Friday will know. You are coming, aren't you? I've got my speech ready, perhaps you could take a look at it and tell me what you think.' He dug into his coat pocket, produced a sheaf of papers and held them out.

'Not just now, William. I'm really very busy looking after papa. And I think you'll have to do without me on Friday unless he improves a lot by then.'

'Surely –'

'Papa comes first, you must see that.'

'I suppose so.' Wharton sighed and reluctantly put the papers back in his pocket. 'His illness really is most untimely.'

Betsey watched him leave and walked thoughtfully back to the kitchen.

Barnard Castle, 5.15pm

'I'VE searched every inch of the castle, there's nothing there, and nobody in town's seen him since Saturday.' Binksley gave a baffled shake of his head as Sandy led them into the Golden Lion. 'It's a complete mystery.'

Sandy nodded in agreement. 'I've known him go missing for a day after a heavy weekend's drinking but never this long.' They reached the bar. 'Two pints plus a chaser for me, George.'

'Coming up, Mr McLeod.' The barman began serving. 'I've been waiting for you coming in, got a message for you from your mate.'

'McQueedie?'

'That's him.'

'We've been looking all over for him. When was he in here?'

'He wasn't. Some kid came in on Sunday night and said a gent had stopped him in the street and paid him to deliver a message to you. I said I'd pass it on. Hang on, I wrote it down.' George delved beneath the bar and emerged with a sheet of paper. 'There you are. "Urgent family crisis, gone to Glasgow. Back sometime. M."'

'Family crisis?' Binksley looked puzzled. 'I didn't think he had any family.'

'He hasn't.' Sandy frowned. 'God knows what the bugger's really up to. We'll just have to wait till he comes back, I suppose.'

Thorpe, 5.45pm

BETSEY gave the simmering rhubarb another stir and was wondering whether it needed yet more sugar when there was a tap on the kitchen door and Craven appeared.

'I've brought your papers from Greta Bridge, thought your father would want them. All right if I come in?'

'Of course.'

'There's the latest *Police Gazette* too, it's got a story about his book being reprinted again which might cheer him up a bit. And some post, just the stuff that won't have him fretting about how we're coping without him.' He laid it down on the table and took a chair. 'How is he today?'

'Much the same. He's had nothing to eat and says he's got no appetite. I'm hoping he'll have some of this.'

'Rhubarb?' Craven looked doubtful. 'Worth a try, I suppose. If there's anything I can do, you've only to ask, you know.'

'Thank you.'

'I wondered...' He paused. 'There's Bucephalus, for instance. Would it help if I gave him some exercise? It can't be good for him, stuck in a stable all the time.'

'I'm sure papa wouldn't mind.' Betsey gave him a grateful smile. 'That would be very good of you.'

'I'd enjoy it. I'll take him out now if you like. Anything else I can do?'

'Well, there is some mail on papa's desk you could take to the post. I'll fetch it.'

She returned with a handful of letters and stopped, examining the addresses. 'He spent most of yesterday writing these. A couple of bill payments, one to his publisher, one to Mr Watson the solicitor... I wonder what that's about?' She frowned as she handed them over.

'I'll get them in the post tonight.' Craven stood up. 'I'll have to be off, I've got a rehearsal at eight. For Friday.'

'The concert, of course.' She hesitated a moment. 'I've been meaning to talk to you about that.'

'It's all right, I can't possibly expect you to come when your father needs you like this. Another time, perhaps.'

'Yes. Thank you, Daniel. You've been very understanding.'

Thorpe, 6.40pm

MATTHEW Graham came downstairs, put his medical case on the hall table and went to find Betsey. She was in the kitchen, tea at the ready, and poured him a cup as he sat down.

'He's no better, is he, doctor?'

'No.' He took a sip of tea. 'I'm sorry, Betsey, but I think he's worse than yesterday. Nothing I've given him seems to have made any difference.'

'He's not been right for weeks.' She joined him at the table. 'I've been telling him to slow down, but you know what he's like. Work, work, work, he never stops. He just needs to take it easy for a bit.'

'Perhaps. Getting a chill after his fainting fit, if that's what it was, hasn't helped. It's gone to his chest and he's having some problems breathing.'

Betsey nodded. 'He's been coughing a lot all day. He is going to get well, though, isn't he?'

'I hope so, Betsey, I hope so.' He drained his cup and stood up. 'I'll drop by again tomorrow. I've left some new pills by the bed, make sure he takes them.'

'Of course.'

As she watched him leave the cat ambled across, wondering if it was time for supper. She picked it up, gave it a cuddle and sat staring out of the window. A lone swallow was swooping among the apple trees.

'Poor, poor papa.' She put the cat down gently on the floor. 'He'll be all right, Tommy. I'm sure he will.'

Saturday May 29th

Yorkshire Gazette, Page 6

Our obituary this week announces the death of Mr. Snowden, the superintendent of the Gilling West Constabulary Force, to whose vigorous exertions the unravelling of the dark mystery that so long enveloped the Barnard Castle murders, was to a great extent most deservedly attributed. Mr. Snowden has long been known as a most zealous officer, and he was held in the greatest esteem by the magistrates of the North Riding. His able work on " The Duties of Constables" shewed that he had an intimate acquaintance with the Criminal Law; and his general reputation as an officer was of the first order. He was taken dangerously ill soon after the last assizes, at which the prisoners Barker, Raine, and Breckon were convicted, and possibly the anxiety and great exertions which he had undergone with reference to this case, may have tended to produce the disease under which he sunk.

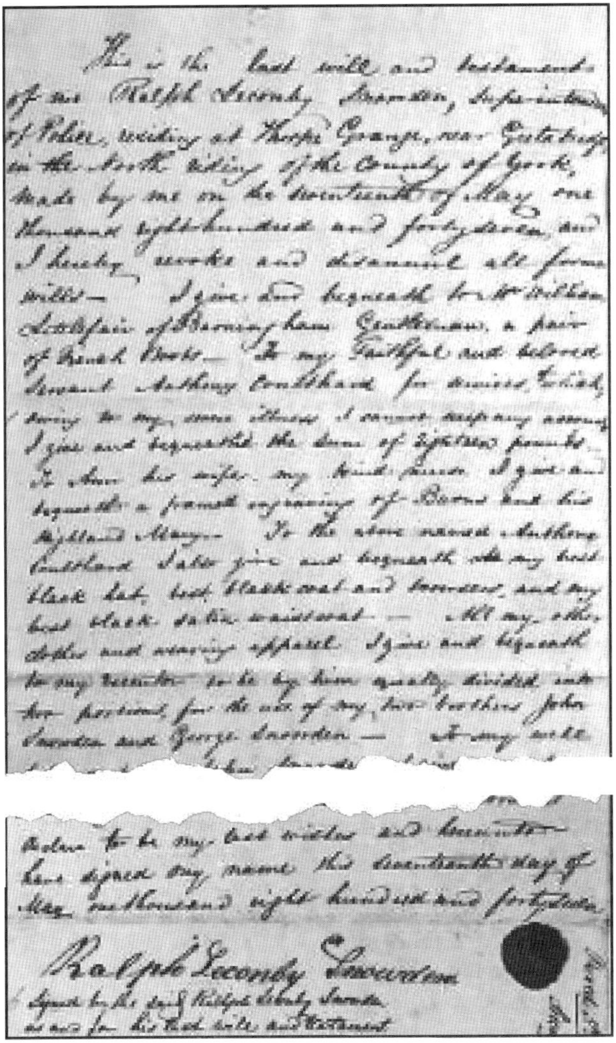

Extracts from Ralph Snowden's will,
dated May 17th 1847

AFTERWORDS

RALPH LECONBY SNOWDEN, just 42 when he died on May 23rd 1847, was buried at Wycliffe. There seems to be no record of his funeral, no gravestone marks where he lies, and the cause of his death remains unknown. His will, written a week before his death, survives. It left most of his estate to Betsey, but there were minor bequests to others, including his brothers John and George, friends in Barningham and Aldbrough, and Anthony Coulthard, to whom he bequeathed £18 and *'my best black hat, my best black coat and trowsers, and my best black satin waistcoat'*. Snowden's book became a bible for magistrates and constables and was reprinted many times over the next four decades.

SUSANNAH SNOWDEN is a mystery. Her family background, her marriage to Ralph and the births of daughters Betsey and Sarah are all on record, but there is no mention of her anywhere after her second baby's death. It seems very likely that she too died in 1831, but the story of her sudden disappearance into a snowstorm is wholly fictional.

BETSEY SNOWDEN became a governess before being married in 1862 to Barnard Castle-born schoolmaster Joseph Lawson, later to become vicar of Brandon near Durham. She had a daughter called Eleanor and died in 1896.

JOHN SNOWDEN, Ralph's brother, made a name for himself as a police officer in York before emigrating with his family to America. His son Ralph Leconby Snowden, named after his uncle, died in Triune, West Virginia, in 1857, aged ten. The rest of the family survived, including William who fought in the Civil War and lived until 1920: descendants are living in Triune today.

GEORGE BARKER and **THOMAS RAINE** spent three years in jails and prison hulks before being put upon the convict ship *Scindian* in 1850 and shipped out to a penal colony in western Australia. Whether either ever returned to England is uncertain, though men of the same names appear in UK court records in the 1870s and later.

JOHN BRECKON disappears from the records after the trial. There is no evidence of him being transported and it may be that he died in jail before the *Scindian* sailed. Or escaped.

ANN HUMPHREYS went back to her job as a winder in a Barnard Castle carpet factory. A quarter of a century later she was in Halifax, unmarried and unemployed. She is believed to have died in 1876.

ANTHONY COULTHARD took over from Ralph at Greta Bridge before becoming police superintendent at Sproatley, near Hull. He died in 1871.

WILLIAM WHARTON stayed single until 1859, when he married a vicar's daughter 22 years his junior. They had no children. He won national fame as a pig-breeder and inventor of agricultural machinery, retired to the south of France and died in 1896.

AUGUSTUS SUSSEX MILBANK remained a bachelor, though he reputedly fathered at least one son by a local farmer's wife. Like Wharton, he was an enthusiastic agriculturalist and created the Hawsteads model farm at Barningham. He died in Monte Carlo in 1887.

ISABELLA CLARKSON, who wondered if she'd ever find a man, married one in 1852, moved to Spennymoor and had five children.

***

MANY other people in this book also existed – judges, magistrates, lawyers and constables, witnesses at the trials, publicans and carpet weavers, land owners and hangmen. But some, of course, are fictitious. There was no McQueedie, McLeod or Binksley, though they may seem nostalgically familiar to anyone who worked in newspapers before computers took over. There was and may still be a Whashton tunnel, but the murder there was dreamed up to keep Snowden (and readers) busy with red herrings when the real murder trail went cold. And as far as I know there have never been satanic gatherings in upper Teesdale, though they're a funny lot up there.

***

THE real murders and subsequent trials were extensively reported in the local and national press, and newspaper extracts are mostly reproduced as they appeared. Where possible I've used the actual words spoken at the time, especially those of witnesses giving evidence, though some testimony has been transformed into interviews with Snowden and his constables to avoid over-lengthy court scenes. I'd like to think much of what you've read is or at least could be true – apart from anything involving bodies in tunnels, exploding pigs or McQueedie, of course.

***

THIS book couldn't have been written without the internet, and I'd like to record my debt to four websites in particular of the many hundreds I've visited in pursuit of Snowden's story: ancestry.co.uk, britishnewspaperarchive.co.uk, teesdalemercuryarchive.org. and uk maps.nls.uk.

If you want to know more about any of the people or events described in this book, I'll be happy to help if I can. Contact details can be found on the Barningham local history group website: barninghamvillage.co.uk.

Jon Smith
Barningham, April 2022

TRUE OR FALSE?

The people listed below were alive in the 1840s and had a role in Snowden's story. All the other characters in the book are fictitious.

ALDERSON, Mary
ALLWOOD, William
ANDERSON, Dr William
ARROWSMITH, Charlie
ARROWSMITH, Jonathan
ASTWOOD, William
BAINBRIDGE, Captain
BARKER, George
BECKWITH, Elizabeth
BEST, Stephen
BIGELOW, Erastus
BLANSHARD, Mr
BLISS, Mr
BRAITHWAITE, Ann
BRECKON, John
BROWNE, John
BUCKERFIELD, John
BULMER, Christopher
BULMER, George
BURRILL, George
BUSSY, Sarah
BUSTIN, Anthony
CALCRAFT, William
CARLOCK, Matty
CARTER, Sarah
CARTER, Tommy
CARTWRIGHT, Joseph
CHATTERWAY, Joshua
CLARKE, Reuben
CLARKSON, Isabella
COATES, John
COATES, William
COOPER, Francis
COULTHARD, Ann
COULTHARD, Anthony
CRADOCK, Col Sheldon
CRAGGS, Elizabeth
CRAGGS, Isabella
CRAGGS, John

CRAMPTON, Robert
CRESSWELL, Cresswell
CROWL, John
CRUDDACE, Matthew
CULBECK, Frances
DALKIN, Mary-Ann
DART, William
DAVIDSON, Rev John
DAWSON, Mary
DENT, William
DIPPLE, John
DIXON, Daniel
DOBSON, George
DROVER, Dorothy
EDWARDS, William
ELLIOTT, William
FAWCETT, Elizabeth
FIELD, William
FISHER, Richard
GALLAND, Martin
GALLAND, Mrs
GARRY, George
GARTHWAITE, Mary
GRAHAM, Dr Matthew
GRAHAM, William
GREENHOW, Joseph
GUNSON, Thomas
HALL, Mary
HEADLAM, Rev John
HILL, Rev Barnabus
HILTON, Cuthbert
HUGLIE, Jane
HUMPHREYS, Ann
HUMPHREYS, Jane
HUMPHREYS, John
JOHNSON, Matthew
KIPLING, Thompson
KNAPTON, James

LACKENBY, Elizabeth
LAIKE, Daniel
LAMBERT, Sarah
LONGSTAFF, George
LONGSTAFF, John
MANNERS, Charles
MARWOOD, Robert
MASON, George
MATTHEWS, Mr
MICHELL, John
MIDDLETON, William
MIDDLETON, Mary
MILBANK, Lady Augusta
MILBANK, Mark
MILBANK, Sussex
MINNIKIN, Ann
MORRITT, John Sawrey
MORRITT, William
NEWTON, Thomas
OLIVER, Ann
OLIVER, Thomas
OVEREND, Mr
PARKIN, Ann
PARKIN, Jane
PEACOCK, Harry
PEARSON, Richard
PICKERING, Mr
PLUNKETT, Lucinda
PLUNKETT, Osbert
PRATT, Matthew
PROCTOR, Sarah
PULLEINE, Mr
PURVISS, Alexander
RAINE, Catherine (Kate)
RAINE, Thomas Routledge
RAINE, Thomas
RAINE, William
RAPER, George

RAPER, Mary
ROBINSON, John
ROLFE, Robert
ROUTLEDGE, Edward
RUTTER, Tom
SCRAFTON, Jane
SHAW & SONS
SIMPSON, Matthew
SMITH, Annie
SMITH, George
SMITHSON, Henry
SNOWDEN, Betsey
SNOWDEN, George
SNOWDEN, Jane
SNOWDEN, John
SNOWDEN, Ralph L snr
SNOWDEN, Ralph L jnr
SNOWDEN, Susannah
SPARROW, George
SPENCELEY, Ann
STEPHENSON, Douthwaite
SUTCLIFFE, Elizabeth
SWEETING, Mark
SWIRE, Mrs
TENWICK, Emmanuel
TODD, Hannah
WARD, John
WALKER, Margaret
WAPPITT, William
WATSON, William
WESTWICK, John
WHARTON, William
WHORTON, John
WILKINSON, John
WILKINSON, Thomas
WINDLASS, Robert
WITHAM, Henry
YATES, Eleanor
YATES, Joseph